W9-AFR-573

ALSO BY NANCY MOWLL MATHEWS

Editor, *Cassatt and Her Circle: Selected Letters*

Mary Cassatt

Mary Cassatt: The Color Prints

Mary Cassatt

MARY CASSATT

A Life

Nancy Mowll Mathews

Villard Books • New York • 1994

Published in the United States by Villard Books, a division of Random House, Inc., New York, and simultaneously in Canada by Random House of Canada Limited, Toronto.

Villard Books is a registered trademark of Random House, Inc.

Library of Congress Cataloging-in-Publication Data
Mathews, Nancy Mowll.
Mary Cassatt: a life / Nancy Mowll Mathews.
p. cm.
Includes index.
ISBN 0-394-58497-X
1. Cassatt, Mary, 1844–1926. 2. Painters—United States—Biography. I. Title.
ND237.C3M28 1994
759.13—dc20
[B] 93-22148

Manufactured in the United States of America on acid-free paper.
9 8 7 6 5 4 3 2
First Edition

Preface

In addition to talent, it takes a strong personality, a receptive historical context, and a great deal of luck to become a successful artist. Mary Cassatt (1844–1926), an American artist who lived and worked in France for sixty years, enjoyed success, and it may be that she even has a chance for immortality. She had talent that was recognized and nurtured from an early age; she had a personality that allowed her to navigate a treacherous art world; she lived among people and in historical circumstances that gave her opportunities; and she had the good fortune to find a group like the Impressionists that made a lasting impact on world culture. Although it is too soon to claim immortality for her, it is undeniable that she has continually appealed to influential critics and historians interested in women and Impressionism, and they have kept her art in the public eye.

A success story such as Cassatt's is always intriguing, and looking back on the twenty years that I studied Mary Cassatt's art, it seems strange to me that I never attempted more than a cursory look at her life. As an art historian, I have studied her mother and child pictures, published the letters most relevant to her art, and dissected her color prints. But it is in Cassatt's life that one finds answers to, or at least ideas about, many of the broader issues posed by her art. Why did she become as prominent as she did during her lifetime and after? Should we consider her an American or a French artist? What role did gender play in shaping her art? How did she balance her personal and professional lives and what effect, if any, did her life as a single woman have on her choice of the mother and child subject? Other questions also arose after I began delving into her life as a professional woman. Was she happy? Did she feel successful? How did she differ from some of her contemporaries, both women and men, in that she became famous and they did not?

These were the questions that I took to the documentary material about Mary Cassatt. The letters, memoirs, and other types of biographical evidence available today, seventy years after Cassatt's death, provide a surprisingly vivid picture of the flesh-and-blood Cassatt. The more human she became, the more confusing she became. A life such as hers incorporated French and American influences simultaneously, it brought success and failure in alternating patterns, and it involved personal and professional decisions that were intertwined.

Mary Cassatt's life and art as understood through historical evidence were so rich that I was reluctant to apply methodology that did not rest on documentation. I did not, therefore, apply Freudian, Lacanian, or any other psychoanalytic method to aid in interpretation. I was also reluctant to use deconstructionist methods whenever they strayed too far from a reasonable account of Cassatt's own motives. But, of course, Cassatt's art and life were often shaped by undocumented inner feelings—either emotions or consciousness of self or identity—and I felt free to make an effort at interpreting them.

Many people helped me with this work over the years, and I would like to take this opportunity to thank them. My research on Cassatt began in 1972 with my dissertation for the Institute of Fine Arts under the direction of Linda Nochlin and the late Gert Schiff. My first book, *Cassatt and Her Circle: Selected Letters,* was researched with the aid of a Smithsonian postdoctoral fellowship under the guidance of Lois Fink of the National Museum of American Art. During these early years, I owed a great deal to the incomparable Adelyn Breeskin, who was senior curatorial consultant at the National Museum of American Art until her death in 1986. Mrs. Breeskin was a model of generosity in sharing her research with all upcoming Mary Cassatt scholars. In recent years my knowledge of the artist has been enriched by Suzanne Lindsay, Frances Weitzenhoffer, and Barbara Shapiro, all of whom have made significant contributions to Cassatt scholarship in the 1980s.

I owe a great debt of gratitude to members of the Cassatt family for their generosity in sharing letters and photographs as well as family lore. Their wish for anonymity makes public acknowledgment difficult but no less heartfelt. I would also like to thank Henry B. and Audrey Haldeman for sharing information from their family archives which brought their great-aunt Eliza Haldeman to life.

Many helpful people associated with archives, museums, and historical societies in the United States and France also deserve to be recognized for their kind assistance. These include Susan Stein and Alice C. Frelinghuysen of the Metropolitan Museum, Caroline Durand-Ruel Godfroy of Durand-Ruel & Cie., Albert Boime of U.C.L.A., Sandra Wheeler of Hill-Stead Museum, Melissa De Medeiros of M. Knoedler, Kevin Shue of the Lancaster County Historical Society, Caroline Carr of the National Portrait Gallery, Pamela Ivinski of Christie's, and Ann Potter of the Archives of American Art. Special thanks goes to C. Gary Allison of the 1st Century Project, United States Olympic Committee, for sharing his information on the Sloane family, and to Susan Sheppard of the Villa Angeletto, and Beatrice Labuset of the Château de Bachivillers. I would also like to acknowledge the contributions of Lee Edwards, Elizabeth Harlan, Honor Moore, and Eunice Lipton in matters of style and subject matter.

In addition, I would like to thank those at Williams College who have made it possible for me to pursue independent research, especially Linda Shearer, director of the Williams College Museum of Art, who has been unfailingly supportive of my work, and my assistant, Ann Greenwood, who has often had to roll with the punches. Thanks also goes to the three who made this book actually happen—my agent, Gail Ross; my editor, Diane Reverand; and my guardian angel, Cathy Hemming—all of whom believed it was possible. For moral support during the daily details which are at the heart of any book, I would like to thank Ingrid Montecino.

August 30, 1993

Nancy Mowll Mathews
Eugénie Prendergast Curator
Williams College Museum of Art

Contents

Mary Cassatt

Chapter I

Background and Early Education (1844–1865)

Even though Mary Cassatt left her homeland for Paris, even though she chose to spend her days in the bohemian world of painters and models, dealers and collectors, there remained in her the sturdy thread of her ancestry—Revolutionary War heroes, Pennsylvania landed gentry, and earnest public servants. She came from the well-bred class that hides its wealth behind modesty and hard work, dresses in a classic style, and prefers whenever possible to lead a country life. Since much of Mary Cassatt's story is about how she departed from this solid background, it is easy to overlook the fact that in her journey beyond the confines of the Pennsylvania gentry she brought certain of its indelible qualities along.

Mary's parents, Robert and Katherine Cassatt, reached the height of American aspirations of their day. Their ancestors had arrived in America from Holland, Scotland, and Ireland in the late seventeenth and early eighteenth centuries bringing with them enough money and position to buy land and establish themselves at once in the American political and professional class. Generation after generation they inched westward, capitalizing on the opportunities in business and the professions offered by the frontiers that were still located in western New Jersey and then Pennsylvania. By the time Mary Cassatt was born, her family enjoyed the social and financial success in Pittsburgh that came from the cumulative efforts of their ancestors and their belief in hard work.

Of the four main branches of Mary Cassatt's ancestors, the Cassatts were the first to arrive in this country. Jacques and Lydia Cossart[1] were French Huguenots who disembarked in New York in 1662 after spending several decades in Holland, where they had fled to escape persecution in France. Their descendants established themselves in New Jersey and, with money earned in land speculation and development there, moved westward to the frontier of Pennsylvania, located in the area around Gettysburg by the 1760s. There, spelling their name "Cassat," they became friendly with another family in the county, the Scots-Irish Simpsons, who had arrived in Gettysburg after having spent one generation in Chester County.

Two Cassat brothers married two Simpson sisters, and one of these couples, Dennis Cassat and Lydia Simpson (who were to become Mary Cassatt's grandparents), took a portion of family money to speculate in land farther west, in the vicinity of Wheeling, West Virginia. They had the support of four other Simpson brothers and sisters who had settled in the booming frontier metropolis of Pittsburgh in the years just before and after 1800. The other Cassat-Simpson couple stayed behind in York, Pennsylvania, where David was a prominent lawyer and was active in local politics, and Margaret raised a family of five children.

In Wheeling, Lydia Simpson Cassat was to lose her husband in 1808 after only three years of marriage. Their son, Robert (Mary Cassatt's father), was two years old, and their daughter, Mary, would not be born until two months after Dennis Cassat's death. The young widow moved her family to Pittsburgh, where they lived in the home of her bachelor brother Robert Simpson for several years. Her son, who was named after this brother, became heir not only to his uncle's gentlemanly estate but to Simpson's prominent social position as well; his uncle was one of the first "gentlemen" in Pittsburgh and one of the city's earliest aldermen.

Robert Simpson Cassat soon gained another mentor in his mother's second husband, Paul Morrow, an attorney who owned property in the nearby town of Greensburg, Pennsylvania. Robert and his sister grew up in Greensburg and Pittsburgh with the man they called Papa, who provided them with additional wealth and social standing. From Paul Morrow, Robert also gained a foothold in the lucrative mercantile interests of this region, which acted as a major depot for the exchange of raw materials brought in from the western territories with the manufacturing and services of the East.

While still a child, Robert Cassat met Alexander Johnston, yet another important figure in his life. The Johnstons had been close neighbors of the Simpsons in Chester County, and Alexander's father had drawn on the old family connection in sending his son out to Pittsburgh to stay with Robert Simpson while the young man studied law in one of the prominent firms. Since Alexander's father had also been a friend of Robert's father, Dennis

Cassat, Alexander became a source of information about a father Robert never knew. Alexander Johnston left the practice of law to join the fledgling Bank of Pittsburgh and was appointed its first "cashier" (director) in 1813. That year he also married. The family of his wife, Mary Stevenson, like the Johnstons, Simpsons, and Cassats, had also spent several generations moving westward and had recently arrived in Pittsburgh. Mary Stevenson's brother, Harry, had become a well-known physician in town.

The marriage of Alexander Johnston and Mary Stevenson produced a son and a daughter. When their daughter, Katherine Kelso Johnston, turned nineteen (in 1835), she married Robert Cassat, who was then twenty-nine. She had known him all her life.

It was a splendid match. Katherine had been given the best upbringing that her banker-father could devise. Although her mother died when she was only four, she had grandparents, aunts, uncles, cousins, and eventually a stepmother to care for her. She received her education in the home of an American woman who had been raised in France and who imparted a Continental education to a few select students. Her father died when she was sixteen, but his investments, particularly in land across the river in Allegheny City, allowed her to come to her marriage with ample funds. At nineteen she was five feet six inches tall, elegant, and mature for her years.

The man she married was lively, engaging and had a twinkle in his blue eyes. By the age of twenty-three he had started his own investment business, the firm of Cook & Cassat. For the next nineteen years (1829–48) he was associated with many mercantile interests in Pittsburgh, including the manufacture of cotton, and for some time headed a firm of commission or forwarding merchants, Irwin, Cassat, & Co. (figure 1). The business involved buying materials—from furs to farm produce—shipped into Pittsburgh along the rivers from Ohio, Kentucky, and elsewhere and reselling them to buyers from the East. A large part of the business rested on investment and speculation, the aspect that held Robert Cassat's interest. His own father, Dennis Cassat, had died before any profits from his own land speculation in West Virginia could be realized. His young family's fortune had been lost. But with the help of a large and important family in Pittsburgh and his own professional zeal, Robert was successful enough to make his own family financially independent by the time he was in his early forties.

This success was not entirely unclouded. Robert Cassat's profession was viewed with some suspicion by the social group to which he and his wife belonged. The other men in the family were doctors, lawyers, and, occasionally, bankers, but a financier was unusual. Robert's brother-in-law, Joseph

IRWIN, CASSAT & CO.
(Late James Irwin,)
COMMISSION
AND
FORWARDING MERCHANTS,
PITTSBURGH, PA.
JAMES IRWIN,
R. S. CASSAT,
WM. DRUM.

1. Advertisement for Irwin, Cassat & Co., 1837, from **Harris's Pittsburgh Business Directory for 1837,** *p. 135*

Gardner, the husband of his beloved sister, Mary, and namesake of his youngest son, Joseph Gardner Cassatt, worked for a time for Cook & Cassat in the mid-1830s. Gardner, scion of an old Chester County family, had been trained as a doctor, but after several years of touring Europe and other travels, found that the medical profession did not suit him. Robert offered him a job representing the firm in the growing city of Cincinnati and Gardner accepted, but not without some reservations about becoming a "money changer."[2]

Robert and Katherine Cassatt, with all their family history and entanglements, stood just slightly apart from the rest because of his open enjoyment of business and her French upbringing. Both husband and wife dressed impeccably and their home always had more luxuries and antiques than those of their friends and relatives. For generations these families had followed the westward course of American settlements and had displayed certain pioneer qualities. With Katherine and Robert Cassat the trend began to reverse itself; these successful people—like many in their generation—began to look eastward once again. They now wanted to take their wealth and social position back to the more cosmopolitan capitals of the United States and, ultimately, to Europe.

The Cassats, now Cassatts, began their trek eastward in 1848 after six of their seven children had been born. In the first thirteen years of marriage, Katherine Cassatt had given birth to three daughters and three sons, although one daughter and one son had died in infancy. The children who survived were Lydia Simpson (born 1837), Alexander Johnston (born 1839), Robert Kelso (born 1842), and Mary Stevenson (born 1844). They lived in various houses in Pittsburgh and Pittsburgh's "twin," Allegheny City, which had grown up across the river. Between 1840 and 1847 they lived on Rebecca Street (now Reedsdale), which led away from town to a residential area overlooking the Ohio River.

Allegheny City was wealthier and more cultured than Pittsburgh in the 1840s. In addition, it was the terminus of the Pennsylvania Railroad/Canal system and thus a better location than Pittsburgh for a forwarding merchant like Cassatt. The canalboats that came over the Allegheny Mountains from the end of the railroad in Altoona docked in Allegheny City and from there were taken over the river to Pittsburgh by means of an elevated aqueduct. Following in the footsteps of his uncle Robert Simpson, Robert Cassatt volunteered for public service. He served on the Select Council of Allegheny City in 1845 and 1846 and was mayor in 1847.

Cassatt, like many men of his social class, was ready for retirement in his early forties. He had been in business for twenty years and had already made his political contribution. He had four growing children whom he now wanted to enjoy. As of 1848 he joined the ranks of men who in directories and censuses simply listed themselves as "gentleman."

After a brief move back into Pittsburgh, the Cassatts decided to leave the area for good. Setting their sights on a quieter life, Robert, Katherine, and their four children said good-bye to their old friends and family and moved eastward over the mountains to Lancaster, Pennsylvania. Lancaster was centrally located between York, where Robert's aunt Margaret Simpson Cassatt and several of his cousins still resided, and Coatesville, where Robert's sister Mary Cassatt Gardner and her family lived. Robert's mother had also recently moved from Pittsburgh after the death of her husband to live with her daughter in Coatesville. Robert's cousin Hannah Cassatt Coleman and her family also lived in Lancaster. Hannah Cassatt's husband, Thomas Byrd Coleman, was a son of Robert Coleman, the wealthiest man in Lancaster. Robert Cassatt's connections in this region—the Colemans and the Gardners—were both in the iron industry, which was, at this time of rapid expansion of the railroad, a very lucrative business. Cassatt continued his investment business privately during these years, for the benefit of close family and friends.

Robert and Katherine Cassatt may also have been attracted to Lancaster by the availability of what was considered to be one of the finest mansions in the state of Pennsylvania (figure 2). Called Hardwicke at the time (now usually spelled Hardwick), its graceful curved entrance portico overlooked 103 acres of rolling meadows. The house had been built in 1795 and had been occupied by some of the most illustrious citizens of Lancaster, including William Coleman, Thomas Byrd Coleman's older brother, and David Longenecker, who was president of the Lancaster Bank and owner of the nearby Conestoga Cotton Mills. The Palace, as it was known locally, was assessed for tax purposes at $7,994, while another local mansion, Wheatland, which was purchased by James Buchanan a year after the Cassatts bought Hardwicke (and used by him during his presidency and later retirement), was assessed at only $4,430. Unfortunately the Hardwicke mansion no longer exists; it was torn down in the 1880s, when a branch of the Pennsylvania railroad was built through the grounds.

This was the Cassatts' first country house, although Robert Cassatt, and possibly Katherine as well, had grown up with homes in the country (Greensburg) and the city (Pittsburgh). Now that he had made his fortune,

2. Watercolor sketch of Hardwicke, ***c. 1830***
Lancaster County Historical Society Collection

Robert wanted his own children to enjoy country life. The Cassatts lived well. The house was furnished with family heirlooms, including much household silver and a clock that had once belonged to Marie Antoinette. As Katherine Cassatt was musical, they were never without a piano, and the family always maintained a carriage. Mary Cassatt, who lived at Hardwicke for two years from the age of four, would not have remembered too much from this period, but the pattern was indelibly set—she and her two brothers bought and/or built their own country mansions as soon as they became financially able.

The four Cassatt children had acres of woods and meadows to explore and horses, dogs, and farm animals to play with. Unlike their routine in Allegheny City and Pittsburgh, the children did not attend local private schools but had a governess who gave them lessons in their own home. Lydia, Aleck, and Robbie, now eleven, nine, and seven, would be continuing studies already begun in school while Mary, aged four, probably began her formal education at this time. The children soon had an extra diversion in the form of a new brother, Joseph Gardner Cassatt. He was born three years after another brother, George Johnston Cassatt, had died in infancy, and five years after Mary. Young Mary may not have liked losing her privileged status to a new infant who would now receive all the attention she was used to, but the fact that she had five years of being the youngest child gave her a lifelong sense of being special and entitled to extra consideration from those around her.

While the family welcomed its new arrival, it soon mourned the departure of two others. Mary's grandmother, Lydia Simpson Cassat Morrow, died at the home of her daughter in April of 1849 after a long and productive life. A month before, Mary's uncle, Joseph Gardner, who had left Cook & Cassat in the late 1830s to join his brother and other partners in buying an iron mill, Rokeby, south of Coatesville, died suddenly, leaving her aunt Mary a widow with six children. Mary Gardner, a spirited and resourceful woman, sold out her share of the mill and moved to nearby West Chester, Pennsylvania, where, with her brother's help in investing her money, she gave her children a genteel upbringing. While Mary Cassatt may not have known her grandmother or uncle who died when she was so young, the widowed aunt and houseful of cousins in West Chester became especially important people in her life as her father took on new responsibilities to his sister and her children.

Once the Cassatts had moved east of the mountains, their ties to Pittsburgh diminished, and they came under the influence of what their neighbors in Lancaster and Chester counties called "our city": Philadelphia. After only a little over a year at Hardwicke, the Cassatts were drawn inexorably to the city itself. By November 1849 they had sold Hardwicke and bought two plots of land in Philadelphia—one in the city, the other in the outskirts. The family rented a town house from which, presumably, they would oversee the construction of their own city and suburban homes. Their reasons for leaving their sumptuous country estate to take up urban life once again can only be guessed at, but there were probably many factors. Robert Cassatt's private investment business, the education of the children, and the disturbing pains experienced by their son Robbie (the early stages of an unidentified bone disease) all would have benefited from the resources of Philadelphia. Also, the fact that Robert and Katherine Cassatt were accustomed to big-city life may have made Lancaster seem too limited.

Moving to Philadelphia from Hardwicke, the Cassatts did not arrive as nobodies. Their connections to the Colemans and the Gardners, as well as their own Philadelphia relatives, the Johnstons, gave them entrée into exclusive clubs and social circles. As the Gardners had done even while living in Coatesville, the Cassatts would dance at the Assembly and send their children to the best private schools. Katherine Cassatt's great-uncle, Francis Johnston, had been a Revolutionary War colonel and one of the original members of the Pennsylvania Society of the Cincinnati (a prestigious association for Revolutionary War officers and their descendants). He settled in Philadelphia and was receiver general of the Pennsylvania Land Office as well as sheriff for the city and county of Philadelphia. His wife, Alice Erwin Johnston, was recognized for her heroic actions during the Revolutionary War in organizing shipments of supplies to Valley Forge and other humanitarian wartime services. The Johnston children, Katherine's second cousins, lived quiet lives in Philadelphia society. When the Cassatts moved to Philadelphia in 1849 they lived in the old Southward district, on Chestnut Street only a block away from the home of Katherine's cousin Alexander W. Johnston and his family. Mary and the other Cassatt children, although younger than the Johnston children, grew up as close friends of their second cousins. Once again the children were enrolled in local schools and the family participated in the life of the city. They retreated to the suburbs during the summer and made frequent trips to West Chester to visit the Gardners.

Even Philadelphia did not satisfy the expanding horizons of the successful Cassatts. After another short stay of a year and a half in Philadelphia, they were on their way farther east, to Europe. An immediate attraction might have been the Great Exhibition, which opened at London's Crystal Palace in the summer of 1851. The Cassatts sailed for England soon after receiving their passports in late June of 1851 and spent about a month in London before applying for visas for France in August. They were to spend almost two years in Paris and then another two years in Germany. Again, they were motivated by a combination of educational advantages for the children, medical care for Robbie, who was growing worse, and a general desire for a "grand tour" that neither Robert nor Katherine Cassatt had when they were growing up. At times, Robert Cassatt traveled on his own in Europe to pursue investment interests.

The years after Hardwicke, when the Cassatts immersed themselves in the increasingly sophisticated cultural arenas of Philadelphia, London, Paris, Heidelberg, and Darmstadt, were the years of Mary Cassatt's earliest intellectual orientation. She was attending school in Philadelphia by the age of six, and by the time she returned from Europe at the age of eleven she had received her fundamental education. She had attended classes in both French and German and was fluent in both; she had received a background in classical French and German literature, as was the custom in European schools, and studied a range of other academic subjects. In addition, she had probably already begun drawing and music lessons. When the earliest known likeness of her was taken in Heidelberg in a family portrait (figure 3), she has the air of a ten-year-old who is unintimidated by the world. Standing over the chessboard of her father and brother Robbie, she looks out with the narrowed eyes and calm expression of someone used to assessing her environment. Her youngest brother, Gardie, on the other hand, is shown in the left foreground with the open, wondering gaze of a still-impressionable five-year-old. Mary's reserved, judgmental expression may have been especially visible during the drawing of the portrait. She no doubt observed the artist, Peter Baumgärtner, with much interest and an already practiced and critical eye.

The Cassatts enjoyed living abroad. They had the means to rent comfortable apartments and hire trouble-free servants—two areas of common complaint by Americans living in Europe. They had enough American friends visiting from back home to allay homesickness, and they were sufficiently socially acceptable to make new friends in the American and international communities wherever they went. Robert Cassatt's liveliness and courtly manners and Katherine Cassatt's personal charm and her fluency in French gave them advantages other American visitors did not have. They stayed in Paris, sending all the children (except Gard) to local schools and partaking of the vast cultural offerings of the city, until Aleck (figure 4) showed he needed more technical training for a budding career in engineering. At this point, in the spring of 1853, they left for Heidelberg, where they stayed for a year to let Aleck attend a local boarding school and then went to Darmstadt, where Aleck was enrolled in the world-famous technical university.

The Cassatts' residence in Europe ended almost a year before they had intended it to when Robbie, at age thirteen, succumbed to the bone disease that had gradually been weakening him for the last five years. He died two days after Mary's eleventh birthday. The loss of a child is always a family tragedy, and this one was no less so for all the care and worry that had been lavished on him for so long. It affected Mary especially, since Robbie was the closest to her in age and was her steady companion during the many moves of her childhood. With the loss of Robbie she was forced to become more self-sufficient. Her nearest siblings now were Aleck (five years older) and Gard (five years younger); Lydia, seven years her senior, was more like a parent than a sister during her childhood. Leaving Aleck to finish his last

3. *Peter Baumgärtner,* **Robert Cassatt and his children,** *1854 (from left: Gard, Robbie, Mary, and Robert Cassatt)*
Pencil drawing, inscribed "Baumgärtner/1854/Heidelberg"
Private collection

4. Photograph of Alexander J. Cassatt, c. 1856 Private collection

year of school in Darmstadt, the rest of the family turned sadly home. Stopping in Paris briefly on their way, they no doubt visited the International Exposition of 1855, with its famous exhibitions of Ingres, Delacroix, and Courbet, but their experience of it would have been clouded by grief.

Although Robert Cassatt still owned property in Philadelphia he could build on, he and his family bypassed the city and established themselves in West Chester, where his sister, Mary Gardner, lived since the death of her husband in 1849. In 1855 the Gardner children were close in age to the Cassatts. The cousins were: Lydia (nineteen), Frank (seventeen), Sarah (fifteen), Katie (thirteen), Annie (ten), and Mary (seven). Robert's interest in his sister's affairs extended to their joint purchase of a large lot on the corner of Church and Union streets while he was still abroad in Germany in 1853. Although they never built on this lot, by the fall of 1855 the Cassatts had taken up residence in a nearby house on the southeast corner of High and Miner streets (figure 5), only a few houses away from the Gardners.

Proximity to their closest relatives after four years abroad and the loss of a child would have been a great comfort. Three Cassatt children were still at home, Lydia (eighteen), Mary (eleven), and Gard (six). Aleck at sixteen was in Darmstadt, then away at college. All had cousins of about the same age to provide instant best friends.

For three years (1855–58) the Cassatts rented houses in West Chester but kept their ties to Philadelphia, as if they were reluctant to give up the city altogether. Robert Cassatt, for instance, renewed his membership in the Athenaeum of Philadelphia, an exclusive library association he had first joined in 1849. Travel between West Chester and Philadelphia was made fast and easy by the Pennsylvania Railroad, and many Philadelphia families, such as the Dalletts and the Blisses, had second homes in West Chester or elsewhere in beautiful Chester County. Where Mary went to school during these years is not known; she may have attended one of the academies in West Chester, or she may have been sent to board in Philadelphia as her older cousin Lydia had been. The Cassatts' style of life was considerably more subdued than it had been at Hardwicke, Philadelphia, or their various residences in Europe, and may reflect the economic downturn of the late 1850s that affected many families with investment income. The houses the Cassatts inhabited in the late 1850s still stand in West Chester, and, although comfortable, suggest a middle-class life rather than the upper-class opulence of Hardwicke.

5. A view of the house at the southeast corner of High and Miner streets, West Chester, Pa., believed to have been the residence of the Cassatt family from 1855 to 1856

By 1858 the family felt once again that they needed to be in the city. The Cassatts purchased a house on what is now South Penn Square in the same district they had lived in before. By now Gard was ready for the best schools, and Mary at age fourteen was academically advanced. It is also possible that the Cassatts wanted to be in Philadelphia for their talented daughter's coming of age and her entrance into Philadelphia society. Although they did not sever their ties with West Chester—they purchased land there to build a permanent country retreat in 1860—they became true Philadelphians for the next four years. Mary Cassatt spent her teenage years (from fourteen to eighteen) in that city. Since she lived there longer than anywhere else in her pre-adult life, it would not be wrong to consider her "from" Philadelphia.

Although Philadelphia was not London or Paris, it was the second-largest city in the United States and the fourth largest in the world. For a teenaged girl who had spent much of her youth in Europe, it offered enough challenges to occupy her until she could step into a larger arena. Mary Cassatt had grown into a tall (five feet six), athletic young woman whose cool independence was punctuated by fervently held and passionately expressed opinions (figure 6). Her parents had encouraged the children to develop their own talents and treated them as equals as they grew up. As a consequence, Mary developed mature interests and engaged in a lifelong study of literature, politics, and the foibles of modern society. Most of all, she felt "a passion for line and color,"[3] and by the age of fifteen she knew she would become an artist. On April 25, a month before her sixteenth birthday, she signed up for the next winter's Antique Class at the Pennsylvania Academy of the Fine Arts in Philadelphia. In her haste to begin, she was first on the list.[4]

Considering Mary Cassatt's European education and the fact that she would have had drawing lessons from an early age, she very likely thought of herself, in spite of her extreme youth, as a very sophisticated observer of the Philadelphia art scene in the late 1850s and early 1860s. The interest of her parents in cultural matters would have made her familiar with public exhibitions, artists' studios, and the galleries of private collectors. Since her parents' own friends were among the prominent art patrons of the city, they were able to introduce her into homes that would otherwise have been inaccessible to a young art student. For example, an old acquaintance of her father's and a neighbor of the Cassatts' in Chester County was the financier Caleb Cope, who served as president of the Pennsylvania Academy of the Fine Arts from 1859 to 1872. When her parents failed her as escorts, she could easily persuade her sister, Lydia (with whom she began to have a more

6. *Photograph of Mary Cassatt, c. 1863*
Private collection

equal relationship as she got older), or her friends from school to accompany her to exhibitions at the academy or local art galleries. From her house Mary had to walk east five or six blocks along Chestnut Street to the old downtown of Philadelphia concentrated around the statehouse (now Independence Hall). There, interspersed with shops and businesses were located the old Pennsylvania Academy of the Fine Arts (between Tenth and Eleventh streets), the Art Union of Philadelphia, the city's most prominent commercial gallery, James S. Earle's Looking Glass, Picture Frame, and Art Gallery (between Eighth and Ninth streets), and Barnum's Museum (between Seventh and Eighth), as well as the studios of the painters John Neagle, J. R. Lambdin, and numerous engravers and daguerreotypists.

Of all the art institutions in Philadelphia, the Pennsylvania Academy of the Fine Arts (figure 7) towered above the rest in influence and importance. Founded in 1807, it was still the most prestigious academy in the United States in spite of the growth of the rival National Academy of Design in New York. Shares bought by the academy's patrons funded the acquisition of European and American works of art as well as copies and casts of famous monuments abroad. Special exhibitions of contemporary art and old master

7. ***John Sartain after J. Hamilton,*** **The Pennsylvania Academy of the Fine Arts, Erected 1806—Partially Burned and Rebuilt 1845–6—Finally Demolished 1870 [*sic*]**
Etching, engraving, and aquatint, 4 x 8⅞ in.
The Pennsylvania Academy of the Fine Arts

art were held regularly in the galleries. These events were well publicized in the newspapers. The public was invited, although the admission fees were high by the standards of the time and excluded all but the upper classes.

Since most of the students at the academy devoted full-time to their art studies, Cassatt most likely discontinued her general education at this point, although she may have continued to study the languages needed for art—French, Italian, and German—as did many of the students. Leaving school at fifteen to study art would have been quite young for girls of this class, who normally continued until they were seventeen or eighteen. Mary's desire to do this would probably have been of some concern to her parents. Of further concern to them would have been the fact that at the academy much time was spent studying the human anatomy. In the early days of the academy, public sensitivity to these matters had been so high that men and women could not even view at the same time works of art featuring the nude body. By Mary Cassatt's day not only did men and women mix in the galleries, but might often be copying the same works of art side by side. Mary's parents had to be quite modern in their attitudes to allow their sixteen-year-old daughter to spend her days in such a way.

The Cassatts were reconciled to Mary's choice of study by the knowledge that their daughter would be among her social peers at the academy and that her best friend, Eliza Haldeman (figure 8), was from as distinguished and upright a family as their own. The Cassatts might have become acquainted with the Haldemans during their brief residence in Lancaster, since the Haldemans lived to the west of the city along the Susquehanna River. The family business was an iron mill like the Gardners' Rokeby, and Samuel Haldeman, Eliza's father, was a silent partner in the mill. His own occupation was scholarly—he was a naturalist and geologist who wrote extensively and taught at the University of Pennsylvania. The Haldemans lived as opulently as the Cassatts did in Lancaster; in fact, their own mansion at Chickies Rock resembled Hardwicke with its grand portico and marble columns. Eliza Haldeman inherited her father's abilities in drawing and music. She boarded in Philadelphia while she attended classes at the Pennsylvania Academy. She also took French and music lessons from private teachers elsewhere in the city.

The letters Eliza Haldeman wrote home during the time she studied at the academy (1860–63) allow us a glimpse of the life led by these students. Although young—sixteen to nineteen years old—they were surprisingly independent. Unlike Mary Cassatt, who lived at home, Eliza Haldeman boarded with a respectable woman, Miss Howe, who also served as her

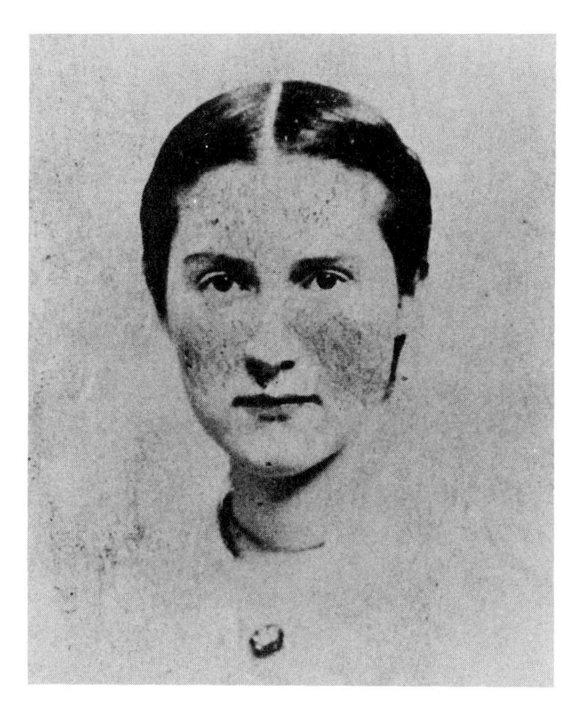

8. Photograph of Eliza Haldeman, c. 1863 Private collection

companion to cultural and social events. Eliza, who was an accomplished pianist, attended a great many concerts and recitals around the city with Miss Howe, or with numerous relatives who often stayed in town, or with friends from the academy, both male and female. Eliza and her art-student friends primarily devoted their free time to seeing art in exhibitions or in private collections. While they hardly had the advantages of any of the European cities in this regard, they did comb Philadelphia for any examples of modern or old master art—of which there were several respectable collections—and studied engravings and photographs of those they could not actually see. They soon became experts on the art they had at hand and learned to speak about it with authority.

Eliza Haldeman and Mary Cassatt had similar competitive temperaments. When they were not jockeying with each other for position in their class, they engaged their colleagues in half-serious badinage. Instruction at the academy was conducted in the form of occasional visits from the staff to look over the students' shoulder as they copied other works of art or drew from a model. Since this instruction was spotty at best, the older students filled in when the instructors were absent and assumed a tutorial role toward the newer students. Thus Mary and Eliza found themselves receiving wanted and unwanted advice particularly from the older male students. This they took with some spirit and often found themselves defending women artists in general and themselves in particular. Haldeman wrote to her father, "Today I asked Mr. Wylie [the academy "Curator"] to look at my drawing. While he was correcting it Mr. Wharton [one of the older students] came up and said 'I might as well try to cross Mount Blanc as to draw that head it was one of the hardest ones in the Academy.' I had a mind to tell him that no less than three ladies had crossed it. . . ."[5]

Both Cassatt and Haldeman were unabashed feminists when it came to the rights of women in the arts. They knew so many women artists locally and abroad by reputation that they did not feel their sex would prevent them from achieving their goals. Twenty-one out of the one hundred students signed up for the Antique Class at the academy in the years from 1859 to 1861 were women, including Fidelia Bridges and Anne Whitney from New York and Emily Sartain from Philadelphia. These three would go on to earn national reputations as professional artists. A sprinkling of women were also represented in the annual exhibitions during the early 1860s, when Cassatt and Haldeman were there. These included Mary Smith (after whom an academy prize would be named), Lilly Martin Spencer, Fidelia Bridges, Eliza Greatorex, and Ida Waugh, all of whom would be important names in American art circles for decades. Rosa Bonheur, the best-known European woman artist of the 1850s and 1860s, exhibited at the academy along with her friend and fellow artist Nathalie Micas. Haldeman and Cassatt saw the sculpture of Emma Stebbins at the gallery of Philadelphia art dealer James Earle, and were familiar with Stebbins's well-known circle of American women sculptors working at that time in Rome.

The academy students also knew the great women artists of the past. They had on daily view two paintings by the Swiss Angelica Kauffmann (1741–1807), which were in the academy's permanent collection, and could read about others in the recently published *Women Artists in All Ages and Countries* (1859) by the popular feminist writer Elizabeth Ellet, or in such memoirs as that of Elizabeth Vigée-Lebrun, published in 1835. Cassatt and Haldeman were well aware that their path would not be easy. They had suffered enough of their male colleagues' patronizing jabs to understand that women artists faced persistent skepticism in the pursuit of their goals, but nevertheless they had enough proof that women could and had made it as artists and enough encouragement to set off on that course themselves.

The students who were at the Pennsylvania Academy in those years found it a heady, romantic experience. The increasing number of spirited women in the classes and the threat of the Civil War draft that hung over the young men caused a heightened emotional atmosphere. Cassatt, Haldeman, Fidelia Bridges, Anne Whitney, and Emily Sartain were counterbalanced by Robert Wylie, Thomas Eakins, Harry Moore, Earl Shinn, and Howard Roberts, the successful men who came out of the academy at that time. This was the last decade the old academy building was used. The building had been completed in 1808 and was torn down in 1872 after increasing dilapidation. Former student Earl Shinn eulogized its last days:

> Certain months ago there tumbled away from the sight of men a silent pale building in the Greek style. . . . A pair of Ionic columns, of very just model and impressively tall, supported the pediment: through the softening stucco, threaded with long zigzag cracks like black lightning, you could see the checkered brick and mortar of which the shafts were built. . . .[6]
>
> Connoisseurs paced the grave old halls immersed in the history of art from the Etruscans downward. Sightseers from the interior took up the Academy as a matter of conscience, entering the first gallery, and telling the whole rosary of the catalogue with the unskeptical regularity of their kind. Lovers made rendezvous, their backs turned to the masterpieces with Love's inimitable contempt. On warm nights of June the externals alone—the cool leafy courts, the shadowy statues, the hawthorn built of scented snow, the open doors through which Lough's "Centaurs" tossed in a flood of light—were an advertisement, and invited to the detailed study within.[7]

Earl Shinn's sensual evocation of the "silent" temple where he and so many others spent their late teens and early twenties suggests not only the power of art but the romanticism of youth. The students, all highly educated and from similar social backgrounds, mixed freely in this atmosphere. As a release from their studies they laughed and flirted. They dated and played pranks on one another. Eliza Haldeman was escorted to cultural events by Robert Wylie and Howard Roberts, while Cassatt and Roberts visited exhibitions together. One of the students, a Miss Welch (Rebecca M. Welsh?) invited a gentleman friend to the academy, promising to make a cast of his hand in plaster. Cassatt and Haldeman, along with their friend and fellow student Inez Lewis, could not resist interrupting the innocently flirtatious game until Miss Welch "finally found it would be well to have some assistance, introduced us to the gentleman, and asked us to help her which we did, making an excellent cast and flattering the specimen of Genus 'Homo' exceedingly."[8] They immortalized the event in a photograph (figure 9) taken in the academy galleries in front of a cast of Ghiberti's Gates of

Paradise from the Florence Baptistry. The willowy eighteen-year-old Cassatt is seen on the right; Haldeman poses opposite her on the left; the honored gentleman looks out from the rear. They worked hard, but at the same time indulged their romantic view of life and art whenever possible. The sentimental Cassatt left the academy's annual exhibition in 1861 and recorded the following in the guest register: "Mary S. Cassatt Phila— bewitched."[9]

As soon as Mary's classes were over in April 1862, the Cassatts moved from Philadelphia to their newly completed country estate in Westtown, near West Chester. This move by no means ended her art studies, since she continued to come into the city periodically to work on copies at the academy and to visit exhibitions. At this point she most likely discontinued the drawing lessons she had been taking with Christian Schussele and the painting lessons with Peter Rothermel outside of her work at the academy. Although she was a conscientious student, she always preferred to work on her own. Years later the instruction she had received while at the academy grew dim in her memory, and she told her biographer, Achille Segard, that she had had none.[10] What she did remember was what she liked best

9. Photograph of Eliza Haldeman, Inez Lewis, Edmund Smith, Rebecca M. Welsh (?), and Mary Cassatt taken in the Pennsylvania Academy of the Fine Arts, 1862 The Pennsylvania Academy of the Fine Arts Archives

at the time and could do at her own furious pace—studying the art of the museums and learning from the great masters beyond the confines of Philadelphia.

The people of Westtown, the small village neighboring the Cassatts' estate, remembered her vividly as an art student. Fresh from the academy, she apparently used the local people as her own private stock of models. While her younger brother, Gard, by this time in his early teens, endeared himself to the community by sharing his pony with the neighborhood boys, Mary was forever bringing the children into the house to sketch their portraits. M. Filmore Taylor, a Westtown resident, recalled such an experience when he was "a little lad."[11] Sometimes her young models were more than she could handle; a Mrs. Gilpin of Wilmington had been a good friend of Mary's during this time and tried to get two of her children to sit for the young artist. She and Mary finally had to give up the idea in the face of absolute noncooperation from the children.[12]

Cassatt kept up with Haldeman, who remained in Philadelphia for two more academic years and visited her at Miss Howe's in town or at the Haldeman home in Chickies. The two worked on paintings together—Cassatt did a portrait of Haldeman, while Haldeman did a portrait of her younger cousin Alice—hoping in vain for the rare honor of having their paintings accepted into the academy's annual exhibitions. Cassatt and Haldeman got to know each other's brothers, sisters, and cousins on their frequent visits back and forth and developed crushes on each other's older brothers. Carsten M. Haldeman, seven years older than Eliza, was an engineer like Cassatt's own brother Alexander.

Mary could be herself with Eliza. In the few letters that remain from their long friendship she is touchingly affectionate toward Eliza, mixing high-flown terms of endearment ("Dearest Love") with quick flashes of dry, self-deprecating humor that allowed her to express her very real self-confidence and ambition without sounding pompous:

> Now please dont let your ambition sleep but finish your portrait of Alice so that I may bring it to town with me & have it framed with mine, sent to the Exhibition with mine, hung side by side with mine, be praised, criticised with mine & finally that some enthusiastic admirer of art and beauty may offer us a thousand dollars a piece for them. "Picture it—think of it!"[13]

Mary could also confide her romantic adventures to her friend. When they were both at their respective homes in the country, they settled for whatever amusements they could find, and Mary tended to find flirtations in every corner. "If I were talking to you instead of writing, I would tell you of a notable flirtation I am carrying on, but I will leave that now until we meet. I find it quite an agreable employment 'Pour passez [*sic*] le temps.' "[14]

These were idyllic days for Mary Cassatt. She spent her time painting and horseback riding—a pleasure she shared with Alexander, who was now home after earning his engineering degree at Renssalaer Polytechnic Institute in Troy, New York. He had originally started college at Yale, but his technical interests led him to transfer to RPI, possibly on the advice of Thomas Scott, president of the Pennsylvania Railroad. Scott was the husband of his mother's cousin Anna Riddle Scott. Alexander's decision to transfer may have been the first step in a long association with Scott, who became his mentor and assured his rise in the Pennsylvania Railroad. But in the early 1860s Alexander got his first job out of college as a rodman and worked briefly in the West Chester area while he lived at home.

It is surely this period that Aleck remembered when he wrote to his future wife that Mary was "always a great favorite of mine. I suppose because our taste was a good deal alike—whenever it was a question of a walk or a ride or a gallop on horseback it didn't matter when or what the weather, Mary was always ready, so when I was at home we were together a great deal—We used to have plenty of fights, for she had a pretty quick temper, and I was not always exempt from that feeling myself, but we very soon made friends again."[15] Mary and Alexander's closeness as Mary approached twenty and Aleck twenty-five was part of a general tightening of the family unit. Since Robbie's death the children had been so spread out in age that only as they got older did they develop lasting common bonds.

Ironically, this period of peace within the Cassatt family coincided with the Civil War that was being waged around them, profoundly altering the fabric of American society. The tragic loss of life did not affect their immediate family because Alexander, like many "gentlemen," apparently paid a bounty to hire a substitute to fill the draft quotas.[16] Many in their circle of friends did serve in the war, and many died. Frank Gardner, a West Chester cousin and Mary Cassatt Gardner's only son, was killed in 1862 while on naval duty. Branches of the Cassatt and Simpson families still resided in the old family homes outside Gettysburg and bore the direct brunt of the military action in 1863. The beauty of the Chester County countryside could not silence the war news or calm the anxieties of those at home, who, as Mrs. Cassatt's aunt had done in the Revolutionary War, made bandages and sewed flags for the men at the front (figure 10).

10. Photograph of Academy students making a flag, 1862
The Pennsylvania Academy of the Fine Arts Archives

The Cassatt family's views on Civil War issues are not known, but as long-standing Democrats they may not have supported either the Republican Abraham Lincoln or the war he fought over slavery. Many Pennsylvania gentry, including the Cassatts and the Haldemans, agreed with fellow Pennsylvanian James Buchanan's policy of conciliation toward the South for the sake of the economic and political well-being of the union. Although many were personally antislavery, they questioned Lincoln's judgment and kept a tight-lipped silence while the war was being waged.[17] Nevertheless, they were pro-Union and the human toll did not fail to move them.

The tragic aspects of the Civil War were balanced by the economic changes that affected the Cassatt family beneficially. In 1863 Alexander Cassatt had become an assistant engineer on the Pennsylvania Railroad headquartered in Philadelphia. Playing a role in the railroad expansion brought about by the war, he was a wealthy man by 1870. His father, Robert Cassatt, took advantage of the wave of new investments and financing opportunities in this period and opened a brokerage office in the Philadelphia Merchant's Exchange in 1865, almost twenty years after he had closed his last one in Pittsburgh. Cassatt & Co. became a respected investment firm with a long history into the twentieth century continued by Robert's son Gardner and his grandsons.

As much as Mary enjoyed life in the country, and as productive as she may have been alternating between painting from local models and going to Philadelphia to continue the exercise of copying, she must have looked upon this period of rustication as merely temporary. As the war drew to a close in 1865 she began planning the inevitable next step of any American art student: study abroad. She was twenty-one years old; her passion for painting had only increased with the years of academy exercises and work on her own; and she had a taste for Europe that was formed in her childhood and continued undiminished until the day she died. Chester County, at first a haven, now began to seem a prison.

As Cassatt's restlessness grew, it became evident to her parents that they would not be able to keep her at home much longer. Her father was the most distressed by his daughter's plans (figure 11). Mary remembered for years that in a burst of anger he had told her he would almost rather see her dead than have her go to Europe by herself to become an artist.[18] Partly this stemmed from his pain at losing her. He liked to keep his children nearby and had been successful with Lydia, who was now twenty-eight and still living at home. Gard, of course, was still in school, and even Aleck, although he was now on his own, only lived as far away as Philadelphia. The parents kept these three close to them for another twelve years. But Mary was different. Independent by nature, her tendency to keep her own counsel only deepened with time. Tempted by seeing her friends, including Eliza Haldeman, live away from home and plan for their own trips to Europe, she

11. Mary Cassatt,
Portrait of Robert S. Cassatt, *1871*
Oil on canvas,
26½ x 22⅛ in.
Private collection

could not be dissuaded. Although her father's disapproval did not stop her, his opposition to her plans gave her pause and left an irreparable rent in what had been a close relationship.

Cassatt's mother accompanied Mary to Europe. The two applied for their passports in West Chester on October 4, 1865.[19] In the shorthand used for personal descriptions in passports in the days before photographs became universal, the twenty-one-year-old Mary Cassatt was summed up as follows:

Stature	—five and half feet
Eyes	—Grey
Nose	—small
Mouth	—Large
Chin	—Large
Hair	—Brown
Complexion	—Ruddy
Face	—Medium

Her ruddy complexion and large chin diminished the beauty that was promised by her other Cassatt family features, especially the small nose and fine gray eyes. But her face was pleasant enough, and, coupled with her interesting personality and elegant figure, made her a sociably acceptable young woman with her pick of male and female friends. If she had wanted to marry, her personal attributes, as well as her family's standing and wealth, would have attracted serious suitors. It was plain that she, like many young women of her generation, was in no hurry to marry when she had such a compelling alternative in her art career. In her own family, she joined her sister, Lydia, and her cousins Lydia, Catherine, and Mary Gardner in choosing an unmarried life. Unencumbered by a desire for an American home and hearth, Mary Cassatt could board the steamer for Europe with unalloyed joy.

Chapter II

Studies in Europe (1866–1870)

Mary Cassatt and her mother arrived in Paris for the Christmas season late in 1865. The parties and balls in Philadelphia in December and January would have been enjoyable, but the season in Paris was brilliant. For Americans, much of the entertainment revolved around parties and dinners held by the American consul and special services at the American Chapel. Everywhere in Paris there were festive decorations, eye-catching gifts in store windows, and large-scale celebrations. Since they had numerous friends in Paris, the Cassatt mother and daughter would have been drawn into the magical season. It was a fitting welcome for the young artist who had celebrated her last Christmas in Paris when she was eight years old.

In her eagerness to be off to Paris, she forged ahead of her friends from the academy, including Eliza Haldeman, Howard Roberts, and Thomas Eakins, who began arriving about six months later. Her mother stayed with her for some time, probably returning home in early summer. She saw that her daughter was well established as a boarder in the home of a trusted family. Other Philadelphians, such as her old teacher, Christian Schussele, had sailed for Europe earlier in 1865. The art collector James Claghorn sailed just before the Cassatts. There were also American art students from other parts of the country who had come to Paris before the Civil War ended and had already learned the ropes.

One of these students was Elizabeth Gardner (figure 12), a well-connected young woman from Exeter, New Hampshire, who, in 1864 at the age of twenty-seven, came to Paris to learn painting and make her fortune. Her family's money had been drastically diminished in the late 1850s, leaving

12. Photograph of Elizabeth Gardner, c. 1858
Elizabeth Gardner Bouguereau Papers
Archives of American Art
Smithsonian Institution

her with the resolve to recoup their lost wealth. Her talent had been little developed in the United States, since she had not attended an important academy as Cassatt had done, but she worked feverishly and advanced quickly once in the hands of various French masters. Although seven years older and never a close friend of Cassatt, Gardner's life paralleled Cassatt's as the two continued decade after decade to live in Paris and become the best-known American women artists in France. Her letters and those of the many young American men and women trying their luck in Paris round out our understanding of Cassatt's own experience there. Very few of Cassatt's letter from this period have survived, so we often have to be satisfied with hearing her thoughts and actions in the voices of those around her.

Once settled, Cassatt's main objective was to get back to work. This meant finding instruction from a recognized master and setting up other opportunities to work on her own. Since women were not admitted to the principal academy of France, the École des Beaux-Arts, they typically petitioned an established painter who was known to give private lessons to take them on. It was common practice for successful artists to teach. An aspiring student had a range of masters to choose from, as long as she could meet the standards of that particular master and could afford the fee. Elizabeth Gardner, who had had little previous training, was taken on by a less important artist, Jean-Baptiste-Ange Tissier, while her more advanced friend from Exeter, Imogene Robinson, managed to be accepted by the well-known Thomas Couture.

It is a measure of Cassatt's skill at this time that she was accepted by one of the most sought after teachers in Paris, Jean-Léon Gérôme (figure 13). Gérôme, a younger master, was considered to be one of the most talented draftsmen of his generation and represented a new wave of realist precision of detail applied to exotic and historic subjects. Her friends back home in Philadelphia, who knew Gérôme only by reputation, were stunned. When Thomas Eakins (figure 14) began studying with Gérôme later that year, he was bombarded with letters from such friends demanding details about Mary Cassatt's great coup. To their mutual friend Emily Sartain he wrote that he did not know much about it, but "from what I know of Gérôme I think the whole story extremely probable"[1] and later another astonished friend, Charles Fussell, wrote back to Eakins asking for all the details of "how Miss Cassatt was honored by Gérôme's private lessons."[2]

Aside from her lessons with Gérôme, Cassatt plunged into the other round of activities that filled the days of Parisian art students. She very

13. Jean-Léon Gérôme, **Death of Caesar,** *1859*
Oil on canvas, 33⅝ x 57¼ in.
Walters Art Gallery, Baltimore

quickly obtained a permit to copy paintings in the Louvre, and began to spend a good part of every day there. If contemporary drawings and prints of the galleries of the Louvre are reliable, the corridors were filled with a thicket of easels clustered around the more popular paintings (figure 15). Most of the easels belonged to art students who were copying as a means of studying the techniques of color, brushwork, and composition of the old masters. Others in the crowd would turn their copies into something more than an exercise. As professional copyists, they took orders primarily from tourists for copies of famous paintings in the Louvre and made a respectable amount of money for their efforts. In the years immediately after the Civil War, American tourists constituted a major market for such copies. Elizabeth Gardner, for instance, very quickly became proficient enough to subsidize her education by executing copies for clients. Even Cassatt later earned money in this way.

In the period from 1865 to 1870, when Cassatt haunted these corridors as a student, she was joined by such American friends as Eliza Haldeman, Howard Roberts, Thomas Eakins, William Sartain, Henry Bacon, Frederick Bridgman, Howard Helmick, Elizabeth Gardner, and Imogene Robinson. Of the French artists of importance to Cassatt, one finds listed in the copyists' register the names of Jenny Sisley, Edgar Degas, Eugène Delacroix, Louise

14. Photograph of Thomas Eakins, 1866 The Pennsylvania Academy of the Fine Arts Archives, Philadelphia Purchased with funds donated by the Pennsylvania Academy Women's Committee

Abbéma, Pierre Cabanel, Paul Cézanne, Berthe and Edma Morisot, and M. and Mme. Joseph Tourny. This international group did not necessarily mix, and letters indicate that the French and American women were particularly cool toward each other. For those who did know one another, the Louvre was unquestionably the social center of the young cliques in Paris.

Not only did the copyists have their daily interaction, but other, more romantic assignations were carried out in the hallowed halls. Even in America, museums and galleries were favorite meeting places for young men and women, but in Paris, with social life heavily chaperoned, the young people turned to the Louvre and the Luxembourg (the museum of modern art) for a freer atmosphere in which to talk and laugh. Since many of the hotels and lodgings of the American students did not allow visitors of the opposite sex, they naturally turned to the Louvre as a second home.

Many an American parent worried about the possible dangers of the social and romantic environment in Paris. Eliza Haldeman laughingly brushed off her mother's fears in response to a story about an American woman abducted in Paris: "Do not trouble about me disappearing in

15. Winslow Homer, **Art-Students and Copyists in the Louvre Gallery, Paris,** *wood engraving in* **Harper's Weekly,** *January 11, 1868, p. 25*

Paris. I know it thoroughly and I think [it] likely the lady you read of *ran* off with some good looking frenchman. As I am to be an old maid there is no danger for me in that quarter."[3] In spite of Eliza's jests, there was some basis for parental concern for their artistic daughters in Paris. They may not have been in serious danger of abduction, but they sometimes did develop inappropriate attachments to their teachers—older men who responded to the flattering attentions of these fresh, self-confident young Americans. Usually these relationships ended innocently, but not without some pain, when the student returned to America. Occasionally the two married. Elizabeth Gardner married William Bouguereau after a twenty-year engagement.

The other danger of concern to parents was to the young woman's reputation. Copying in the Louvre, unlike copying in the Pennsylvania Academy, was an extremely public occupation. The copyists at their easels were in full view of the thousands of tourists and museum-goers who dutifully tramped the miles of art-filled corridors everyday. Since copyists were very often women—copying being a relatively low-paying and noncompetitive branch of art—looking at the copyists had become a part of the pleasure of visiting a museum. Nathaniel Hawthorne in his 1860 classic, *The Marble Faun,* created the character of Hilda, a copyist in Rome whose beauty competed with the city's venerable art treasures:

> All the Anglo-Saxon denizens of Rome, by this time, knew Hilda by sight. Unconsciously, the poor child had become one of the spectacles of the Eternal City, and was often pointed out to strangers sitting at her easel among the wild-bearded young men, the white-haired old ones, and the shabbily dressed, painfully plain women, who make up the throng of copyists. . . . Sometimes a young artist, instead of going on with a copy of the picture before which he had placed his easel, would enrich his canvas with an original portrait of Hilda at her work. A lovelier subject could not have been selected, nor one which required nicer skill and insight in doing it anything like justice.[4]

Many days the young women at their easels would overhear tributes from the onlookers. Eliza Haldeman confessed her pleasure at overhearing a compliment while working at the Louvre: "An old gentleman said to his wife a few days ago 'that's a right pretty girl.' I was glad to have unbiased testimony on the subject for I was afraid my hard work had taken away all the little pretentions I ever had that way and that you would find me old and ugly."[5]

However, the woman who put herself in such a public position was not always respected by the visitor. Perhaps worse than being judged pretty or plain was being judged loose. Henry James countered Hawthorne's pure heroine-copyist with his own corrupt copyist Néomie Nioche in *The American* (first serialized in the *Atlantic Monthly,* 1876–77). The archetypal American traveler, Christopher Newman, comes across Néomie in the Louvre and sits down to observe her:

> As the little copyist proceeded with her work, she sent every now and then a responsive glance toward her admirer. The cultivation of the fine arts appeared to necessitate, to her mind, a great deal of by-play, a great standing off with folded arms and head drooping from side to side, stroking of a dimpled chin with a dimpled hand, sighing and frowning and patting of the foot, fumbling in disordered tresses for wandering hair-pins. These performances were accompanied by a restless glance, which lingered longer than elsewhere upon the gentleman we have described. At last he rose abruptly, put on his hat, and approached the young lady. He placed himself before her picture and looked at it for some moments, during which she pretended to be quite unconscious of his inspection. Then, addressing her with the single word which constituted the strength of his French vocabulary, and holding

> up one finger in a manner which appeared to him to illuminate his meaning, "*Combien?*" he abruptly demanded.[6]

In James's character, the combination of public posturing and offering something for sale add up to a refined type of prostitution. While our earnest American art students would have been outraged at the thought, there was enough whispering about the young women at the Louvre that American parents like the Cassatts or the Haldemans might have had cause to be genuinely concerned. This ultimate lapse, or perceived lapse, in morality—"a fate worse than death"—is curiously like Mr. Cassatt's pronouncement to Mary upon her departure for an artist's life in Paris: "I would almost rather see you dead."[7] He knew she was extremely impulsive and independent, and for her to be whispered about in the Louvre was not what he wanted for his beloved but troublesome daughter (figure 16).

She already had something of a reputation for unconventional behavior. Eliza's parents were extremely fond of her, but at the same time they couldn't help urging Eliza to be cautious in following Mary's fearless lead around Paris:

> I hope you will not run any risk of being waylaid or insulted. I fear that you with Miss Cassatt may venture too far, do not rely on her judgment as she has no religion to guide her and from the impulse of a moment you may rush with her into things that may injure you. So my dear child do be careful.[8]

Mary probably underestimated what her own reaction would be to the moral and ethical miasma that enveloped the Parisian art world in the 1860s. The glittering reign of Napoleon III brought art into new prominence in French culture. The pursuit of fame as well as money from exhibition prizes and commissions drove artists to new competitive heights and put increasing pressure on art students to make their mark early. Cassatt found that she was confronted not only with issues of personal morality in the relaxed social atmosphere of the Louvre but with the issues of professional ethics as well.

Since art students were not yet concerned about marketing and selling, their lives revolved around currying the favor of their teachers and having their first pictures accepted into the huge and prestigious Salon—the annual exhibition sponsored by the French government. Securing the goodwill of

16. *Photograph of Mary Cassatt taken in Paris, c. 1867*
Private collection

the first would help them achieve the second, which would, in turn, give them the visibility and imprimatur they needed to turn from student to professional. Teachers and students thus played a delicate game. The students wanted to attach themselves to the most prestigious and influential teacher possible without joining a class so far above their ability level that the teacher would overlook them in favor of more accomplished students. The teacher in turn wanted to make such a public commitment only to students who would be a credit to him. Thus teachers were often distant in class, uttering only the slightest encouragement (*"Pas mal"*) to students ready to go to any lengths for approval.

When the time came to prepare a work for submission to the Salon jury, students tried to get as much advice on their pictures as possible and took their compositions through sketch after sketch before they received approval to begin the painting itself. Students entangled their teachers so deeply in this process that teachers often ended up painting whole passages of their students' canvases themselves. Then, having invested so much of their own time and talent, teachers used their influence as members of the Salon jury (or, if not members, they pressed their colleagues who were) to have their students' paintings accepted into the exhibition. At first Cassatt accepted this process of behind-the-scenes influence without comment and was as successful in winning the favor of her teachers—and thus their influence at the Salon—as anyone. But after a year of immersion in a system that revolved around ego, flattery, and favoritism, she fled what she jokingly called Paris's "moral depravement," and headed for the countryside.

Cassatt's companion in what would become an almost two-year stay in small villages outside Paris was her old friend Eliza Haldeman (figure 17). The two had undoubtedly been dreaming of this trip to Europe ever since their early days at the Pennsylvania Academy of the Fine Arts. When the time came to put plans into action, Cassatt preceded Haldeman by a full six months; Eliza sailed with her father in May of 1866. But as Mary and Eliza settled into their studies, their fellow students in Paris were distressed to see that the two friends were no longer speaking. The rift had occurred by mail. Something Mary had written caused Eliza to make a cool reply; this in turn caused Mary to stop writing. By the fall of 1866 their quarrel was known to all their friends and family. Finally Howard Roberts, the sculpture student from the Pennsylvania Academy who had been close to both of them, played peacemaker. In late October, Eliza wrote to her mother:

17. Photograph of Eliza Haldeman taken in Paris, 1867
Private collection

What will be your surprise when I tell you that Miss Cassatt and I are friends again. I think it is all through the kindness of Mr. Roberts for he was very anxious we should make up and told me it was as much my fault as hers, & finally, how, I cant say made her come to see me. We met at the door of the

> Louvre one day. She came up and said she was just coming to see me. We took a walk on neutral ground—the garden of the Tuileries—and had a talk.[9]

And to her father:

> I am so happy that Mary and I are friends, she is the only bit of home I have here and she never would have stopped writing if there had not been a misunderstanding; she is as kind as she can be.[10]

This kind of rift was not uncommon when friends had to rely on infrequent letters to nourish their relationships. In a group of competitive and sensitive art students, epistolary estrangements happened with alarming frequency. The gossip and backbiting that went on in the American art cliques of Paris and Rome were made more lethal when conveyed by letter to those back home who spread it second and third hand. Cassatt was often enmeshed in these melodramas in her early days in Europe because, with the best intentions, she would freely express her own thoughts and opinions without thinking of the consequences. She was shocked and mortified when her remarks were repeated to a wider circle causing unintended insult to someone who would then lash out at her in return. In the face of such criticism, her response was to recoil. She was insecure enough to be wounded by her friends and independent enough to seek relief by turning her back. Fortunately she had throughout her life friends like Howard Roberts who could talk her out of her insecurity and aloofness and others like Eliza Haldeman whose affectionate hearts would forgive her. Once forgiven, Cassatt could again exert her power to beguile friends like Eliza. The Haldemans urged their daughter, now that she and Mary had made up, not to neglect her other friends and "be entirely enchanted with [Mary]."[11] Eliza, trusting her own judgement, spent the next two years with Mary Cassatt in as close a friendship as either would ever have.

When Cassatt and Haldeman reconciled, Cassatt joined the class that Haldeman had entered under the tutelage of Charles Chaplin. Chaplin, like Gérôme, was well known to Americans, but practiced a more decorative portrait and genre style (figure 18). He was one of the small group of masters in Paris who held classes specifically for women (figure 19). While Cassatt probably kept up her private lessons with Gérôme, joining Haldeman allowed her to receive the benefits of a structured class, which included having models to draw and paint from at all times. After their years of drawing

18. *Charles Chaplin,* Devotion, *1857*
Oil on canvas, $10^{3}/_{4} \times 8^{1}/_{2}$ *in.*
Walters Art Gallery, Baltimore

19. Detail of photograph of painting class of Charles Chaplin, Paris, 1866 (Mary Cassatt is at top left; Eliza Haldeman is second from right) Present location unknown

from plaster casts and copying other works of art at the Pennsylvania Academy, Cassatt and Haldeman were hungry for practice from the live model. This passion was so great among young art students in Paris that they often supplemented their formal classes with informal study groups that met in the evenings and shared the cost of engaging regular models. Haldeman and Cassatt were involved in one on the Left Bank, as Eliza reported to her father: "Our evening school goes on finely three evenings every week. It is in the quartier Latin and I feel quite like a student when I go there. . . . The days are never long enough for me and I only know the week has passed by Sunday coming and not painting."[12]

Their hard work of the fall caused Cassatt and Haldeman to advance to the forefront of Chaplin's class. They then decided to leave the artificial environment of the classroom for the "real world" of the countryside. In February 1867 they took up residence in the village of Courances, not far from Barbizon and the Fontainebleau Forest, where they could engage actual villagers as models and paint them in their natural setting. They went to Paris regularly. Haldeman and probably Cassatt kept lodgings there. While in Paris they showed their work to Chaplin and received advice. Chaplin was encouraging and they were pleased with their progress, feeling that they were learning more in Courances than they could in Paris.

They were unprepared for the plunge into the past that they, and generations of American artists, took upon entering the primitive, picturesque French villages. Although glad to be back in the country, they looked with a mixture of horror and fascination at the human habitations that seemed unchanged from the beginnings of civilization. At twenty-three years old they struggled to maintain their polite open-mindedness, but could not overcome the fear that dirt and disease lurked in the tile floors and blackened beams of the tiny dwellings or in the pancakes offered in the bare hands of an unpretentious hostess. As time went on they found more of the simple customs to enjoy—such as using a bed warmer and making candy—and fewer to fear. They were also drawn more into the workings of peasant society and set their American minds to work on the puzzle of French class distinctions, seeing in these peasants simplicity tempered with a graceful nobility. Eliza tried to convey the unusual effect to her mother: "It is surprising to see how polite the children are, if we pass a group of boys playing when we are walking they all get up and take off their hats and say good morning though they are only peasants and some but five years old. The men and women are the same and invite us into their houses with as much grace as if they were ladys."[13]

The courtly manners of the poor in Europe were in sharp contrast to the straightforward "democratic" manners of the working classes in the United States. In travel literature of the time, this became one of the most remarked upon differences between the two cultures.[14] To American artists like Cassatt and Haldeman this difference made European peasants interesting and picturesque, and one of their primary aims in painting them was to capture the effect of noble simplicity. They began painting the villagers at once and soon developed ideas for major pictures that they could show to Chaplin. Not

20. ***Pierre-Édouard Frère,* Preparing Dinner, *1858***
Oil on canvas, 16⅛ x 20⅞ in.
Walters Art Gallery, Baltimore

only did he approve of their work, but he encouraged them to finish their paintings in time to submit them to that year's Salon. Although neither painting is known to have survived, they apparently depicted village children posed in one of the romantic peasant cottages. Although the children "tease us nearly to death, sing, dance, and cut up all sorts of capers,"[15] in quieter moments the two artists found contentment as they painted while being "entertained with the music of a spinning wheel and the ticking of a clock."[16]

The paintings did not make it into the Salon that year, but Cassatt and Haldeman were pleased enough with their work that they decided to go more seriously into this style of painting, called genre painting, which was characterized by a grab bag of subjects having to do with pleasant scenes of daily life, usually showing peasants or lower classes. After only a month in Courances, they decided to take up a lengthy residence in another village, Écouen, thirty miles north of Paris, which was the center of a well-known school of genre painting. The two most famous French genre painters, Pierre

Édouard Frère and Paul Constant Soyer, lived in the village and accepted students. Cassatt and Haldeman petitioned Soyer for instruction and were taken on. By April they were settled in the town they would make their home for the next year and a half.

In Écouen they were once again part of an artists' colony that included a number of Americans, including two married couples. Now that they were again among Americans, they spent less time with the villagers themselves, although they continued to paint the local peasants in their country environment. Instead, their social lives consisted of a round of dinners, picnics, and visits that drew the painters together in their off-hours and into conversations that revolved around art and career advancement. Because of the shared interests and ambitions of the group, and because the important resident artists, Frère and Soyer, were prominent in official art circles, Cassatt and Haldeman, as well as the other students, saw their stay in Écouen as an important step in gaining recognition. Ironically, their ties to the Paris art world were almost as strong as if they had stayed in the city.

Perhaps their best friends in Écouen were Henry Bacon and his wife, who was also an artist. Bacon, wounded in the Civil War, left Massachusetts for Paris soon after and was an early convert to the Écouen genre style. Although he and his wife struggled in their early days in France, his pictures were recently beginning to sell and they lived quite comfortably in Écouen.[17] Another good friend was a French landscapist, Léonide Bourges, who lived in Écouen for many years while maintaining a studio in Paris. They also became quite fond of their teacher, Paul Soyer, and his wife, just as they had enjoyed good relations with Gérôme and Chaplin in Paris. Soyer did not hold formal classes, but made his young friends feel welcome to come to him regularly for advice. His practice of interspersing praise with instruction, as well as the fact that he did not charge a fee, endeared him to the group. Eliza Haldeman repeated all his compliments to her parents and was especially pleased when he told her, "Indeed I find that you are a good colorist, an extremely good colorist."[18]

Cassatt attracted the most attention from their teachers and colleagues, and it was Cassatt whom Eliza herself praised unreservedly. While Haldeman had a great deal of talent and interest in painting, Cassatt had a passion for it. Haldeman had come to Europe thinking she would stay only a year, but, caught up in the excitement, eventually extended her stay to about two and a half. Cassatt, on the other hand, intended to stay for three or four years, and was the one who was always thinking ahead, making plans, and pushing her friend to join her as she moved about sampling the diverse wares that the French art world offered. When Mrs. Haldeman sent a word of encouragement to Mary through Eliza, Eliza wrote back, "Mary wishes to be remembered to you, she laughed when I told her your message and said she wanted to paint *better* than the old masters. . . . Mary expects to stay two years more abroad, she is getting on very well and studies hard. I think she has a great deal of talent and industry. One acquires the latter living in France. The people study so hard and the results are wonderful."[19]

Although Écouen was their home base from April of 1867 to May of 1868, they made two short excursions elsewhere in the French countryside during this time. The first was necessitated by a stomach illness that struck Mary Cassatt in August but lingered so long that by the end of September a change of air was recommended. The two friends took this opportunity for a seaside holiday in the town of St.-Valéry-sur-Somme on the Normandy coast. Sea bathing and walking along the ramparts worked the desired cure. Soon they talked of painting again, seeing genre pictures everywhere in the picturesque fishing village. However, it is most likely that they wended their way through Eu, le Tréport, Dieppe, and Rouen back to Écouen without having put brush to canvas.

Another excursion was for purely art purposes and was productive for both of them. In the middle of April 1868 Cassatt and Haldeman went back to Courances for a short visit and to investigate the teachers to be had in the nearby town of Barbizon. Cassatt intended to spend the summer away from Écouen, and to broaden her skills studying landscape painting. The Barbizon style, which stressed simple, more direct compositions than traditional landscape paintings had used, was just becoming known to Americans and was considered by them to be on the cutting edge of modern painting. The masters of the style best known to Cassatt were Constant Troyen, Jules Breton, Jean Millet, and Charles Jacque, although many others, including Théodore Rousseau and Camille Corot, were associated with the school. As much as she admired the style of painting, Cassatt was horrified to find that they neglected the figures in their compositions—in fact, did not draw them from life. Since her main objective was to learn landscape as a background for her figures, she decided against spending the summer there. Although she eventually picked up enough to paint credible landscape backgrounds, it was never the strongest part of her oeuvre. Nevertheless the time in Courances was not wasted because Cassatt and Haldeman began new pictures.

After being back in Écouen for only about a week, Cassatt and Haldeman received the news they had been waiting for all spring—their paintings had been accepted into the Salon of 1868. Haldeman's painting, now lost, was a typical Écouen subject: a girl peeling potatoes in front of a buffet full of dishes. Cassatt's was more romantic: a peasant girl playing a mandoline (figure 21). This work, which stayed in the Cassatt family and is now her earliest documented painting, establishes Cassatt not so much as a genre painter but as a figure painter. Against a neutral background, a melancholy child of about twelve looks away from the viewer as she absently plucks the strings of her instrument. Cassatt has placed more emphasis on the romantic mood set by the face and gesture of the figure than on the ordinary daily-life activity so characteristic of the Écouen school. It is clear that she is aiming for a type of art that transcends the mere anecdotal. Even though she acknowledges both Soyer and Chaplin as her teachers in the Salon catalog, the painting comes instead from the romantic style of very different artists: Corot and Couture. Although Cassatt was a good and loyal student, liked and encouraged by her teachers, her willfulness and innate sense of purpose led her in her own direction.

There was no greater thrill for the art student in Paris than to have a painting accepted at the Salon. Elizabeth Gardner, who had two paintings accepted that same year, explained the process and its significance to her sister:

> I am afraid that you all thought my last letter a crazy epistle. I was very anxious when I wrote it. I had sent two original pictures to the annual Paris exhibition. Twelve of the first artists are chosen as judges. They look over the pictures and decide whether or not they shall be hung in the Salon. It is very difficult for young aspirants to be accepted especially on their first trial and I had never sent before. We were kept waiting six weeks. One after another of my friends were written to that their pictures were refused. There were 800 unfortunates in all but when the exhibition opened *both of mine* were hung in full view among the accepted. I did want to get one admitted but had not dared to hope for both. I know you will all be glad for me. It gives one at once a position among foreign artists and raises the value of what I paint. I have just received $400 in gold for one of the pictures, and have spent it nearly all for curious things to paint.[20]

Eliza Haldeman echoed Gardner's sense of shock: "I did not know until the day of the opening that my picture had been sent and when I heard it was in I took a good crying spell which lasted three hours."[21]

In spite of their deep pleasure in having their pictures accepted at the

21. Mary Cassatt, **A Mandoline Player,** *1868*
Oil on canvas, 36½ x 28¾ in.
Private collection

Salon, Haldeman and Cassatt were also somewhat cynical about the honor. They knew that the jury that year had been especially lenient, particularly with young artists, and that they had accepted many more works than had been customary in the past. Haldeman showed uncharacteristic harshness in sniping at the event and very likely echoed the more strident and opinionated voice of her friend Mary Cassatt:

> The Exposition is very poor this year as there has been 1200 more pictures accepted than usual, in fact almost anything would have passed; there is to be forty medals given though I cannot imagine who there is to deserve them all. . . . In fact the waste of good colors frames and canvas this year is astonishing.[22]

Although there was an element of self-deprecation in Haldeman's and Cassatt's assessment of the Salon, the critical attitude of the two young Americans also reflects the larger artistic discontent surfacing in Paris at the time. Criticism focused on the old-guard artists like Alexandre Cabanel, whose *Birth of Venus* had been the sensation of the Salon of 1863, and who had come to epitomize the style of the French Academy, which sponsored the annual Salons. Cassatt and others around her saw that there was a rebellion afoot in the ateliers outside the official École des Beaux-Arts. Describing the unrest, Haldeman wrote that artists "are leaving the Academy style and each one seaking a new way, consequently just now everything is Chaos. But I suppose in the end they will be better for the change."[23]

Cassatt's and Haldeman's keen interpretation of the artistic upheavals they witnessed in Paris in the 1860s was not shared by everyone in the American colony. Elizabeth Gardner, whose joy in being accepted by the Salon was unclouded by cynicism, did not question the strength of the Academic tradition. Her own pictures in the Salon of 1868 showed that she had worked hard to master the polished style of the old guard, and she would proceed as planned within the system (figure 22). She certainly acknowledged the swarm of other styles that developed during her early years in Paris, but held firm in her belief that the official style, as practiced by such masters as Cabanel and her own favorite, Bouguereau, would bring her the highest rewards in terms of money and prizes. And she was not disappointed.

Cassatt, on the other hand, showed her ambivalence toward the system early on. She saw that the Academic style was being challenged from all quarters—from the most radical artists like Courbet and Manet to the new generation of academics like Gérôme and Lefebvre. The latter were very visible as newcomers in the Salon, whereas the former had proclaimed their independence altogether, most notably when they both staged their own exhibitions outside the official halls of the 1867 international exposition in

22. Elizabeth Gardner Oil on canvas, $60\frac{1}{2} \times 41\frac{3}{8}$ in. The National Museum of Women in the Arts, gift of Wallace and Wilhelmina Holladay

Paris. Cassatt also knew the "outsiders" of Écouen: Frère and Soyer were rewarded by the system, but their genre style was considered a step down from official neoclassicism; their neighbor in nearby Villiers-le-Bel, Thomas Couture, had been a celebrated Academic artist in the 1850s but recently rejected the system and staged a well-publicized and dramatic withdrawal to the countryside.

Cassatt's own withdrawal to Écouen after a year in Paris showed her innate distaste for the moral compromises necessary to make in following the path to establishment success. However, whether she approved of the system or not, she still intended to be embraced by it and, like Elizabeth Gardner, she wanted to reap the benefits of official recognition. She believed that her talent and hard work would so dazzle the artists of the Salon jury that she would soon rise to the top without having to play the political games that were the key to success for lesser artists. What Cassatt didn't realize was that her opposing attitudes were on a collision course. Her anti-

Academic feelings and stylistic experimentation became so well known to Salon juries that, in spite of their respect for her art, they could no longer condone her independent direction. The great tragedy of Cassatt's early career was that after a brilliant beginning, she could not reconcile her clashing attitudes sufficiently to be inside the system or out of it. For ten years Cassatt submitted paintings to the Salon. Toward the end of that time, as the rejections grew more numerous in spite of the obvious flowering of her abilities, her mood grew blacker and more bitter.

In May of 1868 the cracks in Cassatt's career plans were far from alarming. Her initial criticisms of the Salon experience gave way to the pure enjoyment of youthful success and Paris in the springtime. She and Eliza gave up their apartment in Écouen to stay in a hotel in the city for several weeks for the exhibition. They used their special exhibitors' passes to take their friends into the exhibit in the morning before the public was allowed in at ten o'clock. They passed through a private entrance of the Palais de l'Industrie on the Champs-Élysées (figure 23), which has since been torn down to make way for the Grand Palais and Petit Palais on the Champs-Élysées, and they wended their way through the barnlike galleries, pointing out their small paintings hanging cheek by jowl with the other thirty-five hundred works of art crowded into the space (figure 24).

Cassatt had every right to be satisfied with her painting *La Mandoline.*

23. **Palais de l'Industrie, Champs-Élysées, *c. 1865***
Photo Bibliothèque Nationale

24. Gustave Doré, **Palais de l'Industrie, Salon de 1868,** *Paris, Bibliothèque Nationale, Départment des Estampes*

Unlike Haldeman's, which was "skyed," hung toward the top of the wall, Cassatt's was "on the line" at eye-level, indicating that the jury felt it was of more than average interest. This was partly because of its quality, but also, according to Haldeman, it was a reward for being the artist's own work, and not "painted on" by her teachèr. Haldeman confessed that Soyer had lent a hand to her own piece, whereas Cassatt's was done by herself alone.

Cassatt and Haldeman also had a chance to listen surreptitiously to comments about their paintings made by the crowd and to observe fashionable Paris. The annual Salon was one of the most festive events of the year. For the six weeks it was open, hundreds of thousands of people dressed in their finest to promenade the long gallery halls. Cassatt, Haldeman, Gardner, and other young American women carefully observed the length of skirts, the type of sashes, and the amount of Chantilly lace worn by the fashionable crowd not only to keep their own wardrobes up to date, but to report the latest styles to sisters and cousins back home. All three were vain about their dress and felt that they could elicit admiration when the occasion demanded it. Since they were all on limited budgets, they were not among the American patrons of the great fashion houses such as Worth, Doucet, or Pingat. Cassatt and Haldeman lived on lump sums from their parents that had to last for specified periods of time and Gardner had to stretch her small fortune and her as yet modest earnings.

Besides spending as much time as they could at the exhibition, Cassatt and Haldeman took advantage of the other high points in Paris life. Escorted by cousins and family friends in town for the season, they went to operas, concerts in the Tuileries, drives in the Bois de Boulogne, and dinners at their relatives' hotels. The social rounds were always punctuated by sightings of Napoleon III and Empress Eugénie, who moved through Paris with the utmost elegance and dramatic spectacle. Haldeman reported one such glimpse to her sister: "I saw the Empress ride by yesterday on the Champs Elysee looking very lovely in a purple dress and white bonnet; four horses in the carriage, a postillion and the Emperor sitting at her side. They had about a dozen outriders and another carriage following with some of the ladies at her court."[24]

The most daring thing Cassatt and Haldeman did during their month-long fête was to go to the infamous Jardin Mabille, an outdoor dance hall and theater known for its risqué dancers. The energetic cancan with dancing women who tossed their skirts up over their heads, revealing a minimum of undergarments, was enough to make respectable women blush. The two friends were able to watch with some degree of ease only because their escort politely turned his back to the stage.[25]

Cassatt and Haldeman made an effort to do some work while they were in Paris. At the very least, they tried to set aside some time every morning to draw from works of art in the Louvre, an aspect of their education that they missed while working in Écouen. Even if they managed to avoid engagements that would prevent them from going to the Louvre, they often found that the galleries were not as conducive to work as they wished. "There is a quantity of our old Artist acquaintances over here just now and I am afraid the Louvre will become a second [Pennsylvania] Academy for talking and amusing ourselves. I have only been drawing there one day as I have had so much to do since I arrived. But as gentlemen cannot come to see us at the Hotel, we are obliged to receive them at the Louvre."[26] Furthermore, none of their gentleman friends from the Pennsylvania Academy, such as Robert Wylie, Howard Roberts, or Thomas Eakins, had works in the Salon that year, so Cassatt and Haldeman got to host them at the exhibition during the early morning hours of exhibitors' private viewing. Eliza's "Cousin" Sarah (her father's cousin), who was thrilled to take Eliza and Mary under her wing during her stay in Paris, saw romance in all these meetings with gentlemen in artistic settings. But Eliza and Mary steadfastly dismissed all such kindly insinuations: "Cousin Sarah amuses herself saying that [Howard] Roberts is what she calls smitten with both of us; if she had said neither, she would have been nearer the mark."[27]

Toward the end of May, Cassatt had had enough of the entertainments of Paris and was ready to get back to serious work in the Écouen area. Her move to the country may have been hastened by the horrible heat that suddenly descended on Paris in late May of that year. Eliza went out to help

Mary get settled, but since her brother Carsten was arriving from home, she felt it best to stay on in Paris another month or so. This time Cassatt did not stay in Écouen itself, but took a room at a boarding school in Villiers-le-Bel, a half mile away. Her purpose was to switch teachers from the genre painter Soyer, who represented the Écouen style, to the infamous Thomas Couture, whose bravura painting style and rebellious attitude were intriguing to Cassatt. Couture's large studio in the small town of Villiers-le-Bel accommodated many students, particularly Americans, who came out from Paris in search of a more fluid and spontaneous painting style. Couture's own work was a marriage of dramatic brushwork with romantic or melancholy subjects, usually drawn from the peasant population (figure 25). He was also known for having been the teacher of Édouard Manet, who was applying Couture's style to new subjects drawn from modern urban life. With the help of Couture, Cassatt followed her romantic leanings and returned again and again to the theme of the melancholy woman, a version of which she had used for her Salon picture, *La Mandoline.*

Once settled in Villiers-le-Bel, she set up a studio of her own and began several pictures using local models and wistful themes. She wrote to her brother that she was starting a painting based on Tennyson's "Mariana of the Moated Grange," the story of a woman waiting tearfully for her lost love.[28] This evidence that Cassatt used literary themes for her pictures is intriguing, since none of her paintings have survived with literary references to their titles, nor was it common in the styles she was studying to base a work on poetry or novels. Since the romantic Cassatt devoured fiction and poetry of all kinds, it would have been natural for her to combine her literary and artistic interests. As her brother wrote to his future wife, "Mary is an enthusiastic admirer of Tennyson, and she always said she would paint a picture of Mariana."[29] Tragically, this picture and the many others she painted during these years in Europe are lost or misidentified. Aside from *La Mandoline* and one other, we have no documented works from the first decade of her career.

As soon as Eliza's brother Carsten arrived in Paris in July and then departed again for Germany, Eliza joined Mary in Villiers-le-Bel and also began studying with Couture. Neither Cassatt nor Haldeman left us their impressions of Thomas Couture, but others found him an extraordinarily idiosyncratic man. Thomas Eakins reported the stories about Couture he heard from the American Howard Helmick, who was studying at Écouen at the same time as Cassatt and Haldeman. Couture, according to these stories, was a slow-moving, unkempt man (figure 26): "He wore a big straw hat to

25. *Thomas Couture,* Soap Bubbles, *c. 1859*
Oil on canvas, 51½ x 38⅝ in.
The Metropolitan Museum of Art; bequest of Catherine Lorillard Wolfe

keep off the sun & had an old coat or none on & his shirt always open all the way & he would go along the road till he came to some nice shady place & then sleep. The ladies were scandalized till they became so well acquainted with his belly button that it no longer shocked them, for they'd meet him every day. A cold or rainy day he would go about from one studio to another of the artist and blow blow [*sic*] & talk about his book he was writing."[30] Nevertheless Couture was brilliant when he painted, and even if he finished only a fraction of the canvases he started, they were sensual and authoritative. As Eakins wrote to his sister, "He is the Phidias of painting & drawing. Who that has ever looked in a girl's eyes or run his fingers through her soft hair or smoothed her cheek with his hand or kissed her lips or their corners that plexus of all that is beautiful in modelling but must love Couture. . . ."[31]

Such sensuality in art appealed to Cassatt, but one wonders how she reacted to the man. She apparently stayed with him for almost a year and she revisited his studio for a few months several years later (in 1874), which indicates that she, like the ladies in Eakins's letter, grew accustomed to his belly button. However, she never listed him as her teacher either at the time

26. Photograph of Thomas Couture, c. 1855 Private collection

or in later years when she was asked for a biographical account of her training. Nor did she go to him for help when she was trying to get started in Paris as she did all her other teachers, including her first, Gérôme. Very likely, it was Couture's voice of dissent that moved her. He became the prototype for other brilliant but difficult outsiders to whom she was inevitably drawn.

The nonconformist Thomas Couture contrasted violently with the other most important man in Cassatt's life in the summer and fall of 1868: Carsten Haldeman. Carsten, now thirty-one and still unmarried, was an engineer by profession, but a persistent tumor in his throat dictated that he seek the advice of doctors abroad. He had been planning a trip to Europe since the spring. During the numerous delays the doctor in Vienna he intended to see died, leaving his trip even more tentative. Eliza waited in Paris for his arrival. Although she expected him in May, he did not appear in the city until July. The reunion that took place was not only between brother and sister but between Carsten and his sister's friend, whom he had known since she was sixteen years old.

Their ease with one another stemmed from their long acquaintance and probably from Carsten's similarity in age and profession with Mary's own older brother, Aleck. He was probably also aware of Mary's teenage infatuation with him. Carsten was a charming man, the admirer of many women, including more than one of his sisters' friends, and a great tease. When he appeared in Europe in the summer of 1868, both Mary and Eliza loved having him there to see the sights and to show off their artistic lives. One day the three of them saw a beautiful but very expensive veil priced at one thousand dollars in the window of a Parisian shop, Frainais-Gramagnac, which specialized in shawls and lace. Mary, coveting the exquisite object, turned to Carsten and said she would marry him if he bought it for her. Without hesitation he said he would; and for weeks after, he claimed that he and Mary were engaged. Obviously their engagement was in jest, as Eliza wrote to her mother, "Needless to say the veil is not yet bought."[32] But the two were on warm enough terms to joke about such a subject. Since the joke was carried on by Carsten, one senses that if Mary had pressed they might indeed have gotten married eventually. Mary did not press. Although she continued to send him her "kind regards" through Eliza, the relationship remained merely cordial.

If Cassatt ever considered marriage, it most likely would have been with someone like Carsten Haldeman. Similar in social, economic, and cultural background, the two had the added advantage of a long acquaintance and a type of brother-sister relationship. Since both were devoted to family, this sibling familiarity would have been the basis of a comfortable and long-lasting relationship, one that many of their friends had in their own marriages. Cassatt might have had additional impetus for marriage at this time because her brother Aleck had just announced his own engagement. In light of this impending loss, Carsten would have made a convenient brother-substitute. But faced with the real possibility of marriage, Cassatt, at twenty-four, would have had too much to give up. She would have had to leave Europe, prune back her blossoming career, and give up such people as Thomas Couture—for whom there was no American equivalent. Although after Carsten's and Eliza's departure she was often depressed and racked with self-doubt about her progress, she ultimately clung to her belief that life as an artist was preferable to life as a wife.

She and Eliza often discussed the dilemma they faced in regard to marriage. They were well aware that their career ambitions clashed with the housekeeping role expected of women with husband and children. As they continued on into their twenties, they faced increasing skepticism about their willingness to hold on to their art in the face of a marriage proposal from some "nice young man."[33] Even their families, who had shown unquestioned support for them, accepted this inevitability, as Eliza's father wrote: "You will get married and settle down into a good housekeeper like all married women & send off your paints into the garret! There is a prediction for you, and one founded upon almost universal experience."[34] In response, Mary and Eliza tightened their resolve not to give up—even if it meant never marrying. Once away from the heady artistic community of Paris, Eliza did marry and fulfill her father's prediction, but Mary stayed and believed that she had made the right choice.

While Mary Cassatt may have had ambivalent feelings in saying good-bye to Carsten, she had no such questions about the departure of Eliza; she let her best friend go with the deepest sadness. Eliza Haldeman sailed home from Liverpool with her brother in December 1868 after two and a half years of study in France. Most of that time was spent at the side of Mary Cassatt. After their initial quarrel was forgotten, the two expressed nothing but utter contentment with their lives together. Mary, forceful and opinionated, but a warm friend, was put at ease by Eliza's pliant and relaxed nature. Eliza, on the other hand, was goaded into greater ambition and accomplishment by Cassatt and benefited from the intense intellectual stimulation. Had it not been for Eliza's ties to her family, which eventually drew her back home, the two might have continued on for many years in much the same way.

Their relationship does not appear to have been sexual or passionately romantic, unlike relationships between such contemporary women artists as Rosa Bonheur and Nathalie Micas or among the women sculptors in Rome, including Anne Whitney, Emma Stebbins, and Edmonia Lewis. Cassatt and Haldeman very likely knew of lesbianism in artistic circles, or at least had heard the gossip, but there is no evidence that they saw their own relationship in that light or were drawn to those cliques. Nevertheless, their affection was strong. When Eliza left Europe, Mary was never able to re-create the closeness with any of her other friends. They corresponded after their separation, but soon began misunderstanding each other by mail. Remembering their quarrel three years before, Mary panicked when she did not hear from Eliza: "I cannot therefore imagine why you have not written, & am afraid I said something to offend you, if so I did not mean it & hope this will meet with a response."[35]

Haldeman gradually drifted out of Cassatt's life and in the mid-1870s married a Hungarian military man, Philip Figyelmesy, who had come to the United States to fight in the Civil War. Colonel and Mrs. Figyelmesy lived in British Guyana and Switzerland on diplomatic missions and had two sons. They returned in the 1890s to Philadelphia, where Eliza picked up her art again, making small bronze figurines and decorative ceramics. She published a book in 1910 based on the family's experiences in British Guyana titled *Two Boys in the Tropics.* She died that same year. Carsten Haldeman became a major landowner in Florida near Tallahassee. He never married and died in 1892 at the age of fifty-five.

Mary Cassatt stayed on in Europe for another year and a half after the departure of the Haldemans, but without the faithful correspondence of Eliza, we have only an imperfect knowledge of Cassatt's travels and studies during this time. At least until April of 1869 she stayed on in the vicinity of Écouen, where she had access to Couture, Soyer, and Frère. There she prepared her entry for the Salon of 1869, thinking that she would have one more picture in the great exhibition and then head for home. It was a large painting, now lost or misidentified. She hurried to get it in by the deadline, but it was rejected by the jury as not sufficiently finished. This rejection was especially humiliating after last year's triumph and because others like Elizabeth Gardner, Howard Roberts, Robert Wylie, and Howard Helmick were all accepted. From her friend Mlle. Bourges in Écouen she learned that it was possible to reverse negative decisions because that year Bourges had had Frère get one of her rejected pictures in. Cassatt went to Gérôme to enlist his aid. Gérôme was willing, but she had asked too late—a day earlier and he could have gotten her picture in. She was willing to exploit the system, but privately the idea rankled; she wrote to Haldeman, "So you see they are not so very just after all."[36]

Perhaps as a kind of penance, Cassatt left the country for Paris, where she stayed for three months, intending to improve herself by studying in the museums. Her plan of returning home in triumph quietly evaporated. She applied for a copyist's permit and joined the ranks at the Louvre. The contrast to the previous year when she and Eliza reveled in their success made this year's experience especially deadening. She was so discouraged that for the first time since she had been in Europe she was unable to keep up her unrelenting pace. Finally, on the tenth of July, she packed off her paintings from the previous year home to her parents and left Paris with a Miss Gordon from Philadelphia for a sketching trip through the Alps.

Once again the beautiful country and the picturesque costumes of the peasants revived Cassatt's desire to paint. She and Miss Gordon tramped about the countryside often reaching the most remote places. They settled down for a few weeks in the tiny village of Beaufort on the Doron River after a lengthy and treacherous drive from Albertville in a country diligence along streams and through mountain passes (figure 27). Once settled in a local hotel they went about hiring models and setting up poses. As in Courances, the accommodations were primitive ("the dirt & fleas exceed anything we have ever experienced before"[37]), but they overlooked the inconvenience and the unsanitary conditions in view of the artistic opportunities. On their days off they took hikes along the mountain paths to see the famous peaks of that region and escape the summer heat. Cassatt's friends Mr. and Mrs. Howard Helmick were nearby in St. Gervais, Mrs. Helmick to take the baths and Mr. Helmick to paint. Helmick often joined them on their sketching outings.

Cassatt's plans were so uncertain that on the eve of their departure from Beaufort they had not decided where to go next. Longer-range plans included returning to Écouen for the fall and Paris for the winter. As of August, Cassatt was still hesitant to make decisions. Very likely this period of depression and uncertainty lasted well into the fall, with Cassatt going through the familiar motions in the familiar places of Écouen and Paris. Perhaps Katherine Cassatt sensed her daughter's distress, or she simply felt it was time for another visit; in any event she arrived in Paris just before Christmas of 1869, four years after she and her daughter had come with such high hopes. After rousing her daughter to action, she left with her for Rome. For Mary, this was the first time she left France since her arrival in Europe.

27. View of Beaufort-sur-Doron, La Savoie, France

Once in Rome, Cassatt moved quickly. She took yet another master, Charles Bellay, a Frenchman who divided his time between Paris and Rome, and set about executing for the Salon of 1870 a painting (now lost) based on her travels through the Alps the previous summer. By May she was on her feet again—her painting had been accepted, she was recognized by the art colonies of Rome and Paris—and now she was ready to go home. She and her mother returned to Paris in July and were back in the United States by the end of the summer.

Chapter III

Becoming Professional (1870–1874)

Mary Cassatt's reentry into her homeland in 1870 was not particularly smooth. She was sincerely happy to rejoin the family she had left behind, and she could certainly revel in the professional recognition her work had brought her. Nevertheless the changes she encountered at home combined with the changes in her own expectations and attitudes since she left in 1865 made being in her own country increasingly difficult. She gamely went about reviving old family ties and taking proper career steps in engaging studios, models, and dealers, but she soon saw she could not be happy in this environment.

Aside from the many intangible differences between what she had left and what she now confronted at home, there were some seriously concrete ones. First among these was the marriage and extraordinary professional success of her older brother, Aleck, who was now thirty-one (figure 28). When she left he had just begun to move up in the Pennsylvania Railroad Company. With his engineer's degree from Rensselaer Polytechnic, he had at first gotten only lowly jobs, but in 1864 had been promoted to resident engineer of the middle division of the Philadelphia & Erie branch of the system. At that time he moved away from Philadelphia, where he had been able to spend weekends with his family in Chester County, and found lodgings in the small town of Renovo in central Pennsylvania. A few months after Mary and her mother left for Europe in late 1865, Mr. Cassatt sold the Chester County farm and took Lydia and Gard to be with Aleck in Renovo. At that point Aleck became the de facto head of the family. While Robert Cassatt kept his brokerage firm in Philadelphia until at least 1867, it was his son whose fortunes were increasing at a geometric rate.

28. Photograph of Alexander Cassatt, c. 1867
Private collection

Alexander Cassatt took after his father in many ways. He was tall and elegant, and always wore a silk top hat. He had extraordinary powers of concentration and organization. In addition, he had great physical stamina that allowed him to work long hours and thrive on the enormous amount of traveling required by his job. In the 1860s Aleck's power and energy stood out in relief against a family at home that now consisted of his aging father, his frequently ill sister, Lydia, and his teenage brother, Gard. His energy was most closely matched by that of his mother who, ten years younger than her husband, was still a commanding figure. But it was only Mary, developing on her own in Europe, who shared the intense intellectual drive and physical capabilities of her brother.

While she was away, the family followed Aleck from Renovo to the even more remote town of Irvine in Warren County, located in northwestern Pennsylvania. When he was promoted yet again and transferred to Altoona in late 1867, his family did not move with him but stayed on for another year in Warren County. For this cultured, cosmopolitan family the years from 1866 to 1870 were a kind of Babylonian captivity, which meant isolation not only from civilization but even from Aleck.

The identifiable cause of this last phase of isolation in the backwoods was one Maria Lois Buchanan (called Lois or "Lodie"), the twenty-year-old woman Aleck had suddenly fallen in love with, proposed to, and planned to install as the mistress of his new house in Altoona in place of his mother. Accordingly, the Cassatts did not follow Aleck to Altoona, nor did they exercise the option of returning to Philadelphia. In a kind of paralysis, they stayed on in the most remote place they had ever lived in. The relationship between the Cassatts and Lois began with a shock to the family system and continued to reverberate for some time to come.

The initial upheaval in the family caused by Aleck's courtship and marriage was communicated to Mary only through letters. When she returned, she saw that it had made a very real difference to all the Cassatts. The unfolding of this family drama was shaped equally by the personalities of Lois, Aleck, and the family as a whole.

Lois Buchanan had a high level of self-confidence. A lively young woman, she was the favorite sister in a family of eight children and a successful belle in the social circles into which her family's position introduced her. The Buchanans were an old Pennsylvania family. Although her own father was a respectable clergyman in north Philadelphia, they were brought into the limelight because of her uncle James Buchanan, whose political and diplomatic career culminated in his presidency (1857–61). James Buchanan, a bachelor, was very fond of his brother's children and often entertained them at his home, Wheatland, in Lancaster. Although Lois was not a classic beauty, her bee-stung lips and high complexion were irresistible to the young gentlemen she met, and she entered into numerous flirtations without always meaning to. It took only a matter of days for her to captivate Aleck Cassatt during a visit to the home of her brother James, a lawyer for the oil companies in western Pennsylvania, in Tidioute, not far from the Cassatts' in Irvine. Aleck and James were friends from Aleck's days working on the railroad in the Philadelphia area. Aleck in fact had met the entire Buchanan family who lived outside of Frankford, a suburban town north of Philadelphia. Sometime around 1864–65 he had flirted with Lois's older sister Harriet but she had not returned his affection.

Aleck had not known Lois in those days because she was away at boarding school in Philadelphia, where she stayed until she was eighteen. When she appeared with another sister, Henrietta, in far-off Irvine, her beauty and vivaciousness must have been striking. Aleck exerted his own best social skills, which were considerable, and charmed her into responding with more than her usual friendly flirtatiousness. After she left, he proposed by letter and she accepted. The shortness of the courtship worried both families, but since Aleck had been acquainted with the Buchanans for a number of years and since Katherine Cassatt and Lois's mother, Eliza Foster Buchanan, were childhood acquaintances in Pittsburgh, they agreed to go along with the wishes of their children.

After making such a hasty commitment, Lois immediately began to have second thoughts. Once back in Philadelphia, she saw how much it would cost her to give up the pleasures of youth and beauty, and she began weighing Aleck against other men. While this response was natural in a twenty-year-old, her hesitation had repercussions throughout both families. Her own family wanted to protect her as she examined Aleck critically but urged her to conduct herself honorably in light of her commitment. Aleck's family wanted to welcome her graciously as a daughter, but were kept from making plans about their own situation until she made up her mind.

One month after she agreed to become engaged, Aleck was transferred to Altoona. Naturally, he wanted to marry soon and bring Lois there to live. In deference to his plans, the elder Cassatts did not move to Altoona with him. When Lois began delaying the announcement of the engagement and postponed the wedding, Aleck was caught alone in Altoona and the Cassatts remained in limbo in Warren County. It was almost a year before Lois made her decision. A few months after that the two were married (figure 29).

Although Lois's indecision was not viewed kindly by the Cassatts, it was their son's quickness and single-mindedness—good qualities for business but not for love—that were equally to blame for the distress. His decision to marry Lois was made almost by instinct and his firmness in maintaining his purpose throughout was extraordinary. A more yielding man might have seen Lois's vacillation and released her from her promise; that way she would have had time to mature and he would have been able to solve his parents' dilemma about where to live. But Aleck was positive in his resolve to have Lois and exerted considerable pressure on her. Fortunately, the decision was a good one. They had a happy lifelong marriage and his affection for her never wavered. Lois, for her part, grew into the relationship and found a worthy outlet for her social skills in the role of the wife of a wealthy and successful business man.

Gradually the Cassatts warmed to Lois. Gard finished his schooling and went to Altoona while Aleck was waiting for Lois to resolve the question of their marriage. Aleck had found him a position in the First National Bank of Altoona through his connections with the Lloyd family, the founders of the bank. Aleck and Gard were welcomed into the first circles of Altoona society, as was Lois when she finally settled there as Mrs. Cassatt in December of 1868. Gard at age nineteen was everyone's pet; Lois, her four sisters, and their innumerable cousins were among those who indulged him, and he was universally referred to as "the boy." Although equally businesslike, Gard was not as commanding as Aleck and preferred to follow his father's career

29. *Photograph of Lois Buchanan Cassatt on her wedding day, November 25, 1868*
Private collection

in finance rather than Aleck's route up the corporate ladder. He joked about having no more ambition than "to marry some rich girl and go to Europe"; as Aleck wrote to Lois, "He says he has no idea of working for his living. Cool, isn't he."[1]

Lois also grew quite close to Aleck's older sister, Lydia, or "Lydy," as she was called by the family. Two years older than Aleck, Lydia was now in her early thirties and shared with her mother the domestic responsibilities at home. She was not as healthy as the rest of the family, often suffering inexplicable periods of illness that some doctors later attributed to a progressive kidney disorder, Bright's disease. At this time, however, she was by no means an invalid. She traveled frequently to Altoona and Philadelphia, or, in the summer, to mountain and seashore resorts with friends. Before Lois's arrival, her visits to Altoona were relished by Aleck and Gard because she added a more civilized aspect to their bachelor existence, and she babied them when they fell ill or had accidents with their horses. Lydia was also very maternal toward Lois when she arrived. In fact, she and Lois's sister, Henrietta, traveled to Altoona from Philadelphia after the wedding to prepare the house for the return of the bride and groom from their honeymoon.

Lydia's attendance at the wedding itself was marked by a comedy of errors. Lydia never received her invitation to the wedding (Lois's brother, James, didn't get one either), and her dress was stolen before it even arrived at her house. Mary had had a dress made in Paris for Lydia to wear to the wedding and entrusted it to Eliza Haldeman, who at the time was packing her trunk for the voyage home. Unfortunately Eliza's trunk was broken into before it left on the steamer. As Mary wrote to her mother with philosophic good humor, "I am very sorry for poor Lyd as the dress was a beauty but fortunately I got one wear out of it."[2]

Lois had an opportunity to get to know Lydia quite well in 1870, when Lydia and her father moved to Altoona during Mrs. Cassatt's protracted trip to Europe to be with Mary. While Mary and her mother were traveling between Rome and Paris, the rest of the Cassatts congregated in Altoona: Aleck and Lois in their house provided by the railroad, and Gard, Lydia, and Mr. Cassatt at Altoona's finest hotel, the Logan House. Lydia again showed her helpfulness, particularly with the various frightening infant illnesses of Aleck and Lois's new baby, Edward, who was born in the summer of 1869. The family group, rather than the cozy circle of Cassatts in their estate in Chester County, is what Mary encountered upon her return.

Mary and her mother swept into Altoona in late August 1870. Suddenly the fragile family structure, so lately reestablished after years of travel in the backwoods of Pennsylvania and the dramatic inclusion of a new wife and new baby, flew apart once more. When Mary and her mother—two commanding presences—arrived together, they diverted attention not only from Lois but even from the baby, who had been fussed over by the five adult

Cassatts for the last year. Even Aleck, who had previously shown total devotion to his new family, was riveted by the new arrivals.

Within days, Lois was plaintively penning her woes to her own sympathetic parents, brothers, and sisters. Her mother, while advising Lois to have patience with her new family, could not help expressing some bitterness: "I do not think that I have ever had a greater disappointment than in the course Mr. C's family have pursued towards you, as, the fact that he was the son of someone whom I had known and been attached to so long ago, was greatly in his favor as your suitor. I had built up for myself a small 'castle' in hoping that when taken away, you would have one who would be a second Mother to you not withstanding the unpromising commencement however."[3] Mrs. Buchanan does not seem to have had any contact with Mrs. Cassatt since they left Pittsburgh almost thirty years before and seems willing to believe that Katherine Cassatt had wronged her daughter. Lois's brother James, who knew the Cassatts recently and very well in Irvine, defended them to Lois: "Mrs. Cassatt is a very fine woman (I mean the senior) and a woman whose society I always enjoyed very much. She is smart and wide awake and has a good heart. If there has been any apparent want of attention or enthusiasm towards you I think I could explain it in a few words of conversation. . . ."[4] It is obvious that Mrs. Cassatt was not someone who was easily understood, but once acquainted with her, she was very well liked and much admired. But as this episode illustrates, Lois's trouble with her arose particularly when she was coupled with her daughter Mary.

Lois's assessment of Mary could not have been lower or more bitter. Ten years later she still complained: "The truth is I cannot abide Mary & never will—I can't tell why but there is something to me so utterly obnoxious about that girl. I have never yet heard her criticize any human being in any but the most disagreeable way. She is too self important, & I can't put up with it."[5] The conflict between Lois and Mary Cassatt was inevitable and underscores not only the personal qualities of the two women but also the conflicting paths they took.

Lois and Mary Cassatt were both intelligent, well-educated, and determined women who achieved great success in their lifetimes. In many ways Lois was even more successful than Mary. By the age of twenty-three, when Mary greeted her for the first time as her sister-in-law, Lois was already the mistress of the second most important household in Altoona and a sponsor of the prestigious Assembly, the annual society ball in Philadelphia. She was in command of an income far greater than her father's and had a healthy baby and loving husband. As time went on, she became one of the wealthiest women in the United States, oversaw the management of four homes and numerous servants, and was a leader in Philadelphia society. Furthermore, she had the undying affection of her husband and proudly raised four attractive, productive children. She was the acknowledged mentor of her unmarried sisters—even those older than she was. In all these respects Lois triumphed over her sister-in-law, who accumulated only a small fraction of Lois's wealth, had virtually no power in society, lived quietly with few servants (although she eventually acquired two residences), and had no lifelong companion or children. And yet, as Lois's diatribe against Mary reveals, Lois was frustrated by what Mary did have and the importance that Mary and the world attached to it. Mary's "self-importance" rankled in Lois's competitive heart.

While Lois acquired money and influence, she gave up personal power. The two women started out with strong personalities, but their decisions early in life affected the power they would have as adults. Lois exerted her youthful influence by making Aleck wait for her decision about marriage, but she never came up with an alternative plan to marrying him. In the end, the most important decision she would make in her life was made before she was twenty-one. From then on, the important decisions would be made by him and her worldly success was in fact his success.

Mary Cassatt, on the other hand, was by nature the planner and organizer of her own life, and, as such, often swept others along in her schemes. Unlike Lois, she made decisions by the age of twenty-one that ensured that the decision-making power would always be hers. Not only did she decide not to marry at an early age, but she decided to pursue a life work, to have employment beyond domestic concerns. If it could not be art, it would have been something else. This need to plan and to accomplish gave her an air of self-absorption because she was not accustomed to fielding the wishes and decisions of those around her. Instead, she found that others like Eliza Haldeman were interested in hearing her decisions and letting her guide them.

Lois, who was herself guided by her husband, saw with horror the influence Mary had on her husband and his whole family. In her own family it was Lois—the only married sister—who had the biggest say. She probably felt that her voice should carry the same weight with her unmarried sisters-in-law, Lydia and Mary. Instead, Mary Cassatt's influence over people's thoughts and opinions was reluctantly recognized by Lois and others. Indeed, years before, her older sister Annie, who apparently knew Mary, asked Lois after she had had a chance meeting with Mary, "How do you like Miss C. Something of a genious, isn't she?"[6]

Mary, with no more formal education or intelligence than Lois, was an intellectual. She read and thought deeply about art, literature, politics, and the state of modern civilization. In conversation, therefore, she expressed opinions and aired thoughts that seemed interesting and original to others. Men and women listened to her with greater attention than they did to Lois. The respect that she discerned in her listeners gave her increased confidence to express herself and convinced her of her "self-importance." Lois, the family favorite, the social belle, and the beloved wife of Aleck was not used to sharing the limelight, much less having to give it up entirely. Throughout her life Lois was dogged by the suspicion that others found her insignificant, as in one Philadelphian's cutting reference to her as "that little nobody, a niece of President Buchanan."[7] Throughout her life, Mary was noticed and deferred to; through her personal power and accomplishment, people always felt she was "somebody."

Given the clash of personalities and paths the two sisters-in-law had chosen, it is understandable that Lois found Mary unconcerned with those around her. However, Lois's charge that Mary criticized people "in the most disagreeable way" was indeed a failing that Mary Cassatt had. In fact, it was a common failing within the Cassatt family. As a group they presented a cool and assessing face to the world. In contrast to the Buchanans, who used an easy, teasing tone with one another and frequently joked about people they knew, the Cassatts often revealed an edge of cynicism in otherwise innocent remarks about people and places. Both Aleck and his father commonly made remarks about people of lower social status that indicated an acute awareness of class distinctions and a sincere respect only for those in "our set." While Aleck was a fair and popular manager of the men and machines of the Pennsylvania Railroad, his benevolent treatment of the employees masked the common prejudices of his day against social inferiors, Jews, and blacks. In a letter to Lois, Aleck described a friend of Gard's: "I expected to hear him crying oi oi! oi oi! He has a very decidedly Jewish cast of countenance, and [they] are evidentally descendants of that nation—though they now prefer the Catholic (Romish) faith.—Why is it that we have such a prejudice against the Jews? It is very strong, I am ashamed to say, with me.—"[8] Although Mary was more cosmopolitan than Aleck and decried many forms of intolerance, her own cleverness with words and keen perception of people made her acid comments biting and at times offensive. When pushed, she too could make anti-Semitic remarks, such as those against Gertrude and Leo Stein.

The natural antipathy between Mary and Lois as representatives of the two poles of success for women in their day was exacerbated by the exotic European "essence" that clung to Mary after her return. Since all of the Cassatts had spent years in Europe in the 1850s and were avidly interested in the cultural and political affairs of the Old World, Lois, who had never been there, was once again at a disadvantage. In fact, everything about Altoona that Lois prized—her beautifully furnished house and her important husband—paled in contrast to the immensely interesting world that Mary inhabited. That larger world filled Aleck and Lois's parlor in the conversations of Mary and her mother and the fascination for the subject shared by Mr. Cassatt, Lydia, Gard, and especially Aleck. The subjects of art, literature, the currently raging Franco-Prussian War, and the fate of Napoleon III were fresh news brought by the European travelers. Before long, the lure of the larger world affected them all. By the fall Mary had persuaded her parents and Lydia to return with her at least as far as Philadelphia. They left Aleck and Lois, as well as Gard, who was still at the bank, to suffer the confining Altoona winter alone.

After Mary Cassatt's stay in Altoona, Philadelphia must have been a significant improvement. She hadn't lived in the "good city of P." since the Civil War days when soldiers in Union uniform were everywhere and the city struggled to accommodate the demands of being a depot for men and supplies. The city was once again stabilized with a flourishing peacetime economy. The trend toward "modernization" was quickly dismantling the landmarks of her youth, such as the gracious old Pennsylvania Academy building, which had been engulfed by the commercial sector of the city and sold in 1870. Without the "Cad," the artistic community in Philadelphia lost its center, but artists continued to congregate in private studios and informal sketch clubs.

Cassatt's first order of business was to look up her old friends, most of whom had also just recently returned from Europe. Thomas Eakins, William Sartain, and Humphrey Moore arrived just after Cassatt, but most had trickled home over the previous few years. Earl Shinn, who eulogized the demise of the academy building, had returned in 1868, the same year as Eliza Haldeman. Having left Paris in the summer of 1869, Howard Roberts set up his sculpture studio downtown. By the time Cassatt saw him again, Roberts had already drummed up a business in portrait heads and busts among prosperous Philadelphians and was executing large-scale classical and literary works as well. Eliza Haldeman was living with her parents in Chickies, but she still came into Philadelphia often enough to catch up with her old friend.

A favorite spot for reunions among these former academy students was the home of John Sartain, one of America's foremost engravers and a pillar of the Philadelphia art establishment (figure 30). In the years between the closing of the old academy and the opening of the new building in 1876, the Sartain household on Samson Street with its floor-to-ceiling art collection was the next best place to be. John Sartain was always available to give advice to the young professionals, and his numerous children, who were all artists themselves, offered congenial company. The youngest, William Sartain, was a particular friend of Eakins, while the other siblings, Emily and Samuel Sartain, were established as engravers and were well known throughout the city. Emily Sartain had been enrolled in academy classes in the days of Mary Cassatt and Eliza Haldeman and had traveled to Europe twice in the intervening decade although not for prolonged study. She was in Paris during the summer of 1868 after Cassatt and Haldeman had their triumphal debut at the Salon.

Mary Cassatt greeted her old friends with pleasure. After her stay in Altoona she was relieved to be once again with people who were still as full of European studies, travel experiences, and ideas as she was. In addition to treating her to their reminiscences and rousing debates, her old friends helped her to reorient herself in Philadelphia, giving her leads on studios, models, art supplies, and ways of exhibiting and selling. Early in 1871 she was set up with a studio and tapped into a source of male and female models. These she dressed in picturesque costumes that had been collected in Europe and were shared by all the artists. Because good models were too rare a commodity in Philadelphia to be used by only one artist, Cassatt would often work with others once a costumed model had been arranged. In this way she became better acquainted with Emily Sartain, who was

30. Photograph of John Sartain and his children in their home on Sansom Street, Philadelphia, 1868 (From left: John, Henry, William, and Emily) Collection of the Library of Congress

trying to broaden her scope as an artist from engraving to painting. As the two painted side by side, they discovered a mutual desire to return to Europe. As they listened to the tales told by Will Sartain and Tom Eakins they decided that Spain would be their destination.

In Emily Sartain, Cassatt found a friend who was more her professional equal than Eliza Haldeman had been. Sartain was three years older than Cassatt, from a nationally important artistic family, and already a highly paid career woman. Although well recognized by her teachers and colleagues and despite two Salon entries to her credit, Cassatt had not yet begun to sell. She could offer Sartain the benefit of her experience in painting in exchange for Sartain's knowledge of and connections in the art market. Cassatt had managed to place two pictures with the dealer Goupil in New York, perhaps with Sartain's help. Selling was foremost on her mind now that she felt ready to leave behind her student status and set herself up as an independent artist. As she had written to Eliza Haldeman from Europe, "Have you been exhibiting & above all things selling?"[9] Pressure to sell was also coming from her parents, who, now that she was under their roof again, could not condone the extra expenses of studio rental and model fees without evidence that these would eventually produce income. They were not inclined to indulge Mary's art as a pleasant hobby or a respectable feminine "accomplishment." Mary's own businesslike approach was consistent with that of the whole family. In addition, she may have been particularly motivated by seeing Aleck's tremendous financial success.

Cassatt worked all spring in Philadelphia. With the coming of summer, she was persuaded to accompany her family to a country residence near Aleck and Lois, who were awaiting the birth of their second child. The family engaged a house in Hollidaysburg, a beautiful riverside town several miles outside Altoona, where they were joined by Gard. Mary was still full of steam from her spring in Philadelphia. She quickly found a studio in Hollidaysburg that had previously been used by a portrait painter. In the absence of professional models, she began pressing everyone around her to pose. Although she was happy to be in such a beautiful spot for the summer, her longing for Europe engendered a deep dissatisfaction with her circumstances. Even her good sense and dutiful activity did not help her rise above it. In her letters to Emily Sartain she alternated between calm descriptions of her situation and wild, half-serious ravings about Europe. Spain had become such an obsession for her that she called her pain "homesickness" because, as she explained to Emily, "I really feel as if it was intended I should be a Spaniard & quite a mistake that I was born in America."[10] Even the mountains that made Hollidaysburg picturesque were not to her liking: "The mountains are too tame for my taste, I should prefer the Sierra Nevada."[11] In the face of frustration, she tried to be reasonable. " 'Patience' is my motto," she concluded.[12]

Youthful romanticism and exaggeration were strong in the twenty-seven-year-old Cassatt, but her problems that summer were very real. In addition to the uncomfortable proximity to her disapproving sister-in-law, she found herself for the first time at a professional dead end, which was all the more galling because only one year before, she was reveling in her latest Salon acceptance and the prospect of imminent success. Renting a makeshift studio and trying to make a model out of the family's mulatto servant was a far cry from painting the obliging citizens of Écouen in the midst of a colony of young, ambitious artists. Furthermore, whatever hopes Cassatt had of capitalizing on her success at the Paris Salon by selling her two paintings in New York were soon dashed. The paintings attracted many admirers but no purchasers, and Cassatt remained an unsold artist. She was unable to raise enough money to finance a trip to Europe. Another factor contributing to her malaise was her need to have great art at her fingertips. While she was in Europe she spent most of her time in the country, eschewing life in the big art centers. Nevertheless, wherever she was, Paris or Rome with their treasures were only a short train ride away. Even in the remotest village, she needed to look no farther than the easel set up a few yards away to see good examples of contemporary art. As she wrote to Emily, "I cannot tell you what I suffer for the want of seeing a good picture, no amount of bodily suffering occassioned by the want of comforts would seem to be too great a price for the pleasure of living in a country where one could have some art advantages."[13]

Finally, she came as close as she ever would to giving up art altogether. After about two months of struggling to keep up her career and her spirits, the disappointments and the intense July heat were too much. She began to think of other ways of living her life: "I too am ravenous for money & am determined to try & make some, not by painting though. I have fully made up my mind that it [is] impossible for me unless I choose to set to work & manufacture pictures by the aid of photographs. I have given up my studio & torn up my father's portrait, & have not touched a brush for six weeks nor ever will again until I see some prospect of getting back to Europe. I am very anxious to go out west next fall & get some employment, but I have not yet decided where."[14] What kind of "employment" was Cassatt thinking of? Would she have become a teacher or a journalist or perhaps worked for a bank or the railroad with the help of her father and brothers? Determined women could find employment in America in 1871, particularly "out west." It is an important clue to Mary Cassatt's character that when faced with the failure of her art career, she looked for other employment rather than choosing to be "at home," as the census takers described the occupations of women like Lydia Cassatt or Eliza Haldeman. Although Cassatt became an artist because she was driven by her talent for art, she also became an artist because she was driven by a strong desire for work and money. No matter how much talent she had, she would not have chosen this path if she did not think she could earn money doing it.

Not only did she crave independence for her own sake, but her parents made it clear that they would not subsidize the expenses of a practicing artist. They were well-off—in 1860 Robert Cassatt reported personal wealth of forty thousand dollars[15]—but not extraordinarily wealthy. They might have been happy to support their daughter in their own comfortable home but were unable or unwilling to commit funds for studios, models, supplies, or trips to Europe.

Cassatt's depression lifted somewhat with the cooler weather, and she did not abandon art after all. She did go West, not to find employment, but rather to try a different market for her art. She retrieved her two paintings from Goupil's in New York and took them first to Pittsburgh and then to Chicago either to sell or use them to attract commissions for other paintings. This tactic brought immediate success in Pittsburgh, where she was contracted by the (Catholic) bishop to paint two copies of Correggio's paintings for the cathedral. This commission was enough to pay her way back to Europe. At long last her American exile would be over. The commission for copies for the Cathedral of Pittsburgh would pay Mary three hundred dollars, which would support her for about six months in Europe (a young art student typically budgeted five hundred to six hundred dollars for a year, more if they were staying in Paris). Obviously, this would not cover all her expenses for a protracted stay, but was enough to reassure her parents that Mary was beginning to receive some income from her work.

In Pittsburgh she and her mother met with relatives from the Johnston side of the family. While her mother stayed and visited her old Pittsburgh friends, Mary and her two cousins Aleck and Mimie Johnston went on to Chicago. She was equally well received there. Before she could either sell her paintings or get orders for new ones, she was caught in the great Chicago fire of October 8, 1871. No one in her party was hurt, but her paintings, which had been on display in a large jewelry store were burned. She returned from Chicago empty-handed but was still gratified that she had gotten the Pittsburgh commissions and was on her way back "home." "O how wild I am to get to work, my fingers farely itch & my eyes water to see a fine picture again," she wrote to Emily Sartain from Hollidaysburg.[16] Already she began to sweep up her friend in her enthusiasm. In a little more than a month the two were on a steamer headed for Liverpool.

Emily Sartain discovered, as Eliza Haldeman had, that Mary Cassatt was a delightful traveling companion. She was at her best when she was on the move. She loved reading maps and guidebooks, railroad timetables, and descriptions of local customs. By 1871 she could draw on her now considerable European experience to lead the way to the best hotels in all the major cities, persuade cabdrivers to provide courteous service even in the middle of the night, and, of course, cajole keepers into letting her into museums and little-known private collections. She was in high spirits as she entered villages that had potential for genre subjects or cities where she hoped to get special permission to make copies in art galleries. Unfamiliar languages never bothered her; she was fluent in French and German from childhood, picked up Italian in her general education, and, if necessary, took lessons in a new language, as she did when she got to Spain. With such an extensive linguistic background and her forthright manner, she had no trouble communicating her needs and desires in every new country. She must have inherited her wanderlust from her parents, who moved twenty times in the first twenty-three years of their marriage. She spent the first ten years of her European residence (1865–75) staying nowhere longer than the year she spent in Écouen in 1867–68, and even during that time she lived at two different addresses.

When Cassatt went back to Europe in 1871, she was a woman with a mission (figure 31). She and Sartain barely stopped in London long enough to allow Emily to call on a few old friends. Emily's parents were both English and had many ties there. They rushed through Paris, taking quick note of the damage inflicted on the city during the Franco-Prussian War and under the Commune, and then took the twenty-eight-hour train ride to Parma, Italy. Cassatt wanted to get right to work on her copies for Pittsburgh, which were to be of Correggio paintings in Parma museums. It is less clear why Sartain accompanied her there rather than going to the larger art centers of Paris or Rome. No doubt she was carried along by Cassatt's enthusiasm and assurances that she, Emily, could also gain much from a study of Correggio and other masterpieces on view in Parma and by working side by side with Cassatt.

31. Photograph of Mary Cassatt taken in Parma, Italy, 1872 The Pennsylvania Academy of the Fine Arts Archives

Sartain did indeed benefit from her studies in Parma, which lasted about four months, until May of 1872. But her experience paled beside the tremendous and unexpected success Cassatt encountered in this small Italian city. Cassatt leaped from the depths of despair in the summer of 1871 in Hollidaysburg, Pennsylvania, to being hailed six months later in Parma as one of the best artists working in that city. In addition, she received the best response she had gotten so far in the Paris Salon. This success, which came within months of stepping back on European shores, no doubt clinched her belief that only in Europe could she do her best work and receive the recognition she deserved. Returning to America was now out of the question.

The two young women arrived in Parma without knowing anyone there but carrying letters of introduction to the art and music communities. In short order, they had seats at the opera thanks to Signor Rossi, the director, and special consideration at the Parma Academy. They met Signor Caggiati, the director of the academy, and several professors in the school. Cassatt quickly drew the attention of Carlo Raimondi, a professor of engraving, who assumed an elaborately protective role toward the Americans. He put all the resources of the academy at their disposal, helping them find studios and models, allowing them to work in the academy itself, providing guidance and praise, and worrying over them when they were sick. Cassatt and Sartain came to know the whole Raimondi family, including Carlo's son Edouardo, who was himself a painter. Young Raimondi was attentive to both young women, and each referred to him as "your" Edouardo while he displayed a helpful friendship to them both.

The reception Cassatt received in Parma in the spring of 1872 was remarkable. For an unknown American artist to be taken into the bosom of the Parmesan art community and high society, extraordinary factors must have been at work. Surely the relative novelty of two women setting to work in studios around town helped bring out the gallantry of the Italian men. That they were Americans was also in their favor, since Parma, though well known for its art collections, was not a normal gathering place for the American "colony," as were Rome, Florence, or Venice. Americans were looked upon kindly in the days when the U.S. dollar was very strong against the lira.

Furthermore, Cassatt and Sartain conducted themselves as if they deserved the best consideration of the Parmesans. Cassatt, with her Salon credits to her name, and Sartain, daughter of a famous engraver and well known in her own right, were clearly serious artists. Cassatt's commission to copy from Correggio paintings gave them a sense of purpose that elevated them above the level of casual tourists or art students. Furthermore, they took pains to fit into the culture; they both spoke Italian, and they behaved with scrupulous respectability, even turning down invitations if they could not be properly "matronized." They mixed with the local artists and got to know the work of the more famous Italian artists of the day, such as Alberto Pasini, Francesco Pollice, and Federico Maldarelli. Cassatt and Sartain also discovered that the women they met in Parma were highly intellectual and shared their interest in contemporary art and literature; in fact, many of them were artists themselves. Cassatt, with her European background and sophisticated sense of style, particularly enjoyed herself in this cosmopolitan society.

Their air of professionalism may have gotten them initial cooperation, but it was Cassatt's artistic talent and intelligence that brought them into prominence in the community. Not long after their arrival, Cassatt put aside her commission in order to begin work on a painting for the Paris Salon that spring. The Salon had not been held during the battle of the Paris Commune in 1871, so the Salon of 1872 was eagerly awaited and promised to attract even more and better entries. Cassatt couldn't resist trying her luck again, since she had been successful in 1870. She hired a local artist to do the mechanical work of blocking out the copy. In the meantime she began a work titled *During the Carnival* using live models. Although this, like virtually all her paintings up to this time, cannot be positively identified, it may be the work now called *Two Women Throwing Flowers During Carnival* (figure 32). This painting shows the models—one slightly behind the other—throwing pink flowers downward as if from a balcony. Her choice of a scene from the Lenten festival, Carnival, reflects her own experience of such parades in the small towns of France and in Rome but not yet in Parma, since she started the picture in January before Carnival began. The European custom of women in balconies throwing nosegays to the men in fancy costume dancing through the streets below was considered particularly romantic by Americans and may have struck Cassatt as an interesting subject. It was more elaborate than the single-figure studies she had submitted to the Salon in previous years, yet had the same romantic mood as her earlier peasant studies, such as *La Mandoline* or the proposed "Mariana of the Moated Grange."

As Cassatt brought the picture to completion under the watchful eye of Professor Raimondi and the other teachers and students at the Parma Academy, where she painted in an unused classroom, the response grew louder and more enthusiastic. Emily Sartain watched this tidal wave of approval swell and wrote of the phenomenon to her father: "All Parma is talking of Miss Cassatt and her picture, and everyone is anxious to know her—The compliments she receives are overwhelming—At Prof. Caggiati's [director of the academy] reception men of talent and distinction to say nothing of titled people, are brought up to be presented, having requested the honor of an introduction. . . . One of the custodes [assistants in the academy] yesterday, looking around carefully first to be sure he was not overheard, assured her she was much more 'brava' than any of the professors —One of the professors has begged her to come to his study and give him criticism and advice—"[17] All this acclaim for her friend was hard for the accomplished Sartain to bear, but she generally took it with good humor, noting "I shine a little, by her reflection."[18] The picture and Cassatt's talent were further endorsed when *Pendant le Carnival* was shipped off to Paris and

32. *Mary Cassatt,* **Two Women Throwing Flowers During Carnival,** *1872*
Oil on canvas, 21½ x 25 in.
Collection of James J. O. Anderson, Baltimore

duly accepted into the Salon. Parma was proud of its adopted daughter; the art community begged her to stay and make Italy her home.[19] Cassatt outwardly pooh-poohed all the attention, but secretly loved it. Whenever anything appeared in print about her, she got copies and sent them to her family and all her friends. Writing to Emily, she joked about one tribute that was published in Parma, "If the enclosed dont give you a half hour's laugh, I shall think that you have lost all sense of humor."[20]

Toward the end of April, Emily Sartain left Parma to meet her mother and brother William in Paris. Both she and Will entered painting classes there while escorting their mother around to the sights all summer. Cassatt stayed in Parma for several more months to finish her copy for the Cathedral of Pittsburgh and complete a few more studies from local models. In the end, she does not appear to have painted a copy from Correggio's *Madonna and Child with St. Gerome,* which had been her original commission, but instead executed a copy of Correggio's *Virgin Crowned* (this fresco had been partially removed from the ceiling of San Giovanni and was in the Parma Gallery). This she shipped off with some trepidation because she was not pleased with the final effect, nor, as she discovered too late, did she pack it properly. The copy and her Salon painting went first to Philadelphia to her parents' house, where all her friends got a chance to see what Parma had been raving about. The copy was then sent to Pittsburgh. Unfortunately, it too has been lost. Cassatt stayed on in Parma even after the copy was shipped in order to paint a picture to enter in the annual exhibition held at Milan. Later that fall she tasted the first fruits of her labor. She was paid by the bishop of Pittsburgh for the copy and also sold her Salon picture for two hundred dollars. She had every reason to believe she was now established.

At the height of Cassatt's fame in Parma, she had her photograph taken (figure 31). Her smiling face eludes us because it is averted from the camera in a standard feminine pose, but her velvet dress, fringed fichu, and dangling earrings give the impression of a very prosperous woman. In her typical fashion, she gave these photos to all her friends with copies of glowing newspaper reviews and sent one to Sartain, who was now in Paris. The conceit of such a gesture—the kind of thing that infuriated her sister-in-law—was mitigated by the generosity implied in the photo's inscription, "alla distinta pittrice, Emilia Sartain" (to the distinguished painter, Emily Sartain).

Cassatt's glory, however, was over as quickly as it came. The first eight months after she returned to Europe were the most splendid she would ever have. She was surrounded by great art and intelligent friends with whom to discuss it; her work was highly praised and won the most cherished international honor—being shown at the Paris Salon. As soon as she left Parma, however, the extraordinary combination of circumstances that brought her such approval and celebrity could never be re-created, even on subsequent trips to that small Italian city. She forged ahead, honing her skills, making new friends in new places, and receiving ever greater recognition for her art, but never again did she experience the thrill of that golden moment.

In late September of 1872 Cassatt spent four days on the train to Madrid. At last she arrived in the land that had haunted her during those dark hours in Hollidaysburg, Pennsylvania. Although she was bowled over by the art she found in the museums, her impression of the country itself was now colored by her new attachment to Italy. She found the countryside desolate in comparison to the countryside she had just left, which had been dotted with cozy villages. The landscape matched her mood. She was suddenly lonely without Emily and the whole Parma contingent. She wrote plaintively to Paris: "Oh Emily *do do* come, you will never regret it"[21] "Must you stay in Paris?"[22] "Indeed Emily you *must* come."[23] But Emily was obstinate. She wanted to stay with her painting classes in Paris, and on that trip she never did see the country that had filled her dreams in Philadelphia.

Instead of Emily, Mary was inadequately paired for a few days with friends of Emily's who were traveling in Spain at the same time. Her mood was wild while the three went around Madrid. Partly this was because she had a powerful response to the art she saw there, particularly Velásquez, Murillo, Titian, and Rubens. Partly this was because she felt abandoned by Emily, who had fallen under the spell of her painting teacher, Evariste Luminais, in Paris. Like Raimondi, Luminais was quite a bit older than she, was married and had grown children. Luminais was just beginning to have an impact on the art scene with his paintings of classical subjects and episodes from the early history of France, which earned him the nickname Le Gaulois. As was customary for successful artists, he took on a small number of students, both men and women, and was considered a very thorough teacher. Emily Sartain fell immediately into his orbit when she arrived in Paris. She became not only his faithful pupil but practically a member of the family, and soon moved into an apartment above his. Cassatt, who had never heard of him when she was living in and around Paris in the 1860s, knew his work only by a few recently published woodcuts and was appalled that Sartain had put herself so completely in his hands. She was worried that her friend was being taken in by a second-rate artist who charged exorbitant prices. Of course, she was sorry to lose the influence that she herself had exerted over Sartain until so recently. Cassatt did not express her doubts directly to Sartain, but in those lonely days in Madrid bent the ears of Emily's friends. They dutifully repeated Mary's concerns to Emily, who was hurt and angry to hear what Cassatt said about Luminais: "that he was an obscure artist, and for him to demand such a price for teaching is preposterous—She went on that absurd style extensively."[24] After this incident, the two were never as close as they had been in Parma, and Cassatt had once again let her temper injure a friendship. She of course did not know that her ravings had been repeated to Sartain, and continued to write affectionate letters from Spain. In one of these, she innocently and humbly confessed her worst failing, "You know I always tell everything but you are wiser and it is no use to let everyone know your affaires; however I never can remember that all persons don't take my views of things."[25]

Cassatt grew calmer after she moved from Madrid to Seville in late October of 1872. She had obtained a letter of introduction from the bishop of Pittsburgh, who was Spanish, to all the Catholic bishops in Spain. His efforts, coupled with the help of the American consul, were sufficiently influential to establish her in both social and artistic circles in Seville. As in Parma, she soon had a studio in a privileged location (the historic Casa de Pilatos, the palace of the dukes of Medinaceli) and was invited to the studios of other artists and the important local art collections. As in Parma, she was greatly admired by the local art community. She got to know the old master art in the museums, including the large collection of Murillos, and did not neglect the modern Spanish school, which included such artists as Madrazo and Fortuny who had recently been painting in Seville.

Here she began a major cycle of paintings that represents the earliest substantial body of her work that is known today. The unfortunate disappearance of so much of her youthful art gives the six known Seville pictures unusual emphasis. What fascinated her in this bright and colorful city were the people. After years of painting local peasants throughout France and Italy, Cassatt was a connoisseur of exotic features and costumes. She hired as models both women and men who evoked the Sevillian style of beauty and dressed them in traditional costumes. The men were often portrayed as toreadors and the women, swathed in veils, represented the women they fought for. She again portrayed scenes of flirtation like her Parma *Carnival* painting; in fact she executed another balcony subject—this time in Spanish guise—and a scene where a woman offers a bullfighter the *panale,* a traditional drink. She was particularly taken with one model who had full lips and sad dark eyes and used her for a number of studies, including the one called *Spanish Dancer Wearing a Lace Mantilla* (figure 33). As she wrote to Emily, "The great thing here is the odd types and peculiar rich dark coloring of the models, if it were not for that I should not stay."[26]

She was calmer and more productive in Seville than she had been in Madrid, but she was still not happy. She complained that there was nothing to do, no good theater or entertainment, and the people in society, although kind, were not interesting. In her characteristic high-handed way, she judged

33. *Mary Cassatt,* **Spanish Dancer Wearing a Lace Mantilla,** *1873*
Oil on canvas, 26¾ x 19¾ in.
National Museum of American Art, Smithsonian Institution; gift of Victoria Dreyfus

"the Spaniards infinitely inferior in education and breeding to the Italians" and that they were "barbarians" when it came to fashion.[27] It must not have been easy for her as a woman alone in a country where robbery was a way of life and warring political factions made ordinary travel dangerous, but evidently a woman of her class could arrange to be comfortable. She stayed in a protective, respectable boardinghouse and had all the escorts she needed to go about the city. She never complained about being confined or limited by the men of that Latin culture; indeed, she was more disturbed by the poor quality of "the Opera Comique." At last she resorted to taking Spanish lessons to occupy her evenings, although she confessed that she was less interested in learning the language than in having someone handy to translate the hard words in the plays of Lope de Vega as she read them. These months in Spain were the first time she was completely on her own. Although at times she was desperately lonely, she stayed on. Her social needs, however strong, were very rarely strong enough to take precedence over her work.

Toward the end of April 1873, Cassatt made the three-day trek from Seville to Paris by train. She and Sartain had once talked of returning to Italy for the spring, but when the time came, Sartain was even less interested in leaving Luminais, and Cassatt herself could see many good reasons for being in Paris. High among them was the Paris Salon scheduled to open within a week or two. She was eager to know whether or not she would be accepted for the third time in a row, excluding 1871, when the Salon was not held. She had sent the large canvas of a bullfighter and his lady, *Torero and Young Girl* (figure 34), hoping that the judges would see steady improvement in the technique and emotional breadth of her work. To her satisfaction, it was indeed accepted and exhibited under the name Mlle. Mary Stevenson-Cassatt. In 1868, 1870, and 1872 she had used her middle name in the Salon catalog, "Mlle. Mary Stevenson,"[28] in an attempt to deflect unwanted public attention. Now, with the beginnings of an international reputation, she felt it was important to fix her own name in this important professional context.

Cassatt's use of a pseudonym in the early part of her career was somewhat unusual. Although there are many famous examples of women writers using pseudonyms, including one of Cassatt's favorites, George Sand, they usually adopted male names that would give them the competitive edge that men have in the public arena. Some women artists did the same in submitting work to juries. Cassatt gave up this advantage of a pseudonym by retaining a female name, and thus gained only a female anonymity. While Haldeman wished she had done the same because it was "pleasanter" to be anonymous, the notion was extremely old-fashioned by the late 1860s and reflects some of the odd quirks of the Cassatt family. Mr. Cassatt, particularly, was a "gentleman of the old school" and may have been behind his daughter's attempt to keep her name out of print. But after all the publicity she got in Parma under her full name, she may have decided it was a lost cause.

34. Mary Cassatt, **Torero and Young Girl,** *1873*
Oil on canvas, 39⅝ x 33½ in.
Sterling and Francine Clark Art Institute

Cassatt had good reason for wanting her real name to be published in the Salon catalog at last. The first two times she had paintings accepted, the jury was thought to be exceptionally lenient. In 1868 Cassatt and Haldeman knew that newcomers were given extra consideration. In 1869 they were refused when the jury decided to make severer cuts. In 1870 the pendulum swung back to leniency under the leadership of the free-thinking battle painter, Ernest Meissonier. Called the "democratic" Salon, nearly three thousand paintings were accepted and hung without regard to importance or a pleasing arrangement, but in rows, alphabetically by artist.[29] While it was always good to have a painting in the Salon, acceptance into the Salons of 1868 or 1870 was not the honor it might have been. In 1872, when the Salons resumed after the break caused by the Franco-Prussian War and the Commune, the jury was anxious to reinstate rigorous standards and refused more than half of the entries. The same was true in 1873 and would remain in force for several years to come. Not only was the number of Americans in the exhibition down from prewar levels, but during these years the radical French artists around Manet, including Renoir and Pissarro, were unexpectedly humiliated by rejection and began to form plans for alternate exhibitions. In light of the large numbers of artists whose work was not accepted, Cassatt thought more highly of getting in. In fact, she may have regretted staying in Parma for the 1872 Salon and made the trip from Seville especially for the exhibition in 1873.

However proud Cassatt was of earning this form of official recognition, she did not relax her critical perception of the Paris art world. She had always shied away from political jockeying, even on the student level, but now, after spending a considerable amount of time studying the old masters and meeting contemporary artists in Italy and Spain, she could view the modern French school from a broader perspective. She had met French artists studying in Spain and knew that the cool tonalities of Velásquez were in vogue in current French painting. When she saw what such important artists as Léon Bonnat did with Velásquez's style, she felt that something akin to an artistic crime had been committed. She, who had just come from direct contact with the Velásquez masterpieces in the Prado, had been trying to incorporate their realism and solidity into her own work. In comparison she condemned the French school as it was displayed that year in the Salon as "washy, unfleshlike, and grey."[30] The stunning presumption of this twenty-nine-year-old, who had spent only six months of her life in Spain, to take on the entire French establishment for its inaccurate reading of Velásquez was not lost on the people around her. Once again, Sartain was in awe of her friend, "she is entirely too slashing, snubs all modern art, disdains the Salon pictures of Cabanel, Bonnat, and all the names we are used to revere."[31]

Cassatt's opinions, as idiosyncratic as they were, were not unique in Paris. Through the many European and American connections she had, she was soon in touch with others who were also critics of the status quo. The most famous of these were the radical artists who organized their own exhibition in 1874 and became known as Impressionists. Some friends of Cassatt had met Monet and Renoir during their student days in the early 1860s. We have no proof that she had met them, nor do we have any evidence that she was acquainted with Berthe and Edma Morisot, who had been copying in the Louvre during the years Cassatt was similarly occupied. We do know that in 1873 Cassatt painted a small profile head of Mme. Sisley, presumably the wife of the future Impressionist Alfred Sisley. Cassatt's relationship with these artists was undoubtedly slight, but her establishing contacts with a range of artists within the dissident community during this time had momentous repercussions for her future.

At the time, her ravings were addressed to those who were closer to her and more visible in the art world of the early 1870s. In Paris she had met an outspoken collector from Philadelphia, William Hood Stewart, who was living in grand style in a house overlooking the Seine. Stewart, a patron of contemporary art and friend of such important artists as Meissonier and Fortuny, opened his home to the eloquent Miss Cassatt. The conversation there was even more contemptuous of the accepted modern artists. Stewart and his friends went so far as to dismiss the artists upon whom modern art was built, including both Ingres and Delacroix. Although both Meissonier and Fortuny were themselves immensely successful, they were known publicly to criticize academic practices and procedures. Meissonier had headed the jury that selected the "democratic" Salon of 1870, and both practiced styles that were more realistic than standard academic classicism. They served as models for younger artists who wanted an art that had relevance to modern times. In the month that Cassatt stayed in Paris in 1873, she discovered others who felt as she did about the French school and was reinforced in her desire to follow her own path.

Accordingly, she and her mother, who had arrived in Paris about a week after she did, decided to go traveling for the summer. Instead of returning to Spain, which had been Cassatt's original intention, they ended up in Holland and Belgium, where Mary made copies in museums and looked for a studio. She found she could have one in Antwerp for a few months, and took the opportunity to study Rubens in more depth. She painted a portrait of her mother when local models proved too difficult to find (figure 35). Her mother was good-natured about having their lives revolve around her daughter's art, but hoped that she could pry Mary away from the easel long enough to spend August in a seaside or mountain resort. When it came time for her mother to depart in October, Cassatt returned with her to Paris briefly and then took off alone for Italy.

She passed through Parma on her way, but found things much changed, including her relationship with Raimondi, with whom she had been corresponding for the last year. In Rome, this disappointment, coupled with her sadness at finding herself alone in a new place, caused her to chafe at her new surroundings. She was particularly irritated with the American colony, which had all the jealousy and "moral depravement" of the colony in Paris but was even smaller and more inbred. Cassatt revived once she began working. For the next seven months she produced paintings that had little to do with what she could see in Rome but everything to do with her previous summer's study of Rubens.

Aside from two, possibly three, paintings that have survived from Cassatt's stay in Rome, we have very little else to illuminate her response to this very artistic city. In spite of the several months she spent in Rome in 1870, and her extended residence in 1874, she is not commonly recorded as one of the important American artists to have worked there. This may be because she did not mix enough with the other Americans to have been considered a member of the colony and because her teacher and closest adviser in Rome, Charles Bellay, was French. Nevertheless, she was part of

35. *Mary Cassatt,* **Katherine Johnston Cassatt,** ***1873*** ***Oil on panel, 24½ x 22½ in.*** ***Private collection***

the larger international circle of artists whose studios dotted the older parts of town and whose lives were considered so romantic that they were frequently the subject of novels and short fiction. The women artists who worked in Rome were particularly fascinating to American writers. Although no one is known to have based a character on Mary Cassatt, we can have a glimpse of her circumstances in Rome by reading about the numerous women portrayed in this type of fiction. In Henry James's *Roderick Hudson,* which first appeared in serial form in the *Atlantic* in 1875, Rome is viewed through the eyes of an American connoisseur, Rowland Mallet, whose protégé, Roderick Hudson, is a young sculptor. A minor character James creates to flesh out the Roman art world is the painter Augusta Blanchard:

> She was an American, she was young, she was pretty, and she had made her way to Rome alone and unaided. She lived alone, or with no other duenna than a bush-browed old serving-woman, though indeed she had a friendly neighbour in the person of a certain Madame Grandoni, who in various social emergencies lent her a protecting wing and had come with her to Rowland's dinner. Miss Blanchard had a small fortune, but she was not above selling her pictures. . . . Rowland had made her acquaintance early in the winter, and as she kept a saddle horse and rode a great deal he had asked permission to be her cavalier. . . . He admired her, and indeed there was something admirable in her combination of beauty and talent, of isolation and self-support. He used sometimes to go into the little high-niched ordinary room which served her as a studio, and find her working at a panel six inches square, at an open casement, profiled against the deep blue Roman sky.[32]

The saintly Augusta Blanchard is hardly a mirror image of the outspoken Mary Cassatt, but there is much in James's woman artist making her way alone that tempts us to see a glimmer of Cassatt in the character. Cassatt may have known James in Paris about the time he was writing *Roderick Hudson* and may have unconsciously made an impression on him. If Augusta Blanchard is not Mary Cassatt, she may have been one of the many American women like Cassatt—Elizabeth Gardner, Emily Sartain, or many others—who were not uncommon presences in Roman or Parisian society in the 1870s.

Cassatt was least like Augusta Blanchard in the art she created. Blanchard painted delicate, finely wrought flower still lifes. In Rome Cassatt developed her strongest, least polished style. She found a Rubenesque model with white skin and reddish-blond hair, whom she posed with one or two others in musical themes such as singing or playing instruments or alone looking out with a bold and direct gaze. She sent a painting of the red-headed model wearing a mantilla, called *Ida,* to the Paris Salon that spring (figure 36). For the first time, her picture was honored by being included in the series of caricatures of Salon pictures that was published annually by the satiric newspaper *Le Journal amusant*[33] and received more than usual attention among artists and critics. Edgar Degas, an artist who was yet unknown to her, was led to the picture by a mutual friend and openly admired it. Years later, when his praise meant a great deal to her, she was told that he said, "*Voilà quelqu'un qui sent comme moi* [There is someone who feels as I do]."[34]

In spite of this success, Cassatt did not sell the painting, nor the one that she had at a dealer, Rosenquest, on the Boulevard Haussmann. In fact, the sale of her Parma pictures was not followed by a steady stream of buyers, and it was a year and a half since she had sold anything. This was puzzling to her because she had received good reviews and was exhibiting regularly, not only in Paris but in Philadelphia and elsewhere in the United States. Most of the artists blamed the economic downturn of 1873–74 for the depression of the market in those years, but Cassatt focused her blame on what she could do something about—her dealer and herself.

In June 1874 Cassatt arrived in Paris in a black mood. Ever since her first

36. *Mary Cassatt,* **Ida,** *1874*
Oil on canvas, 23 x 18 in.
Collection of Joseph and Carol Anton

year in Paris in 1866 she had only breezed through the art capital on her way to somewhere else or to see her pictures each year in the Salon. In 1869 she had forced herself to stay there for several months as punishment for allowing herself to be rejected by that year's Salon jury. Now, in 1874, she was once again punishing herself for not producing salable works and for not overseeing her dealer properly. She decided to stay in Paris until she got back on the right track. Emily Sartain was once again taken by surprise and reported the momentous event to her father: "I think I told you that Miss Cassatt is in Paris. She astonished me by telling me she is looking for an atelier here, for next winter. She has always detested Paris so much, that I could scarcely believe it possible that she would consent to stay here,—but she says she sees it is necessary to be here to look after her own interests. She thinks it is the fault of her picture dealer that her pictures do not sell."[35] Sartain, who had always been stimulated by Cassatt's brief assaults on Paris, was afraid of her friend's wild mood and did not look forward to a steady diet of it now that they would be living in the same city again. Sartain was still progressing under Luminais and had become deeply entrenched in the official world that her teacher represented. She could foresee being caught in the middle of the inevitable clash between the dissident values of her friend and the academic values of her mentor.

Chapter IV

Changing Direction (1875–1878)

Cassatt's decision to take up residence in Paris in 1874 put an end to the romantic, nomadic life she had led for almost eight years (figure 37). At age thirty, she may have been unconsciously ready for a more settled life. What was more evident was that with her increasing maturity her professional and financial responsibilities weighed heavily on her, and she was ready to make sacrifices for the sake of her career. She began to see it was necessary to confront the Paris art establishment rather than to be critical during her brief stays in Paris before running off to Parma, Antwerp, or Rome. Up to then she had been lucky in getting her pictures accepted into the Salon five out of six times and in attracting the attention of critics and other artists. But her success was only partial, since it did not translate into financial security or professional acceptance. She found that the young artists like Elizabeth Gardner who had stayed in Paris, studied for years under a recognized master, and then gradually made themselves known to the rest of the art community, including the Salon jurors, were reaping more rewards at this point than the brilliant Miss Cassatt, who had so haughtily followed her own path.[1]

Possibly to begin easing back into the Paris community, Cassatt spent the summer of 1874 at Villiers-le-Bel with her old teacher Thomas Couture. Couture had lost none of his charisma in the intervening six years since Cassatt and Haldeman had been part of his entourage. Even Sartain had spent some time in Écouen and went to pay hommage to the infamous master, but in the end didn't have the nerve to knock on his door. In Couture, Cassatt would have had someone to fill her in on the latest Paris

37. *Mary Cassatt,* Portrait of the Artist, *c. 1878*
Gouache on paper, 23½ x 27½ in.
The Metropolitan Museum of Art; bequest of Edith H. Proskauer, 1975

gossip while giving her support for her basically antagonistic view of that world. That summer she may also have tried to rein in the extreme Rubenesque style she had let loose in Rome and, with Couture's help, formulate a style more in keeping with the latest Paris vogue.

When the summer ended, she carried out her plan of taking a studio in the city. Before long, her sister, Lydia, arrived to help ease the transition and lend moral support (figure 38). The two sisters, who had seen little of each other since Mary's first departure for Europe in 1865, established a new intimacy as they shared housekeeping in Mary's apartment and went around Paris together. It was frowned upon for a young, unmarried woman to live alone, and Mary's older sister made an excellent companion and chaperone. At thirty-seven, Lydia had dedicated much of the last ten years to the comfort of her parents, her brothers, and the growing number of Aleck and Lois's children. When she was needed by her sister, she did not hesitate; this was her first trip to Europe since 1855. With Mary's need and Lydia's inclination, this visit also marked the beginning of Lydia's residence in Paris that was at first sporadic but lasted for the rest of her life.

When Cassatt looked back on this period of her art, she felt that she

38. *Mary Cassatt,* **Lydia at a Tapestry Loom,** *c. 1880–81*
Oil on canvas, 25⁵⁄₈ x 36³⁄₈ in.
Flint Institute of Arts; gift of The Whiting Foundation

went astray in these years. She had been so shaken by the lack of public appreciation of her work, as measured by sales, that she cast about for a surer foothold. As she wrote to a friend, "I thought I must be wrong & the painters admired of the public right. . . ."[2] Consequently, she abandoned her old interest in costume genre pictures, such as the peasant paintings, Carnival subjects, and bullfighters, and set about becoming a society portraitist and painter of fashionable life. Although we are once again without many key paintings from this first year in Paris, we know from documentary information that the two pictures she worked on for the Salon of 1875 were portraits: one of her sister, Lydia, and the other of a child.

Paris in 1875 regained the brilliance it had lost during the Franco-Prussian War and the Commune. Foreigners poured into the city in ever-greater numbers and *tout le monde* paraded down the famed Parisian boulevards. The city had undergone drastic changes in the last ten years. Napoleon III had ordered a modernization of the city that resulted in whole sections being torn down to make way for even more boulevards, such as the Boulevard Haussmann, and grand buildings, such as the new Paris Opéra. The emperor was deposed before he could enjoy the fruits of his planning, and the changes graced Paris under the more democratic Third Republic.

Other transformations in the physical appearance of the city were unplanned. Significant destruction resulted from the siege of Paris during the war with Germany in 1870 and France's suppression of the Paris Commune in 1871 in a bloody battle waged inside the city. The palace of the Tuileries, the westernmost structure forming the large courtyard of the Louvre, was completely destroyed and never rebuilt. Badly damaged structures such as the Hôtel de Ville and the Vendôme column, which was toppled with the help of the painter Courbet, were quickly rebuilt, and some, like the Palais Royal, were simply repaired. The process of cleaning, repairing, and reorganizing the city was done in the early 1870s with special zeal since the city would once again be throwing itself open for world inspection during the upcoming International Exposition, or World's Fair, of 1878. Along with the structural improvements came the introduction of electric light and increased police activity that made the city safe and enjoyable around the clock.

Cassatt and her sister joined the many other Americans of the Paris art world in the area off the outer ring of boulevards toward Montmartre. The most popular district for these apartment/studios was along the Boulevard de Clichy at the foot of Montmartre hill. From this location the two women could comfortably join the throngs traversing the grand streets at all hours and dine in local restaurants or have an ice cream in one of the cafés after the theater. Shopping, of course, was the great daytime entertainment in Paris. The endless shops lining the streets offered clothes, jewelry, pictures, and all manner of consumer spectacles. One guidebook described the sensation created by the sumptuous shop windows:

> A heterogeneous crowd, which the delights of the French Capital have attracted from all parts of the world, gaze with rapture upon the scene of wonders. The dazzling display of diamonds and other costly jewels [are] exhibited in the windows, which are illuminated with gas, by means of reflectors, shedding a soft, clear light, and at the same time showing off these treasures to the best advantage. . . . Watches of every variety and style, and every description . . . glitter in the soft and mellow light. Perfumery shops, also arranged with the most consummate skill, impregnating the air with delicious perfume, thereby add to the fairylike impressions of the scene.[3]

The weary pedestrian could continue her journey by horse-drawn omnibus or simply stop in a sweets shop for a bag of chocolate drops as a pick-me-up. Cassatt and her sister took full advantage of the city that catered to all tastes in culture, entertainment, and consumption.

Lydia, an excellent needlewoman with an eye for fashion, went around with Mary to find the lesser-known seamstresses who could carry out the sisters' orders for distinctive clothes. They furnished the small apartment with tables, lamps, and embroideries discovered at shops that sold antiques and imported goods. When they entertained, they served *chocolat* in the finest china and seated their guests among statues and exotic curiosities.[4] While their style of living could not compare with that of the many American millionaires who populated the fashionable sections of the city, it was sufficiently sumptuous to impress the other young American artists and students who lived around them on the Rue Laval and its neighboring streets near the Boulevard de Clichy.

Cassatt, like many artists, saw that visitors to the city were eager for a taste of the Paris art world during their stay. Tourists assiduously visited the Louvre and the Luxembourg galleries as well as the Salon during May and June. Dealers opened up their showrooms to the public and put their best artists' pictures in the windows. The most serious visitors to the capital wanted a picture to take home with them, to bring a little bit of Paris to their drawing rooms in Albany, Altoona, or Cincinnati. Best of all was to take home one's portrait painted by one of the best-known French artists, such as Bonnat, Cabanel, and Carolus-Duran, or an American living abroad like George P. A. Healy or James McNeill Whistler. This was the audience that Cassatt attempted to attract in the mid-1870s.

Since she had never before presented herself as a portraitist, Cassatt had to invest some time gaining the kind of reputation that would draw clients. She had always had a talent for likenesses and often did portraits of family and friends when more formal models failed her. Since she considered portraiture less important than themes of her own invention, she did not think to exhibit them or put them up for sale. Now, having decided to do many things she had once disdained, she gave portraiture the central position in her art. As if to advertise her abilities in this line, she spent the winter of 1874–75 working on two major portraits, a full-length study of her sister and a portrait of a little girl leaning on the arm of a chair. Together these would show all the fashionable visitors to the Salon what she could do for them or their children. Her plan partially failed when the study of her sister was unexpectedly rejected, but the portrait of the child was accepted. It was hung in the gallery of the Palais de l'Industrie that was devoted to the C's (the Salon was usually hung alphabetically by room, although not in order within the room), along with the portraits of Cabanel, Cot, Carolus-Duran, and her old teacher Chaplin, and was charming enough to hold its own in such fashionable company.

Gradually she succeeded in gaining the attention of her intended audience: Americans seeking their portraits painted abroad. One of these was Mary Ellison, daughter of a Philadelphia businessman, who made Cassatt's acquaintance through mutual friends and asked her father to commission Cassatt to paint her portrait (figure 39). Cassatt duly executed commissions like these, but would pose her models in genre-type poses—sewing, reading—and then would produce spin-off genre pictures with similar poses, costumes, and settings that she would offer for sale to the larger public. Although she concentrated on portraiture during the mid-1870s, she never did portraits exclusively, nor did she become identified solely as a portrait painter. Unlike Sargent, who made his sitters appear graceful and at ease with the world, she gave her sitters an air of abstraction and slight melancholy that pleased some but not all clients.

The pressure to adopt a style of painting that did not inherently suit her made Cassatt more than usually agitated in the winter of 1874–75. She entered the American artists' circles in Paris that included such old friends as Emily Sartain, Henry Bacon, whom she knew from Écouen, and the rising star Elizabeth Gardner. She understood that she needed their support as well as their connections, but she also found that her outspoken opinions of

39. *Mary Cassatt,* **Mary Ellison Embroidering,** *1877*
Oil on canvas, 29¼ x 23½ in.
Philadelphia Museum of Art; gift of the children of Jean Thomas Thayer

former days had caused ill will that could not be undone. As much as her friends liked and admired her, they could not offer her the type of professional help she needed to rise in the official art world.

When the jury sat down to deliberate on her two pictures for the Salon of 1875, such old enemies as Luminais were unwilling to go to bat for her. The news that one of her pictures was rejected rippled through the American art community and caused her acute embarrassment. Most onlookers did not realize that another picture she had submitted was accepted. In her agony, Cassatt lashed out at all concerned, but particularly Sartain and Luminais, who she felt were behind not only the rejection but also the unpleasant gossip that was spread about it. Sartain defended herself as best she could in an explanatory letter to Cassatt, who had left for America for a long-delayed visit,[5] but confided to her father, "Miss C. is a tremendous talker and very touchy and selfish, so if you hear of her talking of me at home, as she has done lately in Paris, you will know the origin of it all. I shall never become intimate with her again, no matter how she receives my letter."[6]

Not long after Cassatt returned to Paris in August of 1875, Emily Sartain herself went home to Philadelphia. In 1876 she began teaching at the Philadelphia School of Design for Women and rose to become its principal, a position she held for thirty years. She continued as a painter and engraver and served on many national art committees. She and Cassatt crossed paths again as they both gained in stature but never again were friends.

The bitterness of Cassatt's final quarrel with Sartain reflects the tremendous impact the Salon had on the lives and minds of the artists in Paris. Even Cassatt, who had long established herself as a critic of the official system, could not steel herself against the powerful insult of a Salon rejection. For three years (1875, 1876, and 1877) she threw herself on the mercy of the Salon jury in spite of her knowledge of its weaknesses and injustices. Each year her cynicism deepened: in 1875 one of two pictures was rejected; in 1876 she was bitterly amused to see her previously rejected painting accepted after she darkened the background; in 1877, to her ultimate horror and humiliation, both entries were refused and she was unrepresented in this celebrated forum for the first time in seven years.

Cassatt's struggle with the Salon jury was not unlike that of many radical artists, including the controversial Manet. Émile Zola championed Manet and this group in the press and wrote with great feeling of an artist's emotional response to the Salon in his 1886 novel, *L'Oeuvre.* Zola's artist hero, Claude Lantier, was the leader of an anti-academic faction, but he never overcame his need for the kind of approval only the Salon could give. After many years of rejections, an old friend who had found official success and was now on the Salon jury went to great lengths to make sure Lantier was finally accepted. Lantier's response on hearing the news from his friend was a sharp mixture of emotions.

> Claude, despite the gladness of the tidings, felt a pang at his heart; the note was so brief, and was written in such a protecting, pitying style, that all the humiliating features of the business were apparent to him. For a moment he felt sorry over this victory, so much so that he would have liked to take his work back and hide it. Then his delicacy of feeling, his artistic pride again gave way, so much did protracted waiting for success make his wretched heart bleed. Ah! to be seen, to make his way despite everything! He had reached the point when conscience capitulates; he once more began to long for the opening of the Salon with all the feverish impatience of a beginner, again living in a state of illusion which showed him a crowd, a press of moving heads acclaiming his canvas.[7]

For three years, Cassatt suffered just such tortures of conscience and pride as she saw the Salon jury turn increasingly against her work and saw herself dance faster and more hopelessly to their tune.

Her worst emotional outbursts were against those like Sartain, who symbolized betrayal to Cassatt. To others who knew her in Paris in these years she was the picture of patience in the face of adversity. As she became entrenched in the art circles of the city she became a familiar figure who was known for her talent and generosity as well as for her temper. It was during these years that she established a lifelong friendship with Louisine Elder (later Havemeyer), who first came to Paris with her mother and two sisters in 1874 (figure 40). Daughter of a New York sugar manufacturer, she stayed in the same boardinghouse as Emily Sartain and met Cassatt that summer. The nineteen-year-old Louisine was captivated by the magnetic thirty-year-old Mary Cassatt. "I felt then that Miss Cassatt was the most intelligent woman I had ever met, and I cherished every word she uttered, and remembered almost every remark she made. It seemed to me no one could see art more understandingly, feel it more deeply or express themselves more clearly than she did."[8] Cassatt, in turn, willingly introduced the Paris art world to such an eager student on Louisine's subsequent trips in 1875, 1877, and most years between 1879 and 1883. To Louisine Elder,

40. *Photograph of the Elder Sisters, c. 1872. Left to right: Louisine, age seventeen; Anne, age nineteen; Adeline, age fifteen.*
Courtesy of J. Watson Webb, Jr.
Private collection

Cassatt was a paragon of wisdom and knowledge in art matters, a view that she held for the subsequent fifty years of their friendship.

In the eyes of another Cassatt observer in the mid-1870s, she took on an almost saintly air. May Alcott (figure 41), the daughter of Bronson Alcott, the well-known utopian philosopher, and the sister of Louisa May Alcott, who had become famous with the 1868 publication of *Little Women,* met Mary Cassatt in late 1876, when she arrived in Paris to study painting. For two years Alcott and Cassatt frequented the same circles of American artists in Paris. Alcott's admiration of Cassatt, who was younger than Alcott but far more established professionally, fueled their friendship.

May Alcott's letters home to her sister Louisa and her parents were wonderfully descriptive of her life as an art student in Paris and were full of references to her new friend. When Louisa decided to use May's letters as the basis of a new novel, *Diana and Persis* (begun in 1879 but never finished), on the theme of women artists, she sketched out a character, Miss Cassal, who embodied the qualities May had seen in Miss Cassatt. Louisa had never met Mary Cassatt, but was impressed by the role she played as mentor to May and many others within the American circles in Paris. In her novel, Louisa paraphrases May's actual letters in the fictional letters she has her

41. Rose Peckham,* Portrait of May Alcott, *1877 Oil on canvas, 25 x21 in. Louisa May Alcott Memorial Association, Orchard House, Concord, Mass.

heroine, Persis, write to her friend Diana: Miss Cassal "is a grand woman, full of real genius, I think, and but for her sex would have made a name before now, since all who know her acknowledge her power. She has the modesty of true talent and so is content to do fine things and let others get praised for mediocre work, she biding her time."[9] On the subject of her Salon rejections, Persis is keenly sympathetic: "I am told that men are jealous of her, and her 'Joel' [fictional work] was refused at the last Salon merely because of its boldness and power. She smiles and paints on tranquilly, content to be felt if not seen."[10] Alcott's perception of Cassatt as modest, patient, and tranquil in the face of Salon rejection would not have been shared by Emily Sartain, who had felt the full blast of Cassatt's rage.

Alcott's feminist interpretation of Cassatt's rejection—that the men of the jury refused her because they were jealous of her boldness and power—may in some measure reflect Cassatt's own thinking though greatly magnified by the more overt feminism of the Alcott sisters. Cassatt was as aware of discrimination against women as most educated women of her generation were. She pointed out examples of it in her own field, in which she knew women had difficulties obtaining instruction, selling their work, and receiving the proper recognition. Whether she felt her own Salon rejections were due to sexual discrimination is hard to tell. Certainly discrimination existed in the entire subjective selection process of the Salon, but the system was corrupt and fallible in so many ways that discrimination on the basis of sex was hard, but not impossible, to isolate.

Despite the prevalence of women artists and their reasonable success in all aspects of the art world at this time, there was still a pervasive resistance to them in the minds of their male colleagues. Compare, for example, the Alcott description of the scene at the Palais de l'Industrie on the day entries to the Salon were due with the description of the same scene given by Cassatt's old friend Henry Bacon in his book *A Parisian Year* (1882).

In Alcott's eyes the women artists were fully integrated into the event. Persis and Miss Cassal shipped off their paintings and then rushed off to see them arrive at the Palais de l'Industrie, "where an immense crowd was assembled; mostly art students who, as the pictures were carried up the steps and dumped to be registered, sent up howls of derision or cries of admiration at the work of anyone known to them. It was intensely exciting, and we stood with a group of friends as anxious as ourselves. . . . We stood for three mortal hours and forgot weariness in our interest."[11]

Henry Bacon, on the other hand, saw the same excitement, but assigned women a different role in it: "There is a continuous procession of paintings, for the many thousand sent would stretch out as far or farther than the rank and file of the grand army; some carried, facing the sky, on the shoulders of the bearers, can only be admired by the tall men, or those who have good places on the staircase; others, carried perpendicularly, are seen only from one side, and there is a rush from one side to the other to catch a glimpse. Criticisms are freely given. . . . A lone female follows a porter carrying a picture carefully wrapped in a blanket. She passes in silence, for the crowd are there to amuse themselves, not to be cruel. There are very few women present, and those generally models with their protectors, who enjoy the fun and the sensation their effigies create, as a queen or a Venus."[12] Even though Bacon was an old friend of Cassatt and Haldeman from Écouen days, he gives here a view of women artists as isolated and pathetic. The women of interest to him are not the artists—his professional colleagues—but the models, who are grist for artistic fantasies.

If Henry Bacon could maintain such a dismissive view of women artists in the face of his own very different experience of the lively and successful women around him, it is not hard to see how a jury of more hidebound men might react to the entries by women artists as they came to them throughout the judging process. In Zola's scathing description of this process in *L'Oeuvre,* he describes the grueling survey of thousands of paintings and the virtual impossibility of the jurors' giving valid opinions throughout (figure 42). Those paintings that were not "protected" in some way—through an elaborate system of friendships and favors—were fair game for ridicule. The paintings submitted by women, who were the least likely to be part of the established network, were the easiest to dismiss. "In front of the women's paintings the gentlemen were particularly prone to sneer, never displaying the least gallantry."[13] In Zola's view, these paintings were very likely to be passed over unless a juror had a particular interest in a picture done by a student of his or a woman he was acquainted with in some other way: "He was interrupted by loud jeers. Was she pretty?" asked the other jurors when one voted for a painting of flowers by a lady.[14] A man had to have strong convictions to withstand the teasing of the other jurors when he did choose a woman's painting.

Unfortunately Cassatt would not have engendered this kind of loyalty among members of the Salon jury. Although her work was acknowledged to be very strong and she had some old ties to Gérôme and Chaplin, Cassatt's scathing opinions about the official system would not have endeared her to the men who were chosen every year to constitute the Salon jury. While they trudged past miles and miles of paintings, the jurors were very unlikely

42. Henri Gervex,* Une Séance de Jury de Peinture, *c. 1884–85
Oil on canvas, 117¾ x 165¼ in.
Musée d'Orsay; © Photo Réunion des musées nationaux

to make a stand for the work of a woman who would neither flatter nor flirt with them.

As agonizing as those years were for Cassatt, when she was trying desperately to gain acceptance from a system she could not respect, she was one of the fortunate few who managed to escape the system and find greater success in what must have appeared at first as a flimsy alternative. In 1877, after her final humiliation at the hands of the Salon jury, a sympathetic Edgar Degas invited her to join the annual exhibitions of a group that the press had already dubbed Impressionists, a group with good credentials but worrisome notoriety that banned its members from submitting to the Salon. Most of the members, including Monet and Renoir, had been friends for a long time, drawn to one another because of their mutual interest in a fresh style that had a spontaneous, sketchlike quality. They gravitated toward the controversial Manet, who had made a name for himself in the 1860s by exhibiting scandalous scenes of bohemian life, such as *Olympia* and *Déjeuner sur l'Herbe.* In 1874, after being humiliated by rejections from a conservative Salon jury, they banded together to mount their own exhibitions, which were held again in 1875 and 1877. Although Manet declined to exhibit in these renegade shows, he was usually considered one of the group, which included such now-famous names as Degas, Monet, Renoir, Cézanne, Pissarro, Sisley, and Morisot. Many lesser-known artists exhibited with the group over the years, but only by the invitation of one of the core-group members. In the spring of 1877 Degas offered Cassatt such an invitation.

It is safe to say that any artist or art student working in Paris in the 1870s would have known about the Impressionist exhibitions and the radical artistic movement those exhibitions unveiled to the public. Not only did the group advertise widely with posters and sometimes even banners in the streets, but the word-of-mouth publicity was rampant. When the exhibitions opened, they were reviewed by virtually every newspaper and art periodical in Paris and in major publications throughout the capitals of Europe and America. By 1877, the group had mounted three exhibitions in 1874, 1876, and 1877. Reviews by Émile Zola and Henry James had appeared in such far-flung places as St. Petersburg and New York, while Stéphane Mallarmé published a review in London in English. The critical reactions to the exhibitions ranged from the satiric essay by Louis Leroy, which is credited with giving the group its name, *Les Impressionnistes,*[15] to the explanatory articles written by friends of the artists like Edmond Duranty and Georges Rivière.[16] The press coverage was so complete that no artist, regardless of his or her stylistic orientation, could remain ignorant of the Impressionist group.

Where an artist stood on the issue of Impressionism was another matter. While there were those who were passionately for or against it, the majority of artists perceived these developments as merely good dinner conversation. They took a moderate stance that allowed them to borrow freely from the innovations of the Impressionists without going out on a limb professionally. They recognized the talent of certain of the Impressionist artists and applauded the freshness of the open-air style; at the same time they decried the looseness of structure and the exaggerated color effects sometimes achieved. Most artists would quietly absorb what they could of the style without compromising the high standards of academic drawing, composition, and finish that were the badge of accomplishment in the official Paris art world. Furthermore, they could see the advantage of independent exhibitions, and henceforth more exhibiting societies were formed to give artists exposure outside the restrictive walls of the Salon. At the same time they continued to see acceptance into the Salon as their entrée into professional status and Salon medals as their highest reward.

Cassatt's old friend Henry Bacon was one such observer of the Impressionist movement in Paris. He absorbed enough of the Impressionist style to illustrate his book *A Parisian Year* with charming scenes of modern life à la Degas or Cassatt and professed his admiration for some of the artists of the group. But overall he felt that the extremes of the style were ridiculous. He wrote that "they are afflicted with some hitherto unknown disease of the eye."[17] He expressed the feeling that avoiding the Salon was a form of professional cowardice: the "few good painters . . . prefer to shine by comparison [to the extremists] to being lost among their peers at the Salon."[18] Émile Zola portrayed a similar artist-compromiser in his character Fagarolles in *l'Oeuvre.* In the novel, Fagarolles, an old friend of the hero, Claude Lantier, steals key ingredients of Claude's style but grafts them onto an acceptable Salon style and makes a fortune while Claude languishes in poverty. Zola based his character on the painter Henri Gervex, a Salon favorite who was also a friend of several of the Impressionists.

Interestingly enough, it is this intelligent, tolerant, yet moderate majority of artists who are now largely unknown. Their extremist colleagues on both the right and the left have piqued the curiosity of future generations and skewed our perception of this period. In today's museums we are far more likely to see the paintings of the academics Gérôme or Bouguereau hanging nearby the Impressionists rather than the paintings of Henry Bacon or Henri Gervex. This middle-of-the-road course would probably have seemed reasonable to Cassatt, but, as it turned out, impossible for someone of her temperament. She was destined to end up at one extreme or the other.

Given her background and circumstances, extreme conservatism would have made more sense. Elizabeth Gardner, so very like Cassatt in upbringing, social status, and ambition, took the conservative route. Painting in the style of academic perfection, she was a Salon regular and medal winner. With the money and prestige she earned, she took her place in American high society in Paris and survives today as one of the most important women artists of her generation. Cassatt, with her greater financial independence and superior early training, might have easily surpassed Gardner in the academic sphere if she had made more of her extraordinary opportunity to study with Gérôme when she first arrived in Paris. With her desire to achieve greatness, to paint "better than the Old Masters," she would naturally have appreciated the transcendence that came with official praise and position. She might have likened her pursuit of official success to her brother's pursuit of corporate success with the Pennsylvania Railroad.

But as much as she might appreciate her brother's corporate zeal, or even

Elizabeth Gardner's, there was in her a stubborn independence that made her—almost in spite of herself—more comfortable with the radical fringe. As she told her biographer, when she was invited to join the Impressionists she "accepted with joy" and, finally, at the age of thirty-three, she "began to live."[19]

Cassatt's impression of the group she was joining would have been formed almost entirely by studying their art and reading their reviews; almost nothing would have come from personal contact. The only member of the group she was linked to personally before being invited to join was Alfred Sisley, whose wife is believed to be the subject of an 1873 portrait by Cassatt. Sisley, the son of a wealthy British businessman, grew up in Paris. In the 1870s he lived with his wife in the suburban towns of Louveciennes and Marly-le-roi after the Franco-Prussian War had decimated his family's fortune. Many of the Impressionists, like Cassatt, had turned their backs on the Parisian art cliques and sought asylum outside the city. In addition to Sisley, Monet lived at Argenteuil during the 1870s, Pissarro at Pontoise, and M. and Mme. Bracquemond (both Impressionist artists) lived at Sèvres—all of which were small towns west of Paris along the Seine, but within easy commuting distance. Berthe Morisot and her husband, Eugène Manet, lived in Passy, the most suburban section of Paris, which bordered the Bois de Boulogne.

Cassatt would have known some of the more visible members of the Impressionist group by reputation and perhaps by sight. The most notorious of all, Édouard Manet (figure 43), Cassatt would have known ever since his one-man exhibition in a wooden building on the Avenue de l'Alma during the International Exposition of 1867. Following in the footsteps of Courbet, who had mounted a similar "protest" exhibition outside the gates of the International Exposition of 1855, Manet had firmly fixed himself in the public consciousness by this act. While Cassatt may not have had an opportunity to meet this famous rebel, she would have quickly learned to recognize his elegant figure and distinctive swagger as he made the rounds of the Paris *boulevardier.* He could be seen downtown along the inner ring of boulevards where the most important art dealers had their galleries as well as in the sections around the outer ring, including the Boulevard Clichy, where artists lived and frequented such cafés as the Café Guerbois and La Nouvelle Athènes. Manet, according to the memoirs of a friend, "was a kind of dandy. Blond, with a sparse, narrow beard which was forked at the end, he had in the extraordinary vivacity of his gaze, in the mocking expression on his lips—his mouth was narrow-lipped, his teeth irregular and uneven—a very strong dose of the Parisian street urchin."[20] By the time Cassatt

43. Nadar, Photograph of Édouard Manet, c. 1865
Musée d'Orsay; © Photo Réunion des musées nationaux

finally got to know Manet she would have been familiar with him for more than ten years.

Thanks to Manet, Cassatt would have gotten her strongest impression of Berthe Morisot before actually meeting her. While she may have seen Berthe and her sister, Edma, studying and copying in the Louvre during the later 1860s, it was Manet's portrait of her in the left foreground of his famous painting *The Balcony,* shown in the Salon of 1869, that fixed Morisot's haunting beauty in the public consciousness (figure 44). Morisot had met Manet in the 1860s, when she gravitated toward the radical art circles through her friendships with Félix Bracquemond and Pierre Puvis de Chavannes. She began exhibiting in the Salon in 1864, but, after several years of following the academic route, she felt as passionately as Monet and Renoir that artists should have the chance to exhibit outside the Salon. She became one of the founding members of the Impressionist exhibitions in 1874 and came in for her share of praise and blame as a highly visible member of the group.

Morisot, the daughter of a highly placed bureaucrat in the French govern-

44. *Édouard Manet,* The Balcony, *1869*
Oil on canvas, $67^{3}/_{4}$ *x* $49^{1}/_{4}$ *in.*
Musée d'Orsay; Caillebotte bequest; **© Photo Réunion des musées nationaux**

ment, had all the brooding intensity of a Parisian intellectual and was thought of by some as a *femme fatale* (figure 45). Despite living with her parents in suburban Passy, she was welcomed into the fast-paced crowd of young radical artists around the Boulevard Clichy and held her own as one of the few women in that circle who were colleagues rather than spouses or girlfriends. She challenged Cassatt's strongly held belief that a woman could not have both art and a husband by marrying Édouard Manet's brother Eugène in 1874. They had their only child, Julie, in 1879.

Cassatt and Morisot became very good friends after they began exhibiting together. Cassatt soon bought a painting from Morisot and studied her style very closely (figure 46). They often socialized in Paris and during the summers if they had taken summer homes near each other. Since they both had

45. ***Marcellin Desboutin,* Portrait of Berthe Morisot, *1876***
Drypoint, 10¼ x 6⅞ in.
Bibliothèque Nationale

46. *Berthe Morisot,* Young Woman in a Ball Gown, *c. 1876*
Oil on canvas, 33$^{1}/_{8}$ x 20$^{1}/_{8}$ in.
Musée d'Orsay; © Photo Réunion des musées nationaux

strong personalities and were real and imagined rivals, it is to their credit that they formed such close personal and professional ties.

Of all the Impressionists, Cassatt is known to have the least connection to Monet. While she admired his work and bought several of his canvases over the years, her own style as a figure painter was of less interest to him. Since she did not help to swell his faction of landscape painters and since she did not come to him for advice, she did not fit any of his main criteria for friendship. Renoir (figure 47), on the other hand, was a more sociable man who dearly loved debate even though he was not as extensively educated as his colleagues. Renoir had a quick tongue—a trait of virtually all the Impressionists—and in later years was remembered as "nervous and

47. Photograph of Auguste Renoir, c. 1885 Collection Sirot-Angel, Paris

sarcastic, with his mocking voice, and a kind of Mephistophelism which marked with irony and a strange mirth . . . took a mischievous delight in irritating [his opponent]."[21] Renoir's biting personality was at odds with the rosy view of life he showed in his paintings. If Cassatt did not know him previously, she would have formed quite a different idea of his personality from such works as *The Swing* and *The Ball at the Moulin de la Galette,* which were both in the Impressionist exhibition of 1877.

Camille Pissarro and Armand Guillaumin were equally unknown to Cassatt except through their calm and richly colored landscapes shown at the first few exhibitions. Both of these men, unlike Renoir, possessed personalities more consistent with their art, and Cassatt developed lifelong friendships with them both.

When Cassatt was invited to join the Impressionists, it is somewhat surprising that the invitation did not come from Gustave Caillebotte (figure 48). Caillebotte, the wealthy amateur-turned-painter, had joined the group in 1875 and moved quickly to its organizational center. He was a prime mover behind the exhibitions of 1876 and 1877, settling disputes among the sharp-tongued radicals and smoothing ruffled feathers. But whereas he was extremely effective in keeping the core group together, he did not take it upon himself to invite new members. This was a practice that no one enjoyed more than Edgar Degas.

As was the case with Manet, Cassatt knew *of* Degas years before she knew him (figure 49). Although he was not as public a figure as Manet, Degas was fairly well known from his Salon submissions in the 1860s and his exposure at various galleries around town. Cassatt had apparently missed the Impressionist exhibition in 1874, which ended before she returned to Paris from Rome, so very likely the first glimpse she had of his new style was in 1875, when she saw his pastels in a dealer's window on the Boulevard Haussmann. "I used to go and flatten my nose against that window and absorb all I could of his art. It changed my life. I saw art then as I wanted to see it."[22] In April 1876 she got a chance to see more of his works than she had ever seen before in one place when Degas exhibited twenty-four paintings and pastels out of the total of 252 works in the second Impressionist exhibition. The next year he presented a similar number, to which a single room in the exhibition was devoted. While several of the paintings Cassatt would have seen in these exhibitions were portraits, most were not: they were studies of ballerinas, laundresses, café singers, prostitutes, and women getting in and out of bathtubs.

In the past, one of Cassatt's goals had been to imbue her subjects with a

48. Gustave Caillebotte,* Self-Portrait, *1892 Oil on canvas, 16 x 12¾ in. Musée d'Orsay; © Photo Réunion des musées nationaux

resonant inner life, which she depicted as melancholy, yearning, or contemplation. Her interest in this powerful artistic effect tied her art to the older tradition of romanticism that was fast losing ground in the face of modern realism. In Degas's art she found a way of framing her preferred contemplative subjects so that they evinced a "modern" psychological depth rather than the worn-out romanticism of her noble peasants or the lost-love motif of a subject like "Mariana of the Moated Grange." Degas's work, more than Manet's or Morisot's, stressed the darker side of his subjects or the shadows in the elegant apartment of *Portrait, Evening (Mme. Camus)* and gave the old romantic moodiness a modern twist.

When Degas came to Cassatt's studio for their first meeting, the introduction was facilitated by a mutual friend, Léon Tourny. Tourny was a lifelong friend of Degas's and had known Cassatt since making her acquaintance in Antwerp in 1873. At that time, Cassatt became friendly with M. and Mme. Tourny, who were both artists of some success and reputation, although not part of the Impressionist group. When Degas came to her door, he no doubt was as familiar with her by sight as she was with him. They had lived on adjoining streets only blocks south of the Boulevard

49. Photograph of Edgar Degas, c. 1885
Bibliothèque Nationale

Clichy (she on Rue Laval and he on Rue Blanche and then Rue Frochot) and were equally distinctive in appearance. She was tall and tailored, obviously enjoying the fine fabrics and elegant jewelry that her generous allowance and occasional sales allowed. He was round-shouldered and a trifle lumbering, but equally well dressed. He strolled throughout the city and inhabited the cafés, feeding on gossip and challenging wordplay. One observer of the café scene recalled: "Amongst the other figures to be detected in the gaslight of the Café Guerbois against the clicking of billiard balls on the table, I would like to pick out the painter Degas, who never used to stay seated for long. Degas, with his very Parisian, very original looks, infinitely mocking and witty."[23] George Moore, the Irish novelist and critic, remembered Degas sitting next to Manet "round shouldered . . . in suit of pepper-and-salt [with a] large neck-tie; his eyes are hard, and his words are sharp, ironical, cynical."[24]

Rather than being put off by the fierce reputation of Degas, and, for that matter, all the Impressionists, Cassatt seems to have welcomed the chance to be among them. There can be no question that for the first time Mary Cassatt found people whose own biting, critical, opinionated attitudes matched her own. She no longer had to be constricted by the censure of such thin-skinned judges as her sister-in-law Lois or her erstwhile friend Emily Sartain. The Impressionists were more than a match for her.

Once having accepted the invitation to join the Impressionist group, Cassatt faced immediate changes in her professional life. Not only did she have to get to know an entirely new and complicated group of artists, but her working habits, long tied to the rhythm of the Salon, had to be adapted to her new circumstances. Perhaps the biggest change for her was that she was no longer one of a larger international community that met and mixed in classes, art galleries, the Louvre, or the Salon. Now her primary professional group was relatively small, comprising the twenty to thirty artists who exhibited each year in annual Impressionist exhibitions, and was almost exclusively French.

While Cassatt did not abandon her American and other non-French friends in Paris, she was no longer in step with them professionally. Not only did she cease to share their Salon-oriented concerns, but she no longer looked to Americans or other foreign tourists to support her portrait practice and buy her "souvenir of Paris" paintings. The Impressionists attracted attention in other countries from the start, but it would be another ten years before their style would become accepted enough to be of interest to a tourist wanting a "French" painting. The Salon styles would continue to serve this market for many years to come. The Impressionist patrons in the 1870s were almost entirely Parisians who had sophisticated tastes in contemporary art. Cassatt would have had little opportunity to meet such patrons in her former sphere, but now, as an Impressionist, she quickly entered into a level of French society and culture that had been closed to her before. Even though she had lived in Paris on and off since childhood, she had inevitably remained an outsider.

Cassatt now took a drastic step into a foreign culture. Indeed, she was the only American artist in Paris to do so. The other two successful expatriate American artists, Whistler and Sargent, and the great expatriate American writer Henry James found that they were more comfortable in England. The others who swelled the ranks of American artists in Paris either returned home after putting in their time abroad or, like Henry Bacon or Elizabeth Gardner, despite her long engagement and subsequent marriage to Bouguereau, remained tied to the American colony. Bacon, who lived in Paris for forty years, noted this phenomenon with some bitterness: "We English-speaking people are always strangers in Paris. Spaniards and Italians mix easily with the French; but no matter how many years Americans may live amongst the French, the latter regard them always as foreigners. . . . Americans and Englishmen are treated not unlike commercial travellers,—well received at the office and restaurants, but seldom invited 'up to the house.' "[25]

While there was undoubtedly French coolness toward Americans, the problem was compounded by the Americans themselves. Since Americans living abroad tended to come from the privileged classes, they were inclined to look around them with some disdain. An American guidebook to Paris in 1887 put it somewhat crudely: "As the United States is the best customer that France and Paris have abroad, so the American colony is the best customer that Paris has at home."[26] Americans expected to be treated well, and they were. An earlier guidebook (1869) dealt with the cool formality that marked French-American relations: "The politeness of the French may be superficial, but this in no wise detracts from the pleasure which it imparts, the visitor having no time, and doubtless no inclination, to ascertain the depth of sentiment from the universal expression from which he profits."[27]

There were exceptions to the stalemate between French and Americans in Paris. Bacon observed that American women found a warmer welcome in France than did his own sex because of the French admiration for the American style of beauty.[28] This is borne out by the number of American women, such as Elizabeth Gardner and May Alcott, who married Frenchmen or other Europeans. It may even have helped Cassatt to be assimilated even though she was never considered a beauty. All the Impressionists were accustomed to working with members of the opposite sex, since their group had been mixed from the beginning. Their exhibitions included Berthe Morisot and Marie Bracquemond. They counted as friends Eva Gonzalès and the various artist-wives like Jenny Sisley and Mme. Tourny. French gallantry toward the young, well-dressed American woman cannot be counted out as a factor in her ready acceptance as a friend and colleague.

If Cassatt entered this group with some feelings of being an outsider, they quickly faded. Before long she was referring to "our annual exhibition" and lamenting the fact that "we are carrying on a despairing fight & need all our forces."[29] Rather than merely being a passive addendum to the group, she threw herself into the cause body and soul. The organizing skills that had led her and various companions on complex tours of Europe in her earlier days were now put at the service of the group's annual exhibition. She never vied with Degas or Caillebotte for the leadership roles, but she was a passionate salesman for the group and made many of the arrangements possible through her generosity with her time and extra money. She is not known to have taken the liberty of recruiting new members, but she undoubtedly would have liked to. When American friends of hers started a roughly parallel group, the Society of American Artists in New York, she not only pledged her own participation in the next exhibition but wanted others she knew to send something also: "I hope my artist friends here will send with me."[30]

Just how drastic a step she had taken probably dawned on her as she visited and revisited the Impressionist exhibition that would have been on view when she received her Salon rejection and Degas issued his invitation. For the month of April 1877, approximately 250 works by eighteen artists hung in a large rented apartment on the second floor of a building at 6 Rue le Peletier in the heart of downtown Paris. The exhibition, the group's third, had been well publicized and was genuinely successful in attendance and in critical reaction. Cassatt would have caught the excitement of the crowd as she climbed the steps of the new, elegant building from its entrance on the chic Boulevard Haussmann.

The apartment itself had been transformed for one month into an art gallery with panels dividing the rooms and closing off the windows.[31] The paintings were hung as they were in the Salon: one above the other to cover the walls with a dense pattern of paint and frames. As in the Salon, there was the characteristic mixture of styles in a single room, landscapes and figure paintings hanging side by side. However, the similarities between the Impressionist exhibitions and the Salon exhibitions ended there; most visitors were struck instantly by the novelty of what they saw in the Rue Peletier. Not only were the colors in the paintings that lined the walls indeed brighter and the paint dabbed onto the surface in the characteristic Impressionist manner, but there was a breathtaking sense of the modern moment that pervaded all the canvases.

It was a unique opportunity to be surrounded by freshly observed and knowingly painted glimpses of a world that in 1877 had recently suffered the horrors of war and the trials of rebuilding but was affirmed, in these pictures, to be alive and healthy if somewhat raw and imperfect. The nineteenth-century belief in progress on all fronts—social, political, and technological—had been badly battered by the Crimean War, American Civil War, and the Franco-Prussian War at mid-century, and the population in the 1870s emerged sadder but wiser. To look around with new eyes at what remained was both a challenge and a relief. The world-weary connoisseur could survey in the Impressionist paintings the beautiful French countryside, the grand boulevards and train stations of Paris, the sophisticated art of the ballet, and the contemplative portraits of friends. The modern world seen in glaring sunlight or gray steam and mist could be the subject of great art after all. The overall effect of the exhibition was akin to the great novels of contemporary life by Flaubert, Zola, the Goncourts, and others who were beginning to take over the world spotlight in literature. For those sympathetic to the new trends in art and literature, it was a heady experience to finish reading Zola's *L'Assommoir,* which appeared in book form in February of 1877, and go to the Impressionist exhibition in April. Both provided a kaleidoscopic welter of images of life as it was lived at that very moment, with crudeness and refinement inextricably intermingled.

Mary Cassatt must have looked around her with some alarm. How could she, a painter of picturesque peasants and society portraits, fit in with artists and writers whose insolent frankness invited accusations of pornography? Cassatt was not and never would be interested in using the sexual themes that Zola, or even Degas, used to such powerful advantage in their work, nor was she one to push her art to the point of scandal through exaggerated technique or subject matter. However, there is no doubt that she respected, even admired, this type of brutality or sensuality in the arts even if she did not practice it herself.

She does not seem to have known Zola personally, but she was certainly very familiar with his novels, as all the Cassatts were. Her father sent a photograph of Zola to her brother Aleck in Philadelphia with the inscription "The now celebrated author of the Assommoir."[32] The respectable Cassatts were not among those outraged by the sexuality and violence Zola depicted in this novel of lower-class life in Paris. Indeed, they would have shared Zola's anger at such small-mindedness as he expressed it in the preface to the book version of the novel:

> When *L'Assommoir* was serialized in a newspaper [1876] it was attacked with unparalleled ferocity, denounced and accused of every kind of crime. Is it really necessary for me to have to explain here in a few lines my aims as the author? I wanted to depict the inevitable downfall of a working-class family in the polluted atmosphere of our urban areas. The logical sequel to drunkenness and indolence is the loosening of family ties, the filth of promiscuity, and the progressive loss of decent feelings and, as the climax, shame and death. It is morality in action, just that.[33]

Zola's ultimate defense of his use of graphic scenes of brutality and vacuous promiscuity in this book is that it preaches a moral lesson about poverty. His daring produced great literature; his insights into human behavior and his vivid portrayals of people at their worst, or even in their grinding mediocrity, had the power of truth that went beyond moral lessons. This power of truth was what linked his writings to such Impressionists as Degas and Manet, who also looked deeply into the world of the unheroic for their glimpses of modern times. Degas's laundresses were most like Zola's characters in *L'Assommoir* who were also laundresses, but Degas's scenes of bawdy singers in the café-concerts and the prostitutes in the audience were also drawn from the immoral segments of society (figure 50). Degas even made it known that the ballet dancers he depicted in such splendor were merely lower-class girls engaged in a rarefied form of prostitution once out of the glittering spotlight.

Cassatt, who as a respectable woman could not go to the café-concerts or even sit with any comfort at the Impressionists' gathering place, the café La Nouvelle Athènes, did not shrink from the ideas or images that emanated from these places. She went as far as she could go in investigating the less respectable side of Parisian life. She had early on become familiar with that quasi-risqué establishment the Jardin Mabille and frequented the open-air concerts such as the Concert des Champs-Élysées where one met ladies of fashion from all over the world. However, she had to rely on word of mouth or Degas's pictures to learn more about the category of open-air concerts

50. ***Edgar Degas,* Women in Front of a Café, Evening, *1877***
Pastel over monotype, 16⅛ x 23⅝ in.
Musée d'Orsay; © Photo Réunion des musées nationaux

called *café chantants,* such as the Alcazar or Les Ambassadeurs. These were not places Cassatt could have gone without trepidation of the sort one would experience in a dangerous bar today, where the danger comes not only from the threat of violence but from the encounter with an alien world in which one feels painfully conspicuous. This was what kept women like Cassatt away from these places and led guidebook writers to warn unsuspecting tourists:

> English and Americans who visit Paris commit a fatal error when they allow a morbid feeling of curiosity to overcome their better judgment, and allow their wives and daughters to visit either a public ball or a Café Chantant. They will never meet a French lady of rank and respectable position in society at these places. The appearance of our young and carefully trained country-women, therefore, subjects them to comments, which it would be absurd for their companions to resent, inasmuch as the said localities are intended for the entertainment of a class of women our wives and sisters would shrink from mingling with in their native land; why, therefore, should they do so in a foreign capital?[34]

Even cafés like the Nouvelle Athènes or the Café Guerbois were likely to make a woman like Cassatt, Morisot, or any of the other women in their circle feel conspicuous and uncomfortable. If they sat down for a chat with a table full of men, they would have attracted unwanted remarks or attention from the working-class clientele or the artists and writers who imitated working-class behavior. In Zola's novels, only prostitutes or models, women who were normally assumed to be prostitutes or at best "fallen women," were to be found in such surroundings. Cassatt lived near La Nouvelle Athènes, which was in the Place Pigalle, and walked by it every day on the way to her studio at 2 Rue Duperré (figure 51). George Moore, who became her friend and the subject of one of her aquatints, reminisced about his encounters with her during the years he frequented the café. "She did not come to the Nouvelle Athenes it is true, but . . . we used to see her every-day."[35] We picture Moore or Degas or some combination of the group spotting her through the window and running out to have a word with her.

Although she could not be part of the rough-and-ready debates that went on among the smoke and beer, she had gotten as close to it as she could, and no doubt heard the latest gossip or the gist of an argument when the men came out to greet her and stood chatting in front of the café or while Degas or Moore walked with her the few blocks to her apartment. The

51. Photograph of the café Nouvelle Athènes
Bibliothèque Nationale

debates would be rekindled at the dinner parties that she, Morisot, Caillebotte, or others would then host at night. The women of the group were certainly deprived by their lack of access to the café life, but they made sure they missed as little as possible of the important ideas and information. Cassatt was in a particularly good position, since she was the only woman in the Impressionist group to live and work in the artists' *quartier,* and as a consequence she was very much a link in the lines of communication.

Cassatt's no-nonsense attitude toward the world and all its facets—good and evil—certainly put her male colleagues at ease and allowed them to engage her in discussions of risqué subject matter in modern art that they might not have had with other women. Since Cassatt frankly admired the female nude as a subject and was particularly drawn to the deeply sensual qualities in Courbet's nudes and the powerful anti-heroic qualities of Degas's, she showed that her aesthetics were in accord with those of the group. Furthermore, she did not shrink even from Degas's monotypes of brothels or the veiled references to prostitution in his ballet scenes or bathers. While she did not condone prostitution, she admired the power of sensuality and realism that the subject brought into modern art.

Even to become friends with a man who painted prostitutes was a bold step into the new world she entered in the spring of 1877. We can only wonder how she described her new friends to someone like May Alcott and the other Americans she continued to see for some time after she began her association with the Impressionists. Very likely Alcott was open-minded enough to appreciate Cassatt's new direction and discuss its implications for her and for art in general. Alcott continued to see Cassatt as one of the greatest American painters of their generation. It was a sad loss for Cassatt when Alcott died in Paris in 1879 from complications after childbirth. Cassatt also remained friends with J. Alden Weir, who would become one of Impressionism's staunchest supporters in the United States. As the Impressionists gradually took more of her professional time, the American artists she knew were ones she kept up with from the old days.

For a year following her decision to join the Impressionist group, she put her time into building a body of work to be shown in the exhibition planned for the spring of 1878. As is typical of these years, little information remains to illuminate the exact course she took. It is very likely that her first steps were tentative and drew heavily on her past work. In 1877 she was still executing commissioned portraits, such as the one of Mary Ellison. A logical extension of these portraits were works like *The Reader* or her own *Self-Portrait* (figure 37) that show the same well-dressed young women in genteel poses, now brought out of the plush shadows of Paris apartments into a brighter light that highlights white dresses and pale backgrounds. Once Cassatt had taken this step toward the Impressionists' brighter palette, she no doubt began gradually to try new subjects, such as theater and outdoor garden scenes, that required leaving the cocoon of her studio and venturing out into the real world.

At this time she began carrying a sketchbook with her to record settings and poses she saw at the theater or during strolls in the park. This was hard for her. She was not a spontaneous artist by nature and was most comfortable having a model come to her studio, where she would dictate the pose, the lighting, and all other aspects of the composition. The forced exercise of drawing "unplanned" scenes was a great boon to her style because it helped rid her of the stilted qualities that occasionally marred her early work and gave her a more varied vocabulary of poses and gestures. She also found her work changing under the scrutiny of Edgar Degas, who got into the habit of stopping in at her studio and looking over her shoulder. He helped her obtain models, such as the child in *Girl in a Blue Armchair,* who was the daughter of friends of his (figure 52). As he watched the progress of this

52. *Mary Cassatt,* **Little Girl in a Blue Armchair,** *1878*
Oil on canvas, 35¼ x 51⅛ in.
National Gallery of Art, Washington; Collection of Mr. and Mrs. Paul Mellon

painting he made some suggestions about how to handle the background. In a daring move, he even put his brush to her canvas—an event so rare that Cassatt underlined it when she wrote about it years later: "[he] advised me on the background, *he even worked on the background*—"[36] She considered it a privilege but, given her long-standing aversion to anyone working on her pictures, not one she would have easily accepted.

One of the most important works she painted in her first year as an Impressionist was the portrait of her mother called *Reading Le Figaro* (figure 53). Not only did this large, handsome painting celebrate her mastery of the new style but it marks the second drastic change that occurred in Mary Cassatt's life in 1877: the arrival of her parents and Lydia in Paris—to stay for good. Although we are once again without a recorded explanation for the peripatetic Cassatts' move, it is not hard to see what drew them to Paris.

Since their daughter Mary had left them to return to Europe in late 1871 they had been living in Philadelphia. Mary's departure coincided with Aleck's promotion to the rank of manager of the Pennsylvania Railroad and his transfer to the central offices in Philadelphia. He, Lois, and their two children moved into a house on Delancey Place, now part of Rittenhouse Square. The elder Cassatts with Lydia and Gard moved into a house about three blocks away on Twenty-first Street. To help launch his son Gardner in the investment business, Robert Cassatt came out of retirement in 1872 to head a new brokerage firm in the city. This time the firm was founded in partnership with John Lloyd, a young man only a few years older than Gardner whose father was head of the First National Bank of Altoona, where Gardner had worked for several years. John Lloyd remained in residence in Altoona and by 1877 he had withdrawn his name from Lloyd, Cassatt & Company, leaving it as Cassatt & Co., the name carried by the firm into the twentieth century.

The Cassatts on Twenty-first Street found their greatest pleasure in the children being born and growing up on Delancey Place. By 1875 Lois and Aleck had four: Eddie (six), Katharine (four), Robbie (two) and newborn Elsie (Eliza). The active and affectionate towheads were spoiled by their grandparents and aunts and uncles on both the Cassatt and Buchanan sides. By 1873 Aleck had built a country house in nearby Haverford, where they could all release energy by horseback riding and indulging in every imaginable game and sport. The elder Cassatts also tried to exert an educational influence over their grandchildren by giving them books and children's magazines; Mrs. Cassatt even began teaching them French. The decision to leave this comfortable situation in their old age would have been a difficult one for Robert and Katherine Cassatt.

53. *Mary Cassatt,* **Reading Le Figaro,** *1877–78*
Oil on canvas, 39¾ x 32 in.
Private collection

The compelling reason for pulling up stakes once again and settling this time in a foreign country must have been an appeal from Mary. Lydia Cassatt had gone to Paris two years in a row (1875 and 1876), each time returning in early summer. She had undoubtedly become a very important part of her sister's life in Paris as a friend and chaperone, but Lydia's health was not good, and she did not return in the fall of 1876. Quite possibly, the parents finally decided that since Lydia could not go on her own anymore, it would be best all around if they were to move to Paris and become Mary's chaperones themselves. Mary's need for such respectability might have become more urgent when she began seeing more of the Impressionists and moving in French circles. While the international community, particularly Americans, might have accepted a woman living alone, she might have felt some pressure from her French friends to adopt local standards.

She might have also felt that she was settled now. Since she had made a commitment to work with the Impressionists, she made a tacit agreement to make Paris her home and abandon any thoughts she might still be harboring of going back to Rome or Parma. She missed her family and thought more longingly of family life. From the point of view of her parents, the move would suit each of them in some way. Her mother had always been fond of Paris and never needed prompting to set sail. Her father, now seventy-one, might have thought it would be relaxing to retire abroad rather than stay in the same city with Cassatt & Company, which had always had the power to bring him back to work. He was also eager to see the World's Fair of 1878 in Paris, which promised to outdo all previous events of that kind. Finally, Lydia was fond of her sister and enjoyed life in Paris. Furthermore, at forty, she would be closer to the world's best doctors to help diagnose and cure the illness that worsened with age. With all these good reasons to go, the Cassatts gave up the house on Twenty-first Street, let Gard, at twenty-eight, find his own bachelor accommodations, and set sail for Paris in October of 1877.

Mary welcomed her family into a new apartment on the Rue Beaujon that was big enough to accommodate all of them. She had given up her old studio/apartment at 19 Rue de Laval in the artists' quarter and found a new one that was closer to the Champs-Élysées and the more elegant section where the Cassatts had lived in the early 1850s. At the same time, she set up an independent studio for herself in her old neighborhood. One of her first gestures of welcome was to induce her mother to sit for a new portrait, sitting comfortably in Cassatt's studio armchair reading the premier Parisian newspaper, *Le Figaro.* Not only did this give mother and daughter an opportunity to spend long quiet hours together to make up for the many years they had lived apart, but it was meant to be sent back to Philadelphia, where it would in some small way stand in for the mother the Cassatt brothers had lost.

After a few months on the Rue Beaujon, the Cassatts were looking for a new apartment. Mary's need to be in the artists' quarter outweighed the benefits of a fashionable address, so they found an apartment on the top floor of a building at 13 Avenue Trudaine opposite the College Rollin. From their vantage point they could look out over a small park and up to Montmartre to the north and down the sloping city of Paris to the river to the south. Despite the inconvenience of climbing five flights of stairs, they enjoyed the quiet and the view from their high perch. The apartment was only a few blocks from Mary's studio, and they were connected to the rest of the city by the tramway that ran along Avenue Trudaine itself. About a year after they moved in they were surprised and pleased to learn that Aleck had set up a trust for his mother that supplemented the family's income. Although the Cassatts in Paris were quite comfortable, they could not afford expenses like keeping their own carriage—it was a luxury to stable horses, hire a coachman, and garage a carriage in the middle of the city—and Aleck's trust gave them enough for such extras.

This thoughtfulness on Aleck's part suggests an additional reason for the elder Cassatts' retirement to Paris—their income went further abroad. There are hints in some of the earliest letters written home to Aleck that the Cassatts had seen their fortunes go down over time. One investment in land apparently had seen a dramatic decline:

> What do you suppose my share of the Venango land comes to, it is just 425 dollars . . . and I think that twelve years ago they might have had twenty thousand dollars for it! So it goes.[37]

Robert Cassatt in his old age warned his son, who was making money quickly just as he had done in his thirties, "Most anyone they say can make money, only the wise know how to keep it."[38] It is unlikely that the Cassatts were facing any serious financial difficulties, but they were realistic enough about the vagaries of fortune to be careful with their money.

Moving to Paris would have been a saving for the parents not only because it was less expensive than Philadelphia, but also because it was an economy to have both daughters living under their roof. Gardner by this time was self-supporting with the investment firm Cassatt & Company, but Lydia had no income and Mary was still not economically independent. However much the move might have been an economical one for her parents, it turned out to be a more expensive arrangement for Mary. When they all moved in together, Mary set up her own studio outside the home for the first time. It was her responsibility to pay all the studio expenses. Since we do not know that Mary Cassatt had any personal source of income (trusts, bank accounts, investments) other than the sale of her paintings, this was a new burden. Her father recognized that this put pressure on her but evidently felt that he must be conservative with money:

> . . . I have said that the studio must at least support itself. This makes Mame very uneasy, as she must either make sale of the pictures she has on hand or else take to painting *pot boilers* as the artists say—a thing that she never yet has done & cannot bear the idea of being obliged to do.[39]

Apparently she had previously contributed less to her own upkeep while she lived and worked in the same apartment on the Rue de Laval. Her parents' move to Paris might have allowed her to live with greater comfort and elegance, but her father's guarding of the purse strings also meant new financial pressure, which she probably did not anticipate, especially at a time when she had made a daring change in style and her sales would inevitably decline.

The first year of this new family life in Paris was undoubtedly hard on them all. Mary had to trade more of her precious freedom than she realized to have the comforts of a home. Lydia's health declined precipitously in the first six months after the move. Katherine and Robert Cassatt, veterans of scores of moves throughout their lives, found this to be a particularly difficult one. Not only did they have to make the thousands of adjustments that went with becoming Parisians—not the least being the daily climb up five flights of steps, which Americans never seemed to get used to—but they found that they desperately missed their grandchildren and other family and friends back home. When Aleck talked of resigning from the railroad and moving to Paris himself, his mother tried to be objective, but betrayed her own weariness with the process of assimilation:

> As to coming over here to live, think well of it before deciding. However you are still young enough to make friends in a strange land, and you might like it. I am too old for that now and naturally I see things differently.[40]

Even Robert Cassatt, who liked to maintain a hearty, businesslike attitude toward life, was puzzled at their isolation. Writing to Aleck, he noted that "We rarely see any Americans. . . . It is curious that even at the Exposition I did not encounter a single American acquaintance—You see we do not go to either of the [American] chapels or in any way court the *Colony*."[41] Although this isolation kept them safe from the pettiness of the American gossip mill, it also left the sociable Cassatts feeling somewhat lonely.

Gradually the strangeness of the new situation wore off and everyone's spirits began to revive. By the fall of 1878 the work of furnishing and decorating the apartment on Avenue Trudaine was finally completed; the World's Fair came to a close, letting the city get back to normal; and Lydia's health once more stabilized. Bit by bit the entire family was swept up in Mary's concerns—typical of her compelling personality—and they all got a boost from following the dramatic course she was taking with her fellow Impressionists.

The first major upheaval occurred just as they were moving into their new apartment in the spring of 1878: the intense activity and debate over the intended exhibition that year, which was scheduled for June. Cassatt was passionately determined to make the exhibition come about and wrote to J. Alden Weir about the struggle: "We expect to have our annual exhibition here, and there are so few of us that we are each required to contribute all we have. You know how hard it is to inaugurate anything like independent action among French artists, and we are carrying on a despairing fight and need all our forces, as every year there are new deserters."[42] In the end, the effort was in vain. By May, even Degas was pessimistic about pitting their exhibition against the hoopla of the World's Fair, which opened on May 1, and they decided to put it off for another year.

The delay was frustrating for Cassatt after a year of preparation for her debut as an Impressionist, but it may also have been a relief, since the coming of her family took time and energy away from her painting. She still had a number of good new works to show and tried to find other outlets for them.

Cassatt had one painting in the World's Fair itself in the Art Gallery of the American pavilion. While this painting cannot be identified (it was called *Tête de Femme* in the catalog and referred to by May Alcott as Cassatt's "yellow woman"), we know much more about a painting that was rejected. This was the *Little Girl in a Blue Armchair,* which she had done with Degas's model and his help. Cassatt recalled how outraged she was at the jury that refused it. "Since M. Degas had thought it good I was furious especially because he had worked on it—at that time it seemed new, and the jury consisted of three people, of which one was a pharmacist!"[43] We get another view of the proceedings from Elizabeth Gardner, who also exhibited at the World's Fair along with such Americans as Henry Bacon, F. A. Bridgman,

Frederick Church, G.P.A. Healy, Winslow Homer, George Inness, Eastman Johnson, John Kensett, J. S. Sargent, and J. Alden Weir:

> The American picture gallery is small. The three men who managed it were persons "unknown to fame." [They were Augustus Saint-Gaudens, D. Maitland Armstrong, and C. E. Detmold—one of the latter two was the pharmacist.] I never heard of them before. I was in common with the other known American artists invited to send *one* picture. I sent Ruth [*Ruth and Naomi*]. Then came an invitation for another. I hastily finished a little reduction from the Flower Girl which I sold in Boston. To my horror I found that these men considered the little one the best. It is beautifully placed and really does me credit. But Ruth is quite too high, over a door. It was unjust and I wish the man who did it was hung in its place. It will never sell there and there it must stay for six months. Bierstadt's picture they refused entirely.[44]

This description puts Cassatt's rejection into context. Her status as one of the "known American artists" was confirmed by the invitation to submit two paintings, but it was not uncommon for the jury to reject one or both, or, as in Gardner's case, to make odd judgments about their relative importance. In Cassatt's case the rejection may have been because the painting was in the "new" style, but Cassatt's identity as an Impressionist was presumably already known to the jury when she was invited, even though she had not yet exhibited with the group. In the French guidebook to the exposition, her work is pointed out as the "*Portrait,* de miss [*sic*] Cassatt, qui participe de notre école impressionniste."[45] But in spite of the idiosyncrasies of the jury, having a work in this grand fair was no doubt a source of pride for her parents and even (secretly) for her in those rocky early days of family life.

Cassatt also managed to exhibit *Reading Le Figaro,* the portrait of her mother, in some other forum that spring, although it is not known where.[46] Since she did not exhibit at the Salon or with the Impressionists, she may have entered it in an as yet unknown small exhibition in Paris, or had it in a dealer's window, or even "exhibited" it in her studio to prospective clients. She was so proud of it that she had a photograph taken and sent to Aleck to show him what he was getting. By the end of the summer, when she no longer had an excuse to hang on to it, she shipped it off to her brothers in Philadelphia.

Chapter V

Impressionism (1879–1886)

Mary Cassatt made her real debut at the age of thirty-four when the Impressionist exhibition opened on April 10, 1879. While we know little about what kind of "openings" the Impressionists held, it was common at that time to have a reception of some sort for which invitations were sent to friends, family, and VIPs to see the exhibition before it was open to the public. In this setting Cassatt, surrounded by her elegant parents and sister, was presented to the cream of Parisian intellectual society like a popular sixteen-year-old at her coming-out party.

Cassatt had waited two years for this moment. Ever since she decided to join the group in 1877, she had thrown herself into the plans and preparations for the next exhibition, which she hoped would be in 1878 but was put off time and time again. Finally, everything fell into place in March of 1879. Within a month a site was picked, participants decided on, catalog written, and posters distributed. A release was sent to all the newspapers and produced over thirty notices or reviews in Paris alone. As the show took its final form, Cassatt was disappointed that some of the important group members would not be exhibiting that year. Renoir, Sisley, and Cézanne all decided to submit to the Salon—which disqualified them from entering the Impressionist exhibition—although only Renoir was accepted. Morisot, who was pregnant that spring, decided at the last moment not to exhibit.

In spite of the absence of these four, the exhibition turned out to be the most successful of the Impressionist exhibitions to date. They counted almost sixteen thousand visitors, and for the first time each of the artists made a profit from the proceeds. The exhibition costs, such as rent, interior design to transform an apartment into an art gallery for one month, printing of the catalogs and posters, and wages of ticket taker and other assistants, had been covered by asking each artist to contribute a small amount in advance; ticket sales were such that the organizers could return this initial contribution to the participants with 439 francs (approximately $90 in 1879, $1,500 today) to spare.

Degas played a large role in the practical details of the exhibition. The finding of the rooms was, of course, a major step in the process and was pictured by a contemporary critic as happening this way:

> The little group of Independents bravely continues its peregrinations through the unoccupied *entresols* of Paris. Usually M. Degas leads the caravan. About February, he goes out to look, consulting the noticeboards and interrogating the concierges.—"Do you have a free apartment in the house?"—"Yes, sir." —"Would the proprietor consent to let it for a month?" If the proprietor agrees, M. Degas gives a sign to his companions. The interior decorator is informed immediately. As many works are collected as a drawing-room, a dining-room, two bedrooms, a bathroom and a kitchen could contain. A turnstile is installed in the ante-room and the day for the opening is fixed.[1]

In 1879 the apartment engaged for its one-month role as Impressionist art gallery was on the first floor of a building at 28 Avenue de l'Opéra, the new street built to give a grand approach to Garnier's Opéra, which had opened in 1875. It was in the same elegant downtown district that housed the major art galleries, such as Durand-Ruel, and was only a few blocks away from the sites of the previous three Impressionist exhibitions. The apartment was temporarily transformed to make five galleries, which were spacious and well lit, possibly with the new electric lights that were gradually being installed throughout the city. As usual, the works contributed by each artist were carefully hung to create a harmonious whole out of a disparate assortment of objects. This year there were a larger number of drawings and watercolors. Furthermore there were many decorative objects, such as fans painted by Degas and Pissarro, the cartoons for a ceramic wall decoration, and a faience plate by Marie Bracquemond, and even, for the first time, a small sculpture by Paul Gauguin. The hanging was made even more difficult by the fact that not all the entries had arrived by the date of the initial hanging. Degas, for example, at first brought only three of the twenty-five works he listed in the catalog and gradually added the rest as the month went on.

Some of the artists' contributions seemed to demand a unified hanging, such as the collection of watercolors by the late Ludovic Piette and the retrospective-like group of Monets, which were largely borrowed from collectors rather than having been painted specifically for this show. Monet's personal problems, including the grave illness of his wife, kept him out in the country at Vétheuil for the whole time of the exhibition.

The other artist whose works received a unified grouping was Mary Cassatt. All eleven of the paintings, pastels, and gouaches she chose for her first Impressionist exhibition were hung in the third room of the gallery in a mini-one-woman showing. The prominence that this gave her within the group was not lost on the visitors to the gallery, and critics rarely failed to take note of the arrival of an important new member. Seeing such a number of works hung together must have made an impact on Cassatt herself, who had never before had more than two hanging in a single exhibition. It was a great luxury for any artist at that time since single-artist shows were rare tributes only to the greatest artists of the day or were vanity shows put up at the artist's expense or held in his or her own studio.

What Cassatt saw as she walked around "her" gallery of the Impressionist exhibition was very different from what she thought she would be doing when she settled in Paris in 1874. Instead of "arriving" by winning a Salon medal for a Rubenesque peasant painting, she had become a painter of radical figure studies that were being dissected by a buzz of critics in the French and English press. Gone were the costumed Italians, Spaniards, and coy Parisian demoiselles; in their place were angled and cropped compositions of women in theaters and drawing rooms at the mercy of light and shadow that alternately blinded or obscured their exact outlines (figure 54). In addition to these most "modern" pictures, the group was rounded out by two more straightforward portraits of men (one done several years before in her "old" style), two portraits of children, and a study of women in the garden, as if to show the artist's range of subjects. It was a bold but balanced showing.

If Renoir and Morisot had sent their own studies of the theater and fashionable life, Cassatt could have been evaluated in her full and proper context. Since they were not represented, her work stood out in great contrast to the landscapes of Monet, Pissarro, and others, as well as the more precise portraits of Caillebotte and Zandomeneghi. While she attracted more attention this way, she also appeared to be closer to Degas—the only other artist offering similar theater subjects and "Impressionist" portraits—than she normally would have been. To be associated with Degas was no insult and Cassatt reveled in the critical acclaim:

54. *Mary Cassatt,* Woman with a Pearl Necklace in a Loge, *1879*
Oil on canvas, 31⅝ x 23 in.
Philadelphia Museum of Art; bequest of Charlotte Dorrance Wright

> There isn't a painting, nor a pastel by Mlle. Mary Cassatt that is not an exquisite symphony of color. Mlle. Mary Cassatt is fond of pure colors and possesses the secret of blending them in a composition that is bold, mysterious, and fresh. The *Woman Reading,* seen in profile, is a miracle of simplicity and elegance. There is nothing more graciously honest and aristocratic than her portraits of young women, except perhaps her *Woman in a Loge,* with the mirror placed behind her reflecting her shoulders and auburn hair.[2]

And:

> M. Degas and Mlle. Cassatt are perhaps the only artists who distinguish themselves in this group of "dependent" Independents, and who give the only attractiveness and excuse to this pretentious display of rough sketches and childish daubs, in the middle of which one is almost surprised to come across their neglected works. Both have a lively sense of the fragmented lighting in Paris apartments; both find unique nuances of color to render the flesh tints of women fatigued by late nights and the rustling lightness of worldly fashions.[3]

These reviews and many more were assiduously clipped by Mr. Cassatt and sent home to Aleck and Gard in Philadelphia. The Cassatts' pride in Mary may have been mixed with an equal measure of surprise; after almost twenty years of watching her inch her way up the ladder, they were on hand to see her become famous overnight. Her amazed father wrote to Aleck: "In short everybody says now that in [the] future it dont matter what the papers say about her—She is now known to the Art world as well as to the general public in such a way as not to be forgotten again so long as she continues to paint!!"[4]

Even the inevitable bad reviews couldn't put a damper on the Cassatt family jubilation. There were, of course, many outraged condemnations and humorous lampoons of the exhibition just as there had been in years past. This year the American paper published in Paris, *The American Register,* which had over the years published sympathetic notices of Cassatt as well as the radical French artists Courbet and Manet, reviewed its first Impressionist exhibition. Robert Cassatt noted with a sense of the ridiculous that "Every one of the leading daily French papers mentioned the Exposition & nearly all named Mame—most of them in terms of praise, only one of the American papers noticed it and *it* named her rather disparagingly!!!"[5] In fact it did not actually name her, but only referred to her works in the most exaggerated tones:

> For a month past the vacant salons of an apartment on the Avenue de l'Opéra have been occupied by an exhibition of the works of the so-called "Independent artists." Independent of what, we should like to know. Of criticism? of purchasers? or of all ideas of perspective and of color? We pause for a reply.
>
> In the landscapes, Nature seems to have abdicated all her rights. Pink skies overhang a lilac forest, the trees are blue in another picture, and the heavens are brown. The portraits in the exhibition were, however, the most wonderful objects of all. In one corner, a pea-green woman, evidently in the last stages of Asiatic cholera mooed at you from out of the shadows. . . . A poor young woman, very far gone with the Jaundice was shown wrestling with her fan in the depths of an opera-box. We cannot in fact understand the purpose of the new school. . . . We can see in it only the uneasy striving after notoriety of a restless vanity, that prefers celebrity for ill doing rather than an unnoted persistence in the path of true art.[6]

The anonymous critic aimed his barbs directly at Cassatt, who was well known for her lack of "persistence in the path of true art," i.e., toeing the line set by the academy and the Salon. Two years before, this review would have hit Cassatt where it hurt—her frustrated bid for official recognition; but now she could dismiss it as harmless carping. The Salon was indeed becoming irrelevant to an artist's success even though many rebels, including Renoir, Sisley, Cézanne, and, most important, Manet, still knocked at its door. As Caillebotte wrote to Monet after the show was over, ". . . for the painters and for the public, despite the malevolence of the press, we have achieved much. Manet himself is beginning to see that he has taken the wrong road. Courage then!"[7]

From 1879 to 1882 the group held an exhibition each year. Although the roster of artists changed every time, thus altering the character of each show, the group had something as regular as the Salon to work toward each year if they chose. This was especially important for Cassatt, who had always been eager to exhibit as much as possible. In the United States, she found a similar regular outlet in the Society of American Artists exhibitions in New York. These exhibitions meant more to her during these years because she was now temporarily without a dealer. She had given up on the American dealers she had had previously, Goupil in New York and Teubner in Philadelphia, as well as her earlier Paris dealers. It is possible that she sold some work through the dealer Portier, whose shop was in the artists' quarter, but she had not yet been taken up by Durand-Ruel, the downtown gallery that had "discovered" the Impressionists. Her attachment to the Impressionists made dealers less necessary since she had the annual exhibitions and also the informal network of sales that went on within the Impressionists' circle of Parisian intellectuals and collectors. By 1879 she had already executed a portrait of the collector Moyse Dreyfus and had sold an oil sketch of a child to Henri Rouart. The critic Antonin Proust (father of Marcel Proust) bought one of her paintings from the show itself. Cassatt's fears that she would not be able to sell enough even to support her studio were soon dispelled by the interest in her work shown by her new friends.

Energized by her success in the exhibition Cassatt started on a vigorous program of travel during the summer of 1879. In recent years, since she came back from her trip to Philadelphia in 1875, she had stayed in Paris even during the summers. Freed from some of the anxiety that had dogged her since she began her campaign to find recognition in the art capital of the world, she returned to her old footloose ways. After a quick trip across the Channel to the Isle of Wight and England, she then set off with her father on an extensive review of some of her old haunts in the Alps and northern Italy. Her objective was to renew her acquaintance with her favorite art and favorite people. She and her father visited the Italian primitive frescoes in the area around Milan and the people of the small town of Varallo, in the Italian Alps, where she had painted some ten years before.

When she got back to Paris, she was worn out from her trip and anxious because she was not used to letting the summer go by without working. As of October 1, she had only about six months left to produce enough paintings for the next Impressionist exhibition, which would open on April 1, 1880. If she were to equal the size of her showing in 1879, she would have to produce a major work every two weeks, which was possible but very tight. Her father sympathized with her plight in writing to Aleck, "She has been fretting over the fact that for three months she has not been doing any *serious* work etc—and the next Annual Exposition is already staring her in the face & it is more incumbant on her than ever—after her last years success—to have something good to present etc—"[8]

Before she left for the summer, she had agreed to join Degas, Pissarro, and some others in launching a new art journal that would be illustrated by their own etchings. Interest in original prints, particularly etching and lithography, had been high among the more experimental artists in France and England for two decades. As a young artist Degas had joined such friends as Manet, Bracquemond, and Whistler in learning to make etchings and other prints that were as spontaneous and "modern" as their paintings. In 1879 the idea arose to publish a small fine-art journal that would juxtapose short stories and essays by avant-garde writers with etchings by their artist peers. Degas, Pissarro, and Bracquemond had begun developing designs for prints and planning the enterprise while Cassatt was away for the summer. When she got back she was faced with working in a medium she had never tried before.

Unlike the other Impressionists, Cassatt had not yet been caught up in the vogue for printmaking that is known as the Etching Revival. Her only experience with prints was when she was friends with Emily Sartain, whose whole family, including her father, John, and brother Samuel, were all engaged in making reproductive engravings and mezzotints of paintings and photographs for publication. When Cassatt and Sartain were in Parma they gravitated toward the accommodating Carlo Raimondi, professor of engraving at the Parma Academy, who also specialized in reproductive printmaking. At that time, Cassatt showed little interest in the print medium, which she saw as distinctly secondary to painting. As her experience broadened she became familiar with more experimental printmakers and the possibilities of the print as an original work of art rather than a reproduction.

When she settled in Paris in 1874, she witnessed the upsurge in general interest in the exhibiting and collecting of prints and drawings that had taken place in that decade. A high point was the "Exhibition of Works in Black and White" held at Durand-Ruel's gallery in July 1876, an exhibition of etchings that included the works of Manet, Marcellin Desboutin, Fantin-Latour, Alphonse Legros, Ludovic-Napoléon Lepic, and James Tissot. Degas, friendly with all these artists, was completely immersed in printmaking himself at this time. Since prints were multiples of the same composition and thus potentially could serve a larger market, Degas was especially drawn to this medium (figure 55). His family's finances had declined since the death of his father in 1874 and the subsequent failure of the family bank, and Degas was now more attentive to moneymaking opportunities.

Cassatt may have hesitated at first to try such unfamiliar work. After all, not only was she inexperienced as a printmaker, but her love of painting was so great that she seldom even took pains with her drawing—a prerequisite for printmaking. But she had recently seen two of her paintings reproduced in a new art journal, *La Vie Moderne,* by means of specially prepared drawings of them (figure 56) and may have been struck by how much publicity they engendered. Her father sent a copy of the journal to Aleck: "I send you by this mail the number for Aug 9th of the Vie Moderne containing a sketch of Mame's Lady in a loge at the opera—You will see that the front of the figure is in shadow the light coming in from rear of

55. *Edgar Degas,* **Mary Cassatt at the Louvre: The Etruscan Gallery,** *1879–80*
Soft-ground etching, drypoint, aquatint, and etching, 10½ x 9⅛ in.
Museum of Fine Arts, Boston; Katherine E. Bullard Fund in memory of Francis Bullard and proceeds from the sale of duplicate prints, 1984

box etc—The sketch does not do justice to the picture which was original in conception & very well executed—and was as well, the subject of a good deal of controversy among the artists & undoubtedly made her very generally known to the craft."[9] The prospect of a monthly journal in which she could show off prints that were both original works of art and reminiscent of her current paintings appealed to her instinct for self-promotion.

Finally, when she embarked on the actual making of prints, she discovered that she enjoyed the printmaking process. Ever since she was a student she had been too impatient to make the kind of finished drawings that were the mainstay of academic training. Her friend Eliza Haldeman had compared Cassatt's style of drawing with her own when they were both still at the Pennsylvania Academy: "We keep pretty nearly together. She generally getting the shading better and I the form, she the 'ensemble' and I the 'minutia.' "[10] Later, Emily Sartain was less generous, calling Cassatt "defective in drawing"[11] and reporting Luminais's assessment that her talent was merely a "talent of the brush."[12] Cassatt's impatience with "minutia" and a high degree of polish in drawing made her also reject traditional forms of printmaking, particularly ones like wood and steel engraving, mezzotint, and detailed lithography that were used for reproductions. The printmaking she encountered in Degas's studio, however, was a world apart.

For the past few years, Degas had been caught up in an experimental

56. ***Mary Cassatt,* Drawing of Woman with a Pearl Necklace in a Loge, *1879 (This drawing was reproduced in* La Vie Moderne *(August 9, 1879), as* Dans Une Loge.*) Pencil, 10½ x 7½ in. Private collection***

approach to prints that had been pioneered by such artists as Henri Guérard, the husband of Eva Gonzalès, another of the important women painters in the circle of the Impressionists. Degas worked with Guérard, Armand Guillaumin, Dr. Paul Gachet, Henri Somm, and Jean-Louis Forain—all referred to as "Impressionist" printmakers—to develop unusual techniques of etching, aquatint, lithography, and monotype that would bring out the more spontaneous, "painterly" effects of this black-and-white medium. *This* type of printmaking appealed to Cassatt. She was not afraid of hard work; on the contrary, her prints and paintings show constant, painstaking revisions that underlie the "spontaneous" finished product. She resented the facile sterility that she saw in academic work. When given a chance to break out of it, she invariably did.

For the next several months, in the fall and winter of 1879–80, Cassatt lived and breathed prints. During the day she would work at Degas's studio to use Degas's tools and his small etching press. During the evening she would sketch everything around her either directly onto a specially prepared copper etching plate or on paper to be transferred to the plate the next day. Most artists used the lamplit hours for drawing, since the color of their paintings was distorted by anything but pure daylight. Cassatt, who had always despised drawing, now took up evening work herself for the sake of her black-and-white prints. Thanks to the prints, we have a much closer glimpse of the cozy family unit, sitting together in the evenings, reading, sewing, and meditating in front of the fire. Visitors are documented in the parlor of 13 Avenue Trudaine—unidentified women in hats sipping tea from fine china cups; George Moore, the eccentric Irish writer whose observations of the Impressionists have indelibly shaped our understanding of their personalities, is himself captured in an odd moment sitting in the Cassatts' armchair, an open fan held absentmindedly in one hand (figure 57).

From the prints we understand that Cassatt's evenings consisted not just of lamplit homelife but also of the urban dweller's home-away-from-home: the theater. Cassatt did not discover the theater through printmaking—she had been working on pastels and paintings of this subject for two years—but the opportunity to observe and sketch freely outside the home was better seized at the theater than at any other public evening activity.

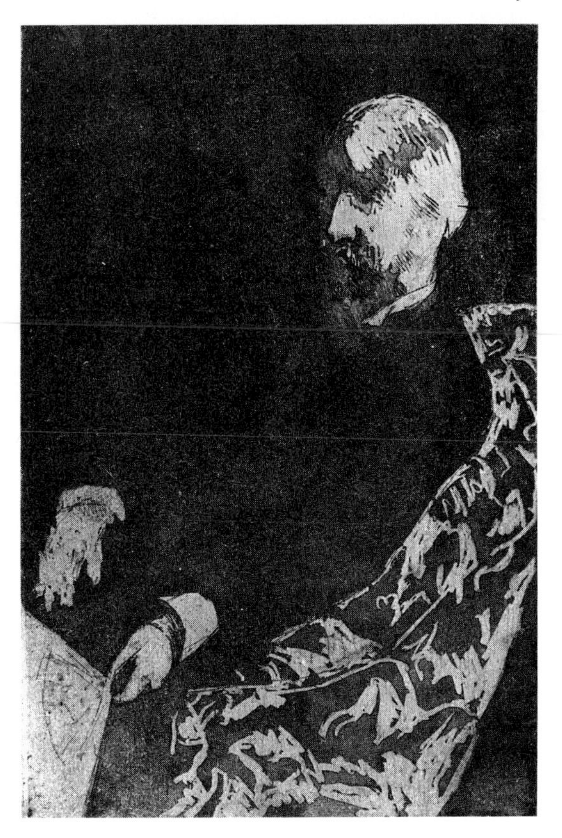

57. *Mary Cassatt,* **George Moore,** *c. 1880* *Soft-ground etching,* *8¾ x 5½ in.* *The Metropolitan Museum of Art, Rogers Fund, 1919 (19.1.1)*

58. *Mary Cassatt,* **In the Opera Box, No. 3,** *1879–80*
Soft-ground, aquatint, and etching, 8¹⁄₆ x 7³⁄₈ in.
Museum of Fine Arts, Boston (on loan)

Cassatt made full use of it, producing ten known versions of this subject in prints (figure 58).

The Cassatts went to the theater once or twice a week. They lived within an easy cab ride of all the major theaters of Paris, and enjoyed virtually every type of performance from the classic theater to the opéra comique. They even took children of their acquaintance (Mary's models, neighbors, children of friends, nieces and nephews) to the children's theaters and to the famous Cirque Fernando, which was only two blocks away. As a member of the intelligentsia, Cassatt was often invited to opening nights of new plays.

In spite of her regular attendance, it is probably safe to say that although she enjoyed the theater, she was not passionate about that art form. She much preferred literature and probably enjoyed reading plays more than seeing them performed. However, she did enjoy socializing, and the theater afforded the most comfortable way of seeing one's friends—indeed, seeing *tout Paris*—in a relaxed, festive atmosphere. Unlike Degas's scrutiny of the performers—singers, dancers, musicians—Cassatt's focus is the audience. Her interest is almost entirely in the romance suggested by beautifully dressed young women watching and being watched, playing with their fans and bouquets, acting out their real-life dramas (figure 59). Cassatt had gravitated toward romantic themes from the start. Her carnival and toreador scenes foreshadowed the shyness, flirtation, and reverie Cassatt caught so well in her images of the modern debutantes appearing nightly in Paris theaters.

While the Impressionists paid homage to the contemporary theater, the theater in turn tipped its hat to the Impressionists. In the fall of 1877 *La Cigale* (The Grasshopper), a play featuring several "Intentionist" painters as main characters, opened in Paris. Almost simultaneously translated into English, the play was performed in London and New York shortly afterward. An American edition was published in 1879 and the play was continuously

59. *Mary Cassatt,* The Loge, *c. 1879–80 Oil on canvas, 31½ x 25⅛ in. National Gallery of Art, Washington; Chester Dale Collection*

performed into the 1880s. Written by friends of Degas's, Ludovic Halévy and Henri Meilhac, *La Cigale* was such a broad farce that the gentle mocking of the bohemian "artists of the future" would hardly have offended the Impressionists, and the knowing public enjoyed a harmless laugh at the radicals in their midst. The play revolves around a beautiful young circus acrobat (called the Grasshopper) who discovers she is the long-lost daughter of an aristocrat and goes from rags to riches overnight. She falls in love with the artist Marignan, but the couple must overcome many misunderstandings and unhappy engagements to others before finally finding happiness in each other. If this situation comedy was the kind of thing Cassatt and the young theatergoers in her pictures were watching, it is little wonder that she found them and their concerns more absorbing than the plays themselves.

After experimenting with several versions of the theater subject, Cassatt settled on one, *In the Opera Box,* to print in a large edition of fifty impressions. Presumably this was to appear in the first issue of the proposed journal, called *Le Jour et la nuit* (Day and Night), they had all been working toward. Perhaps it was meant to accompany a piece by Ludovic Halévy himself, co-author of *La Cigale,* who had asked if he might write for the journal. In the end *Le Jour et la nuit* was never published. After months of work, Degas abruptly declared himself "not ready," and the project simply folded. The plan seems to have been to have its appearance coincide with the opening of the Impressionist exhibition on April 1, 1880. When this deadline was not met, there seemed little point in proceeding. Cassatt was riled by this turn of events, and her irritation was echoed by her loyal mother in writing to Aleck,

> Degas who is the leader undertook to get up a journal of etchings and got them all to work for it so that Mary had no time for painting and as usual with Degas when the time arrived to appear, he wasn't ready—so that "Le jour et la nuit" (the name of the publication) which might have been a great success has not yet appeared—Degas never is ready for anything—This time he has thrown away an excellent chance for all of them—[13]

The pique in Mrs. Cassatt's tone was heard in the voices of virtually all involved with the Impressionist exhibitions and projects in the late 1870s and early 1880s. Sooner or later, Degas exasperated everyone who tried to work closely with him or whose own professional advancement was tied to a group effort led by him. Degas was a strong leader and a convincing orator when he was passionate about an idea or plan. At the same time he was a loner who would ultimately make decisions based on what was best for him —and not necessarily the group he had gathered around him. Projects like *Le Jour et la nuit* propelled him into action and swept others along with him, but when a more lucrative commission came his way or he became distracted by another project, he could just as easily forget his original plans. His shaping of the Impressionist exhibitions of 1879, 1880, and 1881 to include less important or more conventional artists made some members of the group so angry that they took the reins away from him in 1882.

Cassatt may have been aware of Degas's erratic nature when she began the print journal with him, but she had not yet been directly affected by it. When they embarked on this joint venture, they became more intimate than they had ever been before. Now they necessarily worked side by side using the print equipment in Degas's studio and were often engaged in the hard physical labor of operating the press. They were seldom alone, since there were many others also involved or interested in the project who worked alongside them. Many times Cassatt would be accompanied by her sister, who was posing for Degas, along with Mary, for the etching later called *Mary Cassatt at the Louvre* (figure 55).

Nevertheless, the collaboration would have been a heady experience for Cassatt, who had in the past been drawn to older men like Couture and Raimondi who flattered and instructed her. Degas soon became a social friend as well as a professional colleague. He often dined with the Cassatts and invited them to his own soirées. Degas and Cassatt became a frequent sight at the Louvre where they probed each work by the old masters and tested their theories of art. They frequently met in public gatherings at the openings of exhibitions and at the theater. Degas at forty-five had beguiled many women with his caustic humor and his unusual regard for their intelligence and ideas. He could also be extremely thoughtful, as he was in obtaining a puppy for Cassatt from Ludovic Lepic, a mutual friend who bred Brussels griffons. As he wrote to Lepic, the dog was for Mlle. Cassatt: "This distinguished person whose friendship I honour, as you would in my place, asked me to recommend to you the youth of the subject. It is a young dog that she needs, so that he may love her."[14] Cassatt was charmed; and she, at thirty-five, had not yet outgrown her youthful tendency to flirt back. The subjects of her paintings and prints in the first years of their acquaintance, young women at the theater expressing shyness and pleasure at the homage paid them, may have reflected her own feelings at the time.

Possibly Cassatt grew to expect more from Degas than gallantry at the

60. *Edgar Degas,* Mary Cassatt, *c. 1880–84*
Oil on canvas, 28⅛ x 23⅛ in.
National Portrait Gallery, Smithsonian Institution; gift of the Morris and Gwendolyn Cafritz Foundation and the Regents Major Acquisition Fund

printing press (figure 60). Her romantic imagination was always very rich, and Degas elicited from her feelings of respect, even awe, that no other man had. He dominated her thoughts and actions during that winter of making prints and they both rose to new heights from the association. Then he dropped the project, and thus the newfound intimacy with her, quite suddenly. Her anger exposed the extent of her expectations. For the first time she felt the betrayal that others had experienced with Degas and recognized that she had no more power over him than they. Berthe Morisot had observed this tendency in Degas years before when he suddenly ran off to talk to two non-artist friends while Morisot and he were strolling together through the Salon of 1869. She wrote to her sister, "I must admit that I was a little annoyed when a man whom I consider to be very intelligent deserted me to pay compliments to two silly women."[15] Degas's most frustrating trait was to cast aside his colleagues and intellectual equals for people or projects of less significance.

Although she continued to treasure his friendship, Cassatt learned to take what she could of his inspiration, advice, or art when it was offered, knowing full well that it could be withdrawn or altered without warning. She loved him as a friend and as a brilliant artist for the rest of his life, but she never allowed herself to be betrayed again. Curiously, she never again used the theater subject or in any way revived the scenes of flirtation which had occupied her that winter.

Her lifelong friendship with Degas was predicated upon the new armor that Cassatt wore against him. After she told Louisine Havemeyer many stories of Degas's cruelty to other artists (about John Singer Sargent he said, "He is a skillful painter but not an artist"),[16] Louisine asked, "How could you get on with him?"

> "Oh," she answered, "I am independent! I can live alone and I love to work. Sometimes it made him furious that he could not find a chink in my armor, and there would be months when we just could not see each other, and then something I painted would bring us together again and he would go to Durand-Ruel's and say something nice about me, or come to see me himself. . . . When criticism was at its worst, he said to me: 'They are all jealous of us, and wish to steal our art.' But," continued Miss Cassatt after a quiet moment, and I saw her face light up with a beautiful expression, "magnificent! and however dreadful he was, he always lived up to his ideals."[17]

At the time Degas abandoned the journal project, Cassatt had not yet worked out a way of accommodating Degas's idiosyncrasies, and her disappointment with Degas's betrayal was exacerbated by the failure of that year's Impressionist exhibition to live up to the one before. She had fewer major paintings—eight, compared with eleven the previous year—and was thus "in the background."[18]

The exhibition itself suffered from innumerable problems of content and presentation. The defectors, Renoir, Sisley, and Cézanne, were joined by Monet, who was at the heart of the new style in the minds of many. Although with Degas, Pissarro, Morisot, and Guillaumin representing the original core group the show was still a solid one, it lacked the depth that Monet and Renoir had provided in the past. Furthermore, the apartment they had rented was in a building under construction that was located a little farther from the center of the art district, and the installation of works had been done somewhat haphazardly. Finally, there was the odd sight of an empty glass sculpture case that was intended to hold Degas's *Petite danseuse de quatorze ans (The Little Fourteen-year-old Dancer),* but the wax statue, like the print journal, was "not ready."

Cassatt did manage to produce eight major paintings and pastels for the show in addition to eight etchings, some of which she exhibited in two states, unfinished and finished. Although the few paintings we can identify are now considered among her best, such as *Five O'Clock Tea* (figure 61), the critics found them dark, more conservative, or flawed in some other way. She had to suffer the needling of critics like Henry Havard, who claimed "[Cassatt's] talent has remained as lively, but her originality has abated. Of the four portraits that she exhibits, only one is strange"[19] or Philippe Burty's remarks: "Miss Mary Cassatt seeks tonal strength that is not always forthcoming from her pencil. Her beginnings were much applauded. Regrettably we now see her aspiring to the partially completed image."[20]

Fortunately, there was enough encouragement from critics, collectors, and friends to keep her from sinking irrevocably into depression from the year's events. The disappointments of the spring were also mitigated by the news that Aleck and his family were at last booked for a visit that had long been promised but always delayed. His parents had anticipated seeing their son and their beloved grandchildren from the moment they set sail themselves in 1877 (figure 62). For Mary, the visit from the "Americans" was more a matter of curiosity than longing. Although she would be delighted to see her favorite brother again, she had never formed an attachment to his problematic wife, and she was almost completely ignorant of his children. Her trip to Philadelphia in 1875 was timed to witness the birth of the youngest, Elsie, but over the years she had spent only a few

61. Mary Cassatt, **Five O'Clock Tea,** *1880*
Oil on canvas, 25½ x 36½ in.
Museum of Fine Arts, Boston; M. Theresa B. Hopkins Fund

months in the company of her young nieces and nephews. The children knew and loved their Aunt Lydia, but Aunt Mary was merely an abstraction to them.

In honor of Aleck's visit, the Parisian Cassatts decided to forgo their intended visit to spas for Lydia's health and instead rented a villa in the countryside near Paris. The plan was that the four children (and their governess) would stay with their grandparents, freeing Aleck and Lois to enjoy Paris and travel throughout Europe unencumbered. This was Lois's first trip abroad and Aleck's first since he was sixteen years old. The apartment on Avenue Trudaine was to be closed up for the summer while Mary, Lydia, and their parents moved to Marly-le-Roi with the children and Aleck and Lois stayed in town at the elegant Hotel Meurice.

Lois looked forward to her arrival in Paris with some trepidation since she had never entirely erased her feelings of being slighted by Aleck's parents, and time had only hardened her opinion of her sister-in-law Mary (figure 63). Their meeting at the train station in Paris was a scene she wrote about at once to her sister:

62. Photograph of the children of Alexander and Lois Cassatt, c. 1878 From left: Eddie, Katharine ("Sister"), Elsie, and Rob Present location unknown

> You will all be interested to know that on our arrival in Paris on Saturday night the whole family were at the station to meet us, and the reception I got from *all* was all that even I could have hoped for. Mr. Cassatt (pere) stayed at the hotel all night with us to conduct us out to Marly-le-Roi the next day and I was invited in the kindest manner, to stay out there at least for a night. . . . I took them just as I found them and when Lydia offered to come in and go to the dressmaker's with me I at first declined entirely but I found she wanted to do it so I accepted with many thanks. . . . The dressmakers are already after me at the hotel arriving every morning before I am up and one of them brought a huge box in hopes I would try all her dresses, I believe. . . . [however] I am going out among them with Lydia, who is a connoisseur.[21]

The gentler members of the Parisian Cassatts, Lydia and her father, smoothed the way for good family relations that summer. The others, Mary and her mother, did the best they could. Mrs. Cassatt did her part by performing her usual household miracles, providing the best of accommodations and gourmet meals for her guests and devoting herself to the entertainment and instruction of her grandchildren. Mary fell back on her own talents and began to paint them all. She persuaded Aleck to sit for his portrait and won for herself some private time with him after so many years

63. *Photograph of Lois B. Cassatt, c. 1880–85*
Private collection

64. *Mary Cassatt,* **Alexander J. Cassatt,** *1880*
Oil on canvas, 25¾ x 36⅜ in.
The Detroit Institute of Arts; Founders Society Purchase, Robert H. Tannahill Foundation Fund

of separation (figure 64). As the summer went on, the portrait served as her hold over Aleck, who was once again susceptible to the more exotic world his sister opened up to him. Aleck began to spend nights and whole weeks at Marly, leaving Lois to stay in Paris alone.

Aunt Mary also sketched and painted the children, using her art to get to know them gradually without imposing on them a false familiarity. She drew on her experience with other children their age, sons and daughters of friends who had also served as her models, to gain the confidence of the four nieces and nephews—and, before long, their affection. Lois watched this transformation with awe, since, as she confided to her sister, "the truth is I cannot abide Mary and never will."[22] But, she admitted, "The children all seem to prefer her to the others, strange to say."[23] Mary even discovered in her younger nephew Robbie an interest in art and had him painting beside her every day. Lois lamented to her mother, "Poor Rob can do nothing but paint now, his letters are forgotten."[24]

Perhaps Rob, the artist, assisted his aunt in painting what was called by the Cassatts the "Family Group" (*Mrs. Cassatt Reading to Her Grandchildren,* figure 65) since he is not in it. Of all the sketches of her nieces and nephews Aunt Mary made that summer, this was the only finished painting. It shows Eddie (eleven), Elsie (five), and Katharine (called "Sister," nine) crowded around their grandmother as she read fairy tales from a bright red book. Mary's mother was frequently called upon to be a conspirator in getting children to pose attentively for her daughter and probably often brought out the fairy tales for just such a purpose. This time she is shown having accomplished a great feat—getting three lively, impatient children to pose all at once.

The two months the children spent at Marly in 1880 ushered in a new phase in Cassatt's relationship with her brother and his family. Having made their first family trip abroad, they began to come regularly every other year. They also inspired Gard to begin regular visits, starting in 1881. The brothers alternated so that the family in Paris could look forward to annual visits from home. Aleck was undergoing changes in his professional career that would soon allow him greater freedom to indulge his interest in travel, art, and, his great passion, racehorses. Lois, too, was changing in her attitude toward her in-laws and becoming more adventuresome in travel. Once she had had a taste of Paris with its elegant society, its shops, and its dressmakers, she never needed urging to return.

65. ***Mary Cassatt,* Katherine Cassatt Reading to Her Grandchildren, *1880***
(from left: Eddie, Elsie, Mrs. Katherine Cassatt, Katharine)
Oil on canvas, 22 x 39½ in.
Private collection

Lois also saw that frequent trips to Europe satisfied Aleck's yearnings for broader horizons and made him more satisfied to reside in the United States. By the time they made their trip in 1880 Aleck had built up such a longing for foreign life that he talked seriously about expatriating. At the end of their summer, his appetite was somewhat abated and Lois was able to write to her mother with great relief, "On the whole do you know I think even Aleck is going to go back to America very well satisfied with his own country. As for me, although I am entirely enjoying the experience, I know ours is the only country to live in. But isn't it lovely to have Aleck go back so pleased with home?"[25] Lois no doubt felt that this was a triumph over Mary in influencing Aleck's thinking; and it probably was.

Even if Mary could not have Aleck living in Paris permanently, she could be happy with her renewed relationship with him and the promise of more regular contact. More important to her was the acquisition of real nieces and nephews—not just names and photographs mailed across the ocean. She could now join with her parents and Lydia in the outpouring of affection and guidance that characterized the Parisian Cassatts' relationship to the four children in their lives. The bond established that summer was mutual and long-lasting.

Once the Philadelphia branch returned home in September, the remaining Cassatts stayed on for another month and a half in Marly. The site was so pleasant, situated as it was above the broad waters of the Seine and next to the Versailles-like park of Louis XIV's vacation residence, Marly-le-Roi, that they recuperated in good spirits. Mary took the time to finish the "Family Group" and work on some other paintings out of doors. Lacking the pool of professional models she had in Paris, she pressed Lydia into service for works painted *en plein air,* such as *Lydia Crocheting in the Garden at Marly* (figure 66). Even after she returned to Paris she continued to be fascinated by Lydia's image, executing *The Cup of Tea* (figure 67) and *Lydia Working at a Tapestry Frame* (figure 38) in an urban apartment setting. While Lydia had been a frequent model for Mary for a long time, this series of major finished paintings was unprecedented. Lydia had been free from alarming symptoms for over a year at this point and had withstood the onslaught of the children in good health. Perhaps the paintings were a celebration of Lydia's recovery, or simply a holdover of the family feelings that had engulfed them all during the summer. Perhaps Mary turned to Lydia to fill the void left by Degas, now that they were no longer working side by side. For whatever reasons, these paintings stand as a testament to the kind, refined woman that everyone in the family went to for help or solace. Her quiet face with its upturned

66. ***Mary Cassatt,* Lydia Crocheting in the Garden at Marly, *1880***
Oil on canvas, 26 x 37 in.
The Metropolitan Museum of Art; gift of Mrs. Gardner Cassatt, 1965 (65.184)

nose and downturned lips, her hands busy with needlework, teacup, or book are almost all we have been given to help us penetrate her personality. No letters or any other documents from Lydia Cassatt have survived, nor is she given more than a secondary place in anyone else's. Her desire for privacy and a quiet life has been almost completely respected.

The two sisters spent the next winter and spring harmoniously, with no major health setbacks for Lydia and no failed art projects for Mary. They were familiar figures around Paris. The elder, more sedate Lydia, forty-four, accompanied the wiry and tireless Mary to the Louvre, to openings of art exhibitions, and to small gatherings of friends in the art and literary circles. Lydia, without a profession, dedicated herself to household matters and fashion, making sure that all the Cassatt women were dressed by the best seamstresses. In addition, she was a constant reader, as were all the Cassatts. Although she may not have had the intellectual zeal of her sister in contemporary literature, she was nimble and well-enough-informed to be considered good company by the likes of Edgar Degas and his friends.

67. *Mary Cassatt,* The Cup of Tea, *1880–81 Oil on canvas, 36⅜ x 25¾ in. The Metropolitan Museum of Art; from the collection of James Stillman, gift of Dr. Ernest G. Stillman, 1922*

The circle of people intimate with the Cassatt sisters viewed Mary's offerings in the next Impressionist exhibition in 1881 with double pleasure. The exhibition included some of the best-received paintings and pastels she had shown so far, and at least three out of eleven were studies of her sister done in the last year. Lydia was no more of a beauty than Mary, but her features and her complexion had an interesting delicacy that Mary was now skilled enough to capture. The effect was picked up by numerous critics in writing about the show, and Cassatt received some of the most flattering reviews to date:

> How can one not be interested, for example, by the studies and works of Cassatt, whose pictures have such grace, finesse, delicacy and, dare I use the word, distinct femininity. The eleven paintings she shows at the Independents are all of great interest. Among them I especially like her woman seated outdoors with knitting in her hands. Shaded by a large white bonnet, her face has a lovely tonality that is simple and peaceful.[26]

Another critic, Gustave Geffroy, who would follow her work for decades, expressed similar praise in writing about *The Cup of Tea:*

> We prefer above all the woman in the pink dress and bonnet who holds a cup of tea in her gloved hands. She is exquisitely Parisian. The nuances in the pink, the airy lace, and all the lights and reflections that play upon her clothing, hair, and softly pale skin make this *Thé* a delicious work.[27]

Mary Cassatt blushed and dismissed the endless reviews as "too much pudding," said her father,[28] and no doubt Lydia silently seconded her.

Once again Cassatt, Morisot, Degas, and Pissarro stood out in the Impressionist exhibition because of the absence of Renoir, Monet, and now Caillebotte. In their place were such friends of Degas's as Jean-François Raffaelli, Jean-Louis Forain, and Federico Zandomeneghi, who were considered minor artists by other members of the group and by many critics. This turn of events made for a less prestigious exhibition, but in practical terms it bolstered Cassatt's standing and her sales. According to her father, she had either sold or had offers on all eleven pictures in the show. This included the "Family Group" which had been so meaningful to all the Cassatts when it was painted and now provided many happy memories. Her family underestimated how important selling was to Mary when they assumed she would never accept a collector's offer to buy the painting: "She could hardly sell her Mother and nieces and nephews, I think."[29] Cassatt did indeed sell it and then had to retrieve it from the buyer when the family protested. Even the many studies of Lydia were for sale. Years later the artist or her brothers bought them back.

Cassatt was not sentimental when it came to exhibiting and selling her work. When family members posed for paintings—unless they posed for portraits designated in advance for a particular family wall—the paintings were treated as part of Cassatt's professional output. She believed since her student days that the goal of an artist was to exhibit and sell, to achieve fame and fortune. Her success stems largely from the clarity of her vision in this regard.

A corollary to her own sales was the simultaneous purchase of other artists' works, for herself, for other collectors, or for resale. Her motives were largely generous. She believed in the works she purchased and wanted to help the artists monetarily and in other ways. But she was also convinced that these works were good investments and often calculated the increase in the value of a Monet, a Manet, or a Degas she had bought or recommended to someone else. Investments, after all, were the family business, and she did not grow up in the midst of discussions of stock prices and real estate values without gaining the ability to see art in those same terms. The buying and selling of her own and other artists' work intensified by 1881 to such an extent that she became friendly with Paul Durand-Ruel, the proprietor of the well-established art gallery that had first promoted Impressionist work starting in the early 1870s. Durand-Ruel began carrying Cassatt's paintings that year and established a relationship with her that would blossom over the next twenty years.

At the conclusion of the Impressionist exhibition of 1881 Cassatt felt that she had reached a sort of benchmark. She had been exhibiting with the group for three years in a row and had seen her critical fortunes go up, down, and then back up again. Her sales were steady now; her relationships with the other Impressionists had stabilized; and she had established a new pattern of work throughout the year. After their pleasant experience renting a summer home outside Paris in 1880 the Cassatts repeated the arrangement the following year. Mary began to find local models so that she could work during the summer without imposing so heavily on her own family. The addition of outdoor summer scenes in turn gave a new dimension to her oeuvre. She complained that she had less passion for work during the summer, but she nevertheless had a model every day and at least sketched out several major paintings during that time. That summer the family had its first visit from Gard, then thirty-two, who was still running the investment firm, Cassatt & Co., in Philadelphia and still a bachelor.

However, Cassatt's newfound stability was threatened before the summer was out. In July Mrs. Cassatt wrote to Lois all the chitchat from Louveciennes (near Marly-le-Roi), where they had rented the house called Coeur Volant. Among other things she mentioned the damp weather and that "Lydia committed some imprudence in her diet and has not been so well, but as she is now very careful, is getting better."[30] And as for Aleck, she relayed the family's thoughts on the news that Aleck had decided to resign from the Pennsylvania Railroad after twenty-one years. Neither item would have immediate consequences, but a year and a half later all the Cassatt siblings had seen drastic changes in their lives.

The sequence of events started with Mary, who lost her secure place in the Impressionist group when conflicts among the group members caused her to pull out from the annual exhibition of 1882. The exhibitions ceased for three years after that. Aleck's resignation from the Pennsylvania Railroad did eventually take place, although not as swiftly as he had hoped, leaving him, like Mary, somewhat adrift. For Gard, the changes were both good and bad. After many years of playing the field, "the boy" suddenly fell deeply in love with Eugenia Carter from a fine Philadelphia family with Southern roots. They were married about the same time that Aleck resigned in October 1882. Unfortunately, after beginning to build a house and take on new expenses, his business suffered an unexpected loss, and the young couple started out their married life having to retrench.

Mary Cassatt was working away as usual in the winter of 1882 when the bitter arguments began to brew among the Impressionists. Caillebotte and Pissarro again took mediating roles to try to bring together not only the artists who had been exhibiting together for the last three years but also the Impressionists who had defected: principally Renoir, Monet, and Sisley. The rift between the landscapists and the painters of modern life instantly reappeared, and the old objections to Raffaelli, Forain, and Zandomeneghi were voiced again. This year, Degas could not carry the votes necessary to include his adherents and was forced to withdraw along with them. It was made clear that Cassatt's participation was not in question—she was not lumped with the objectionable three—and the group fully expected her to show. In the end she must have been persuaded by Degas to stand with his faction because she did not participate. Her friend Morisot, who was in the South of France at the time, asked her husband in Paris, "Have you seen Miss Cassatt? Why did she back out?"[31] Eugène Manet replied, "I have not yet been able to discover the reason for Degas's and Miss Cassatt's withdrawal. A stupid Gambettist newspaper says tonight that as a result of this withdrawal the Impressionist exhibition was 'decapitated.' "[32]

The distress Cassatt felt over losing her prized exhibition paled next to the overwhelming anxiety caused by the return of her sister's ill health and the sudden new heart problems suffered by her mother. Both women were in pain and needed the kind of attention they usually provided for each other. Neither Mary, who worked in her studio several blocks away during the day, nor her father was accustomed to the new demands of having two invalids in the house. Finally, doctors persuaded them that a warmer climate would be advantageous. Mrs. Cassatt and Lydia managed to get themselves to Pau, in the South of France, to try the cure there. Mrs. Cassatt did indeed improve, but Lydia was on a downward course that demanded more extreme measures.

For a number of years, doctors had been suggesting that Lydia Cassatt had Bright's disease, a degenerative disease of the kidneys, but their diagnoses were not conclusive and the family preferred to believe them wrong. Even six months before her death, two doctors they consulted disagreed about the cause of her illness. Her symptoms were attacks of extreme pain, "neuralgia," in the head and stomach accompanied by debilitating weakness. In the past the attacks were temporary, and the worst of them had not recurred for a year and a half. But now the pain had returned and was almost constant. The extremes of nineteenth-century medicine were called into play. For the last months of the disease, Lydia was treated with doses of arsenic, morphine, and the blood of animals drunk fresh at the abbatoir.

The family once again moved outside the city for the summer, renting a house next to the one they had the previous summer in Louveciennes. There Mary attempted to work and Lydia attempted to get better. By mid-September her condition worsened and, as her father wrote to Aleck,

> Some new and alarming symptoms have developed in Lydia's case and she herself begins to realize her danger and has lately spoken to Mary of her probable death, and made her promise to have her buried in the country and directed her to give keepsakes to you and Gard. Poor dear! This is the first time she has spoken plainly and directly of her death. . . . [she] bears her affliction with wonderful patience and resignation. She suffers fearfully not only from pain but from nausea and greatly also from want of sleep. She has intervals of comparative ease, but they grow shorter and shorter. Last night was a very distressing one to her. Mame keeps up very well and Lydia says has developed into a most excellent nurse. As far as her art is concerned her summer has been lost to her.[33]

The family moved back into Paris a month later and on November 7, 1882, Lydia Cassatt passed away in her sleep.

It is not possible to describe the immense loss felt by all the Cassatts, but especially by Mary. Not only did she lose the patient mainstay of family life that Lydia had become, but she also lost her loving confidante and companion and, to a certain extent, her vision of future domestic tranquillity. Looking beyond the deaths of her parents, she saw living with Lydia as a happy way to glide into old age. She was so confident of this arrangement that she had used Lydia as a shield against the obvious course of action, marriage. Her sister-in-law reported that "she is very lonesome now and says she feels now that perhaps she would have been better off to have married when she thinks of being left alone in the world."[34]

By a strange twist of fate, she turned to Lois, her old nemesis, to fill the void. Aleck, Lois, and the children arrived in Paris barely three weeks after Lydia died, having planned the trip to celebrate Aleck's resignation on October 1. They had expected to see Lydia, even if in ill health, and were saddened to receive the news of her death the day before their departure. This time Lois did not dread her arrival in Paris. The Cassatts who met them at the train station were bowed with grief and hungry for the solace that only family could bring them. Lois wrote with a mixture of surprise and sympathy, "Mary seems to be most anxious to be friendly and proposes something for us to do together everyday. . . . She has not had the heart to touch her paintings for six months and she will scarcely now be persuaded to begin."[35] Relations between Lois and her in-laws continued to improve, and at Christmas Lois was deeply touched that she was now treated as one of the family. Mr. Cassatt gave her an exquisite ring with nine small diamonds arranged on five gold bands, and the gift had great meaning to her. "I was perfectly overcome. You can readily imagine how astonished I was as I had received no intimation that anyone had a present for me."[36] It had taken Lois fifteen years and a death in the family to be accepted by the Cassatts.

This time it was Mary instead of Lydia who went with Lois to the dressmakers' and helped place the children in appropriate schools for their several months' stay in Paris. With Lydia gone and her mother still in a weakened state, Mary had to spend less time in her studio and more time taking care of mundane matters. Although she began to complain about not finding the time to paint, the constant activity suited her energetic personality. She was now thirty-eight and in her physical prime. Eventually she would learn how to carry out the household responsibilities without sacrificing her art, but in the meantime she made all the compromises necessary and began to feel alive again.

Aleck, Lois, and the children were not the only beneficiaries of Cassatt's new desire for outside friendships. For the past several years Degas and her other colleagues in the art world had satisfied her need for professional discourse and networking. Without Lydia she now saw the need to go beyond the family for personal closeness and drew around her a mixed group of old and new friends. Berthe Morisot and her husband were building a house closer into town and became regular social partners with Mary and her parents in the round of dinner parties and outings. Their group often consisted of not only the faithful Degas, but Stéphane Mallarmé, occasionally Georges Clemenceau (then Socialist deputy from Montmartre), Pissarro (when he made his monthly trip in from the country), Renoir, and various patrons, including M. and Mme. Paul Bérard. The Bérards were wealthy collectors with a background in diplomacy and banking. They were special patrons of Renoir, who often visited them in their country house, Wargemont, near Dieppe. The Cassatts enjoyed the company of the Bérards, who had children the same ages as Eddie and Katharine, Mary being particularly friendly with the beautiful Mme. Bérard, and were persuaded in 1886 to take a summer house near Wargemont.

The entire Impressionist community was brought together in unusual harmony by the death of Édouard Manet in the spring of 1883, about six months after Lydia's death. Mary could sympathize deeply with his bereft widow, Suzanne Leenhoff Manet, as well as with his brother Eugène and sister-in-law, Berthe Morisot. Berthe, who was present at Édouard's death, wrote to her sister of the experience:

> These last days were very painful; poor Édouard suffered atrociously. His agony was horrible. In a word, it was death in one of its most appalling forms. . . .
>
> If you add to these almost physical emotions my old bonds of friendship with Édouard, an entire past of youth and work suddenly ending, you will understand that I am crushed. The expressions of sympathy have been intense and universal; his richly endowed nature compelled everyone's friendship; he also had an intellectual charm, a warmth, something indefinable, so that, on the day of his funeral, all the people who came to attend—and who usually are so indifferent on such occasions—seemed to me like one big family mourning one of their own.[37]

Cassatt's relationship to the others in the Impressionist circles was more like "one big family" now that their annual exhibitions had ceased and the fervor of the new movement had abated. She got to know the husbands, wives, and children of her fellow painters, saw them in the country during the summers, and let discussion of personal matters mix with the latest news of the art world.

In addition to her art friends, Cassatt also enjoyed renewing ties with family members beyond her own immediate household. For instance, she had new contact with her Gardner cousins on the occasion of the marriage of Lydia Gardner in 1882 at the age of forty-seven. Having moved from West Chester to be near her sister Anna (Mrs. Luther Smith) and her children, Lydia Gardner led a modest style of life in a boardinghouse. The unmarried Gardner sisters lived off the small trust left to them by their mother in 1869, which continued to be administered by Cassatt & Co. They were so humble that when Aleck increased the amount of the trust out of his own growing wealth, Lydia Gardner was incapable of bringing herself to write and thank him. She confessed to Mr. Cassatt, "I have wanted since my marriage to write to Aleck, and thank him for his handsome addition to my income the last two years and to tell him how comfortable it made me but he is such a great man now that I with my bungling pen have not had the courage to make the attempt."[38] Other correspondence with family members in the old Cassatt hometowns of Pittsburgh, West Chester, and York in the 1880s gave the Paris Cassatts a revived interest in the larger family and genealogy.

One branch of the family from Pennsylvania came to Europe to stay for several years and was an especially welcome addition to the Cassatts' circle in Paris. This group consisted of Annie Riddle Scott, widow of Thomas Scott, former president of the Pennsylvania Railroad and Aleck's mentor, her mother, Mary Dickinson Riddle, and her two children. Mary Cassatt knew the family from Philadelphia, where they had moved in the 1850s, but her parents knew Mrs. Riddle and her daughter, Annie, from Pittsburgh, where they had all grown up. Mrs. Riddle was Mrs. Cassatt's first cousin, the daughter of Alexander Johnston's sister. It was a treat for the elder Cassatts to have such lifelong friends with them in such an unlikely place as Paris. When their tour was over in 1886, Mr. Cassatt, then eighty years old, lamented their departure: "We have lost Mrs. Scott and her mother, and we miss them very much. I miss them I think more than the others as now there is not a soul in Paris that I knew before coming over and nobody that I can talk as freely to as I could to them."[39]

Annie Scott was just beginning to be interested in art at this time and gradually began collecting a few paintings. While they were in London she had her daughter Mary ("Molly") painted by Millais and visited Whistler's studio. When they came over to Paris, Mary Cassatt offered to paint a portrait of her mother, Mrs. Riddle, in return for many kindnesses, including the gift of a Japanese tea set that she intended to show in the portrait itself. The painting, now called *Lady at the Tea Table* (figure 68), progressed rapidly in the fall of 1883. Although she was very pleased with it and received many compliments from her artist friends, including Degas and Raffaelli, she was not sure it would please Mrs. Riddle and her daughter. "As they are not very artistic in their likes and dislikes of pictures and as a likeness is a hard thing to make to please the nearest friends, I don't know what the results will be."[40]

In the end they did not like the portrait. Although their refusal did not cause a rift with Annie or her mother, it did cause lasting ill will between Mary Cassatt and Mrs. Riddle's other daughter, Bessie Fisher, who was also traveling in Europe. Evidently, the spare and elegant treatment of the elderly

68. *Mary Cassatt,* **Lady at the Tea Table,** *1883*
Oil on canvas, 29 x 24 in.
The Metropolitan Museum of Art; gift of the artist, 1923

woman offended the pride Mrs. Riddle and her daughters took in their own beauty, which was legendary in Pittsburgh. In a book on Pittsburgh society women published in 1888, Mrs. Riddle was listed as one of the great beauties of her generation: "Mrs. Riddle, née Dickinson, mother of Mrs. Thomas A. Scott, with a tall, willowy figure, soft expressive eyes, brown hair, a tender, beseeching expression of countenance, was a noted beauty of the long ago."[41] Thirty years later, when museums were squabbling over the picture and Mrs. Riddle's family finally wanted it, Cassatt wrote, "On no account shall Bessie Fisher ever own it. She sent me the most decided messages regretting that there was so little likeness to her Mother! The line of the back & the hand & that is all. Even the worm will turn, & I see no excuse for her too evident desire to snub me. Well let her rejoice in Miss Beaux portraits & leave me alone."[42] Cecilia Beaux, following in Cassatt's footsteps at the Pennsylvania Academy, had established a national reputation as a portraitist. To Cassatt she represented the slick, accommodating approach to art that Cassatt had always disdained.

One final friend who was with her often in the early 1880s was Louisine Elder. Louisine had been in Paris for the summer of 1881 and returned after Lydia's death in the fall of 1882. In that dark time she spent many hours with Cassatt in a companionship that few others could now offer her. Their teacher/student relationship had matured into something more personal and more equal. Louisine, although not an artist herself, had a rare understanding of and passion for the fine arts that endeared her to many artists besides Cassatt, including Degas and Whistler. Not the least important of Louisine's traits, as far as artists were concerned, was her willingness to acquire art and to pay homage to the artist in this most tangible way. By 1882 she had already acquired works by Degas, Pissarro, Monet, and Whistler, as well as Cassatt's self-portrait (figure 37). This particularly impressed Cassatt, not only because she liked advising Louisine on art purchases but because she could only be truly intimate with people who had a deep commitment to art. She had many friends in all walks of life, but she reserved her strongest feelings for those who understood art and thus, she felt, understood her.

In 1883 Louisine married Harry Havemeyer, a man she had known all her life. This new responsibility and birth of her three children caused the two women to be separated for six years. In 1889, when the Havemeyers resumed their regular trips to Europe, they formed with Cassatt an art-collecting team that was unrivaled in the history of American patronage.

In the year after Lydia's death, Cassatt drew on friendship from all corners to help ease the pain of losing the person with whom she had thought she would grow old. But since Cassatt was herself not yet forty, concerns about her old age could easily be pushed aside by the here and now, and life would inevitably go on. Never having finished the Marly portrait of Aleck, she eased back into painting by starting a new portrait of him, which Lois encouraged her to do. She followed that with two pastels of Elsie, then eight years old—one for Philadelphia and one for Paris (figure 69). Meanwhile Lois was itching to have her portrait painted and considered asking Renoir, whom Mary suggested, but ended up asking Whistler. Aleck and Lois again left the children in Paris with their grandparents, although this time they all crowded into the Avenue Trudaine apartment, and spent the month of April in London.

Mary Cassatt had known James McNeill Whistler (figure 70) for some time, although there is no information about when or how they met. Since Whistler came to Paris regularly from his London home, she could easily have met him through Degas or another mutual friend. By 1879 Whistler was the best-known American painter in Europe and was better known than the Impressionists as a radical artist. In *La Cigale,* even though the characters were understood to be Impressionists and the play was written with the help of Degas, the American version of 1879 described them as "color mad, eccentric, and followers of James Whistler."[43] Lois's choice was a daring one, and her experience with him was consistent with his reputation. She and Aleck quickly fell into socializing with the outgoing "butterfly" artist,

69. ***Mary Cassatt,* Elsie in a Blue Chair,** ***1883***
Pastel, 35 x 25 in.
Private collection

70. *Mortimer Menpes,* **Portrait of Whistler with Monocle,** *Lithograph The Metropolitan Museum of Art; gift of Paul E. Walter, 1985 (1985.1161.22)*

going out together to dinner, to his club, and to the theater. They went to see his famous Peacock Room at the home of Mr. and Mrs. Frederick Leyland and thought it "perfectly lovely."[44] But Whistler's eccentricities did surface. Lois was annoyed that he dispensed with all her beautiful clothes and had her pose instead in a drab riding habit (figure 71). She also wrote in her diary with some alarm: "[At the theater] Mr. Whistler came to our box and came home with us and it is now at 12:30 [and] he is sitting in the room talking and laughing."[45] At the end of the month all the children but Eddie, who stayed to finish his year at the École Monge, joined them in London, and the whole family departed for home, leaving Whistler to put finishing touches on the portrait and send it after them.

Whistler came to Paris about a week later for the opening of the Salon, to which he had sent a number of recent paintings. He visited the Cassatts, Degas, and in general made the rounds of all his Paris friends and left behind the usual tales of Whistlerian flamboyance. His companion on this trip was the young Oscar Wilde, whose presence exacerbated each encounter. Whistler told the Cassatts he was very pleased with Lois's portrait and expected

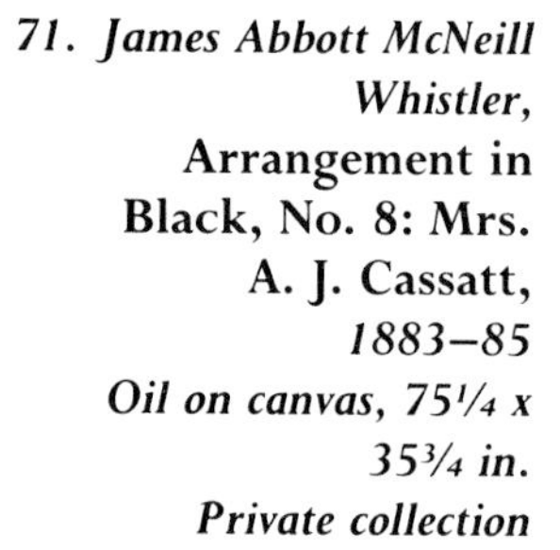

71. James Abbott McNeill Whistler, **Arrangement in Black, No. 8: Mrs. A. J. Cassatt,** *1883–85*
Oil on canvas, 75¼ x 35¾ in.
Private collection

to finish it soon, but to Mary he complained that Lois had not been willing to pose enough. As she wrote to Lois:

> Whistler has been awarded a third class medal at the Salon, he asked for one & the jury were determined to punish him for his nonsense by putting him

> in the 3rd class, he behaved like a fool here, he and Oscar Wilde together; Whistler told me he would have been glad of twenty-five minutes more on your portrait, he told me he did not make you stand much, you gave him but few sittings he said—[46]

The following fall Cassatt herself saw the portrait in London and admired it. As she told Aleck, "After all it is a work of Art, & as young Sargent said to Mother this afternoon, it is a good thing to have a portrait by Whistler in the family."[47] But as time went on the portrait was never sent, and it took several more years before the Cassatts could exert enough pressure on Whistler to finish it. After about a year and a half of waiting, Mary couldn't resist needling Lois, who was actually disappointed with the portrait itself, "I am sorry you don't like it, you remember I recommended Renoir but neither you nor Aleck liked what you saw of his; I think Whistler's picture very fine."[48]

Without the annual Impressionist exhibitions between 1882 and 1886, Cassatt lost the rhythm of the work year that had previously been so important to her. After recovering from Lydia's death in 1883, she was once again interrupted by her mother's ill health in 1884. That spring she took her mother to Spain for a change of climate and commuted back to Paris to find a new apartment with an elevator. The old fifth-floor apartment on Avenue Trudaine with its pure air and sweeping views of the city was no longer feasible for her mother. Cassatt signed a lease on a "small" apartment with three bedrooms, sitting room, dining room, kitchen, and accommodations for the two maids, Anna and Mathilde, located on the part now called Avenue Pierre Ier de Serbie of Rue Pierre Charron not far from the Place d'Iéna. The new apartment was elegant and in a very fashionable part of town, but Cassatt seems to have kept her studio and her ties to the old neighborhood around the Boulevard de Clichy.

The Cassatts began to entertain again after their period of mourning for Lydia. Very often they gathered their French and American friends together with Mary acting as translator whenever necessary. Her father had never become fluent in French and Lois always needed some extra help. They relied on their two maids to keep their home running smoothly, but Katherine Cassatt was the arbiter of excellence when it came to food and Robert Cassatt did the same with wine. Their Continental manners and practices, adopted on their first trip to Europe in the 1850s, were sometimes supplemented with American largess, such as abundant oysters and apples, which Aleck would ship to them whenever possible. Judging from Cassatt's paintings, it appears that her taste in furnishings was lighter and more modern than it had been in her studio on the Rue Laval.[49] Although the apartment was still full of interesting furniture and objects of all sorts, the walls were now painted white and the paintings that hung on them were in the colorful Impressionist palette.

Katherine Cassatt recovered rapidly once in her new home. Just after Christmas the family welcomed Aleck and Robbie for a short stay abroad. Once again Mary persuaded Aleck to sit for a portrait (she was not satisfied with either the 1880 or the 1883 versions), this time sitting with his son Robbie on the arm of his chair (figure 72). This portrait, with its juxtaposition of old and young faces, was her most idiosyncratic to date and did not please her enough to prevent her from making one more attempt at Aleck several years later.

It wasn't until 1885–86 that Cassatt's old work schedule was revived. After Aleck and Robbie went home and Mrs. Cassatt recovered her strength, the family regained a sense of normalcy. Mary worked steadily in her studio and even took up printmaking again, although this time in drypoint rather than etching. In 1884 and 1885 the family once again rented summer houses outside Paris where Cassatt could paint outdoors and ride through the forests to her heart's content. They could not face returning to Marly and Louveciennes, where Lydia was buried, and so looked in the area north of Paris and rented in Viarmes and Presles, successively. In the summer of 1885 Cassatt developed a bad case of bronchitis and was sent to the seashore for a few days to recover. Presumably it was there that she got the idea for her *Children on the Beach* (figure 73), her one and only attempt at a beach scene.

She had been exhibiting a few pictures here and there since 1882, when she no longer had the Impressionist exhibitions. Durand-Ruel showed two works in a small show he held in London in 1882 and three the following year in London in a larger and more important display of Impressionism. In 1884 she showed in the "Exposition du Cercle Artistique de la Seine," which was presumably one of many small group exhibitions that began to spring up in Paris after the Impressionists started theirs. She also sent pictures to New York for the annual exhibitions of the Society of American Artists in 1883, 1884, and 1886. There was talk of another Impressionist exhibition in Paris on and off during this time, and in the late fall of 1885 the idea finally caught hold. At the same time Durand-Ruel was trying to organize a major exhibition of Impressionist art in New York that would bring the style to that city for the first time in full force. After having no

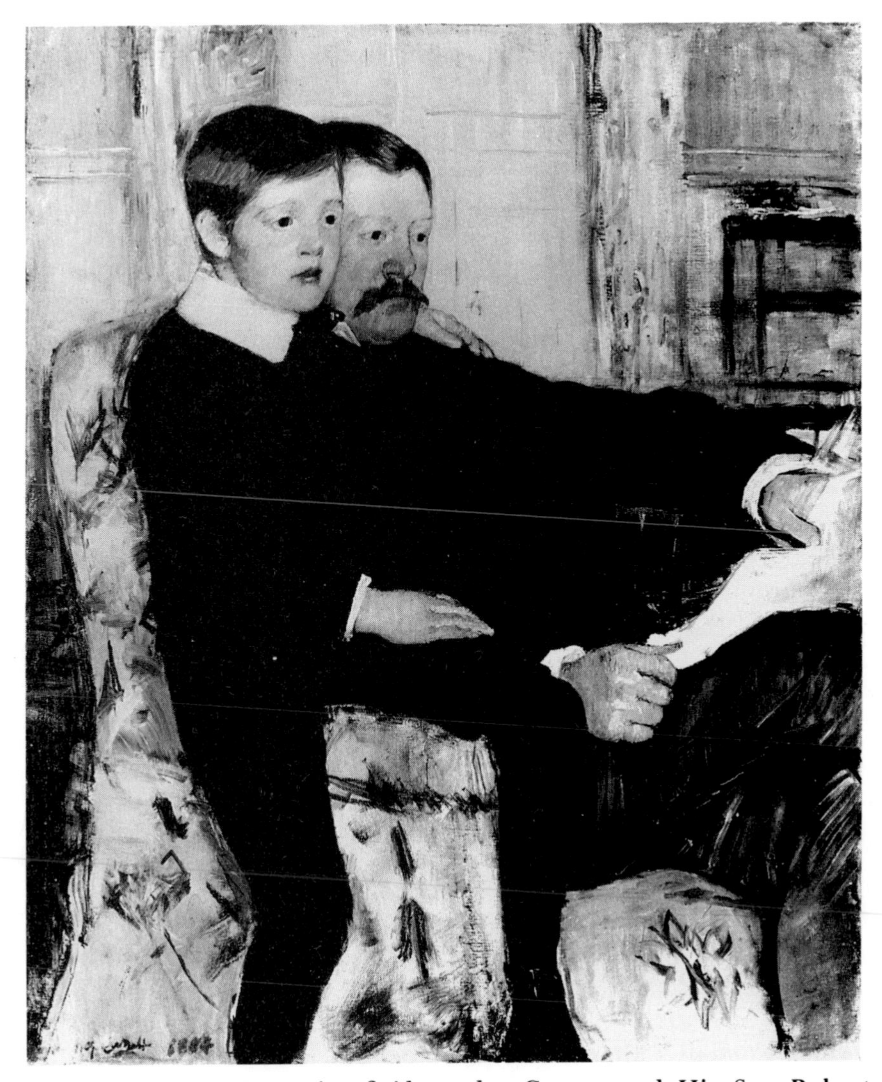

72. *Mary Cassatt,* **Portrait of Alexander Cassatt and His Son Robert Kelso,** *1885*
Oil on canvas, 39½ x 32 in.
Philadelphia Museum of Art; W. P. Wilstach Collection and gift of Mrs. William Cox Wright

exhibitions at all for three years Cassatt was suddenly caught up in two projects, both as an organizer and as an exhibitor.

Cassatt's friendship with Paul Durand-Ruel (figure 74) had grown with her importance in the Paris art market as an artist, a buyer, and an adviser

73. Mary Cassatt, **Children Playing on the Beach,** *1885*
Oil on canvas,
38⅜ x 29¼ in.
National Gallery of Art, Washington; Ailsa Mellon Bruce Collection

to others such as her brother and Louisine Elder. Durand-Ruel had inherited the business from his father in 1865 and immediately pursued two unusual avenues, the support of radical artists and an appeal to American tourists. Up to the mid-1880s neither of these had brought him great success, dependent as they were on the vagaries of the economic outlook, but he nevertheless maintained his gallery in the heart of the gallery district of

Paris. In 1885 Durand-Ruel devised a scheme to get a large number of Impressionist pictures to New York for an exhibition. The art market had been so bad in Paris for the previous few years that he was prepared to go to any lengths to sell the paintings that were languishing in his storeroom. An added twist to the scheme was that by sending the pictures for an exhibition and selling them there, he would circumvent the unusually stiff tariffs imposed by both the French government and the U.S. customs on the export of luxury goods. But, even with a commercial motive, Paul Durand-Ruel argued in his petition to the French ministry to sanction the operation as "cultural" and exempt it from French customs, the exhibition would save the future of French art by "remedying the current stagnant state of the art market which has so cruelly struck down a great number of our artists."[50] His petition was denied, but Durand-Ruel was able to make more money for his artists by his auction and sale of individual works in New York than if he had sold them to the same American collectors in Paris. American artists supported the lifting of the tariffs for Durand-Ruel's exhibition, and also a second exhibition that he immediately proposed, because of its educational value.[51]

Cassatt's role was relatively minor, but she did offer Durand-Ruel moral

74. Photograph of Paul Durand-Ruel, c. 1890
Document Archives Durand-Ruel, Paris

support in the midst of much opposition. She also gave him practical assistance in the form of introductions to her contacts in the New York art world and the full support of her brother Aleck, who lent to the show a large number of Impressionist works from his own collection. In fact, Aleck lent the only two works by his sister that were on view when the exhibition finally opened on April 10, 1886: the much loved "Family Group" and a portrait, probably the one of her mother reading *Le Figaro.* At this time neither Durand-Ruel nor Cassatt made much of Cassatt's potential appeal to an American audience, but that would soon change.

Meanwhile, back in Paris, the eighth group exhibition of the Impressionists was scheduled to open on May 15. This was of more immediate concern to Cassatt, who not only worked "like a beaver"[52] to finish enough new works to have a major showing, but also joined with Degas and Morisot to finance the exhibition. They engaged a posh suite in the art-gallery district where they were not far from the dealers Durand-Ruel, Petit (who was now competing with Durand-Ruel in Impressionist art), and Bernheim-Jeune. As usual the five rooms were apportioned according to what suited the works that finally arrived at the gallery on hanging day. Some artists' works were better hung together, like Degas's *Series of Nudes Bathing, Washing, Drying Themselves, Dressing and Being Dressed,* a group of ten pastels. Others seemed best hung in a group setting—such as the works of Seurat, Signac, Pissarro, and his son Lucien Pissarro that represented the new Neo-Impressionist style and were assigned their own room. Cassatt's seven paintings and one pastel were presumably mixed in with others by Morisot, Degas, Forain, and Marie Braquemond that were figural like hers rather than landscapes. Once again Monet, Renoir, and Sisley declined to participate.

Because of the inclusion of the Neo-Impressionists and also Redon, whose styles were quite removed from original Impressionism, this exhibition did not present to the world the same camaraderie as previous ones had, in spite of internal squabbles. Many beautiful and provocative works were shown, but neither the public nor the critics responded as they had in the past to the exhibition as an exciting wave of the future. Attendance was not as good as in previous years and the reviews were not as passionate. After the exhibition closed there was no talk of another one.

What were Mary Cassatt's thoughts as she walked around this exhibition, nine years after she had thrown in her lot with the Impressionists? Certainly she had the sense of a moment that had come and gone. She had already begun to put her Impressionist style behind her; the paintings hanging in this show were more solid and less "spontaneous" than her earlier theater pictures and interiors. The close-knit group of artists had also unraveled, leaving her on the fringes while Monet, Renoir, and Degas began to achieve not just success but fame. She was now apt to be left out of exhibitions of Impressionism organized by dealers other than Durand-Ruel, who saw the movement primarily in terms of Monet and landscape painting.

Nevertheless, she also had a great deal to be satisfied with after nine years of exhilaration and turbulence in her professional and personal life. She had earned the genuine respect of her colleagues in the Impressionist circle, as well as of the larger Parisian art world. She had taken a daring step with her art that achieved great results in refinement and originality. Her subject matter broadened, but the most extraordinary advances were in her mastery of nuances of light and dark, sensuous materials (including flesh), and psychological suggestion. Her drawing and composition had become more abstract and thus stronger and more interesting. She had brought her art into the modern world, while others like Elizabeth Gardner and Henry Bacon who were following more conservative paths remained in a mode that was soon to become obsolete. Her sales were strong and steady, and even if her prices remained a fraction of what Degas and Monet were getting, she could be sure her work was loved for itself and not for its investment value.

Cassatt knew that Impressionism as she had fallen in love with it was on the wane; she knew her own interests were leading her in other directions. What she did not know in 1886, at age forty-two, was that the best was yet to come.

Chapter VI

Her Prime

(1886–1893)

After having lived in Paris for over ten years and in Europe for twenty, Mary Cassatt no longer felt like a foreigner. Paris had opened up to her more completely than she had ever imagined it would. In fact, as friendly as it had become to Americans in the last ten years, no American was as wholeheartedly accepted as Mary Cassatt herself. She had gone beyond such token symbols of assimilation as acceptance into the Salon, permanent residence in the city, or even, as Elizabeth Gardner was to do, marriage to a Frenchman. By virtue of her wit, curiosity, and creative authority, she gained entry into French intellectual circles that were normally closed to outsiders. Many Americans in Paris in those years, blinded by their quest for acceptance by the French art establishment and high society, did not even perceive the modest groups of artists, writers, and collectors who were quietly producing the paintings and books that were beginning to dominate worldwide culture.

For Cassatt, ensconced as she now was in her French cultural niche, the increasing numbers of Americans flooding the city imposed a burden that would take years for her to adjust to. She had chosen an expatriate life because she preferred, even craved, the intellectual and cultural values of Europeans, particularly the French. She had learned to avoid the American colony, made up as it was of social climbers and pleasure seekers. As more and more Americans found the means and the opportunity to travel abroad, Cassatt found herself surrounded by old friends and family from back home, young eager acolytes in the art world, and others she could not ignore. Cassatt was also brought back into American social circles by her desire to promote modern art. She found that there was interest in her school among American collectors and saw a chance to channel Impressionist art as well as a great deal of important old master art into American public and private galleries. Although she became more French in her personal habits over the years, she became increasingly entangled with American taste and culture in spite of herself.

For the first year after the Impressionist exhibition of 1886, Cassatt busied herself with her regular routine. She spent the summer at Arques-la-Bataille (near Dieppe) with her parents and in the fall continued her dealings with Durand-Ruel, who was attempting to send another batch of Impressionist paintings to New York. There is no way of pinning down the course of her own work at this time, since she did not have the usual Impressionist exhibition in the spring to reveal her previous year's direction, but presumably she picked up where she had left off the spring before. Outside of her work, the two most remarkable occurences of the 1886–87 winter were the birth of a new nephew, Gardner Cassatt's first child, also called Gardner, and the move to a new apartment at 10, Rue de Marignan, where Mary and her parents remained for the rest of their lives.

The following year (1887–88) was much more eventful owing mainly to the year-long residence in Paris of the Alexander Cassatts and the brief visit of Gardner and Jennie Cassatt with their new baby during the winter. Mary and the elder Cassatts had once again taken a house for the summer at Arques-la-Bataille, where they were joined by Alexander, Lois, and the children. In the fall they all settled back in Paris; the children attended French schools and Eddie, now eighteen (figure 75), entered Saint-Cyr, the distinguished military academy.

Mary Cassatt's routine was interrupted not only by the usual demands of her visiting relatives, but by the sudden decline of both her parents. This time her father demanded most of her attention with his first serious illness at the age of eighty-one. All winter he was afflicted with swollen legs that suddenly prevented him from taking his daily miles-long walks through Paris and his usual strenuous rides on horseback. Now he could barely hobble around the apartment with a cane. With Mrs. Cassatt also in poor health, the household at 10, Rue de Marignan was in an upheaval. At times Mary was so consumed with nursing her parents that she felt she could not leave the apartment even to have dinner with her brother. Lois further warmed toward her sister-in-law as she saw Mary under such trying conditions. They put aside their old competitive ways and agreed to respect each other's opinions and accomplishments. Lois even saw the fundamental generosity in

75. Photograph of Edward Buchanan Cassatt, 1885 Private collection

her sister-in-law that had been well hidden from her and many others Mary had turned away from over the years. Lois wrote to her sister Harriet, who had also known Mary Cassatt for decades, "[Mary] is the kindest soul in the world. . . . Don't read this to *all* hands."[1]

A symbol of their hard-won closeness is the pastel portrait Mary did of Lois at this time. After four portraits of Aleck, one for each visit since 1880, Mary finally offered or Lois finally agreed to sit for her own (figure 76). Knowing Lois's objections to the portrait Whistler had done—that he forced her to pose in a drab riding habit and did not make her face enough of a likeness—Mary let her wear one of the sumptuous gowns Lois loved to shop for in Paris and made sure that the face was as "like" as possible. Lois was a brave woman to subject herself to her sister-in-law's scrutiny, knowing as she probably did the fate of even acknowledged beauties, such as Mrs. Riddle, at Mary Cassatt's hands. Lois was never a beauty and Mary was never a flatterer. Consequently the face that looks out from Lois's portrait with its abstracted stare is stark, in contrast to the extravagance of the blue silk gown. Lois's slightly bulbous nose, her unflinching mouth, and her chunky neck, a sign of the weight Lois was powerless to keep from gaining as she approached middle age, are only just counterbalanced by the beauty of her upright posture and soft auburn coloring. Lois's response to the portrait is unrecorded, but it is a good sign that the newfound cordial relationship between the two survived such a confrontation of personalities in the close quarters of Mary's studio.

Aleck's pastel portrait done about the same time is less complicated and more flattering (figure 77). In comparison with Lois's, his face is relaxed and youthful in spite of the commanding pose his sister elicited from him. He was, at age forty-eight, a happy man. In the five years since his retirement from the Pennsylvania Railroad he had done enough railroad business to keep his hand in, and the rest of his time he devoted to raising and competing thoroughbred racehorses. He had set up a farm in Chester County, called Chesterbrook, for this purpose and become internationally known for the quality of his stable. In the 1880s he raced three champions —Rica, the Bard, and Eurus—whose triumphs and losses were closely followed by all the members of the family through the racing news. Aleck's eye for beauty and distinction, very much like his sister's, was his greatest asset in building up his stable. In fact, Aleck's choice of horse racing as an avocation was probably as close as he could come to being an artist. With his love of the finest of horses and his frequent trips abroad, he duplicated his sister's exotic life in his own way.

One last portrait from this year is small in size but of great significance in terms of Mary Cassatt's family relationships and her art. This is the

76. *Mary Cassatt,* **Mrs. Alexander J. Cassatt Seated at a Tapestry Frame,** *1888*
Pastel, 32 x 25 in.
Private collection

portrait of her other sister-in-law, Jennie Carter Cassatt, and her baby, Gardner, which was done as a print (drypoint) rather than as a pastel or painting (figure 78). Jennie and Gard had made several trips to Paris since their marriage in 1882, and Mary had already painted at least one portrait of Jennie, who was a lively woman eleven years younger than her new sister-in-law. On this side of the family it was Jennie, not her husband, who was the willing sitter to Mary's brush. There are several portraits of Jennie over the years, but only one quick drypoint sketch exists of Gard (figure 79) which was probably done at the same time as the sketch of Jennie and the baby, and no other known portraits.

Mary and her parents adored Gard's new wife, who came into the family without the unfortunate baggage that Lois dragged with her. When her first baby was born, they were ecstatic. Jennie had won Mary's heart for good when she diplomatically chose Ellen Mary for the baby's name should it be a girl. Mary was briefly disappointed at the news of a son and blurted out, "I would have been more delighted if it had been a girl,"[2] but in the end she welcomed the baby with great affection.

Little Gardner Cassatt had a difficult beginning; he was weak and sickly, and the family despaired of his surviving his first winter. A year later, when the family came to Paris, he had grown into a fat and happy child. Whether it was this miraculous turnaround in his health, or whether it was his auspicious arrival into the family when the eldest Cassatts seemed on the verge of leaving it, the child inspired in Mary Cassatt deep emotions that she immediately translated into art. Her portrait of Jennie and little Gard is the earliest dated[3] example in a series of mother and child images that would grow into her greatest body of work and her signature theme for the next thirty years. Cassatt had flirted with the theme before, producing a few scattered paintings and pastels mixed among her standard images of modern life, but now she began to repeat the subject in a serial manner, often to the virtual exclusion of any other subject.

Cassatt surely saw the irony in making maternity her signature theme. She who had no husband or children herself broke the rules of nineteenth-century naturalism in devoting herself to a subject outside her own experience. Furthermore, she put herself at risk of having every critic and writer on her art point out her childless state and speculate on her motivation for indulging in the theme. For example, in 1890, in one of the first articles ever written on her the author discusses her mother and child pictures in glowing terms and then cannot resist pointing out her childlessness: "In fact, and I hope she will pardon us for mentioning this detail, which lets the

77. *Mary Cassatt,* Portrait of Alexander J. Cassatt, *1888*
Pastel, 35½ x 27¾ in.
Seattle Art Museum; gift of Mr. and Mrs. Louis Brechemin, by exchange, 88.154
Photo credit: Paul Macapia

78. Mary Cassatt, **Gardner Held by His Mother,** *1888*
Drypoint, 8¼ x 5 7/16 in.
Print Collection, Miriam and Ira D. Wallach Division of Art, Prints and Photographs, The New York Public Library; Astor, Lenox and Tilden Foundations

79. *Mary Cassatt,* **Mr. Gardner Cassatt Reading the Newspaper,** *c. 1888 Etching and drypoint, 10⅞ x 6⅞ in. Print Collection, Miriam and Ira D. Wallach Division of Art, Prints and Photographs, The New York Public Library; Astor, Lenox and Tilden Foundations*

reader glimpse a corner of her private life, Miss Cassatt has devoted herself to Art as other women have to religion. Miss Cassatt is not married."[4] Cassatt could not have been pleased by this picture of herself as an "artistic" nun; nothing could have been further from the truth of her intensely social and richly woven life. A less courageous artist and woman might have backed off from a course that put her own womanhood on trial.

In the final analysis we don't know what motivated her or how she felt about the spotlight that was instantly beamed onto her personal life; she left no record of her thoughts on these matters. A reasonable guess is that she had begun the mother and child subjects quite innocently—with portraits of family and friends—and, in her typical manner, didn't give a thought to what the world's reaction might be. Then, once the theme had entwined itself around her heart, she persevered in what she profoundly sensed was the right track and turned her back on intrusive or demeaning criticism. She probably could not explain, even to herself, why she felt justified in claiming the subject as her own; she only knew that in her hands motherhood was understood and ennobled as it had seldom been before.

Beyond the initial irony, of course, there was a flood of reasons why this childless woman became the great interpreter of maternity. First and foremost were her years of training in old master art as well as the painting of modern life. From the former, she learned the classic subjects and the transcendent themes; from the latter, she learned to penetrate real experience and to paint it with all the subtlety and nuance of the modern world. Her years of painting women lost in thought and children posing without guile made it possible for her to master quickly the possibilities of putting the women and children together. The result was a universality of expression that was worthy of Western artists as far back as Giotto and a freshness that spoke to the present—and the future.

The idea that Cassatt's mother and child paintings broke the rules of naturalism stems from an impossibly narrow reading of the realist theory of the day. Certainly artists went to great lengths to paint from their own environment and experience, but Degas, for example, was not criticized for painting jockeys, ballet dancers, or prostitutes without having been any of them. The requirement was rather to study a familiar subject and enter into its spirit as fully as possible. This Cassatt surely did with ease, taking advantage of the numerous mothers with children among her own family and friends and, when these failed her, engaging professional models to enact the mother and child poses. She had a special way with children, which was acknowledged even by such stern judges as Lois Cassatt, and found that she could call up from her own experience the care, nurturance, and love of a helpless creature. Her nursing of her sister in the final terrifying stages of her degenerative disease was still fresh in her mind. It is hardly coincidental that her first series of images of tender maternal solicitation began when her aging parents began to depend so completely on her. To everyone's surprise, including probably her own, Cassatt turned out to be an excellent nurse. This instinct for calm comfort and silent affection was what made her mother and child pictures so moving and so true.

Did the maternal scenes also reveal a yearning for the children that Mary Cassatt never had? Certainly there is an element of this. The way Cassatt paints a mother pressing her own cheek against the soft, dimpled cheek of her child makes even the most jaded observer yearn for such an exquisite sensory and emotional experience (figure 80). As many nieces and nephews as Cassatt held in her arms over the years, she never knew the complete joy of such intimacy with a child of her own flesh. She believed that motherhood

80. *Mary Cassatt,* **Hélène de Septeuil,** *1889–90* *Pastel,* *25⅞ x 16½ in.* *The William Benton Museum of Art; Louise Crombie Beach Memorial Collection*

was one of the great rights and imperatives of womanhood and was keenly aware that she had missed it.

At the same time, it is safe to say that she did not elevate her own childlessness into a personal tragedy that could be relieved only by painting pictures of children. In many ways she saw herself as an exception among women—she worked, she handled her own money, and she functioned in a largely male professional world. She did not feel the loss that a woman who was childless and "at home" might feel. Her degree of desire for children was enough to enhance her paintings of motherhood, but not enough to force her to turn to painting as a substitute. Nor was her desire great enough to seek a marriage and children, which she might still have done at age forty-three when she began her maternity series. In the end, she preferred to paint children than to have them.

The emphasis on transcendent human emotions rather than the manners and fashions of contemporary life separates Cassatt's mothers and children very neatly from her Impressionist subjects and indicates the general change in cultural direction that had taken place in the mid-1880s. By the time the Impressionists opened their eighth and last exhibition in 1886, the signs of change were everywhere—in music, literature, and art, including the presence of the mysterious art of Redon and the startlingly theoretical style of Seurat and the other neo-Impressionists within the Impressionist exhibition itself. The period now designated as Postimpressionist encouraged deviations from the naturalist norm of the Impressionists and would eventually embrace a range of styles from Cézanne's structural abstractions to the neo-spiritualism of Gauguin and his followers who called themselves Nabis ("prophets"). Cassatt's own departure into the time-honored mother and child subject with its Madonnaesque fragrance suited the temper of the new times.

After the last of the Philadelphia Cassatt family members left in the summer of 1888, the Paris Cassatts retreated to Fontainebleau for the rest of the season. At Fontainebleau and back home in Paris, Mary worked away at her mother and child compositions in prints and in painting (figure 81). Miraculously both her parents recovered from their illnesses of the winter before and left her freer to work than she had been in some time. It began to seem like old times when she and a group of her artist friends, including Degas, Pissarro, and Bracquemond, organized themselves once more into an exhibiting society of "painter-printmakers" and opened a show at the end of January 1889. Cassatt showed only three things—one pastel and two prints—but it was enough to get her back into a regular routine. When the group decided to make this an annual exhibition, spurred by Durand-Ruel, whose gallery hosted the event, Cassatt suddenly had a focus for each year's work as she had had in the Salon and the Impressionist exhibitions earlier in her career.

In the next year Cassatt produced her first great series of prints, she renewed her friendship with Louisine Elder (now Havemeyer), and she broke her leg, all of which were signs that she was back to her old level of activity after several years of emotional and family distractions. In May of 1889 she turned forty-five, a good age for taking stock. She had to acknowledge that she was no longer the rising young star she had been when she first knocked on the establishment's door and then joined the renegade Impressionists. Now others held the spotlight in the Salons and in the increasingly popular independent exhibitions. The younger artists developed new styles that were even more daring than Impressionism, and in her own

81. Mary Cassatt,
Baby's Back,
1889–90
Drypoint,
9 3/16 x 6 7/16
Collection of the Library of Congress

camp the big names—Monet, Renoir, and Degas—were beginning to surpass the rest. Cassatt had pulled back in the mid-1880s, letting this happen with little sign of a struggle while she coped with illness, old age, and death among those dearest to her. Now that her life had stabilized and she had the inspiration of a new baby in the family, she began to fight to regain her rightful place in the Parisian art world. She was no longer young, but she began to realize she was not old either. She had merely entered a new phase: her prime.

Mary Cassatt in her prime was different from the brash, careless, and ambitious young woman who had come to Paris in 1865. Although she was still fond of saying she was intent on "fame and money,"[5] she had become decidedly more polished in seeking it. She continued to see her old friends Degas, Morisot, and Pissarro, but her most important alliances were no longer with artists but with collectors like the Havemeyers and dealers like Paul Durand-Ruel and his sons. She continued to take chances in her art, but she was no longer interested in the excitement of the avant-garde and was happier to be associated with those who tempered their love of modern art with the art of the past. Some of the other Impressionists like Degas and Pissarro had begun showing in Théo van Gogh's more radical gallery of modern art at Boussod and Valadon, but Cassatt grew closer to Durand-Ruel at a time when he was starting to seem a little old-fashioned. She sought the company of those whose artistic statements were less bold, but more meaningful.

Cassatt's appetite for conflict had lessened in her personal manners as well. She now avoided Degas at times when she did not have the strength to defend herself against his wicked tongue and preferred the company of the gentle Camille Pissarro. She was still capable of stunning frankness in her opinions, but had learned to voice them only to her oldest and best friends like Louisine Havemeyer. To others she was now the soul of diplomacy and seldom found herself caught in a web of betrayals and hurt feelings as she had been as a young woman. In appearance she was perhaps more angular than ever, since she tended to be on the thin side when her health was bad, but she was still very strong and graceful and dressed in the most elegant clothes. Like a character in one of Henry James's later novels, Europe had smoothed away her rough edges, just as the character Chad Newsome in *The Ambassadors* was discovered to be changed after his years in Paris:

> Chad was brown and thick and strong, and of old Chad had been rough. Was all the difference therefore that he was actually smooth? Possibly; for that he *was* smooth was as marked as in the taste of a sauce or in the rub of a hand. The effect of it was general—it had retouched his features, drawn them with a cleaner line . . . it had toned his voice, established his accent, encouraged his smile to more play and his other motions to less . . . It was as if in short he had really . . . been put into a firm mold and turned successfully out.[6]

Cassatt's smoothness was not an overrefinement, as in some of James's characters, but it was equally the product of her years in Paris and her increasing love of the finest things of life.

This same smoothness can be seen in Cassatt's art from this time forward. Her brushstrokes no longer have the Impressionist choppiness of the old days; instead her surfaces in oil are creamy, her lines in pastel are long and velvety, and the delicate drypoint hatching in her prints describes the softest materials. There are still many unfinished passages and puzzling areas where she changed her mind, but her new work was intended to beguile rather than challenge the viewer. In fact, in many instances Cassatt deliberately chose a sturdy, unattractive model (figure 82) in order that she might

82. *Mary Cassatt,* **Woman with a Red Zinnia,** *1892*
Oil on canvas, 28¾ x 23¾ in.
The National Gallery of Art, Washington; Chester Dale Collection

transform her model's roughness into the smoothness of her art just as James's character Chad had been given "a form and a surface, almost a design."[7]

Mary Cassatt also began living in a grander style than ever before. Money problems no longer cropped up in the correspondence to Aleck and Gard. The new fifth-floor apartment on Rue de Marignan was large and sunny, with enough rooms to house the family and their two maids and give Mary a studio. The Cassatts were also able to keep their horse and carriage in the stables behind the courtyard. The family's pet was the little Brussels griffon, Battie, who accompanied his mistress everywhere, mostly riding in her arms. In the summer of 1889 they rented their largest summer home yet, the mansion called Les Tournelles, situated on the top of the hill rising behind the small village of Septeuil about thirty miles west of Paris. The three Cassatts with their two servants rattled around the big house and its parklike grounds overlooking the rolling plains of this fertile agricultural region. Septeuil was not a well-known artists' haunt, but several artists lived in Les Tournelles over the years, such as the landscape painter Antoine Chintreuil, who was buried on the grounds, and later the genre painter Léon Lhermitte. Like many of the old French country houses, it is now occupied by a private school. Cassatt broke her leg in a fall from her horse that summer, but not before she managed to engage some local people to pose for the pastels and prints she was working on, including a young child named Hélène, who appears in several mother and child compositions dressed in a chic blue plaid coat and wide-brimmed hat (figure 80). The woman holding Hélène is Cassatt's maid, Mathilde Valet, on one of the rare occasions the artist persuaded Mathilde to pose.

Back in Paris that fall she was reunited with Louisine Havemeyer, who hadn't been to Europe since 1883 (figure 83). "Louie" and her husband had come to see the World's Fair held in Paris that year, featuring the new Eiffel Tower, and to tour the Continent. She found her old friend incapacitated: "I found her in bed with a broken leg. Her horse had slipped upon the pavement of the Champs Élysées[8] and she sustained a bad fracture of the leg. The poor creature was forced to give up work and lie still for several weeks. She was very dear and cordial. . . ."[9] The two women were glad to renew their friendship, since both were entering very active stages when they needed someone of a similar energetic and practical frame of mind. They quickly found that their interests coincided—Havemeyer in collecting and Cassatt in the art market in general—and found much to stimulate their correspondence and frequent rendezvous in Europe. In addition, Mary Cassatt took an instant liking to Harry Havemeyer, the balding, round man Louisine had married, who had a passion for collecting and business, much like Mary's own brother Aleck. The Havemeyers cut their trip short that fall to return home and nurse one of their children through a sudden illness.

83. ***Photograph of the Havemeyer family, 1888***
(from left: Horace, Louisine, Electra, Harry, Adaline)
Courtesy of J. Watson Webb, Jr.

But once contact between the two women had been reestablished, their relationship continued for the rest of their lives.

By the following spring of 1890 Cassatt had finished two series of prints to show in the second exhibition of Painter-Printmakers held in March. The first, a series of twelve drypoints, was so successful among French amateurs that Durand-Ruel was able to sell them as sets rather than as individual prints. Cassatt's method was to draw a delicate web of lines with the diamond-tipped drypoint needle directly into the copper plate and then ink and print the the plates herself on the small press she had bought for her studio. This technique made the images of women and children (six were maternal subjects and six were other scenes of women visiting, playing the mandoline, trying on a bonnet, etc.) seem to materialize partially and then trail off toward the edges (see figure 81). Although the prints were small (all were under nine by six inches), they formed a display as impressive as any Cassatt had had in the earlier Impressionist exhibitions.

Buoyed by the success of her drypoint series, Cassatt was once again full of printmaking—as passionate as she had once been in her first round of experimentation with Degas on the print journal *Le Jour et la nuit.* Barely three weeks later her printmaking was to receive another boost in the form of the enormous exhibition of Japanese woodcut prints that opened at the École des Beaux-Arts on April 15. The sight of hundreds of these ukiyo-e prints, showing scenes of everyday Japanese life usually in bold colors and designs, drove Cassatt into raptures reminiscent of the old days of exploration and discovery. As she had written to Emily Sartain decades ago urging her to come to Madrid to see the Velásquezes, now she wrote to Berthe Morisot with the same urgency. Asking her to come to lunch and go with her to the exhibition, Cassatt once more underlined her words, "Seriously, *you must not* miss it. You who want to make color prints, you couldn't imagine anything more beautiful. I dream of doing it myself and can't think of anything else but color on copper. . . . P.S. You *must* see the Japanese—*come as soon as you can.*"[10]

Berthe Morisot was more accommodating than Emily Sartain and joined her friend for a day of lunch and art in the city (figure 84). She and her family had already moved out to the country for the season on account of her husband's failing health, renting a house in Mézy-sur-Seine, outside Paris in the direction of Septeuil. The two women saw a great deal of each other these days; their social round of dinners with Degas, Mallarmé, and others in Paris still continued and they visited each other frequently during summers in the country. Exhibitions of their art were beginning to pick up again as they both participated in group exhibitions, such as the Painter-Printmakers, and as Durand-Ruel gave them more exposure in his gallery. The vogue of color printmaking set off by the Japanese exhibition at the École des Beaux-Arts that spring also brought them together. When they retired to their neighboring country houses for the summer, both began series or "portfolios" of prints in the Japanese manner. The ten miles between Septeuil, where the Cassatts were once again comfortably ensconced, and Mézy, Morisot's home for the summer, were easily traversed by carriage, and the two spurred each other on in their new endeavors.

84. Berthe Morisot, **The Drawing Lesson (Self-Portrait with Julie),** ***1888–90 Drypoint, 7³⁄₁₆ x 5³⁄₈ in. National Gallery of Art, Washington; Rosenwald Collection***

Morisot's idea was to make a series of color lithographs featuring her daughter Julie, who was just turning eleven years old. Her husband's illness and other demands on her time prevented her from finishing more than a few drawings and one lithograph for the portfolio. Cassatt was more fortunate, for a change, in her family circumstances. Aleck came for a few weeks that summer with Katharine and Robbie but was no trouble. She attacked her project with youthful zeal. Even a second accident did not deter her; the accident, which occurred in Paris days before they were to move out to the country, left Cassatt with a black eye and a vivid story to tell her friends: "You would have heard from me before now . . . if I had not had another accident—I was thrown from my carriage on the stones at the corner of the rue Pierre Charron & the Place de Iena & as I alighted on my forehead, I have had the blackest eye I suppose any one was ever disfigured with—The carriage was kicked to pieces, the coachman pitched out & even the dog wounded; & all because a man driving a van thought he would amuse himself cracking his whip at my cob's head, finding it frightened her. He leaned out of his wagon & continued his amusement until he drove her nearly mad with fright & then he drove off smiling!"[11]

As soon as the doctor allowed her to move, she packed up her printing press and settled at Septeuil. What she began there mushroomed into a project that consumed all her time and energy for the next nine months. It turned out to be a set of ten prints much like her series of twelve the previous year, but with the added challenge of printing in full color rather than in simple black ink (figure 85). Adding color meant not only thinking differently about how the compositions were designed, but it meant complications in technique and printing—involving more than one plate per print—that ultimately called for the assistance of a professional printer. In the end Cassatt printed each composition twenty-five times, for a total of

85. *Mary Cassatt,* **The Letter,** *1890–91*
Soft-ground etching, drypoint, and aquatint, 13⅝ x 8¹⁵⁄₁₆ in.
National Gallery of Art, Washington; Chester Dale Collection

250 color prints, each of which was hand-inked by the artist and became a unique work of art. Today these are among the most valuable prints of the nineteenth century.

Cassatt had planned to unveil her new set of prints at the next Painter-Printmakers' exhibition in the spring of 1891. To her disgust, the organizers of the exhibition gave vent to feelings of xenophobia and declared that the society and its exhibitions would henceforth be only for *French* artists. Their intention was to keep out the American and other foreign artists whose invasion of Paris threatened to overwhelm the native culture and fabric of life. They had not intended to insult their old friends, such as Mary Cassatt and Camille Pissarro, who had been absorbed into French circles but had never become French citizens. Cassatt and Pissarro, a Danish national, did take offense, and went to Durand-Ruel, who was once again hosting the exhibition, to mediate. Durand-Ruel's solution was to give the two "outsiders" their own rooms within his commodious gallery on the Rue Pelletier, with entrance on the Rue Lafitte, where they could show their latest efforts alongside the larger exhibition of the "patriots." Cassatt even had her own catalog printed up and enjoyed the idea that she would have her first solo exhibition. Pissarro apparently did not have a catalog, but Cassatt may have insisted on one because the two concurrent exhibitions at Durand-Ruel—the Painter-Printmakers' exhibition and a small show of the paintings and drawings of Berthe Morisot—both had them.

Cassatt's offerings included the ten color prints she had produced with such difficulty in the last year, hanging alongside two paintings and two pastels of mothers and children probably done at Septeuil. Pissarro's show consisted of about thirty etchings, gouaches, watercolors, pastels, and fans; Morisot's apparently included fewer than fifteen oil sketches and drawings in colored pencil from her summer at Mézy. Cassatt was once again in good company, where the strength of her work guaranteed her share of recognition among distinguished peers. The perceptive Symbolist critic Félix Fénéon surveyed the ten prints of women shown in daily activities—caring for their children, writing letters, being fitted by a seamstress—and recorded his impressions:

> [Cassatt's] physiognomic observation of these women and children is fine, calm. It is without self-consciousness that the letter-writer is caught going over what she has just written in the letter and how she hesitates to finally seal it; or how this "Young woman trying on a dress" betrays a fugitive restlessness that comes from her curiosity to turn and see the whole. And

> always, always, the large hands, the beautiful masculine hands that Cassatt loves to give her women, have a role in the design, especially when they are set off against the bodies of nude children and cause a disruption of the delicate lines; but then all the lines once more flow together to create unexpected arabesques.[12]

Fénéon appreciated Cassatt's subtleties of design and psychology as much as Degas, Pissarro, and Morisot did, and such rare perceptive reviews stood out against the morass of ordinary newspaper criticism that Cassatt had long ago stopped reading. She may have been equally surprised to see that her old nemesis *The American Register* had softened toward her. In its brief notice it pronounced the exhibition by "the well-known American artist, Miss Mary Cassatt" to be "decidedly worth a close inspection."[13]

The success of the exhibition made Cassatt yearn for bigger and better things—a larger exhibition, more publicity, greater visibility in her own country. All these demands she presented to Durand-Ruel, who by now had a contract to be her exclusive dealer. He tried to mollify her with plans for a large exhibition in the fall in New York, but she still felt he should be doing more. Degas and Pissarro were also unhappy with their old dealer, and the three plotted to get ahead without him. Pissarro (figure 86) recounted a meeting he had with her toward the end of April, while their exhibitions were still up at Durand-Ruel's:

86. Photograph of Camille Pissarro, c. 1893
Document Archives Durand-Ruel, Paris

> We had a long talk about the problem of selling pictures, I told her about my position *vis-a-vis* Durand; she is incensed at Durand on her own account and asked me if I would go along with her if she left Durand. We will probably exhibit with Degas. She will use all the influence she has to push our paintings and engravings in New York, she is very desirous of upsetting Durand. She has a lot of influence and Durand, who suspects that she is irritated with him, is trying to calm her down with promises and offers which he does not make good.[14]

In the end Cassatt's ruffled feelings were smoothed over—although she did not have an exhibition in New York in the fall and had to wait two more years before he gave her a major exhibition in Paris.

Success also brought problems in other quarters. After the exhibition opened, a dinner was given at the home of Cassatt's good friend Albert Bartholomé, the painter and sculptor. The group assembled no doubt included all of the old crowd, including Degas, Pissarro, Caillebotte, Renoir, Zandomeneghi and Morisot. Reunions of this sort brought out the biting sarcasm that had gotten them all together in the first place. On this occasion, as Cassatt had been honored with her own gallery in the exhibition, she became the honored target. Although she no doubt held her own in such company, she was no longer accustomed to verbal abuse, and confided to her biographer years later that she left the party "toute bouleversée" (totally upset) and very near tears.[15] Cassatt had had the courage to make these people her friends, and although she gained immensely from the relationships, she also paid a high price.

On the whole, Cassatt went off to the country happy that year. She had found yet another summer home—this time it was the most remote in which the Cassatts had ever lived. The area was northwest of Paris, fifty miles out of the city, an area with which she had become acquainted through Camille Pissarro. In 1883 Pissarro moved his large family to the small town of Eragny, not far from Gisors, on the river Epte. Over the years Pissarro had offered to look in his area for summer estates for the Cassatts, but they had never before needed his help. It is most likely that through Pissarro they found the Château de Bachivillers that year and immediately fell in love with the rolling landscape of the great valley of the Seine and Oise. The house, although only a hundred years old, was built in a classic French style—brick with vast sloping roofs over the central block and its two wings (figure 87). A grand allée bordered by linden trees formed the approach to the house from the countryside, but on

87. *View of the Château de Bachivillers*

the other side the house was close to the main street of Bachivillers and surrounded by the barns of the working farm. The Cassatts enjoyed the fresh farm produce supplied to them by their landlord as well as the "excellent rich milk at 3 sous bottle or quart and the gardener brings us every morning an ample nay generous supply of fruit and vegetables."[16] With no expected visitors from Philadelphia—a proposed trip by Eddie did not materialize—Mary looked forward to a summer of uninterrupted work. Her mother reported her activities with her usual mixture of wit, partiality, and concern:

> Mary is at work again, intent on fame & money she says, & counts on her fellow country men now that she has made a reputation here—I hope she will be more lucky than she is in horseflesh—her new horse has been down—this time when driving him—Mary firmly believes she has bad luck & it looks like it—happily for her she is immensely interested in her painting & bent on doing something on a larger canvas as good as her pictures of last summer which were considered very fine by critics & amateurs, one of them could have been sold ten times but Durand-Ruel said he bought it for himself—you will probably see that one in New York next fall or winter. After all a woman who is not married is lucky if she has a decided love for work of any kind & the more absorbing it is the better.[17]

Mary's mother loved her daughter and admired her accomplishments, but she could not prevent a note of sadness from escaping when she discussed her daughter's professional life. Katherine Johnston Cassatt had taken a different course, and now she was in the mood to look back on it wistfully. Married at nineteen to a man who made his fortune in Pittsburgh and carried her off to Philadelphia and then Paris, she made a rich life out of her concerns for her husband and children and took pride in the excellence of her home. Now the hub of that life for fifty-six years, Robert Simpson Cassatt, was failing. The illness that had struck him four years ago returned and this time could not be set right. Although he loved the country and still took a daily drive, he had not been well since he left Paris. With his usual clear vision, he summed up the situation to Aleck:

> I have been *very* unwell I may say ever since we came out—I need not particularize—Old age—general breaking up probably. . . . Swollen feet and legs, heart and lungs affected, stomach out of order . . . Why I keep on telling you all this I don't know so I stop with a God bless & keep you all.[18]

Robert Cassatt survived until the family moved back to Paris, and he died on December 7, 1891, at the age of eighty-five. His passing left a painful gap in the life Katherine Cassatt and her daughter Mary had constructed for themselves in the country so distant from their birthplace. Katherine Cassatt, at seventy-five, would not recover from the loss, but merely continue on, closer than ever to her daughter. Mary Cassatt, at age forty-six, was still in her prime, and although she would always suffer from the loss of the man Lois once said was "the only being she seems to think of,"[19] she would regain her footing and go on. In the short run, this would be accomplished by a change of scene and her usual cure: hard work.

Days before Robert Cassatt died, Jenny Cassatt and little Gardner arrived in Paris. The sociable sister-in-law was a great help to Mary in the distressing aftermath of her father's death. The two women had planned to travel south that winter in any case, and changed their itinerary to the South of France for the health of Katherine Cassatt. In February of 1892 they found their way from Cannes to the small peninsula of the Cap d'Antibes, where they rented a villa at the highest point. The warm weather and beautiful views from their windows were soothing to all members of the mourning family, and for several years they repeated the journey to the south to escape the dreary Paris winters.

Ever since the success of her exhibition of color prints, Cassatt had longed for bigger projects and a larger audience. The death of her father threw her off course. Normally it would have taken her many months before she could pull herself together and decide what to do next. Instead she was suddenly jolted out of her mourning as soon as she, her mother, Jennie, and little Gard got back to Paris that spring. She was visited by a woman she had met a few years before, Bertha Honoré Palmer, a Chicago art collector and wife of the wealthy hotel owner Potter Palmer. With her was their mutual friend Sarah Hallowell, a woman who had turned her love of art and her organizational genius to the growing business of organizing international art exhibitions. Hallowell had a home in Moret, a village in the Fontainebleau forest, and may have been the reason for the Cassatts' stay there in the summer of 1888.

Palmer and Hallowell were not making a social call to 10, Rue de Marignan, on this occasion. Their mission was to invite Mary Cassatt to paint the most important mural a woman would paint in that century: a mural depicting *Modern Woman* for the imposing pavilion simply called the Woman's Building of the largest world's fair ever held—the World's Columbian Exposition held in Chicago in 1893. The mural was one of two that would face each other from the end walls of the Hall of Honor in 12- by 58-foot spaces that curved to fit the barrel-vaulted glass roof (figure 88). The opposite mural, called *Primitive Woman,* would serve as a counterpoint to *Modern Woman* to show that women have risen to great heights from their original condition of servitude.

Commissioning the two murals was one of the last steps Palmer had to take in the overall completion of the building, which had involved women architects, sculptors, and decorative artists. Palmer, as the president of the Board of Lady Managers, oversaw all aspects of the project and brought her knowledge of modern art to bear on the choice of artists throughout. All along, she had worked closely with fellow Chicagoan Hallowell, who was secretary to the director of fine arts for the fair, but she was especially dependent on Hallowell's expertise in the matter of the muralists. In 1892 the American women artists of greatest renown lived in Paris and Hallowell knew them all. By far the best known, and the team's first choice, was not Mary Cassatt but her old rival Elizabeth Gardner.

By this time, Gardner was a firm fixture in the dual circles of official French art and American society. She had won the Salon medals she so coveted, and, although she could not marry Bouguereau as long as his mother was alive, she had her studio next door to his. She frequently entertained individuals and parties from the American colony in her studio,

88. Photograph of the Hall of Honor, Woman's Building, World's Columbian Exposition, 1893
(View to the south, showing Mary Cassatt's mural mounted at the top of the end wall in the tympanum)
Chicago Historical Society

where she would show off her latest paintings to an admiring crowd. Her style was academic: she showed classical, religious, and peasant scenes polished to a gleaming perfection. Because of her traditional style and her association with Bouguereau, who had executed many murals, the committee for the Woman's Building felt she would be the ideal painter of one or both of their murals. To their surprise, she declined the invitation entirely, claiming that the enormous amount of work and the necessity of climbing up and down ladders was too physically demanding for her at the age of fifty-five.

Hallowell immediately began to make other suggestions of replacements for Gardner and brought up the name of Mary Fairchild MacMonnies, who at thirty-four was much younger than Gardner but who was also allied with a famous artist—her husband, Frederick MacMonnies, who was executing a monumental sculptural commission for the fair. MacMonnies had come to Paris as a promising art student in 1887 and, with the help of her new husband, was rapidly establishing herself in Paris art circles. Palmer and MacMonnies were able to secure her for the *Primitive Woman* mural very quickly, and since her style was as academic as Gardner's, the pair had had to sacrifice very little of their original vision in switching to her.

The other mural, however, demanded an artist who was modern in all respects. Both Hallowell and Palmer had a taste for modern art and openly admired such Impressionists as Degas, whom Palmer had collected at Cassatt's suggestion, and Sisley, Hallowell's neighbor in Moret. The logical choice was the only American member of the Impressionists, Mary Cassatt. They had rejected her at first, since she did not fit their preconceived notion of a muralist, but as time went on and as Palmer relaxed in the more daring atmosphere of Paris during her trip that spring, they began to see Cassatt as a realistic choice. Palmer probably saw Cassatt's recent mother-and-child compositions for the first time and bought one from Durand-Ruel. She also acquired a set of Cassatt's color prints from the year before. There is no question that Cassatt was held in very high regard in Paris, and since Palmer and Hallowell admired her work, they took the bold step of asking her to do the mural.

Cassatt was horrified. This was the kind of project someone like Elizabeth Gardner would do. She had spent her whole career breaking away from traditional forms of art, and the mural was the most traditional. Furthermore, she was also afraid of the physical demands of such an enormous canvas that would be compounded by the pressure of a deadline that was now less than a year away. But, as she wrote Louisine Havemeyer, "gradually I began to think it would be great fun to do something I had never done before. . . ."[20] And while she was thinking it over, she mentioned it to Degas and that clinched it: "The bare idea of such a thing put Degas in a rage and he did not spare every criticism he could think of, I got my spirit up and said I would not give up the idea for anything."[21] So the combination of her own love of the new and her stubbornness in the face of opposition led her to say yes. By agreeing, Cassatt joined a select group of artists and others in Paris whose lives would revolve around Chicago for the next year. Hallowell and Mary and Frederick MacMonnies were only a few of the Americans involved with the fair, while such French friends as Antonin Proust, minister of fine arts, and Albert Bartholomé, on the French sculpture jury, were also tied to Chicago. Degas was furious when he saw so many of his old friends who had previously disdained official art events suddenly capitulate to a world's fair.

Cassatt must have begun planning the mural in May of 1892 while she was still in Paris before moving back out to Bachivillers, where she intended to execute the work. Such a project demanded complex arrangements of the sort she was little used to. Materials had to be ordered: the murals were to be painted on canvas that would then either be glued directly onto the wall of the Woman's Building or be mounted on curved stretchers and fitted into the space—the decision about the method of installation had not yet been made. Enough paint had to be procured to cover the 12- by 58-foot canvas, and, in addition, Cassatt planned for a decorative border that would be highlighted with actual gold leaf. Initial discussions had to be held with Mary MacMonnies to make sure that similar materials were used and to settle questions of design. Bertha Palmer returned to Chicago, but Sarah Hallowell stayed at her home in France through the summer and played a part in the developing designs of both murals. They all judged that the immense height at which the two works would be shown and the distance between the two ends of the hall would make the murals visually quite independent of each other, so that each artist could feel free to develop her ideas without any further consultation. The two women undoubtedly knew each other but had never developed a professional friendship as Cassatt had with Berthe Morisot, for instance, that would have made them wish to work more closely together. When Cassatt moved out to the country, they evidently had no further contact—MacMonnies had chosen to stay in Paris and set up her enormous canvas in one of her husband's large sculpture studios.

Cassatt, thus liberated from the academic MacMonnies, let her ideas flow (figure 89). In fact, it seems that she strove for effects that would be a rebuke to the MacMonnies mural (figure 90). Just as Modern Woman

89. ***Mary Cassatt,*** **Modern Woman,** ***from*** **Art and Handicraft at the Woman's Building of the World's Columbian Exposition,** ***M. H. Elliot, ed., Chicago, 1893, p. 35***
Photo courtesy of the Chicago Historical Society

90. ***Mary Fairchild MacMonnies,*** **Primitive Woman,** ***from*** **Art and Handicraft at the Woman's Building of the World's Columbian Exposition,** ***M. H. Elliot, ed., Chicago, 1893, p. 35***
Photo courtesy of the Chicago Historical Society

triumphed over Primitive Woman, modern art would triumph over the traditional style she knew her rival would use. Where MacMonnies would use soft, harmonious colors, Cassatt chose a bright blue and green palette with accents of purple, pink, and gold. Her model was Giotto, with his rich coloring and realistic human activities and emotions. MacMonnies looked to the era of Botticelli and his successors with their ideal scenes of antiquity. Above all, Cassatt stressed the importance of costume in expressing the ideals of the age and ordered dresses made for her models at such prominent Parisian houses as Doucet and Worth. MacMonnies, on the other hand, strove for an unidentifiable place and time by using generalized draperies and nude figures.

The interpretation of the two subjects, Primitive Woman and Modern Woman, was left entirely up to the artists themselves. The point the committee wanted to make was a simple one: women have thrown off the chains that kept them in servitude since primitive times, and have now emerged as an important force in modern civilization. The Woman's Building as a whole was to be furnished with exhibits demonstrating the achievements of women. MacMonnies interpreted her subject in a clear and straightforward way: she showed women serving men, carrying heavy burdens, and caring for children in vignettes arrayed across the surface of her canvas. Cassatt discarded what would have been the logical counterpart—scenes of women in schools, in the workplace, and in allegorical triumph—and instead sought a more complex interpretation of the condition of modern women.

By her own account, she "tried to make the general effect as bright, as gay, as amusing as possible. The occassion [*sic*] is one of rejoicing, a great national fete"[22] and yet there is great seriousness as well. As she said, "I reserved all the seriousness for the execution, for the drawing & painting,"[23] and consequently the figures move slowly and solemnly in their bright green environment. A later critic described one of the figures as having "the grandeur and simplicity of a young priestess in an antique procession."[24] The mural, like all her work from this period, strikes a fragile balance between the sheer beauty of the design and the contemplative mood of the subject.

Even Cassatt's choice of theme is deceptively simple. She divided the canvas into three zones, each one showing a separate scene that is tied to its neighbors only by a similar grassy background. In the central and most important zone she placed the subject that to her represented the advances, but also the dilemma of Modern Woman: "Young women plucking the fruits of knowledge or science" (figure 91). This choice had an artistic motive in that, as she said, it "enabled me to place my figures out of doors & allowed of brilliancy of color."[25] But it also spoke to the growth of education for women that she had witnessed in her own lifetime and was in full flower in 1892. By this time most of the great women's colleges had been established—such as Mount Holyoke (1837), Vassar (1865), Smith (1871), Wellesley (1875), Bryn Mawr (1880), Goucher (1885), and Randolph-Macon Woman's College (1891). In addition, coeducation was in force in private colleges, such as Oberlin and Swarthmore, as well as in the land grant universities, such as Iowa, Wisconsin, Kansas, Indiana, Minnesota, Missouri, Michigan, and California. Appropriately, in October of 1892, while Cassatt was working on her mural, the University of Chicago opened as a coeducational institution. Cassatt herself had received "higher education" at the Pennsylvania Academy of the Fine Arts, and was actively interested in the education of all her nieces as well as the nephews. In fact, while she was painting the mural, her niece Elsie came to her at Bachivillers to ask her advice on Parisian schools she might attend now that she was seventeen and finished with her preparatory education.

Cassatt's depiction of "women plucking fruit" was not cast in a purely triumphant mood, as an unalloyed celebration of women's gains in education. The seriousness of Cassatt's women conveys her belief in the burden that education brings with it: the responsibility to go forth with that education and make one's way in the world as a professional woman. Yet the simultaneous emphasis on fashion in her mural as well as the scenes of caring for babies and children indicates Cassatt's recognition of a "feminine sphere" that education should not take women away from. The resolution of these two conflicting worlds—the personal and the professional—was one Cassatt solved by choosing her profession over a husband and family, but the

91. *Detail of the central panel of Mary Cassatt,* Modern Woman, *from W. Walton,* World's Columbian Exposition: Art and Architecture, *Philadelphia, 1893*

dilemma had to be confronted and solved by each individual woman, with a great deal of "seriousness" and often pain.

Thus the symbol of the tree of knowledge was not without its darker side. It could not be read without reference to the biblical Eve who plucked the fruit and brought about the collapse of her own safe world. In Cassatt's youth, when education for women was still being debated, the tree of knowledge was used in one of the most famous feminist essays of that time. Titled "Ought Women to Learn the Alphabet," the essay by Thomas Wentworth Higginson that appeared in the *Atlantic Monthly* in February 1859 was credited with inspiring Sophia Smith to found the woman's college that would bear her name. He starts out with a tongue-in-cheek review of previous claims that education for women would bring about "the frightful results which have followed this taste of the fruit of the tree of knowledge [and] that the woman who knows the alphabet has already lost a portion of her innocence."[26] Then he goes on to show the unstoppable movement toward women's education in recent times and concludes with good humor that "Eve's daughters are in danger of swallowing a whole harvest of forbidden fruit, in these revolutionary days, unless something be done to cut off the supply."[27] If Cassatt remembered this essay—or read it in many of its periodic reprints over the years—she, like Higginson, was willing to risk expulsion from "paradise" in order to found a new civilization based on principles of equality for women, but she did so with firsthand knowledge of the sacrifices and perseverance that must go with it.

The two end panels were related only tangentially to the central theme. On the left, she showed "young girls pursuing fame," which was done with her own brand of self-deprecating humor. She made no excuses for her own pursuit of fame and remembered her youthful zeal with some amusement. She showed three girls with hair and dresses blowing in the wind racing across the countryside in pursuit of a nude allegorical figure of fame. The addition of geese snapping at their heels represented both the undignified posture such a pursuit forces the girls into and the annoying squawks of ever-present critics trying to impede women in their advancement. The panel on the right shows three women—perhaps the mature version of the girls on the left—in dignified poses depicting Music (a seated woman playing a banjo) and Dance (a standing woman lifting her skirt for a "skirt dance"). The third woman serves as an audience for the other two and may represent the observant artist or simply the appreciative art lover. Both the banjo and the skirt dance were in vogue in 1892 while Cassatt was painting the mural and, like the fashionable dresses, helped to create the air of utmost modernity.

Once Cassatt had settled on her designs, hired her models, commissioned the costumes, and obtained her materials, she set out for the country. At Bachivillers she had one more preparatory task, and that was to have a large glass studio built on the lawn. Into the soft ground she had a sixty-foot trench dug—approximately six feet deep—so that she could lower the canvas into the trench and paint on the top part without using ladders. She evidently posed her models (whom she housed in the many rooms of the château) directly in front of the mural itself so that she might paint directly from life rather than from smaller sketches. In addition, she employed at least two assistants to help her paint and gild the vast expanses of the border, which was three feet wide and outlined the entire mural as well as divided the three zones.

The work was arduous and unrelenting because of the strict deadline by which the work had to be shipped to Chicago, but, on the whole, Cassatt was exhilarated by the challenge of it and grateful for such intense work that pushed the still-painful memories of her father's death from her mind. While she deliberately exiled herself from other artists like Degas who might demoralize her or Mary MacMonnies who might irritate her, she had no similar defense against the family and friends who thought a ride out to Bachivillers for the day or the week would be charming. Aleck and Lois were in Paris again that August and September with Rob, Katharine, and Elsie. Lois was sorry that the huge panel deprived her of Mary's companionship, which she had grown accustomed to in recent years. Mary came in to Paris only a few times: once to take Aleck around to look at pictures and once to attend the funeral of Paul Durand-Ruel's son, Charles. She combined the latter occasion with a visit to Lois, whom she took to the funeral with her. To Lois's delight they saw Degas there and "all the great artists" as Mary pointed them out to her.[28]

Other relatives who claimed Cassatt's attention during that time might have been more helpful to her in her great endeavor. These were her second cousin Mary (Mimie) Johnston, with whom Cassatt had traveled to Chicago back in 1870, and her husband, William Milligan Sloane, a professor of classics at Princeton.[29] The Sloanes were more intellectual than most of Cassatt's cousins; Mr. Sloane had been educated in Germany, and, as a couple, they traveled frequently to Europe, often spending long periods in Paris. He was so well respected by European scholars that in 1888 the renowned social philosopher Hippolyte Taine recommended Sloane to be the author of an exhaustive study of Napoleon, which was published in Paris and the United States in 1894. Mrs. Sloane was involved in one of the women's committees for the Chicago world's fair and had met Bertha Palmer. The Sloanes were some of the few people Cassatt could talk to that fall at Bachivillers about the content of her mural, including modern education and the status of women.

The work progressed slowly. The summer turned to fall, the fall turned to winter and Cassatt and her mother remained at Bachivillers. The glass studio was nearly impossible to heat, and yet Cassatt had no choice but to spend eight hours a day plugging away at what now seemed an endless task. The feedback she had gotten from the few people she allowed to see it—Sarah Hallowell, Paul Durand-Ruel, André Mellério, and possibly Pissarro—had been good, and the photographs she had sent to Chicago of the central panel were received warmly by Bertha Palmer. In general she was satisfied with the work and wrote, "I think, my dear Mrs. Palmer, that if you were here & I could take you out to my studio & show you what I have done that you would be pleased indeed without too much vanity I may say I am almost sure you would."[30] But at times she got discouraged and wished for advice from Degas—"the only man I know whose judgment would be a help to me"[31]—but could not afford to be crushed if he arrived in a savage mood. Consequently she drew the monumental project to an end trusting her own instincts. She shipped the mural off to Chicago by the middle of February and immediately headed south on a leisurely tour of Italy to recuperate. In looking back on the previous year's work she regretted not having had more time to develop the idea and execute the mural, which she felt she had to ship off in an imperfect state. Over all, she had "enjoyed the new experience in painting very much."[32]

The small group in Chicago privileged to see the mural as it was unpacked was delighted with the freshness of its style and message. These were among the most sophisticated connoisseurs of modern art in the United States—Sarah Hallowell, Bertha Palmer, and the critic Lucy Monroe—and their understanding of Cassatt's theme and experimental style was unusually acute. None of these women were prepared for the bizarre transformation that the mural underwent as it was hoisted fifty feet in the air and gazed upon by the well-meaning but unsophisticated public that began pouring into the building on May 1, the fair's opening day. Suddenly the theme that had seemed so logical became indecipherable to the average viewer, and the style that had seemed so sunny and realistic became a jarring pattern of bright colors that was out of synch with the rest of the building. And the worst blow was that Mary MacMonnies's mural, which had seemed so uninspired on the ground, actually improved at a distance, and, in comparison with Cassatt's, seemed to have all the grace and dignity that hers lacked. Those interested in modern art continued to admire what Cassatt had done and express boredom at Macmonnies's traditional "Primitive Woman," but, as the summer of the fair wore on, it became painfully obvious how few of them there really were in the United States in 1892.

Cassatt herself was spared the full shock of the public rejection of her mural, since she had no intention of traveling to Chicago herself, nor did she read much of the American newspaper and magazine criticism of it. Besides, she was uniquely armored against such criticism because she had experienced much worse throughout her career as a radical artist. She may have temporarily forgotten, but she would quickly remember that a world's fair was very little different from a Salon, and she could have anticipated her fate in that type of setting. Bertha Palmer had no such experience to give her perspective and was genuinely surprised and embarrassed that her daring choice of an Impressionist for this mural did not have the positive result she had expected.

The failure of Cassatt's mural was not just the result of public misunderstanding of a radical art style. Cassatt herself misjudged the necessary elements of mural painting. As was pointed out many times by critics, her approach was pictorial rather than decorative. The three separate scenes of her mural resembled three independent easel paintings that had inexplicably been elevated to the top of the wall. Her color, which she had deliberately intensified to compensate for the great viewing distance, harmonized with nothing else in the building and made the figures, which were too small to begin with, seem even smaller. MacMonnies had a more modest goal for her mural, explaining to Palmer that "a decoration, like a tapestry, should be a superior sort of wall-paper, which gives first and above all a charming and agreeable effect as a whole, but does not strike the eye or disturb the attention by any vigorous or salient 'spots.'"[33] Palmer had worried that MacMonnies's use of monumental nudes would offend some of their more sensitive visitors, but MacMonnies defended her use of nudes as "virile" and added, "I think you will scarcely see my semi-nude women at all (I mean be aware of them), if the work is successful *as a decoration.*"[34]

Cassatt had also claimed she used tapestries as her model, "brilliant yet soft,"[35] but she was obviously not as interested in turning her picture into "a superior sort of wallpaper." Her loyalty to the tightly constructed picture did not allow her to sacrifice the qualities of each of her three compositions for the sake of the building as a whole. Degas had warned her about just this problem and spoke heatedly to Pissarro about the "decoration": "It is an ornament that should be made with a view to its place in an ensemble, it requires the collaboration of architect and painter."[36] Cassatt disagreed, advocating something called a "decorative picture," which Degas dismissed as an "absurdity, a picture complete in itself is not a decoration."[37] Degas, as it turns out, was right, but Cassatt was the one who got the opportunity to do the mural and boldly went forward with a radical new interpretation of a traditional format. Even if it did not receive public approval, it was the beginning of a process of reevaluating the mural to make it adapt to new ideas in art and become once again a vital art form for expressing modern ideas.

At the close of the fair on October 31, 1893, all the buildings of the White City had to be removed from their temporary homes in Chicago's Logan Park. The Woman's Building was duly stripped of its exhibits and its decorations in preparation for the wrecker's ball. All items that had been lent to the Woman's Building were returned to their owners, and those works that had been commissioned and paid for, as were the Cassatt and MacMonnies murals, were put into storage. There had been some talk of erecting a permanent respository of women's art and industry, called the Woman's Memorial Building, in which the murals would be placed, but when that didn't materialize no other plans were made for their preservation. There is no trace of them today, and presumably they were left to the storage company to dispose of once the fees ceased to be paid.

Cassatt herself was not concerned about the fate of her mural; once it was finished and shipped, she evinced very little curiosity about it. She had been paid three thousand dollars for her year's work, which just about covered her expenses in materials, models' fees, assistants, and the cost of the glass studio. She was pleased, however, in knowing that she was paid the same amount as the men who executed similar murals for the fair and wrote the whole experience off as positive.

Even if she made no monetary profit, she did finish the year with a host of new pictures and ideas for color prints, all using the same models and the same garden setting, with many continuing the themes of plucking fruit and playing the banjo. These works, formulated without the restrictions of the mural format, were some of the strongest and most beautiful Cassatt had ever done. Durand-Ruel, who admired the mural as he saw it develop at Bachivillers, was eager for the mural-related pictures and brought them into his gallery as soon as she finished them (figure 92). The interest in her work

92. *Mary Cassatt,* Young Women Picking Fruit, *1891 Oil on canvas, 51½ x 35½ in. The Carnegie Museum of Art, Patrons Art Fund, 22.8*

was so strong that he felt the time was right finally to accede to her wishes and give her her first major retrospective exhibition. During the summer of 1893, when her mural was being lambasted by American critics, she worked away quite happily on new paintings and prints for her upcoming November show.

Cassatt and her mother returned to Bachivillers for their third summer, drawn by the rolling green countryside that offered an abundance of fresh poultry and produce as well as endless paths for horseback riding and drives in the carriage. Both mother and daughter may well have been struck by the similarity of the landscape to that of Chester County, where they had lived thirty years before. By this time they were getting to know their neighbors, both the villagers of Bachivillers, to whom they were very generous, and the other prominent families who owned or rented estates in the region. One such neighbor was Paul Durand-Ruel's daughter, Mme. Aude, who had married and lived nearby. The ties between Cassatt and Durand-Ruel strengthened because of this friendly proximity.

This summer also marked the beginning of Cassatt's willingness to execute portraits, usually in pastel, of friends and family beyond her immediate circle. Her rare excursions into portraiture beyond those of her parents and her brothers and their families, as in the case of Mrs. Riddle, were so disastrous that she seldom gave in to requests or even her own occasional interest. In June 1893 she agreed to do a pastel portrait of the youngest daughter of her cousin Mimie Johnston Sloane, with whom she had spent much time in the last few years. As she had done many years before, when she was trying to build up a portrait practice in Paris, she not only finished the portrait for the family but created a second version for herself—one that she could exhibit and sell (figure 93). Once the stunning *Child with an Orange* was shown at her Durand-Ruel exhibition that fall, she was deluged with requests for child portraits and did them with increasing frequency in the next twenty years.

Just as the Chicago world's fair closed, Cassatt's first major exhibition in Paris opened. Almost one hundred works were installed in the same Durand-Ruel galleries that had held her exhibition of color prints two years before. This time, instead of sharing the commodious space with Pissarro, Morisot, and the Société Française des Peintres-Gravures, she had the gallery all to herself for a month. The size of the show and the detailed catalog

93. ***Mary Cassatt,*** **Portrait of Margaret Milligan Sloane (No. 2),** ***1893***
Pastel, 32 x 25¾ in.
Private collection
Photo courtesy of Hirschl & Adler Galleries, Inc.

consoled her for the fact that such friends as Degas, Renoir, and Gauguin had all had exhibitions here within the last year and Berthe Morisot had had a large one in May and June 1892 at Boussod and Valadon. Cassatt's envy had apparently been noticeable to Morisot, who remarked wryly to a mutual friend that she had not heard any news of her exhibition since she left town, least of all from her old friend: "Miss Cassatt is not one to write me about an exhibition of mine."[38]

Cassatt had been well occupied with the mural project while her friends had been having exhibitions, and now could enjoy at her leisure the summing up that came with a retrospective look at her accomplishments. The exhibition covered only the years since 1878 when she joined the Impressionists, when she "began to live," but it included enough representative paintings to cover the various phases she had gone through since then: paintings of the theater and tea parties, paintings of Lydia at home and in the garden, the mother and child pictures, and the most recent mural-related works. In addition to the thirty-one paintings and pastels, Cassatt showed almost sixty prints ranging from her earliest Impressionist prints made for the journal project *Le Jour et la nuit* to the color prints she made from mural designs, *Gathering Fruit* and *The Banjo Lesson.* Most of the works were for sale, and according to a review of the show, half had been sold within a few weeks. Those that were not for sale were those loaned to the exhibition by such Parisian collectors as Henri Rouart, Dr. Peyrot, G. Murat, Dr. Georges Viau, Antoine Personnaz, Paul Gallimard, the dealers Michel Manzi, MM. Martin et Camentron and Paul Durand-Ruel, and by Cassatt's loyal friend Edgar Degas. Many of the prints were owned by André Mellério, the critic and writer, who also contributed the introduction to the exhibition catalog.

All the writing that surrounded the show—both the catalog essay and the reviews—demonstrates how seriously Mary Cassatt's art was taken in Paris. A critic might prefer her prints to her paintings, or her Impressionist works to her mother and child pictures, but all were discussed with the utmost respect and appreciation. French intellectual trends had veered away from naturalism and toward symbolism in the past ten years, which, of course, led reviewers to see the spiritualism in her modern "Madonnas" and a sacred quality to her women plucking fruit. Reviewers expressed a greater appreciation of the depth of feeling of even her Impressionist work, which had previously been discussed only in terms of its quality of light and faithfulness to modern life. The ingredients that had been present in Cassatt's art from the start, particularly her uncanny ability to represent *thought* on canvas, were discussed in full.[39] The theme that had intrigued her from her earliest days—the contemplative woman—had come into its own. Paris's acceptance of Mary Cassatt, signaled by the understanding and recognition of critics, was underscored by an official request for a painting by the Luxembourg Museum, which was the repository of the art of living artists chosen to be honored by the French state. All this was in stark contrast to the treatment she suffered at the hands of American critics writing on her Chicago mural, and it was with some feeling that she wrote to Sarah Hallowell, "After all give me France—women do not have to fight for recognition here, if they do serious work."[40]

Chapter VII

American Connections (1894–1899)

When her retrospective exhibition closed in December of 1893, Mary Cassatt instinctively closed a chapter in her life. It was inevitable that the exhibition, which summed up the last fifteen years of her art, put a period to her previous work. When she next sat down to her easel, it would be with a new self-consciousness about her past and an awareness that the next mark she made on the canvas would begin a new era.

Furthermore, by this time she was physically tired. She had just completed five years of intense work, which included two major projects—the series of color prints and the mural—that required physically demanding materials and techniques. She had held her first two solo exhibitions in Paris as well as the exhibition of her mural in Chicago. Added to the labor of producing so much new work was the pressure of constant and relentless deadlines.

Finally, personal matters had begun to weigh heavily on her. Just as she was beginning to adjust to the changes brought about by the death of her father, she was forced to face the increasing frailty and the prospect of impending death of her mother. All these factors forced Cassatt to take a few months to get away from Paris and pull herself together. When she returned to Paris, she had successfully reoriented herself and would spend the next five or six years making her life slower, more manageable, and more suited to her own tastes and comforts. After all, in 1894 she would turn fifty and had earned the right to indulge herself.

As soon as the paintings from the exhibition had been taken down, and all the loose ends of such an undertaking attended to, she and her mother traveled south for the third winter in a row. In 1894 her mother was ailing, and so, rather than subject her to strenuous sightseeing, they headed to the Cap d'Antibes, where the two of them could rent a quiet villa and recuperate.

Cannes and its surrounding coastline had been discovered as a winter resort in the 1860s and by the 1890s were crowded with luxury hotels and private villas that dotted the hillsides overlooking the sea. French, British, and American socialites gathered there in January and February to enjoy the balmy weather and worldly amusements. The Cassatts were familiar with this type of resort from assorted vacations to the Isle of Wight (1879), Biarritz (1884), and Arques-la-Bataille, near Dieppe (1887–88). Although neither of them liked the sea, they both enjoyed the panoramic views and the proximity to a wider circle of friends and acquaintances.

They rented a large villa called La Cigaronne (figure 94) about halfway up the peninsula of the Cap d'Antibes. From the front of the house they looked across the bay to the small town of Juan-les-Pins on the mainland, and, farther to the west, a smaller peninsula, which hid the city of Cannes from their view. In the distance, they could see the mountain ranges of the Alpes-Maritimes rising behind the coastal towns. They were not as high up as they had been in the Villa Ste.-Anne two years before, but this new house

94. View of the Villa La Cigaronne, Cap d'Antibes

was larger, had level grounds and gardens to enjoy, and was closer to the edge of the bay.

Cassatt was energized by the Mediterranean environment. In addition to caring for her mother, she kept up a steady stream of correspondence, generated by her recent high visibility, that often mixed business and friendship. She was in touch with a large number of artists, collectors, museums, agents, such as Sara Hallowell and George Lucas, and, of course, her dealer, Durand-Ruel.

While in the south, she saw the end of her negotiations with the Luxembourg Museum. Unfortunately, they had chosen a painting that was owned by Durand-Ruel. Since their policy was to buy only from the artist (and Durand-Ruel would not give the painting back to her, nor would the Luxembourg choose another painting), the transaction could go no further. Cassatt declared that it didn't matter to her, but in fact she was peeved at the stubbornness of both sides and frustrated that the matter was out of her hands. It wasn't until three years later that negotiations reopened, this time with another picture, which was owned by Cassatt herself, and she had the satisfaction of seeing her first work enter a museum collection. The work, a pastel mother and child, has now been incorporated into the Louvre.

The irony of this honor coming from France rather than her own country was not lost on her, as she wrote to a friend while the first round of negotiations were going on, "I can hardly imagine . . . that the Metropolitan Museum will propose to buy one of [my] pictures as the Musée du Luxemburg [*sic*] has just made me the compliment of doing—"[1] She was right about the Metropolitan; they did not purchase a Cassatt painting until 1909. She herself eventually donated a major painting to the Metropolitan Museum in 1923.

Cassatt's days were not entirely taken up with business correspondence. She was also inspired by her surroundings to get back to work and somewhat grudgingly take advantage of the picturesqueness of the area. To one correspondent she wrote that "the country is too beautiful, it grows wearisome," and that, conversely, the people were not beautiful enough.[2] The scenery revived her old antipathy to landscape painting, particularly the way it was practiced by Americans in the now-outmoded Hudson River grand manner so popular in her youth. Finding that there were a number of American landscape painters in the area, she groused, "It [the landscape] is rather too panoramic for my taste, but doubtless could be interpreted by a great man, in an artistic way; I have never yet seen it done to my satisfaction."[3]

For all her complaining, Cassatt was not immune to the seductive scenery all around her. She appreciated the color and light, and was charmed by the brightly painted boats that populated the shores of every inlet. By the end of her first month there she had settled on a major composition now called *The Boating Party* (figure 95) that took advantage of the sun, the color, and one of those picturesque Provençal boats. She hired local models, even though they were not beautiful, and posed them in the boat as a family taking a Sunday-afternoon outing. The woman holds her child sprawled across her lap, while the man, dressed in a refined version of the local Provençal fisherman costume, which features a sash around the waist and a large floppy beret, rows the boat. The boat has the typical rounded shape of the local style and has short pegs to which the oars are lashed for rowing. The boat also has a sail, which may have been a feature of these boats at the time, since they usually sport a small mast and old photographs show rigging on the occasional small fishing boat; or the sail may have been Cassatt's own addition as a compositional device, just as the colors of the sea, the boat, and the costumes were carefully chosen for their "artistic" effect.

95. ***Mary Cassatt,* The Boating Party, *1894***
Oil on canvas, 35½ x 46⅛ in.
National Gallery of Art, Washington; Chester Dale Collection

The landlord of the Villa La Cigaronne kept one of these boats for the convenience of its tenants in the small inlet at the water's edge. Since the boat was pulled up onto the beach when not in use, Cassatt could have posed her models in it with the water forming a middle ground and the main coastline forming the background. We can picture her thus with her easel set up on the beach, transferring the scene before her to the enormous canvas. Although she was not accustomed to working in public places and probably attracted a small, unwanted crowd on the fringes of the beach, she worked happily and was "thankful for the sun & the long days."[4]

As the only work Cassatt is known to have painted on the Cap d'Antibes in 1894, *The Boating Party* was unusual in many respects. It had been years since Cassatt went out to all parts of France, Italy, and Spain in search of interesting local costumes, ethnic physiognomy, and regional activities. The last time she had done this was for her Spanish bullfight series, done in Seville in 1873. The Spanish series was also the last time she had used a male figure in a major compositional role, apart from portraits of family members and friends. The boatsman in this painting is a throwback to those early days, and Cassatt has placed him in dark colors in the foreground, facing the brightly lit mother and child—Cassatt's current subject—as if to bind together the art of her past and her present.

Cassatt kept the painting in her own possession for many years and was sentimentally attached to it. She allowed it to be exhibited and to be reproduced in publications on her art, but she did not offer it for sale until, in her old age, she got the impression that her heirs—her family—did not value it as much as she did, and she consented to put it on the market. Part of her sentimental attachment, which she rarely had for pictures other than portraits of her family, came from the special period of her life spent on the Cap d'Antibes, poised as she was between past and future, just as she was about to cross the half-century mark.

Another fond association she had with the painting was the birth of another niece, Ellen Mary, which took place in January of that year, twenty-five years after the birth of her first nephew, Eddie, in 1869. Ellen Mary was the daughter of Jennie and Gardner Cassatt, who were closer to Mary than Lois and Aleck now that they traveled to Europe more often and spent more time with her. Cassatt had already formed an attachment to their firstborn, "little" Gardner, who was now almost eight years old, and who had spent a significant amount of his young life with his aunt. The birth of Ellen Mary was something Cassatt had waited many years for—a niece who was her namesake, with whom she would always have a special bond.

Cassatt's ties to her brothers' families were changing at this time. Aleck and Lois's children were all growing up, going to college, and beginning their adult lives. Although they had strong ties to their aunt, they now began to come to Europe with friends or spouses rather than together as a family, and it was harder to maintain the same closeness. On the other hand, Jennie and Gard had young children, which allowed Cassatt to transfer her attention to the new nieces and nephew and have a second round of watching "her" children grow up.

While Cassatt was still on the Cap d'Antibes, she made one bold move that, more than anything, opened a new phase in her life. This was the purchase of a country mansion that was called Mesnil-Beaufresne, "château" of the village of Mesnil-Théribus, which was located in the same area as Bachivillers, about fifty miles northwest of Paris, where she had spent the last three summers (figure 96). For more than twenty years the Cassatts had rented summer homes in various locations around Paris or Dieppe. The houses had become progressively grand as time went by, until they ended up with the château of Bachivillers, where Cassatt had begun her series of color prints, and where she had built her glass studio for the Chicago mural. She and her mother loved this region, and were stunned to hear, during their stay in 1893, that the landlord would no longer rent the house to them. She wrote acidly to a friend, "We were turned out of the [Bachivillers

96. *Postcard showing the front view of the Château de Beaufresne*
F. A. Sweet Papers, Archives of American Art, Smithsonian Institution

house] by the marriage of our fat landlord to a young woman desirous of living in a 'chateau.' "[5] Responding swiftly to this unfortunate turn of events, Cassatt discovered that the château of the next town, Mesnil-Théribus (three miles away), was for sale, and offered to buy it. It took several months for the deal to be struck and the funds transferred, the final transactions taking place while the Cassatts were in the south.

For the first time since she came to Europe in 1865, Cassatt would live in a house that she owned. While she was a struggling young artist this had been impossible, but even after the arrival of her parents and sister, the family continued to rent both apartments in Paris and summer houses in the country. The unfortunate circumstance of losing the Bachivillers house was the catalyst for the sudden excursion into landowning, but it had really been made possible by the death of the peripatetic and parsimonious Robert Cassatt. As long as Mary's father was alive, he dictated the major circumstances of their housing. His urge to change residence frequently had decreased only slightly in old age. His decisions were behind the four apartments in Paris; his whims dictated the nearly annual change of summer location. Furthermore, he was happy only with a bargain rate, which could be obtained on grand summer houses some distance from Paris and on the smaller apartments in the desirable districts in Paris itself. When the Aleck and Gardner Cassatts visited, they remarked on the smallness of the rooms of the Paris apartments, and the inconvenience of the locations of the summer houses; their own style of living was far more luxurious than that practiced by their father.

When Robert Cassatt died, not only did his funds go to his wife and daughter, but at last the financial reins were turned over to them.[6] Thus, when Cassatt found she could no longer rent the house she wanted, she did not hesitate to buy, nor did she hesitate to buy an even grander house than any she had lived in with her family. When she had the chance to dictate her own style of living, she, like her brothers, chose comfort and elegance over economy. Furthermore, once Cassatt bought Mesnil-Beaufresne, she never moved again, as if to underscore the fact that the constant moving was her father's idea, not hers. She kept the same Paris apartment and the same country house until her death, more than thirty years later.

When she and her mother returned from the south in March, Cassatt acquainted herself with the château she had bought so hastily. Leaving her mother in Paris, she made excursions out to Mesnil-Théribus to meet with architects and workmen to determine the true condition of the house and what work would be necessary. She had bought the house, but apparently at first only rented the grounds from the de Grasse family, which had owned the property for centuries. She leased about ten acres (four hectares) for her own private use for gardens, stables, later a garage, and other outbuildings.

After extensive examinations of the house, she was relieved to hear that it was structurally very sound, especially since some parts of it were thought to be earlier than 1600. The main part of the house was thought to date to the time of Louis XIII (c. 1630), although in style it appears to be around 1730, which may indicate a history of additions and remodeling. A long, porchlike gallery had been added to the back of the house in the nineteenth century, which offered views of the garden and pond from its continuous row of windows (figure 97). Cassatt did not substantially alter the house during the time she owned it, but she immediately set about bringing it up to modern American standards, particularly in matters of indoor plumbing.

While the purchase price and the cost of the renovations to the house may have been more than Cassatt's father would have paid if he had still been alive, the house was still a remarkable bargain. Cassatt paid thirty-nine thousand francs (approximately eight thousand dollars) at a time when a similar house in the United States would have cost at least three times that amount. Her own father, forty-five years before, had bought the Hardwicke estate for almost the same price. In many ways the Mesnil-Beaufresne

97. *Postcard showing the back view of the Château de Beaufresne*
F. A. Sweet Papers, Archives of American Art, Smithsonian Institution

château resembled Hardwicke, with its brick-and-stone exterior and rows of shuttered windows. The wide-open landscape also resembled the rolling meadows of Pennsylvania in Lancaster and Chester counties, where Mary had grown up. She was in a position now to indulge herself, and setting up a country house reminiscent of those of her childhood gave her great pleasure. Her brothers had done the same thing as they became able: both owned vast country estates outside Philadelphia, and both eventually owned property in Chester County itself.

However, it must be noted that this landscape did not appeal to most visitors to France, who looked for charming old villages and signs of an ancient civilization. After a visit to Cassatt in 1895, the British writer Vernon Lee described the area around Mesnil-Beaufresne as "that high-lying, monotonous, not at all beautiful French country, crude or dingy in colour, composed of blunt lines, without romance or suavity of village or old house," but, she added, "[it] has yet a charm of breadth, of belonging to an endless continent . . . [of] there being *enough land,* and enough sky especially, leagues of cloud and air. . . ." She concluded, "I liked immensely being at Mesnil."[7]

Vernon Lee found similar qualities in Cassatt herself. Cassatt was "very nice, simple, an odd mixture of a self-recognising artist, with passionate appreciation in literature, and the almost childish garrulous American provincial."[8] To Vernon Lee, who cultivated an aesthetic style of writing and living, Cassatt was surprisingly blunt for a highly educated, artistic person. In fact, to most "consciously-European" connoisseurs, Cassatt's personality and her choice of countryside seemed stereotypically American. In spite of their differences, the two women took a liking to each other. Cassatt executed one of her rare on-the-spot portrait sketches of her new friend (figure 98).

Cassatt's initial excitement over home-ownership quickly faded as the summer of 1894 wore on. The simple renovations she had planned turned into months of upheaval as she encountered the dual obstacles of working on an old house and coping with armies of workmen. Although her father had built their house in Westtown, Chester County, when she was in her late teens, that was the last experience she had had with construction. She was unprepared for the frustrating delays and setbacks caused by this type of work. Even more difficult for her was dealing with the workmen, who required endless direction and proceeded with what was, to her, a snail's pace. Judging from her treatment of the assistant she hired to help her with her mural two years before, she held her workmen to her own standards of productivity and efficiency and was doomed to disappointment. By the end

98. ***Mary Cassatt,*** **Sketch of Vernon Lee,** ***1895*** ***Watercolor,*** **9½ x 16¾ *in.*** ***Present location unknown***

of July, after three months of construction, she was so seriously frustrated that she was willing to give up the whole thing. She wrote to Durand-Ruel that she wanted to put the property up for sale. Although the house was fine, she did "not want to give any more orders to workmen, who don't follow them anyway."[9]

Adding to her distress was the fact that she was scheduled to have a long-awaited exhibition in New York in the spring of 1895, just more than a year after her last one in Paris, and she needed to produce a new group of works. Even without the exhibition, she counted on the summers as the most pleasurable and relaxed time for painting, and her desire to get back to her easel was very great. In the past, her parents had been able to shield her from household matters, but now, with her father gone and her mother ill, she had to address problems that were a burden to her. As for the care of the grounds, she wrote, "My mother is no longer of the age or the strength to concern herself with the outdoors, and I don't have the interest." As for the house, "I have given nearly three months of my time and I know that I still have a part of the summer to devote to giving orders, and I ask myself when will I find the time to do a bit of painting!" Her needs were simple, she explained, "What I want is the freedom to work."[10]

As with all construction, progress was eventually made. Cassatt and her mother moved in. Although the work continued into the fall, they began to appreciate not having a landlord and an absolute date by which they had to vacate the house and return to Paris. The summer turned cool and rainy, and Cassatt consoled herself that she would not be able to paint out of doors anyway. She relaxed both about completing the work on the house in one summer and about producing a large amount of new work for her upcoming exhibition. She decided not to sell the house after all.

Sadly, Cassatt's year got worse rather than better, especially after she and her mother returned to Paris. In December her mother came down with a grippe that was so severe that for the next month Cassatt had to give up everything else in order to care for her. Cassatt's devotion to her mother and her skill at nursing certainly prolonged her seventy-nine-year-old mother's life. Others caught in the influenza epidemic were not so fortunate; tragically Berthe Morisot fell victim to it and was swept to her death in five days. Morisot's death was a stunning loss to the entire artistic and intellectual community of Paris and a great personal blow to Cassatt. In this anxious period, Cassatt worked fitfully, but managed to produce several pastels, such as *Mother and Child—Young Thomas and His Mother* (figure 99), that show a solicitous mother and an unusually solemn child.

As the time grew near, Cassatt wanted to postpone the exhibition that was scheduled to open in the middle of April, but Durand-Ruel was reluctant to change and pressed forward with it. On April 1 Mrs. Cassatt took a turn for the worse and Gard and Jennie were on the point of sailing to be with her. When she improved, the Gardner Cassatts canceled their trip, and Mary Cassatt's first New York exhibition opened as scheduled.

Since her mother's health was so precarious, Cassatt had no thought of going to New York for the exhibition. Even under better circumstances, it is doubtful that she would have considered it. Judging from her complete lack of curiosity about the Chicago Exposition two years before, we may assume that New York would have had no greater appeal. Cassatt wanted recognition in her homeland and knew that New York was the only arena worth pursuing, but she was without any concrete experience of the art world there. She routinely socialized with the New York artists like William Merritt Chase and J. Alden Weir when they came to Paris, and looked after their students when they came with letters of introduction. She also had an intimate acquaintance with the New York art market through her friendship

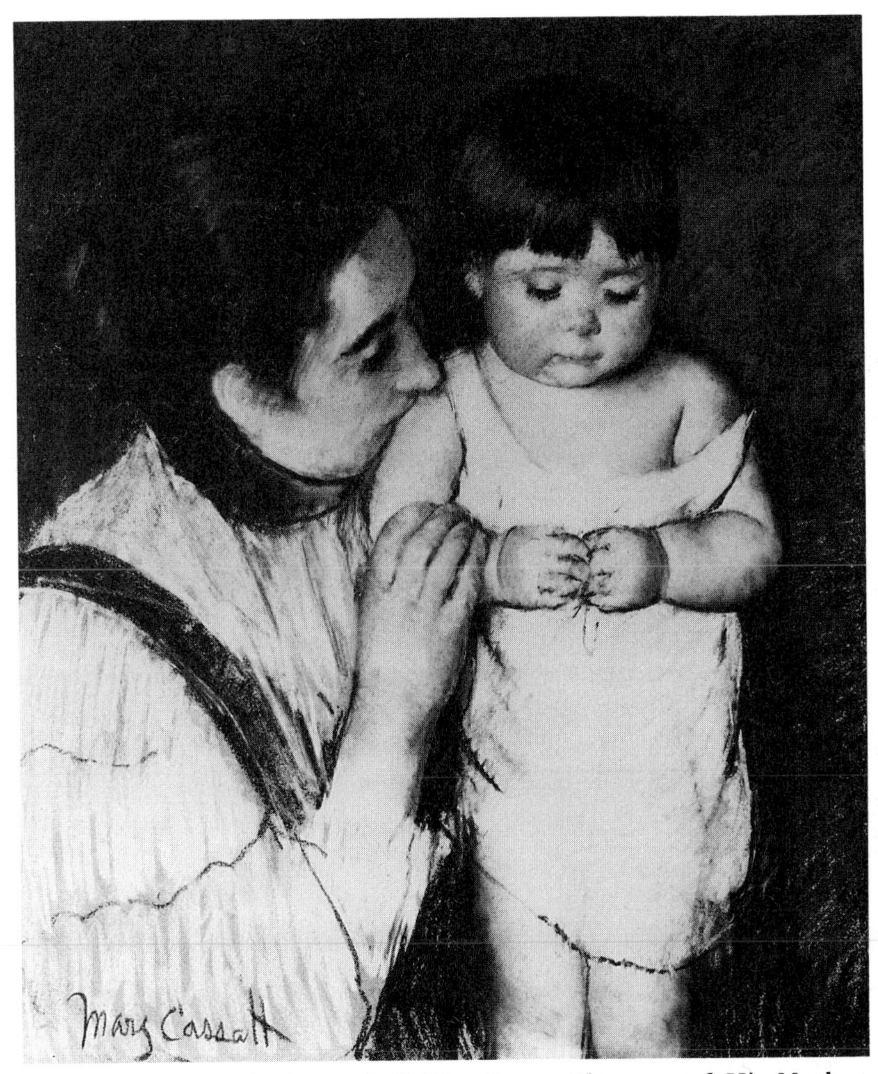

99. ***Mary Cassatt,*** **Mother and Child—Young Thomas and His Mother,** ***1895***
Pastel, 23⅝ x 19¾ in.
The Pennsylvania Academy of the Fine Arts

with Harry and Louisine Havemeyer and the Durand-Ruel family. But since she had been away so long and had so slight an acquaintance with the city even when she lived in the United States, New York must have seemed too great an abstraction for her to be closely engaged in it. After this exhibition, her ties became much stronger. When she had her next exhibition there, three years later, she broke her long exile for a firsthand glimpse of the streets paved with gold.

The exhibition that opened in the elegant midtown galleries of Durand-Ruel, located at Thirty-sixth Street and Fifth Avenue, was not as large as the previous one in Paris, but was similar to it in many ways. Durand-Ruel showed the mother and child paintings and the mural-related works from 1893 that had not yet been sold and added her most recent mother and child pastels. Only seventeen of the sixty-four works were shipped from Durand-Ruel's Paris gallery. Nineteen were borrowed from American collections, including those of her brothers, the Havemeyers, her cousins the Scotts, and other collectors such as John H. Whittemore. The remaining twenty-eight works in the exhibition were her drypoints and color prints, most of which had been shown at the New York gallery before. The result was a less perfect show than the one in Paris, since her best works were in Parisian private collections and had not been lent to the New York venue, but it served as a similar kind of retrospective.

The New York critics treated her with great respect; they all knew her work and knew her reputation in Paris. For most, this was the first time they could see a large group of objects representing her full range. There were works dating from early to late—paintings, pastels, and prints. Such a variety naturally elicited different responses, and Cassatt may have been surprised by the depth of American critical judgments. After her experience with Chicago, she tended to dismiss American opinions as superficial. Although there were fatuous reviews by both extreme admirers and detractors, the critics who fell in the middle, such as the anonymous critic for *The New York Times,* wrote thoughtfully and judged each piece individually.

The *Times* reviewer preferred the earlier, "softer" Impressionist paintings to the more recent, carefully drawn paintings and pastels of the period around the time she worked on the mural, but he found her work in general "rarely, if ever, uninteresting."[11] William Walton, who wrote for *Scribner's Magazine,* had followed her work for years and felt her more recent work was her best and praised her talent for bringing flesh to life on the canvas. He was also fully aware of her choice of strong art over mere prettiness, "The old doctrine of 'Beauty' has been superseded among the moderns by a haunting fear of falling into the pretty-pretty. Miss Cassatt is probably too conscious of her strength to be much troubled by this dread, but the unregenerate spectator will sometimes wish for a little more pandering to his prejudices in this matter."[12] Most reviewers also stressed that although she was a member of the Impressionist group and learned from Manet and Degas, she "manages to preserve a powerful personality and a strong originality that are extremely attractive."[13] Although the American critics did not tend to be literary figures as were the Paris critics such as Mellério, Geoffroy, and Fénéon, not to mention Mallarmé or Zola, nevertheless they were earnest and well informed and strove for fair judgments. The American press's handling of her exhibition had much to do with rekindling her interest in the American art world and the fostering of closer ties in the years to come.

This first exposure in her own country was the beginning of the general public's acquaintance with her. While she had always been known by the small circle of artists and collectors who went beyond conventional bounds, she had not reached a sizable audience before this time. In the next few years, thanks to exhibitions and related reproductions of her work in mass publications, she struck a chord beyond the art community—a phenomenon that would never have been predicted from her initial debut at the Chicago fair. Popularity on this level was not something she had ever sought, and, in fact, her career was calculated, if anything, to discourage it; but to her great surprise, from this point on, it was something she would have to reckon with.

Admiration of a more substantial sort came from sales of works from the New York exhibition. Some sales were to those with personal ties to the artist: the Havemeyers bought a painting and a pastel, and her cousin Annie Scott bought a pastel mother and child to go with the theater painting she had bought some ten years earlier. Both the Havemeyers and Mrs. Scott were building handsome collections of Impressionist art. Other purchasers included John H. Whittemore, an amateur artist and collector who had made Cassatt's acquaintance in Paris and was beginning to add her work to his growing collection of Impressionism. He may have in turn introduced his friend Alfred Pope, a wealthy industrialist from Cleveland, to Cassatt's art, since Pope bought his second painting by Cassatt from that exhibition. Another American collector who was to amass a large number of Cassatt paintings beginning in 1895 was Cyrus J. Lawrence, who was already a leading collector of Impressionist canvases, particularly by Monet.

The sales from the show totaled $7,100, almost enough to cover the cost of Mesnil-Beaufresne, although Cassatt would not have received the full amount. It is difficult to tell what percentage Durand-Ruel took as his commission, since at times he made standard lump-sum payments to Cassatt at regular intervals, and at other times he seems to have passed on the proceeds from the sale of a particular work. At any rate, Cassatt's sales in these years were certainly sufficient not only to support her but also to allow her to buy a country home. She added this money to the family account at the Paris branch of the Philadelphia-based Drexel Harjes bank, now under her mother's name. She did not think of her earnings as "her" money, but she was sufficiently proud of her income to feel that she was not beholden to her family for support.

She settled into the Beaufresne château for the summer of 1895 with great pleasure. The work on the house was more or less completed, the grounds were less of a chore than she had imagined they would be, and she had a summer of work planned without the pressure of an exhibition or any other deadline. Her mother's health was a nagging worry, but it was mitigated by a round of visits from old and new friends who relieved the sadness of her mother's slow decline.

Her work from this summer shows that she was delighted to be outdoors after the long bleak winter. In fact, what intrigued her most of all was the reflecting pool, long and rectangular in the formal manner of bygone centuries, that stretched out behind the house (figure 100). With *The Boating Party* from the Cap d'Antibes still fresh in her mind, she posed her models in a small boat on the pond and painted them floating leisurely across the

100. View of the pond, Château de Beaufresne

101. Mary Cassatt,* Feeding the Ducks, *1895
Third State
Drypoint and aquatint, 11⅝ x 15¾ in.
Collection of Mr. and Mrs. Jem Hom

surface in the company of a resident flock of ducks. The sensations of color, sunlight, and floating were so appealing that she set up her printing press in the small architectural "folly" built on the dam at the far edge of the pond and made a color print of the subject, *Feeding the Ducks,* while immersed in the picturesque setting (figure 101).

Louisine Havemeyer found Mary in her pond-studio at the end of the summer. The Havemeyers had come to Europe to travel and make some art purchases. While Harry was transacting business in Paris in late August, Louisine and the children slipped out to Beaufresne to see Cassatt and her new château. "Eight o'clock in the morning would find her in her grey blouse in the small pavillion over the dam which fed her 'piece d'eau' and where she had installed her printing press. There she would work while daylight lasted with the aid of a printer [brought out from Paris at Cassatt's expense]. She did her own coloring and wiping of the plates; it was at the cost of much physical strain for she actually did the manual work."[14]

That summer Cassatt was thinking about producing a new series of color prints along the lines of the set of ten she had done in 1890–91. She had been impressed by recent arguments in the art world that art should be democratized, that art should not be restricted just to paintings and other fine art media, but should be adapted to all types of useful objects. Prints were once again in vogue because they could be mass-produced and offered to the general public at lower prices. She saw this as particularly urgent in America:

> I believe [nothing] will inspire a taste for art more than the possibility of having it in the home. I should like to feel that amateurs in America could have an example of my work, a print or an etching for a few dollars. That is what they do in France. It is not left to the rich alone to buy art; the people —even the poor—have taste and buy according to their means, and here they can always find something they can afford.[15]

Cassatt was undoubtedly already feeling the demand for her art from the general American public and looked for a way to satisfy it. To this end, she thought of publishing a portfolio that would include not only her own work but that of other American artists, such as John Singer Sargent. She asked Vernon Lee, when she visited in July, if she would consider writing an introduction for the portfolio. Lee related their discussion in a letter to a friend:

> [Miss Cassatt] wants to make art cheap, to bring it within reach of the comparatively poor, and projects a series of coloured etchings, for which she wants me to write a little preface. She wants other artists to do something similar, suggested Sargent—do you think he would? She has most generously given me one of her new and most beautiful etchings, a mother and baby, green on green, quite lovely.[16]

Cassatt's plan for a new series of color prints was forgotten in September, when her mother entered a crisis phase in her illness. Louisine Havemeyer, who had known Mrs. Cassatt for more than fifteen years, was devoted to her in her last illness and sat for hours holding her hand. Perhaps to distract Mary, she posed for the first of a series of portraits her friend was to do of her and her daughters in the next few years (figure 102).

The death of Mary's mother, Katherine Kelso Johnston Cassatt, on October 21, 1895, at Beaufresne, brought forth an outpouring of sympathy from her friends all over the world. In the years since her mother had come

102. Mary Cassatt,* Portrait of Mrs. Havemeyer and Her Daughter Electra, *1895
Pastel, 24 x 30½ in.
Private collection

to live with her in Paris, and since the death of her sister Lydia, she had grown closer to her mother than to any other person in her life. Katherine Cassatt had become her mainstay and source of encouragement in her art and her life, as well as being an intelligent, charming companion. Mary's artistic and intellectual friends viewed her not just as her daughter's elderly parent, a shadowy figure always in the background, but as an active presence who sometimes charmed friends away from her daughter. Louisine Havemeyer, who was admittedly partial to Mrs. Cassatt, spoke of her in the strongest terms:

> Anyone who had the privilege of knowing Mary Cassatt's mother would know at once that it could be from her and from her alone that she, as well as her brother A. J. Cassatt, inherited their ability. . . . I think Mrs. Cassatt had the most alert mind I ever met. She was a fine linguist, an admirable

housekeeper, remarkably well read, was interested in everything, and spoke with more conviction, and possibly more charm than Miss Cassatt.[17]

Louisine Havemeyer sailed for New York before Mrs. Cassatt's death, but she returned in the spring, only a few months later. Outside Cassatt's family, she was probably the principal support for her friend in her time of grief. Havemeyer in her memoirs wrote simply, "To poor Miss Cassatt the loss was irreparable. She struggled bravely."[18] Cassatt herself, when she began to bring her life back to normal, explained her breaches of courtesy during those dark days, "Please give my regards to Mr. Weir when you see him & tell him I have not had the courage to thank him for his letter, it reached me when I was in great trouble—"[19] In fact, she confessed to a friend two years later that she was struck to her very core, "[I] was so bereft & so tired of life that I thought I could not live. . . ."[20]

At the age of fifty-one Mary Cassatt was alone. She had forgone the opportunity to marry and have her own family; her sister, who ordinarily would have been her companion in old age, had died thirteen years before; the long lives of her parents had prevented her from establishing any other kind of living situation with a companion or close friend. She was faced with an unusually hard burden of loneliness, and she missed her mother acutely for the rest of her life. However, she had had years to plan for this moment. Losing elderly parents was to be expected sooner or later, and basically she was mentally prepared. The period of mourning was no doubt extraordinarily painful, but it was not as devastating to her as had been the death of Lydia, which had seemed so unexpected and unjust. In the end, although she thought she would not be able to go on living, she eventually wrote to her friend, "now I know I must."[21]

A sign of her ability to cope with this sadness was the speed with which she returned to work, and the large output of the next two years. She began with portraits of her namesake niece, Ellen Mary (figure 103), whom she saw for the first time when Gard and Jennie sailed to Europe to be with her at their mothers' death. Thirteen years before, Cassatt had used portraiture as a form of healing after Lydia died; she started with a portrait of Aleck and went on to do two pastel portraits of her youngest niece, Elsie, in 1883. One of the portraits of Elsie stayed in the Cassatts' Paris apartment (the other went to Aleck in Philadelphia), where it hung over the fireplace (see figure 69). When Cassatt turned to paint Ellen Mary, the new "Elsie," she copied the pose and composition of the beloved portrait over the fireplace and went over in her mind the last years of her parents' lives as they

103. *Mary Cassatt,* Ellen Mary Cassatt in a White Coat, *1896*
Oil on canvas, 32¼ x 24 in.
Anonymous fractional gift in honor of Ellen Mary Cassatt
Courtesy, Museum of Fine Arts, Boston

unfolded under Elsie's watchful gaze. The portrait of Ellen Mary was a chance to relive and honor the past, but at the same time it symbolized the beginning of a new life.

Other portraits followed in the year after her mother's death. Since Gardner and Jennie had come to Europe for a stay of two years, Cassatt also had a chance to paint Jennie and "little" Gard. When Louisine Havemeyer and her family returned to Paris in the spring of 1896, Cassatt executed a formal portrait of Louisine and one of her older daughter, Adaline. These were therapeutic for Cassatt, since she could gain the benefit of getting back to work while at the same time she could spend long hours with the people she loved best. It is telling that there are no portraits of Aleck, Lois, or any of their children from this period—or, indeed, ever again. In spite of the fact that they also came to Europe for short trips during this time, Cassatt turned to others as her main source of comfort.

In addition to the portraits of family and friends, Cassatt was also able to produce a number of other works to turn over to Durand-Ruel, who immediately shipped them to the New York gallery, where they found ready sales. Although she was free of the stress of preparing for an exhibition, she seems to have been under a similar kind of pressure to finish new works to meet a demand in the market. She worked alternately in oil and pastel, but did not immediately execute her idea of a new series of prints. The new works did not continue her experiments with boating subjects that had occupied her during the summer of 1895. Instead, she returned to the mother and child theme—perhaps inspired by the presence of Ellen Mary.

Although she kept a watchful eye during this period on new developments in the Paris art world while, at the same time, doing more research into old master art, she was at a point in her career at which none of the art she saw around her would have much influence over her direction. Now that she was no longer working within the framework of a group or new movement, and since her art was exhibited often and selling well, she forged ahead on her own. She used an exquisite pastel technique, refined to old master standards by studying the work of Maurice Quentin de La Tour, to depict the simplest of subjects: the embrace of mother and child, a mother holding a glass for her child to drink from, a mother and child playing patty-cake (figure 104). These are neither Impressionist nor symbolist works; nor are they Postimpressionist in the style of Gauguin, Cézanne, Seurat, or the Nabis such as Vuillard or Bonnard. People who did not know her past would not have been able to place her within any of the current major styles.

Cassatt's departure from Impressionism and any of the succeeding

104. Mary Cassatt,* Patty-Cake, *1897
Pastel, 23¼ x 28¼
The Denver Art Museum

avant-garde styles in Paris caused her to be treated less and less as a member of the Impressionist group. The demand for Impressionist art grew rapidly throughout Europe and the United States in the 1890s. She was often included in group exhibitions, but just as often she was not. Her friend Pissarro, whom she now saw more of than any other member of the old group because of the proximity of their country homes, was also beginning to be seen as on the fringes of Impressionism, and the two no doubt spent much time discussing the change in attitude. Pissarro, who went through a period of Neo-Impressionist pointillist brushwork, returned to a version of his earlier, classic Impressionist style in the mid-1890s, when he was asked by Durand-Ruel to paint a series of the boulevards of Paris. He worried about the ascendancy of Monet and Renoir, who were now firmly fixed in the public's concept of Impressionism, and his own value in comparison with them. When he heard that a group of his paintings on view in Berlin had received a lukewarm reception, he wrote in anguish to his son:

> Why should people there be interested in my paintings when even in Paris where I am known, known by everybody, people scorn or don't understand them. Moreover, as a result of this incomprehension I myself am ending up by wondering whether my work isn't poor and empty, without a hint of talent. It is said that money is scarce, but that is only relatively true; doesn't Monet sell his work, and at very high prices, don't Renoir and Degas sell? No, like Sisley, I remain in the rear of the impressionist line.[22]

This period of reevaluation of the Impressionists, producing a hierarchy among the old comrades, was excruciatingly painful for those not at the top of the list. Although Cassatt certainly shared Pissarro's dismay at the unevenness of the group's success, she did not feel it as strongly. She, unlike Pissarro, did not return to the motifs and style of her Impressionist days to win acceptance in the public's new vision of the group. Instead, she developed a unique style, unlike any she had used before. Since she was not a landscapist, she did not feel Pissarro's rivalry with Monet and Renoir. Of her closest rivals, Morisot was now dead and could no longer challenge her, and she could feel no enmity toward Degas, whom she had always seen as the greatest artist of her day. When Degas's prices rose to a high of thirty thousand francs in the 1890s, compared with Cassatt's high of fifteen thousand francs, Cassatt would only look at her Degas paintings with greater satisfaction. Since Cassatt's paintings were exhibited more and sold for higher prices than Pissarro's, whose highest prices were five thousand to six thousand francs, she could observe history's reshuffling of Impressionism with greater equanimity.

By the beginning of 1897 Cassatt had probably already settled with Durand-Ruel that he would hold another exhibition of her work in New York in the spring of 1898, because that year was one of the most productive of her entire career. Not only did she turn over to her dealer at least twelve new paintings and pastels, but she also was finally able to get back to her idea of a new series of color prints.

She lived that year the way she had always wanted to—she spent the winter in Paris and the summer and fall at Mesnil-Beaufresne. Both the apartment and the house were now run in an orderly fashion by her longtime maid, Mathilde Valet (figure 105). Valet had joined the Cassatt household around the time of Lydia's death in 1882, and was held in such high esteem by the Cassatts that Aleck hired her sister Bertha to run his household in Philadelphia. The Valets were Alsatian German by birth, but the sisters, and apparently a cousin, Susan, were all in service in Paris. They were educated

105. Photograph of Mathilde Valet, 1914 F. A. Sweet Papers, Archives of American Art, Smithsonian Institution

and spoke several languages, and were considered a cut above the average household servant. When Cassatt's mother died, Valet took over some of the management of the house that Mrs. Cassatt had once handled. Although Cassatt was conscientious about her domestic responsibilities, she relied on Valet to relieve her of many duties that the lady of the house would normally have performed. Valet understood Cassatt's lifestyle—her need for uninterrupted work, her discriminating taste, and that of her wealthy and cultured visitors, as well as her high standards for herself and those who worked for her. Cassatt in turn respected Valet's skill and appreciated her intelligence and loyalty; she gave her a great deal of responsibility that Valet might not have had in another situation. Although there were other servants in Cassatt's household, Cassatt and Valet formed the team that made it run smoothly. In the absence of other family, the two women also formed a close emotional bond that lasted until Cassatt's death in 1926. In later years Valet nursed Cassatt through her last illnesses and, in return, Cassatt provided her with a nest egg for her own old age.

At the end of this tranquil and productive year, 1897, Cassatt submitted herself to the torture of sea travel so that she might revisit the country of her birth for the first time since 1875. She had always suffered from acute seasickness. As she got older she found fewer compelling reasons to put up with it, even for short distances. She refused to cross the English Channel again, after 1883, or take a cruise on the Mediterranean in her brother Gardner's yacht. She even confessed to getting seasick when she went out in a boat to study the reflections on the water for *The Boating Party* (figure 95).[23] Her decision later that year to make the trip across the Atlantic, therefore, was courageous, and must be attributed to the persuasion of those closest to her—the Gardner Cassatts and the Havemeyers. Her recent success in New York and the opportunity to see her exhibition there in March were also factors.

The impact of her homecoming on January 4, 1898—arriving in New York and departing immediately for Philadelphia—was dulled by her wretched condition after a week on the waves. She had to be carried off the boat on a stretcher. When she finally revived, she was settled in Gardner's town house at 1418 Spruce Street ready to assess the changes to Philadelphia that had taken place in the more than twenty-two years since her last visit. Philadelphia, like Paris, was now in its modern guise—electricity, telephone, and rapid transit had transformed the pace of life as much as new construction befitting the Gilded Age had changed its appearance. "This is a curious experience to me, after twenty two years absence everything is so different that I wonder if I really remember anything."[24]

While she saw much of her brother Aleck and his family, she was more comfortable staying with Gardner, Jennie, and their children. Jennie had just had her third and last child, Eugenia, in August. Cassatt came on this trip prepared to work and soon had her pastels out making sketches of Ellen Mary that she kept for herself and completed a finished pastel portrait of Ellen Mary and her brother Gardner that she gave to the family.

The energetic Jennie Cassatt (figure 106) openly admired her sister-in-law and pressed her to do family portraits whenever she could. She and Gardner were not as avid about collecting art as Aleck was, but they decorated their house with Barbizon and Impressionist paintings and hung the examples of Mary's work that she was willing to give them. Jenny would probably have enjoyed having the professional life her sister-in-law had; she loved her children but spaced them out in age so that they were not all-consuming, and thus she was always able to keep up the activities she enjoyed outside the home. She and Mary were so similar in temperament that no rivalry developed between them.

106. Photograph of Jennie C. Cassatt at Kelso, c. 1908
Private collection

Mary's relationship with Lois, however, had worsened in the last few years. This was partly aggravated by Mary's friendship with Jennie, of whom Lois had been critical since Gard married her. After Jennie's trip to Paris in 1891, when she was such a comfort to Mary at the death of her father, Lois allowed her old dislike of both of them to resurface. Lois was also jealous of the attention the Paris Cassatts paid to Jennie's children, which she felt deprived her own. This feeling, which arose at the birth of Gardner, was exacerbated when Jennie suddenly had Ellen Mary eight years later and Eugenia three years after that. Mary Cassatt's obvious delight in her new nieces was galling to Lois.

Lois was an extraordinarily devoted mother. She was wrapped up in her children when they were young and developed friendships with them as they grew older. Her passion for her children was very nearly matched by Aleck's, so watching their children enter their twenties and begin to scatter was a difficult adjustment for them. Both Lois and Aleck increased their outside activities to fill the void. Aleck maintained his thoroughbred stock farm in Chester County, he served as supervisor for Lower Merion Township, and he acted as consultant to his old friend Frank Thomson, who had just become president of the Pennsylvania Railroad. Lois put more time into clubs and organizations, especially those based on family heritage such as the Colonial Dames and the Society of Daughters of the Cincinnati, the female counterpart of the Society of the Cincinnati, which Aleck joined. Because of the research needed to document ancestry dating back to the American Revolution and beyond for membership in these organizations, they both developed an interest in family genealogy. Another outlet for them was the summer house in Bar Harbor in addition to the town house in Philadelphia, the country estate, Cheswold, in Lower Merion Township, and the farm in Chester County.

None of the interests that filled Lois and Aleck's lives when Mary Cassatt visited them in 1898 were of the sort that would bring the three closer together. Aleck's interest in art and collecting waned as he grew busier with other things, and some of Lois's long-standing indifference to his sister's art seemed to rub off on him. The loss of this shared passion was a blow to the relationship of brother and sister, as was the recent loss of both their parents, whose health Mary and Aleck had agonized over for the past ten years. Now in their fifties, they were left with a great deal of mutual affection, but little else in common.

Mary Cassatt may have looked at her adult nieces and nephews with the same detachment. She had seen them often since making their acquaintance in 1880, and could not but be affectionately curious about them now that she could see them as adults in their home setting. So little concerned was she about keeping them as children that she enthusiastically embraced their fiancés or fiancées and spouses as each one in turn entered into a permanent relationship. Her favorite, Eddie, then twenty-nine, who had spent long periods of time living in Paris, had been married for three years and already had a young child. His year at Saint-Cyr led to West Point and a promising military career. His wife, Emily, was a lively young woman who warmly embraced her "aunt" Mary and shared with her the young daughter, Lois or "Baby," who was the first to make Mary Cassatt a great-aunt.

Rob, twenty-five, who had displayed some artistic talent as a child, grew up wanting to follow his father into engineering and a railroad career. His path was rocky, however, since he was not admitted into the engineering program at Harvard and at the moment was trying to work his way up in the railroad instead. In 1898 he was working in Altoona and living at the Logan House, just as his father had done years before. Katharine, twenty-seven, and Elsie, twenty-three, were still living at home at this time and followed their mother into clubs and charitable occupations. Katharine had a long-standing relationship with her childhood beau, James Hutchinson, a rising physician in Philadelphia, and would soon become engaged to him. Elsie was also on the verge of becoming engaged to Plunkett Stewart, another longtime friend. The girls were among the ten wealthiest heiresses in Philadelphia and their relationships were carefully monitored by their anxious parents.

This group of attractive and useful young people gave Cassatt much to be proud of. However, she surely missed in them the zeal that had marked her and her brother in their early days, and still drove them to lead complicated, demanding lives. Faced with these young adults who had turned out to bear little resemblance to their father or herself, she looked to her other, brand-new nieces and nephews who still held promise.

As Cassatt struggled with the loss of common interests with her Philadelphia family, those family members also must have struggled with having her as a relative—an artist whose controversial style was freely debated in the local newspapers, bringing unwanted attention to them all. Cassatt had allowed two works to be sent to the annual exhibition of her old alma mater, the Pennsylvania Academy, so that they would be on view when she arrived in January. She was surprised to find that the Philadelphia critics were still arguing the issues of Impressionism, and that her own work was being criticized for its lack of "academic" polish. The attacks on her style and her mastery of the craft were so virulent that a defender was forced to point out that "If she is unconventional, it is not because she is ignorant of conventions, but because after having served an apprenticeship and learning her trade thoroughly, she has been given original power to go forth in absolute independence, working out her own ideals in her own way . . ."[25] Mary Cassatt herself would have brushed off the whole debate as hopelessly old-fashioned, but Lois Cassatt would have been embarrassed and would have had trouble explaining it to her friends in the Colonial Dames. In Paris, Cassatt was considered a proper Philadelphia lady. But in Philadelphia, it became clear just how far she had strayed from that refined path.

It was with mutual relief that she left Philadelphia and the family for a tour of other sites—New York, Boston, and Naugatuck, Connecticut—where she would again be in the company of artists and collectors. Foremost on the long list of friends she was scheduled to visit on this trip were the Havemeyers, whom she had known for over twenty years, but only on French soil. When she arrived in New York she finally got a chance to see them in their home setting, as people powerful in New York business and social circles and not only as wealthy American travelers.

Just as interesting to Cassatt was the collection she had helped Harry and Louisine Havemeyer amass and the sumptuous house on Fifth Avenue they had commissioned and moved into in 1891. In 1898 their collection was still heavily weighted in favor of old master paintings, Oriental ceramics, and other decorative arts. Their collection of modern art, which included the purchases Louisine had made as early as the 1870s, family portraits and other works by their friend Cassatt, and an assortment of Degas and Manet canvases, was beginning to grow very quickly. While Cassatt was in New York she exerted her influence over Harry Havemeyer to buy a number of Impressionist works that were currently on the market in New York and Paris.

While a guest of the Havemeyers, Cassatt could renew old ties with artists and other friends now living in New York. In addition to specially arranged dinners and receptions, Cassatt could also mix with the crowd that came for the Havemeyers' Sunday-afternoon musicales in the Rembrandt Room. Here she might find, as the young Homer St. Gaudens did, "painters like Thomas Dewing, architects like Stanford White, sculptors like Frederick MacMonnies,"[26] or friends from her past like Will Sartain, William Merritt Chase, or J. Alden Weir.

In addition to sizing up the New York art scene, Cassatt also spent some time in preparation for her upcoming exhibition at Durand-Ruel. She had hand-carried some of the works for the show, finished too late to be shipped with the others from the Durand-Ruel gallery in Paris. These were a group of color prints, all done using the same models, satisfying her long-standing desire to design another series like the one she exhibited in 1891. She finished three of a proposed four plates for this series, obviously working up to the last minute, and finally had to leave the fourth behind in Paris uncompleted.

When the show opened on February 28, Cassatt got a firsthand glimpse of the New York art world at work. Unlike Paris, where her exhibitions would be attended mainly by artists and intellectuals, the most prominent visitors in New York were the wealthy, for whom art was a leisure-time activity, and behind them came newspaper critics and other artists. Fortunately for Cassatt, her art appealed to both the educated eye and to the layman, and thus received a warm reception. Her reviews this time were almost universally positive, with special praise going to her color prints and her mother and child compositions. "The conventional woman, elegant, sickly, and insipid, and the conventional infant are nowise to Miss Cassatt's taste. She likes them strong, lusty, brown or rosy, alive and glad of it."[27]

Cassatt also came to New York intending to work. Although it had been years since she had practiced as a portraitist, she was persuaded by various American collectors to take up this trade once again. One of her most fervent admirers, Cyrus J. Lawrence, commissioned her to do a pastel portrait of his wife and grandson (figure 107) as well as a sketch of his daughter, Mary Say Lawrence. Cyrus Lawrence paid her one thousand dollars, and Cassatt's American tour as a portraitist was begun.

It is interesting that Durand-Ruel recorded all Cassatt's commissioned works from this trip and presumably took the gallery's standard cut of the sales price, implying that the firm acted in some way as Cassatt's agent in setting up these commissions. Their records also show a portrait for a Mrs. B. Thayer that is today unidentified.

Portrait commissions were the reason Cassatt went to Boston after her stay in New York. Although she also had many friends among the artists' and collectors' circles in that city, it is doubtful she would have included it on her itinerary if it had not been for a portrait commission she had taken on. This time the subjects were to be the three children of Mr. and Mrs. Gardiner Greene Hammond. The parents had their own portraits done by John Singer Sargent; but he declined the request to do the children, recommending Mary Cassatt instead. Surprisingly, Cassatt agreed, even though the family was not personally known to her, nor were they collectors of her work. The experience was an agreeable one; the Hammonds introduced her to a wide circle of collectors in Boston, and she added as a favor a third, uncommissioned portrait to the two she had contracted to do. She typically set up her drawing board in a temporary studio in the sitter's house and endeavored to keep the children quiet by telling stories or having someone read to them. At the Hammonds' she caught a glimpse of Gardiner dressed for the park in such a dashing cape that she couldn't resist sketching him in it (figure 108).

She stayed in a hotel in Boston that would accommodate both her maid, Mathilde Valet, and her dog, who were her constant traveling companions. From the hotel she made contact with other friends she had met in Paris, including the painter Rose Lamb and the artist and collector Sarah Choate Sears. Cassatt had made the acquaintance of both women in the late 1880s or early 1890s and found an instant rapport with them both. Mrs. Sears also became an early collector of Cassatt's work, and by the time Cassatt visited Boston she owned a pastel mother and child and a color print. Sears's own work in watercolor and pastel was widely exhibited in Boston and New York, and the two saw in each other a similar energetic and inquiring

107. Mary Cassatt, **Portrait of Mrs. Cyrus J. Lawrence with Grandson R. Lawrence Oakley,** *1898*
Pastel, 28 x 23 in.
Sterling and Francine Clark Art Institute; gift of Mrs. R. Lawrence Oakley

108. Mary Cassatt, **Head of Small Boy (Master Gardiner Green Hammond, Jr.),** *1898 Pastel, 20 x 19½ in. Phoenix Art Museum, Harrington Collection*

personality. Sears later took up photography and became a member of the New York Photo Secession, led by the progressive artist and gallery owner Alfred Stieglitz. Sears kept in touch with Cassatt during her frequent trips to Paris in years after this and became Cassatt's link to many of the radical developments in American art after 1900.

Cassatt moved on from Boston to the small town of Naugatuck, Connecticut (near Waterbury), where she was commissioned to do a portrait for the Whittemore family. The wealthy Whittemores had purchased important paintings of hers in New York and now wanted an example of her portraiture. As happened with the Hammonds, Cassatt finished the portrait she was commissioned to do and then went on to do others out of friendship. In all, she finished three portraits for the family—one of Mrs. John Howard Whittemore, one of Mrs. Harris Whittemore with her baby daughter, Helen, and one of the young Harris Whittemore, Jr., and established a lifelong association with them.

While staying with the Whittemores, Cassatt was introduced to their friends and fellow collectors Mr. and Mrs. Alfred Pope and their thirty-year-old daughter, Theodate (figure 109). Alfred Pope, although not an artist himself, was a discerning collector of modern French art and was eager for Cassatt to see his collection of Degas, Manet, Monet, and others and to receive her advice on future purchases. His daughter had persuaded her parents to move from Cleveland to Farmington, Connecticut (near where

109. Gertrude Kasebier, photograph of Theodate Pope, c. 1900 Hill-Stead Museum Archives

she had gone to school), and was busy designing a house for them that would show off their collection.

As impressed as Cassatt was with the taste of the Popes, she was even more impressed by their extraordinary daughter. Theodate Pope—short and rotund—had the personality of a zealot. She was a supporter of various political causes, including feminism and socialism, and was determined to make her mark on the world. She chose architecture as her field of endeavor, because it combined art and usefulness, and taught herself enough to design a series of houses, schools, and monuments during a thirty-year period. Her great wealth was both a help and a hindrance; she used her advantages to construct her family's house, Hill-Stead, with the help of the most famous architect of the day, Stanford White, while at the same time advocating a universal distribution of wealth and an end to household servants. Cassatt delighted in this flamboyant yet serious young woman—arguing with her at every turn—but reveling in the contact with such an original mind. Theodate was only a year older than her own oldest nephew, Ed, and seemed more like "family" to her than any of her own young relatives.

At the end of Cassatt's American trip, she had executed some twenty portraits and portrait sketches. The length of her stay is in some doubt. Frederick Sweet, after interviewing descendants of the Whittemores and Hammonds, believed that she stayed through the fall of 1898 and into 1899. She had projected a short trip, writing to Rose Lamb upon her arrival that she would return to France that same spring (1898); and the stock books of Durand-Ruel show that all the portraits were recorded as executed and paid for by May of 1898. The stock books also show that she finished and turned over other works to the dealer by the fall of 1898, and, although they do not reveal her location when she painted them, it seems likely they were done in France. Until other definitive information about her whereabouts surfaces, we must assume that she followed her own plan and was back in her beloved Beaufresne for the summer of 1898.

After this short but intense reacquaintance with her homeland, Cassatt's ties to America were stronger than they had been at any time since she left as a young art student in the 1860s. As her circle of professional French friends scattered—either retiring to the country or passing away (Morisot in 1895, Sisley in 1899)—she replaced them with Americans. Her trip to the United States cemented her friendship with such people as Sarah Sears, Theodate Pope, and, of course, the Havemeyers. Since she had lost interest in the contemporary art scene, which became more extreme every year, she turned her back on the artists' circles and found a more congenial atmosphere among collectors of Impressionism, many of whom were American. She continued her own work, and agreed to two portraits in the style of her American series during the next year. She continued her studies of mothers and children, often using the interiors or gardens at Beaufresne as a setting. In this calm manner, secure in a new set of friends and in the solace of her work, she passed the last year of the nineteenth century.

Chapter VIII

"THE MOST EMINENT OF LIVING AMERICAN WOMEN PAINTERS" (1900–1910)

Mary Cassatt was fifty-five years old when the new century began (figure 110). Hers was the generation fortunate enough to be in charge when assessments were being made of the outgoing century and plans were being made for the new one. She was also unlucky enough to see the power of her own generation decline rapidly—within the first decade—and be replaced by a rebellious new order. She rode the crest of the wave for the first ten years of the century, engaging in minor skirmishes with the emerging "modernists," but enjoying a period in which she received international recognition for her art and her ideas. She was lauded for her participation in Impressionism, which had now fully emerged as a major movement, and, because of her increasing conservatism in style and subject matter, she also had the support of the art-world establishment.

Ironically, recognition on such a scale began to have a deleterious effect on her current art production. The clamor for more and more mother and child paintings prevented her from exploring new subject matter and mediums, which had kept her art fresh in the past. Instead, to keep up her interest, she sought grander effects by using old master techniques and more elaborate costumes. The result was too often mannered and heavy. Although she received gold medals in exhibitions and unstinting praise from critics, after the decade was over she looked back and felt she had gotten off track.

Paris greeted the twentieth century with all the bombast it could muster. As the undisputed capital of world culture, it claimed the right to hold the world's fair of 1900. For six months, it welcomed visitors from every land to its extravagant displays. Of all the great expositions of this sort in Paris,

110. Photograph of Mary Cassatt, after 1900
F. A. Sweet papers, Archives of American Art, Smithsonian Institution

the 1900 world's fair is the only one still available to revisit, since many of the major buildings, which transformed a section of Paris on both sides of the Seine, are still standing, and are being restored, one by one, to their original glory. The new train station and hotel built just for the 1900 exposition, the Gare d'Orsay, is now the Musée d'Orsay; the Grand Palais and the Petit Palais are both still in use as exhibition sites; and the Pont Alexandre III, the bridge that connected the two "palais" with the exhibition halls on the opposite side of the river, the Esplanade des Invalides, still serves as a monument to the opulence of style and scale that characterized this world's fair.

Mary Cassatt's friends and family from across the ocean did not need prompting to come to Paris in 1900. Aleck and Lois traveled in great style. Aleck, after spending seventeen years away from the Pennsylvania Railroad, was brought back as president in 1899. Although reluctant at first to give up his freedom, once he agreed to take on the job he began systematically to attack the enormous problems the railroad faced in the late 1890s. With dizzying speed and boldness, he began to consolidate railroad lines and to build a tunnel that would allow the Pennsylvania railroad to enter the lucrative port of New York City for the first time. While his new responsibilities naturally put an end to his life as a country gentleman, it did not prevent him from taking his annual trips to Europe or stop his regular visits to his sister. Lois, however, was now used to putting as much distance as she could between Mary and herself and found excuses to cut short their obligatory stays in Paris.

That summer Lois was particularly careful not to stay too long because her nemesis, Jennie Cassatt, was also a visitor to Paris. Jennie and Gard, unlike Aleck and Lois, were eager to see Mary and brought the children out to Beaufresne for a leisurely stay. The Gardner Cassatts, whose daughters, Ellen Mary and Eugenia, were only six and four, were still a family unit and filled the house with the warmth that Alexander's children had once brought. Gard was still the head of the investment firm, Cassatt & Co., and quietly shepherded the family fortunes; he was as retiring a figure in Philadelphia as his brother was a visible one (figure 111).

The most extended visit to Paris that summer was made by Cassatt's nephew Eddie, who had just finished a tour of duty in the Philippines, which Spain had ceded to the United States after the Spanish-American War. Through the influence of his father he had been reassigned to London, where he was to be military attaché at the United States embassy and was also a special representative to the International Exposition in Paris. For the next year, Cassatt saw a great deal of her nephew, who had become her favorite of Aleck's children after he spent long periods in Paris during his youth. She also had the opportunity to get to know his wife, Emily, and their beloved only child, Lois or "Baby," who was only a few months younger than Ellen Mary. Cassatt typically reached out to the spouses and

111. Photograph of J. Gardner Cassatt, after 1900
Private collection

children of her nieces and nephews and not only entertained them all in France, but established long-standing correspondences with them when they returned to the United States.

When Ed and Emily's marriage cooled, Emily fled to Paris with Baby to be comforted by Aunt Mary. Cassatt did her best to effect a reconciliation, but privately sympathized with Emily over Ed's indiscretions in London. The fact that she seemingly took Emily's side in the quarrel outraged Lois and even made Aleck turn a deaf ear to her appeals on Emily's behalf. When Ed and Emily divorced in 1901, the rift between aunt and nephew was never healed, and Mary and Lois grew even further apart. Mary and Jennie Cassatt kept up their relationship with Emily, however, for two more decades.

As inundated as she was with family during the world's fair of 1900, Cassatt still welcomed as many friends as showed up on her doorstep. Many of the American artists she had recently visited during her trip to the United States in 1898 were represented in the American section of the fine arts exhibition and came to Paris that summer, including Sarah Sears and J. Alden Weir. She also tried to persuade the Havemeyers and the Popes to come, writing to the latter, "Do come over this summer you won't regret it, Paris has changed. The fine opening from the Champs Elysées through to the 'Invalides' & the new bridge add much to one part of the town, & the exhibition is going to be very fine."[1]

Cassatt's enthusiasm for the upcoming exhibition is remarkable, since she does not appear to have been included. As with the Chicago exposition of 1893, there were various art exhibitions throughout the fair, but her name is listed under none of them. The major exhibition of contemporary art was the "Exposition Décennale," which was a ten-year survey of the best of the Paris Salon. Here could be found the work of her old conservative colleagues Bouguereau, Bonnat, Carolus-Duran, Gervex, and many others. A smaller exhibition featured the Impressionists, but showed only a limited number of early works by Monet, Pissarro, Sisley, Renoir, Degas, Cézanne, Morisot, Guillaumin, and Boudin. The American section of the large display at the Grand Palais also showed the work of many of Cassatt's old friends and colleagues, including Eakins, Whistler, Sargent, and Chase, as well as Homer, Beaux, Robinson, and Hassam. Cassatt might have been included in either the exhibition of the Impressionists or that of American paintings, and judging from her goodwill toward the whole affair was probably absent by her own choice, presumably shy of getting involved in another world's fair after her experience with Chicago.

While her work may not have been on view at the exposition, she was by no means forgotten. A small volume published by André Mellério, *L'Exposition de 1900 et l'Impressionnisme,*[2] was one of many overviews of Impressionism prompted by the end of the old century, and includes Cassatt without question in what was now considered a heroic group. A more extensive survey prepared by Camille Mauclair and published first in English as *The French Impressionists* (1903) includes Cassatt with the "minor impressionists, Pissarro, Sisley, Cézanne, Morisot, Caillebotte" and others.[3] In addition, her art could be seen at any time at Durand-Ruel's, either displayed in small groupings that constituted informal exhibitions, or by request. Other dealers such as Ambroise Vollard and the Bernheim brothers began acquiring her works as they came back on the market (Durand-Ruel had rights to all new works by her), and she began to be promoted by them through publications and exhibitions as well. Camille Mauclair published a long, laudatory article on her in *L'Art Décoratif* (1902) that featured works that were currently on the market.[4] With these signs of support in Paris and the growing demand for her art in the United States (she exhibited in Pittsburgh and Cincinnati in 1899 and 1900), she could afford to pass up the bombastic world's fair of 1900.

Cassatt spent the summers at Beaufresne and found herself more and more reluctant to leave even when the weather turned cold. The brief trips she took into Paris satisfied her need to conduct her affairs and keep an eye on the art world. Gradually she prolonged her season in the country until after the New Year. Then, in January or February, it was her practice to move back to the Rue de Marignan for the important events of the spring season in Paris. By 1900 most of her work was being done at Beaufresne and her studio in the Paris apartment was used for final touches, for executing the occasional portrait that had to be done in town, or simply for storage.

In 1901 Louisine and Harry Havemeyer offered her a different way to spend her spring. On impulse, finding they had more time on their hands than usual, they booked passage on a ship taking a southern route to Europe and disembarked at Genoa for a sightseeing tour in the warmer climates of Italy and Spain. Accompanying them was Louisine's older sister Annie Elder Munn. They sent an appeal to Paris to have Cassatt meet them when they landed. Since the trip involved no traveling on the sea, Cassatt consented, and they found her, in her punctual way, waiting on the dock in Genoa. Cassatt hadn't been to Italy since her trip with her mother in 1893, after finishing the mural for the Chicago world's fair. In fact, her most vivid memories were from the extended periods of time she spent there while based in Parma and Rome in 1872 to 1874. Louisine Havemeyer and her sister also had memories of Italy from their first trip there as teenagers in the 1870s. The three of them saw this return to Italy as something of a sentimental journey.

Harry Havemeyer had no such notion. After ten years of serious attention to the buying and selling of art, he was searching for "finds" of old master art in private collections or unpretentious art galleries. Like many businessman-collectors, Harry Havemeyer resented the control that major international dealers and auction houses exerted over the prices and availability of valuable paintings. He thought he might beat the system by going directly to the source of supply. He knew that Italian and Spanish paintings from the early Renaissance to the Baroque periods were coming into vogue among American collectors who could afford to pay astronomical prices, but it was still possible to find good-quality works—not by Leonardo or Raphael—but by Andrea del Sarto, Domenichino, Paolo Veronese, Francisco Goya, or, finally, El Greco.

He had been able to circumvent the system to a certain extent in the area of modern French paintings. Although he generally bought through major dealers or auction houses, he and Louisine had been able to see paintings first in artists' studios or the homes of private collectors because of their friendship with Mary Cassatt. Not only was Cassatt a superb connoisseur of modern French painting, but she was known and trusted by every important painter and collector of Realism and Impressionism.

The plan to do the same in Italy and Spain was something of a long shot, but was entered into eagerly by both the Havemeyers and Cassatt. Cassatt, of course, had nothing in Italy or Spain like the network she had built up in Paris over the years, but had kept her eyes and ears open to the gossip and paintings coming from the southern climes and still had many contacts there. It was also a problem that her knowledge of old master art, while based on many years of study in the major museums of Europe and extensive reading, could not rival her firsthand acquaintance with modern French art. But she trusted her keen eye and judicious temperament to be able to judge "quality" even in works and artists unfamiliar to her. The Havemeyers also felt they had learned much in their years of collecting and could sense great art to some extent as their friend could.

Armed with optimism, the group set out at a furious pace to cover the length and breadth of Italy. They traveled light, as was the Havemeyers' practice. They left their servants at home and packed only what they could manage and carry themselves. More than ten years older than the others and accustomed as she was to having Mathilde at her side and her dog in her arms, Cassatt would have preferred more comfort, but she gamely went along with the plan and enjoyed the quick pace of people as zealous as she was. They braved many discomforts stemming from the unusually cold winter in Italy and often had to take trains without first-class accommodations because they took many a side trip to see art in out-of-the-way places. In about a month's time, they had explored Genoa, Turin, Milan, Naples, Reggio, and, crossing to Sicily, Messina, Taormina, Syracuse, Girgenti, Palermo, and then back up to Rome, Bologna, Ravenna, Venice, Mantua, Padua, Florence, Milan, Brescia, and Bergamo.

The only record of this trip survives in Louisine Havemeyer's memoirs, which she began to write in the 1910s and were published after her death as *Sixteen to Sixty: Memoirs of a Collector* (1930). To Havemeyer looking back, this trip was the highlight of her life as a collector. To be on the road, surrounded by those she loved most—her husband, her sister, and her best friend—delving into the dark musty villas of a past and faded aristocracy, turning up treasures by poking around in what at first appeared to be junk: she couldn't ask for anything more. Indeed few Americans could resist such a combination of treasure hunting and immersion in the distant past, a combination that simply was not available in the United States. The Havemeyers joined the ranks of American collectors who tramped through Italy on such a quest in the first few decades of the new century.

For the first part of the trip, the group visited museums and dealers in each city and bargained in antique shops for minor pieces of jewelry and the decorative arts. By the time they got to Rome they were increasingly anxious for a major find and impressed upon one of the larger dealers that they were interested in important works. When the gallery owner in Rome showed them a picture they had already seen and refused in Milan, they lost all respect for Italian dealers. They moved on, increasingly disappointed with their inability to turn up the treasures they sought. Upon their arrival in Florence, the capital of the Italian market in old master paintings, they were ready to take extreme measures. During a visit to a large gallery, they discovered that one of the salesmen, Arthur Harnisch, was someone Cassatt had known many years before when she had been working in Italy. Their encounter was described by Louisine Havemeyer:

> "How ill he looked," said Mr. Havemeyer, "and altogether disgusted with his job. When he saw you he appeared embarrassed, as if he feared you would not care to recognize him."
>
> "I knew him so many years ago," answered Miss Cassatt, "but his face

puzzled me at first. He was an artist then, doing small things, *putti,* etc., and seemed rather successful. He married an Italian woman about the time I left Italy, and I never saw him again until today. He did indeed look ill and very poor, didn't he?"[5]

In a spirit of pity mixed with opportunism, Mary Cassatt and Harry Havemeyer saw in Arthur Harnisch the means of getting around big dealers to make direct contact with the private families who still had Italian Renaissance and Baroque paintings in their possession. For his part, Harnisch saw his own opportunity when he recognized Mary Cassatt, whom he had known as a rising young star in Rome and remembered that she was from a rich American family. When she entered the gallery with Harry Havemeyer, who was probably not previously known to Harnisch, it took him only minutes to assess the wealth and ambition of this American collector. The friendliness of the Americans and their subsequent invitation to join them that evening in their hotel boded well for the middle-aged man who lived in modest circumstances with his younger Italian wife. Harnisch quickly agreed to act as their agent, independent of the gallery, and eventually left the gallery to work full-time for the Havemeyers.

The very next day after this initial encounter, the Harnisches arranged for the Havemeyer party to see a private collection in which "the pictures were all for sale."[6] As in a fantasy treasure hunt, Louisine Havemeyer remembered that "we drew up before a shabby building, too far from Florence to be a *palazzo* and not far enough to be a villa, we followed La Signora and soon found ourselves in a large dark room, which, when some wooden shutters were thrown open, we found contained many pictures, most of them as dark as the room. . . . At an exclamation from Miss Cassatt, we turned around to see what she had found. From its hinges upon the wall she had swung a huge frame directly across the window and was looking at a portrait. As we gathered about her, La Signora said: 'That is by Paolo Veronese; it is a portrait of his wife.'"[7]

Cassatt fell in love with the picture, and although the woman depicted in it was not handsome, she felt that the quality of the technique made it a great painting. She took the Havemeyers to the Uffizi to study the Veroneses there and to convince them that this one was equal to those hanging in museums; she even swore that she would buy the painting herself if they didn't. Under such pressure from their adviser, the Havemeyers began a long and tortuous negotiation through Harnisch and were thrilled when the painting finally arrived in New York two years later.

Several romantic treasure hunts with Harnisch and his wife produced other Veroneses, a Fra Filippo Lippi, an Andrea del Sarto, a Raphael, and many more Italian works of art. Unfortunately these, like many Italian art treasures bought by American collectors, were eventually proved to be by hands other than the famous artists they were attributed to at the time. Cassatt and the Havemeyers had let their pride in their aesthetic discernment and their desire to beat the system lead them into a well-worn trap.[8] Since the authenticity of these and their other finds was not questioned until many years later, they basked, temporarily at least, in the glow of their success.

After their breakneck trip through Italy, the group lost its fourth member when they returned to Paris. Annie Munn decided to spend the next month in Cassatt's comfortable apartment on the Rue de Marignan and let the three others go to Spain without her. Cassatt was in the lead, since she was the only one who had been to Spain. Although she had not gone back to southern Spain after her lengthy stay there in 1873, it was still vivid in her mind. She took the Havemeyers first to Madrid, where they could study works of the period they were most interested in at the Prado and use this collection as a touchstone for any old master art that might be offered to them during the trip. While there, they became acquainted with El Greco's portraits, which even Cassatt had not fully appreciated before, and they became some of the earliest admirers in what would become a virtual cult of El Greco in the next few decades. "Back and back we went, and always the fascination of that painter threw a spell over us. We could not resist his art; its intensity, its individuality, its freedom and its color attracted us with irresistible force."[9]

After their conversion to El Greco, the three were driven to find a major example of his work, preferably a portrait, for the Havemeyer collection. Most driven of all was Mary Cassatt, who suddenly changed her travel plans, sent the Havemeyers on without her to visit Toledo, Seville, Cordova, and Granada, and went about finding El Grecos in Madrid by herself. She must have let her intentions be known among dealers and acquaintances in Madrid because before long she had found Joseph Wicht, who had family connections in Madrid and was obviously experienced in the Spanish art market. Through Wicht she was able to see some of the most important El Grecos and Goyas in Madrid and started the long process of untangling them from their complicated family ownership.

Probably because the Spanish old masters were less in demand than the Italian, the Spanish paintings offered to her were for the most part genuine and of very high quality. When the Havemeyers returned to Madrid, she was able to show off masterpieces such as El Greco's *Cardinal Don Fernando Niño de Guevara,* which was bought by the Havemeyers and is now in the Metropolitan Museum, and El Greco's *Assumption of the Virgin,* now in the Art Institute of Chicago. The Havemeyers' Spanish collection grew slowly but became second in importance only to their holdings of modern French paintings.

Cassatt's trip to Italy and Spain with the Havemeyers was her first extended experience acting as an expert adviser on art other than that produced by her circle of friends. In doing so, she entered a world with which she was only barely acquainted, in spite of her lifetime of activity in the European art community. She soon found that there were people, procedures, and issues of which she was ignorant, and that ignorance was very risky. At first, her supreme confidence in her "eye" was the only resource she felt she needed. She made judgments spontaneously, such as the Veronese she "discovered" in Florence, and an El Greco she spotted in the doorway of a Madrid antiques shop. Before the trip was over, she resorted to a more systematic approach. To acquaint herself with El Greco, for instance, she went out to buy all the photographs of El Greco's work she could find and paid a visit to Manuel Cossío, who was compiling a complete catalog of this artist. She listened to Cossío, who pointed out the high quality of the *Cardinal Guevara* and even had a hand in arranging for them to see the work.

Cassatt as an artist and a lover of art studied paintings closely and learned the secrets of the old master techniques. In the past she had had no need to question their authenticity or to categorize paintings by artists so carefully that she could fit an unknown work into the larger picture of an artist's complete *oeuvre.* She quite naturally relied on her own preference in paintings. If she liked a work, she was convinced it must be by a great artist—whichever one she was told it was. It was not long after this trip that she became fully aware of her own fallibility in judging the authenticity of paintings, when works she had waxed enthusiastic over were quickly found to be copies or documented works by lesser artists. Louisine Havemeyer's faith in her friend was never shaken, however, and she believed in Cassatt's judgments until she died.

Cassatt entered this field at a time when it was beginning to be in the hands of professional connoisseurs, the only ones who could devote themselves to the kind of intense study required to make accurate assessments of authorship and authenticity. With the prices rising astronomically for old master art, the number of paintings misattributed to famous artists and the number of downright fakes rose also. The work being done by Cossío on El Greco, Dmitri Rovinski on Rembrandt, or Bernard Berenson on all the Italian artists was the only safeguard against unscrupulous or careless art agents or dealers. Berenson had been assembling his massive photographic file of Italian Renaissance artists and exercising his exacting judgments about authorship for ten years before Cassatt and the Havemeyers took their buying trip through Italy. It is not to their credit that they did not hear of him for another two years.

Although they did not attempt to become experts themselves or to employ the services of an expert like Berenson, Cassatt and the Havemeyers learned to be extremely cautious in the minefield of old master art. Louisine Havemeyer arrived at this conclusion:

> It is hard to destroy the faith of a collector . . . or dampen the ardor of an enthusiast; but I believe he who relies on his own judgment, or on the appearances of things, or in the proofs of seals or dates, or on style, or on the texture of fabrics or the composition of color, or on any other test under the sun, will in ninety-nine cases out of a hundred be taken in. . . . If you wish to enjoy the subtleties of deceit, to enter the inner sanctuary of art's legerdemain, or to learn the mystery of mystification, seek them all in the revelations of art imitation, and if one has philosophy enough to surmount the disappointment, he cannot fail to be amused at the clever shrewdness of the master thief when the fraud is revealed. This experience is not easily acquired, sometimes it is very costly and we, like everyone else, paid for our knowledge.[10]

In the years after this trip, when Cassatt handled negotiations for the Havemeyers in the purchase of an old master painting, she learned to show the work to two or three other knowledgeable people, such as Theodore Duret or Roger Marx, whose opinions she valued, before allowing her friends to proceed. She had the further advantage of conducting future business in Paris (rather than in an out-of-the-way villa in Italy), where she could consult dealers, collectors, and critics before making any decisions. Furthermore, the actual purchases were very often made with the help of Durand-Ruel, who could bring his expertise as a dealer to the proceedings.

In spite of the mistakes Cassatt made in regard to the authorship of some of the old master paintings she urged the Havemeyers to buy, her exercises in connoisseurship nevertheless revealed an approach to collecting that was an extension of her own art and personality. Although as a typical American she was thrilled by the romantic European past, she nevertheless tended to judge old master artists first and foremost by their relationship to modern art. Years before, she had written to Berthe Morisot that she saw in Italian frescoes the same experimentation with color that the Impressionists had recently developed, "Really I don't see that the moderns have discovered anything about color."[11] In 1901 she was still looking for the correspondences between past and present, and called Veronese "the father of modern art"[12] because of his brilliant color and luminous shadows and asserted that El Greco's "merit is that he was two centuries ahead of his time, that is why painters, Manet amongst others thought so much of him."[13] Furthermore, true to her realist orientation, she was convinced that style overcame subject matter, and that in most cases a painting was the greater for having a less-than-beautiful subject transformed by a beautiful technique.

Her habit of seeing old master and modern art in a dialogue with each other led her to encourage the Havemeyers to broaden their old master holdings in tandem with their purchases of modern art. She wanted their collection to illustrate her own belief that great art is constantly being reborn through the centuries, and that a Degas hanging next to a Vermeer and a Courbet next to a Rembrandt would bring out the best in both of them. She disapproved of collectors who bought only old master or modern, or who didn't manage the mix properly. She thought Charles Lang Freer's collection of Oriental art mixed with contemporary American painters, such as Whistler and Dewing, was a good idea, but wondered at his selection of moderns, since he left out the French. She also looked down on Isabella Stewart Gardner's collection because she had mixed her old masters with Sargents and Zorns. Since American collectors tended toward the more conservative areas of old master art, she stressed that a great collection must have "the modern note" in it, and that, of course, came only from her French circle.

She likened the making of a great collection to the making of a great painting, and she went on to say that the painter, like the collector, "must be classic as well as modern."[14] This advice came directly from her own aesthetic as it had developed over the years. When Cassatt was assessing old master paintings for the Havemeyers in 1901, she couldn't help looking at them and comparing them with her own. Occasionally she defended something unusual, such as El Greco's depiction of eyeglasses on the Havemeyer's *Cardinal* because she herself had done the same thing in her 1879 portrait of Moyse Dreyfus. Her defense of Veronese's use of an unattractive model was at the same time a defense of her own controversial habit of hiring only the least beautiful.

Cassatt's response to the paintings she and the Havemeyers were drawn to on this trip was so personal and so powerful that at times she actually felt she had to shield herself from this art. While in Rome, she insisted that they see all the Domenichinos they could and then complained, "It upsets me terribly to see all this art. . . . It will be months before I can settle down to work again."[15] And later, in Madrid, she resisted an El Greco she was tempted to buy "as it might upset her in her work."[16]

When she was younger, she felt that the paintings hanging in museums and collections throughout Europe were put there for her own convenience, and in her youthful arrogance she copied and studied them so that she might "paint better than the Old Masters." Now that she was older and facing the ultimate judgment of history on her own work, she became humbler in the face of the giants of the past. She was increasingly awed by their accomplishments and, in an ambivalent manner, alternately borrowed and protected herself from them.

Interestingly, she did not buy any of these pictures herself, although she was tempted to and often talked of it. She had a modest collection of decorative objects from many periods and styles, including jewelry, furniture, Japanese prints, and Persian miniatures, but had only a few old masters (a Donatello relief and a Simon Vouet painting) over the years to hang among her paintings by Degas, Monet, Morisot, and Cézanne. She, like many artists, preferred the company of her own pictures and those of a few of her friends rather than admit any others that might spark her competitive spirit and disturb the tranquillity and confidence she needed to enter her studio day after day and once again face the blank canvases.

The furious trip to Italy and Spain in 1901 lasted only about two months, but its impact was felt by all the participants for years afterward. In terms of collecting, Cassatt continued for the next three of four years to try to obtain for the Havemeyers the Italian and Spanish paintings they had seen. She was not only their representative in Paris to whom photographs and letters of opinion were to be sent but also their banker, since they deposited large sums of money with her to be used for the quick payment of fees whenever the pictures might suddenly become available. She enjoyed this role immensely. Being known as the Havemeyers' trusted adviser gave her added importance in the Paris art world and gave her a new circle of friends among critics and connoisseurs with whom she spent endless hours in discussions about the history of art. She would even, on occasion, take a sudden trip to Italy or Spain to conclude a negotiation or to see a new picture.

She took great pride in the collection that was shaping up in the Havemeyers' opulent house on Fifth Avenue. As she looked at the collecting going on around her, she could not always conceal her sense of superiority. Speaking of George Lucas, the American art agent who had been in Paris as long as she had and who was now advising the collector Henry Walters of Baltimore, she sniffed, "Lucas is a dear old man, & so upright but I don't think he knows enough about old masters."[17] The Philadelphia collectors John G. Johnson, P.A.B. Widener, and William Elkins, she felt, "cannot conceive what the Havemeyer collection is,"[18] and as for Isabella Stewart Gardner and Sarah Sears in Boston, she assured Louisine Havemeyer, "No my dear, you & I are about the only two . . . we two must just do the best we can, helped by men."[19]

The trip also had a great impact on her own art. She set to work as soon as she got back to Paris and wrote with the mixture of enthusiasm and uncertainty with which the immersion in the old masters had left her: "All day long I work! I am wild to do something decent after all the fine things we have seen. Oh! if only I could! Goya's unhesitating firmness upsets me."[20] Over the next two years, as she continued to see old master paintings in Paris being offered to the Havemeyers, she occasionally rose above the trembling that constant comparisons with the greats triggered in her. One day, after a session at a dealer who was offering inferior pictures labeled with great names, she went back to her studio with relief. As she wrote to Havemeyer, "To give you a perfect insight of my state of mind, when I got back here I sat down before the last little picture I painted & *admired* it! & felt that it would be a better investment than those!"[21]

When she first got back to work, she had to finish some portraits in her Paris studio, but by the middle of June 1901 she moved to Beaufresne for the summer. Although she promised the Havemeyers she would come to New York a year later, she decided against the trip and instead stayed home to devote herself to a long year and a half of work. What she produced in that time was, as usual, turned over to Durand-Ruel. By 1903 he decided it was time for another exhibition in New York. This group of oils and pastels was executed in direct response to the trip to Italy and Spain. The dominant theme is a mother with two children, and in each the three figures are arranged so that the composition has the utmost fluidity (figure 112). Often they are arranged so that the heads are lined up or so that the mother looms large on one side or the other and the children flow downward toward the other side. The group of three suggests a traditional composition of Madonna and Child with Saint John. The flowing lines echo the sixteenth- and sev-

112. Mary Cassatt, **The Caress,** *1902*
Oil on canvas, 32⅞ x 27⅜ in.
National Museum of American Art, Smithsonian Institution; gift of William T. Evans

enteenth-century masters she had just been looking at. Although there is a grandeur to these new works, one looks in vain for any direct link to Veronese, to Goya, or El Greco—or any of the artists who figured so greatly in her recent trip and her continuing correspondence. Her absorption of the old masters colored her style, but in such an indirect way that her sources are difficult, if not impossible, to detect.

Once these works had been shown in Paris and New York, they were lent to exhibitions elsewhere in the United States. One painting, *The Caress* (figure 112), was entered into the Seventy-third Annual Exhibition of the Pennsylvania Academy of the Fine Arts in early 1904. For the first time, Philadelphia officially recognized its expatriate daughter. The painting was awarded the Walter Lippincott Prize and grudgingly accepted by the Philadelphia critics. In an interesting juxtaposition of old colleagues who had traveled vastly different paths, *The Caress* was hung next to a large painting by Thomas Eakins, *Portrait of Archibishop Elder, of Cincinnati.* The contrast was not lost on those who knew the work of both artists. A New York critic writing in *International Studio,* however, gave the most succinct summary of why Cassatt was finally accepted in Philadelphia:

> By the side of [Eakins' portrait], yet parted by an ocean of difference in purpose and manner, was Mary Cassatt's *Caress;* certainly one of her most beautiful examples, since she has deferred on this occasion to popular prejudice as to choose types of humanity that are not positively disconcerting in their homeliness. As a result, there is nothing to interfere with our enjoyment of her mastery of composition and drawing, of tone and lighting. It is truly a lovely canvas![22]

The critic's obvious relief that Cassatt had not used a homely model would not have pleased her; but she did in fact make concessions to popular taste that she had seldom made before. Not only are the models attractive, but they are richly dressed and imposing in stature. The mother has the air of a Renaissance noblewoman; she is dressed in the velvets that Titian and Veronese loved to paint. The painting is made even more ingratiating by the kiss that the daughter plants on the baby's cheek, in violation of Cassatt's usual non-anecdotal, unsentimental standards. Altogether, the painting is calculated to please tastes shaped by knowledge of the old masters but susceptible to sentimentality—the taste of the typical American art lover in 1904. Cassatt knew her audience well and, for the first time, had decided to cater to it. After its triumph in Philadelphia, *The Caress* went on to Chicago, where it was awarded the Norman Wait Harris Prize at the Art Institute of Chicago's Seventeenth Annual Exhibition.

Even though *The Caress* and other paintings of this period made concessions to American taste, Cassatt had by no means capitulated to establishment values. She still saw herself as a standard-bearer for the new freedom in art that had been won by the Impressionists, and was seen that way by others. After she gained greater visibility in America through her regular exhibitions in New York and her participation in the important exhibitions elsewhere in the country, many museums and arts organizations wanted to gain her cooperation and goodwill. With artists of Cassatt's stature, this was usually accomplished by inviting them to serve on juries of important exhibitions of contemporary art, which most American museums and academies at that time held annually. The Pennsylvania Academy, for instance, after honoring her with its Lippincott Prize for *The Caress,* followed up with an invitation to serve on the jury for the next annual exhibition.

A few years before, Cassatt had consented to be an honorary juror for the Carnegie Institute in Pittsburgh, thinking that she might use her influence to get the museum to add fine old masters to its collection. When she found this was an unrealistic expectation on her part, she saw no other reason to serve. In fact, she indulged her natural prejudice against juries and used every future invitation as an opportunity to preach against them. Remembering her own bitter experience with the Salon, she wrote, "I would never be able to forgive myself if through my means any pictures were refused. I know too well what that means to a young painter. . . ."[23] She knew that the process itself was unworkable, "One of the men who served oftenest in the Paris Jury, told me that after seeing a few pictures, some hundreds say, he was *abruti* [senseless] and could not tell good from bad. . . . I abominate the system and I think entire liberty the only way."[24] She became even more eloquent when she was asked the following year to serve again for the Carnegie Institute. She allowed that the jury system assured some measure of quality, but, she said, that was merely a "high average."[25] That might do for other fields of endeavor, but "in art what we want is the certainty that the one spark of original genius shall not be extinguished, that is better than average excellence, that is what will survive, what it is essential to foster."[26] On the same principles of fairness and equal opportunity, she disapproved of prizes other than those given in cash to young, struggling students and thus also refused the Lippincott and Harris prizes awarded her in 1904. The Harris Prize of five hundred dollars was at her request turned over to Alan Philbrick, who had recently graduated from the school of the Art Institute of Chicago and was currently working in Paris.

Her outspoken criticism of the art establishment and her concern for the struggling art student caused her to become something of a hero to the new crop of young Americans making their way to Paris after 1900. Not only was she admirable because she had been an Impressionist, but keen observers saw how her work embodied the modern values that would soon take art on its dizzying antinaturalistic course through the twentieth century. In an

113. Mary Cassatt,* Breakfast in Bed, *1897
Oil on canvas, 25⅝ x 29 in.
Virginia Steele Scott Collection, Huntington Library and Art Gallery

article in the radical art journal *Camera Work* titled "The Value of the Apparently Meaningless and Inaccurate," the author claims that "Modern art, in its best examples, is the very antithesis of accuracy" and that "accuracy is the bane of art."[27] He offers as an example a painting by Mary Cassatt, *Breakfast in Bed* (figure 113), which could then be seen at Durand-Ruel. Although he feels she is "by no means a great artist," he finds that "on almost every one of her canvases, roughly, sometimes brutally composed, drawn, and painted, there is that touch, which by imparting to form and color some particular quality of effect, impossible to analyze, endows all her figures with the energy of life."[28] For the restless young artists of New York, impatient with the still-powerful conservative art establishment, Cassatt could teach more about freedom than any other American artist of her generation.

In Paris, Cassatt became associated with the Art League, an American group that was connected with the Hostel for American Students. She was frequently asked by the women students to be a speaker and chose topics exploring the various aspects of "art for art's sake." She even attempted to persuade them to give up the jury system for their own exhibitions, but was unsuccessful. To encourage more students to learn fine pastel technique she donated money to be used as a scholarship for two of the women students to spend a year in St. Quentin studying the seventeenth- and eighteenth-century pastels in the museum there. Finally, to everyone's surprise, she consented to become honorary president of the Art League, and probably did so hoping to have more influence over the group.

Cassatt's well-known interest in American art students led many to seek her out in a kind of pilgrimage. Alan Philbrick, the recipient of her five hundred dollars from the Chicago prize, came to her apartment in Paris to thank her for her generosity and found her a "fiery and peppery lady, a very vivid, determined personality, positive in her opinions." He confessed that he "was scared to death of her."[29] Another Chicago native, Grace Gassette, had the courage to approach Cassatt while she studied in Paris in 1906. Gassette spent many hours absorbing all she could of Cassatt's advice and opinions, and wrote a laudatory article on her for the Chicago *Post.* In later years, after having returned to the United States, Gassette would list Cassatt as her teacher in the catalogs of exhibitions she entered. Cassatt, for her part, was vastly amused by the young woman who had nerve enough to call not only on her but also on Degas, even though she did not believe that Gassette had the makings of an artist. She wrote candidly to Louisine Havemeyer that "Art is not at all her affair, except to talk; she will never paint anything of account."[30]

Another young art student, Anna Thorne, from Toledo, Ohio, bought a bouquet of violets and took the train out from Paris to pay homage to Cassatt at Beaufresne (figure 114). A guide at the Louvre had given her directions, and when she got off at the wrong station, she decided to walk back and needed only to ask for "the chateau of the celebrated lady painter." When the door was opened to her,

> A rather lovely woman stood in the shadowed interior. "I am Mademoiselle Mathilde," she said graciously, "companion and maid to Miss Cassatt. Will you come this way?" The inside of the chateau was glorious. It was like walking through some grand, unknown castle, filled with elegant beauty. . . . There at the far end, where the shades were drawn, sitting almost as one on a throne, I saw her, my idol, the painter of "La Loge" and "A Cup of Tea" —Mary Cassatt! We came close. She did not smile, only sat there, arrogantly proud, austere; her white hair done in a precise, little, bright embroidered

114. Photograph of Mary Cassatt at Beaufresne, 1910
(from left: Mme. Joseph Durand-Ruel, Mary Cassatt, unidentified woman, Marie-Louise Durand-Ruel)
Document Archives Durand-Ruel, Paris

> French cap; her thin hands folded in her lap. Then, suddenly, her proud head lowered and her eyes caught mine. Nervously, I clutched the violets. "How do you do," she said with a Pennsylvania accent. "So, you're an American? I don't like Americans. I've been in France too long. But sit down. You've come a long way to see me and we'll talk."[31]

The interview lasted only a short time, but long enough for Thorne to show Cassatt her sketchbook and hear Cassatt's lecture on how long it takes to become an artist. Like many another young pilgrim, Thorne was cowed by Cassatt's fierceness, but grateful for the concern for art and for the young that was behind it.

Cassatt's good citizenship in advising collectors and promoting the careers of young artists more than made up for her unwillingness to serve on juries. She was at this point recognized both in France and the United States, and it may not have surprised her to learn that she had been named Chevalier of the Légion d'Honneur on December 31, 1904. This was one award she did not refuse. She wore the red ribbon infrequently, but proudly, although it took the government another six years to elicit from her the birth certificate and other official documents it needed to close her file.

Cassatt's life in the art world after 1900 was complex, but it was not all-consuming. She pursued other interests with the same intensity—from gardening to spiritualism to world politics. The sophisticated smoothness she had acquired in her forties began now to give way to a wiry, imperious image as she neared sixty. She had always been active and talkative; now she seemed to cut a swath through life, stopping only to hold selective audiences in thrall with her observations and opinions. Since she lived alone, she lost the habit of taking others into consideration. Although she was a gracious hostess and loving friend, she followed her own path and dismissed with a characteristic wave of the hand all people and ideas that did not seem relevant.

She loved the physical life she led at Beaufresne. She would attack her canvases and pastels with the utmost concentration during the morning hours, and then get relief from the constant standing by working in her rose gardens or taking a drive in her carriage or her new automobile. Lifelong stomach trouble,[32] which ultimately led to diabetes, drove her to take up a vegetarian diet. To indulge herself, she grew an abundance of vegetables, including her childhood favorites such as American corn and eggplant. She read gardening books voraciously for hints about improving the beauty and productivity of her small estate, and would work tirelessly with her gardener to have her new ideas carried out. She was also keenly interested in medical cures, largely because she did not trust doctors and because she herself had a talent for nursing. She believed people should be able to care for their own health. Years later, when her brother fell ill on their trip to Egypt, she felt humiliated that the family insisted on sending for outside help. Over the years she touted the value of such natural medicinal aids she discovered in her reading as camphor, corbelic smoke balls, and morning dew.

Since she believed strongly in the healing properties of nature and the power of the mind, she was swept up in the spiritualist movement that came into vogue in Paris after 1900. She read the influential book by Frederick Myers, *Human Personality and Its Survival of Bodily Death,* published in 1903, with great interest because she still grieved for her mother and wished there were a possibility of communicating with the dead. Myers was a British scholar of the classics and philosophy whose work with the Society for Psychical Research in London attracted the attention of many intellectuals, including the Harvard professor of philosophy William James. Cassatt admired both Myers and James for their emphasis on the value of the individual's subjective response and their theories of the "subliminal self." She was also fascinated by the popular manifestation of spiritualism in the form of séances conducted by mediums. She attended the séances of one, Mme. Ley Fontvielle, with Theodate Pope in 1903. She described another to Louisine Havemeyer's daughter, Electra, in which the table they were sitting around "rose four feet off the ground *twice*."[33] As curious as these experiences were, Cassatt had to relinquish her high hopes of a reunion with her beloved mother and settle for a more general result: a greater insight into the workings of the human mind. This was satisfying enough for her to recommend spiritualism to all her friends in her characteristic eloquent and persuasive way.

At Beaufresne, after the sun went down Cassatt ceased her physical activity and switched to an equally vigorous mental activity (figure 115). If she did not have houseguests to lead on explorations of a myriad topics, she would bury herself in her books. Aside from her gardening and spiritualist reading, she loved cultural history, such as Lenormant's *La Grande Grèce*; natural history, such as J. H. Fabre's *Social Life in the Insect World*; biography and memoirs, such as those of Sir Richard Burton and Lady Burton; and literature, in both French and English. She devoured contemporary fiction of all kinds, but was not fond of the "society" novels of Henry James, Edith Wharton, and Paul Bourget. She read so fast she was always looking for new books and she complained to Louisine Havemeyer:

> It is hard to get anything interesting to read, I have here a novel I have been urged to try, "The House of Mirth" by Mrs. Wharton, literally I could not read it, such an imitation of Bourget, a writer I cannot endure, by the way, so a copy isn't made to please me. Those people arn't Americans, the heroine just such a one as Bourget makes or rather the situations are. She tries James for the Character. I would rather go back and read Miss Austen's novels over again for the 100th time. Dear Dear No Art! at home or here either.[34]

She avoided the circles that Edith Wharton, Henry James, and her houseguest of 1895, Vernon Lee, moved in when they came to Paris, although she knew all of them. Her animosity toward this crowd extended now to Lee, for whom she had developed an intense dislike. She wrote again to Havemeyer, "Someone has just sent me Mrs. Whartons book on Italian Gardens dedicated to Vernon Lee, the latter once staid with me, she never will again."[35]

More than anything else, Cassatt hated social climbers and poseurs, people

115. Theodate Pope, photograph of Mary Cassatt at Beaufresne, 1903 Hill-Stead Museum Archives

who wasted their own time and hers with the petty concerns of society. She found Wharton's *House of Mirth,* with its story of an impoverished woman attempting to marry a rich husband, hollow and unworthy of literary effort compared with the great social themes of Zola or the elegant simplicity of Jane Austen. She felt the same about the authors of such books; they were pretentious and shallow compared with those who had passions for art or a social cause that drew them out of their narrow personal interests. When she found them, she drew people of substance to her side, and her circle included friends of a wide variety of professions, ages, and incomes.

These people Cassatt entertained regularly, and particularly enjoyed it when friends came out from Paris for the day. Degas made the trip every few months (figure 116), if he and Cassatt were currently on speaking terms, as would her friends among the critics, Theodore Duret and Roger Marx. Degas continued to work on pastels and sculptures although his eyesight gradually deteriorated and he grew thin and unkempt after periodic illnesses sapped his strength. He had gone on to champion other women artists, such as Suzanne Valadon, but he never married. He and Cassatt had many breaks

116. Albert Bartholomé, photograph of Edgar Degas in Bartholomé's garden, 1908 Bibliothèque Nationale

in their friendship over the years, such as over the Dreyfus affair, but they always managed to patch it up. While Cassatt was an ardent supporter of the pardon of the Jewish officer convicted of treason, Degas was so outraged that he stopped talking to many of his oldest Jewish friends, such as the Halévy family and even Pissarro. A friend arranged a luncheon to bring Cassatt and Degas back together again. She was reluctant to go because, as she told Havemeyer, " '. . . you don't know what a dreadful man he is, he can say anything.' 'So can you,' " Havemeyer replied, and she went.[36]

Her favorite relative, William Milligan Sloane, professor of classics at Princeton, would visit whenever he was in Paris for a rousing argument on some topic of current interest such as the Boer War. Lilla Cabot Perry, a Boston artist and society woman who spent part of every year at Giverny, would come to call with the latest news of Monet and his admirers in that nearby town. In 1903 Cassatt acquired a new neighbor in the art dealer and publisher Michel Manzi, who bought a château in Chaumont-en-Vexin for his family. Manzi collected her art and had a lavishly illustrated article on her published in his magazine, *Les Modes,* in 1904. The Durand-Ruels continued to be close friends and neighbors. Cassatt's greatest loss was in the sudden death of Pissarro, who was preparing to paint a new series of canvases from an apartment window in Paris when a cold led to prostate problems and then to blood poisoning. He died on November 12, 1903.

Considering that she was not free of the stereotypes of Jews, blacks, and the poor that characterized her age, she was remarkably democratic in her outlook. She thought nothing of using labels such as "Jew" or "niggerbaby" in a derogatory manner, but did not seem to be affected by racial bias in her friendships or treatment of others. As for her treatment of the lower classes, she was reasonable with her servants and a generous neighbor to the less fortunate in Mesnil-Théribus. She got to know a great number of the local people because she was always on the lookout for models, and most were happy to come with their children and pose for her. When she discovered that one young model was being abused by her father, she went to court to intervene, although without success. Her relationship with Mathilde Valet deepened as the years went on until she became more of a companion than

117. John Singer Sargent,* Portrait of Alexander J. Cassatt, *1903 Oil on canvas Railroad Museum of Pennsylvania

a maid. Cassatt's friends and relatives also befriended Valet. Cassatt frequently passed messages to and from Mathilde in her own correspondence with them.

During these years Cassatt's routine was altered to some degree by the sudden fame of her brother Aleck, who, by accepting the presidency of the Pennsylvania Railroad, became one of the leaders of his country (figure 117). Cassatt had always led a privileged life because of her family's wealth and impeccable ancestry. After her brother's ascension to such a high post, however, she began to see what real privilege was. Suddenly he was one of the most powerful men in the United States as well as one of the best known. His name was in newspapers across the country on a daily basis and his influence was sought by politicians, businessmen, and cultural leaders. He was in the same league of giants as Frick, Carnegie, and J. P. Morgan. If he had established a museum or library, he would be just as well known today.

Aleck's position from 1899 to 1906 undoubtedly had an impact on the status of his sister in the United States. Although she had already made a name for herself in the 1890s and was clearly poised for success, the fact that she bore a very powerful name undoubtedly brought her attention from museum directors, exhibition organizers, and the press, that she might not otherwise have had. One cannot discount the possibility that her sudden popularity in Philadelphia in 1904, which brought her the Lippincott Prize and an invitation to serve on the jury, was partially due to the Pennsylvania Academy's attempt to win not only her favor but her brother's. A recent portrait of her brother by John Singer Sargent was shown in the annual exhibition that year, symbolizing her brother's sudden appearance in what had been her own sphere—the world of art.

For a number of years after 1900, reviews of her work routinely pointed out that she was the sister of A. J. Cassatt. In one instance, she was included in an article on marine painters in a popular weekly, *The Hampton Magazine,* as the sister of Alexander J. Cassatt.[37] In the same issue, "The Summer Hostesses of Society: The Chatelaines of Bar Harbor," Lois was discussed as the mistress of Four Acres, the Cassatt "cottage," in Bar Harbor. Mary Cassatt, to her horror, found herself embroiled in the society news and the world of social climbing she had always abhorred.

Journalists more interested in the power and status of the Alexander Cassatts than in art began finding their way to Mary Cassatt's door. Although she had many friends who were writers and critics in Paris, she was always shy of the popular press and in no way condoned the interjection of her personal life into published discussions of her art. Now that she had the double attraction of being a successful artist and the sister of a corporate celebrity, she actively had to discourage the prying eyes of the press. About one request for an interview she wrote to Louisine Havemeyer from Beaufresne, "Here is a Miss Henderson commissioned to write of my work in the Century, she proposed to come out here to see me to get 'what *we* call local color'—Not if I [can help] it. I answered I would meet her in Paris."[38] For those who did get to interview her, Cassatt was ready with set answers about her past, and so the information about her published during her lifetime tends to be repetitious and superficial. Furthermore, she gave the same negative answer to requests for photographs of her, and explained by rote that she would rather be known for her art: "It is always unpleasant to me to see the photographs of the artists accompany their work, what has the public to do with the personal appearance of the author of picture or statue? Why should such curiosity if it exists be gratified?"[39]

If it irritated her that the more unwelcome aspects of celebrity were due more to her brother's accomplishments than her own, she was outraged when people assumed that her brother subsidized her and made her a wealthy woman. One Philadelphia newspaper called her "Heiress to millions, the richest artist living,"[40] calculating her worth on the basis of the massive fortune of Alexander Cassatt. While Aleck's actual holdings cannot be known, newspaper reports after his death set his fortune at $50 million. If this is an accurate accounting, his wealth would have exceeded that of such other art-world figures as Harry Havemeyer, whose fortune was probably around $25 million, or of Isabella Stewart Gardner, who inherited under $3 million from her father.

While Aleck was generous with his parents and sisters in Paris, there is no evidence that he supplemented their income substantially on a regular basis; nor does he seem to have had any financial arrangement with Mary after the death of their parents. Mary undoubtedly had inherited the bulk of the elder Cassatts' holdings, since Aleck and Gard were far more wealthy than their parents. Judging from Gard's will, Mary would have received a substantial token of ten thousand dollars from each of her brothers upon their deaths. Cassatt's total fortune in 1911, when she made her own will, could be calculated at around two hundred thousand dollars. This sum enabled her to support two homes and a small staff of servants, to buy her clothes at the best dressmakers, and to collect antique jewelry, but it was not sufficient to amass a major art collection or practice philanthropy on a grand scale as her friends such as the Havemeyers, Popes, or Whittemores did. She was, of course, fortunate to have such friends, but was always in the position of having to persuade others to carry out the grand plans for cultural betterment of her country that she believed in so fervently.

Because of the contrast between Aleck's fortune and her own, Cassatt could only chuckle at the world's assumption that she benefited financially from her famous brother. She had only to compare the Alexander Cassatts' recently built fourth home, Four Acres, with servants' quarters for sixteen maids and four men, with her own modest establishment at Beaufresne to demonstrate the difference. As she pointed out to Havemeyer, it was *she* who increased *his* wealth by arranging for him to buy Impressionist pictures that increased astronomically in value over the years. As much as she resented the false conclusions drawn by others, she never resented her brothers because of the imbalance of fortune. Because she had sufficient money to live exactly as she wished, she was able to rejoice in their success and take comfort in the fact that if she ever needed money their coffers would be opened to her in an instant.

By 1904 the great wealth of people closest to her became a liability as trust-busting launched into full swing. Alexander Cassatt and Harry Havemeyer were at the helm of empires that became targets of Theodore Roosevelt's antitrust drive. First came the attack on the railroads, which, by 1906, led to an investigation of A. J. Cassatt's personal holdings in coal and the allegation of kickbacks and favoritism in the railroad's dealings with the coal industry. Aleck and Lois were abroad when the crisis came to a head and had just arrived in Paris to see Mary when they had to hurry home to face charges. Also embroiled in the controversy was the investment firm of Cassatt & Co., into which Gard had recently taken his nephew Robbie. Rob had to testify on the company's vast holdings in coal, and the appearance of wrongdoing on the family's part was very strong. Aleck survived the scandal by conducting his own investigation and by standing firm behind his hitherto unimpeachable reputation. The matter was soon under control; but the strain of defending himself against such an attack, coupled with a dose of whooping cough caught from one of his grandchildren, was too much for Aleck. On December 28, 1906, he died at the age of sixty-seven.

Harry Havemeyer faced similar attacks on his conglomerate, the American Sugar Refining Company, in 1907. Although a $30 million antitrust suit against the Havemeyer company was dismissed, accusations of illegal manipulation of stock and other antitrust issues would resurface against Havemeyer a few years later. Another problem soon arose after the discovery of fraudulent weighing of raw sugar on which duty was to be paid. A scandal ensued when employees of Havemeyer's company were implicated. Strikes and an economic downturn in 1907 caused more worries. In a pattern similar to Alexander Cassatt's, Harry Havemeyer fought off the attacks but a few months later was suddenly stricken by kidney failure and died on December 4, 1907, at the age of sixty.

Within a year, Cassatt had lost two of the people closest to her, their premature deaths seemingly brought about by the strain of defending their power and fortune. Cassatt's faith in their personal integrity was never shaken, in spite of the scandals that preceded their deaths, and she developed a lifelong, virulent hatred for Theodore Roosevelt. Her own life was probably more directly affected by the death of Harry Havemeyer than her brother's, since Havemeyer had been her partner in so many of her art activities in recent years. She was also more needed by Harry's widow, Louisine, in the immediate aftermath of his death, and was as distressed by Louisine's pain as she was by Harry's death (figure 118). Louisine and her daughter Electra came to stay with Mary in Paris a few months later, and Mary agreed to return the visit the following fall. Cassatt made her last transatlantic voyage in November of 1908 primarily to be with Louisine on the anniversary of Harry's death. The trip lasted only a month and included a visit to the Gardner Cassatts' as well as the Popes'. Since she had no exhibition in New York, nor any commissioned paintings to execute, it was purely as an act of friendship that she suffered the discomforts of the sea. In the future Louisine would always have to come to her, because once and for all, Cassatt was content to stay on her adopted side of the ocean.

118. Photograph of Electra and Louisine Havemeyer in mourning, December 1907
Courtesy of J. Watson Webb, Jr.

Although Cassatt was deeply affected by the deaths of those close to her, the years from 1905 to 1910 were remarkably productive. Now that she was in her sixties, she might have thought of retiring from the physical labor in the studio and from the stress of exhibitions, but instead she forged ahead with little diminution of her powers. In fact, she felt that since her output was so strong and the demand for her work at its peak, perhaps she was not being promoted actively enough by her old friend Durand-Ruel. She was furious when she found out he had arranged an exhibition of Impressionist work in London in February of 1905 and left her out. Emphasizing that "I consider my place was and is with the others whose works I have admired and upheld for more than a quarter of a century,"[41] she broke her long-standing exclusive contract with him and began to sell to other dealers.

She immediately turned to Ambroise Vollard, who was rivaling Durand-Ruel in the field of Impressionist and now Postimpressionist art (figure 119). She had become acquainted with him while advising the Havemeyers on purchases of modern French art and had been cordial to him when he acquired some of her earlier pieces through resale. In the summer of 1906

119. Pablo Picasso, **Ambroise Vollard,** *1915 Pencil, 18⅜ x 12⁹⁄₁₆ in. The Metropolitan Museum of Art; Elisha Whittelsy Collection The Elisha Whittelsy Fund, 1947 (47.140)*

she invited him out to Beaufresne to choose from her recent work as well as older canvases she still had on hand. After he made his selections, she rashly burned "all that was left to save my heirs the trouble."[42] Sadly, this must have been the moment when so many of her now untraceable early works disappeared.

When Durand-Ruel heard what she had done, it was his turn to be upset, and by the end of the year they were friends again. Cassatt was touched by the emotional attachment the aging Paul Durand-Ruel displayed—"he actually clings to me, which I am rather astonished at."[43] Cassatt still hesitated to reinstate her exclusive relationship with Durand-Ruel. The next time she exhibited, she had a show with Vollard and one with Durand-Ruel in the same year (1908).

It was flattering for Cassatt to have two such respected dealers of modern art vying to handle her work. This attention came at a crucial time, since even she could not deny that the Paris art world was being led in a dangerous direction by those who would later be dubbed "modernists"—those who followed Gauguin, Cézanne, and Seurat in the direction of Neo-Impressionism and Fauvism. As she watched the Postimpressionist styles of the 1890s develop into even more bizarre styles after 1900, she felt sure that the excesses were a passing phase. By 1908, when she had seen Matisse emerge as a leader of the Fauves and other young radicals such as Picasso obtain a firm foothold in the press and in the galleries, she began to feel the pressure of the new. The young art students she met at the Art League were knowledgeable about the new movements even though they maintained a conservative stance themselves. When her friend Sarah Sears began to take the new art seriously, she knew she had to address the situation.

She apparently went with Sarah Sears and her daughter, Helen, to an exhibition of Matisse around 1908 during one of the Searses' trips to Paris.[44] She sized up the artist by paying attention not only to his most recent radical works but to early works that were done in an Impressionist style. Furthermore, she formed her opinion by observing the crowd, which probably included the artist himself as well as Leo, Gertrude, and Michael Stein and Michael's wife, Sarah. She had heard much about the Steins but seems to have formed a firsthand impression as well. The crowd also must have been a largely international one, because Cassatt reacted to the large number of Germans and Scandinavians and the relative absence of the French. Helen Sears Bradley remembered that they had actually gone to the Steins' apartment together, but Cassatt stated clearly that she had never deigned to enter their notorious salon.[45] Nevertheless the conclusion of the evening seems to have been that Cassatt was outraged: "I have never in my life seen so many dreadful paintings in one place; I have never seen so many dreadful people gathered together and I want to be taken home at once."[46]

When Cassatt wrote to her niece Ellen Mary[47] about Matisse and the Steins a few years later, her anger had cooled only slightly. In explaining her negative view of Matisse and the Cubists, she attacked the quality of the art, the use of sensational and manipulative tactics to make it known, and the mistaken assumption that initial rejection is a sign of great art, since it once happened to the Impressionists. Matisse, she felt, was unable to master the Impressionist style in his early days, so he got the idea of developing a style in which he would not have the competition of truly great artists, and would achieve fame through notoriety. Matisse found the Steins, who had a similar desire for fame, and they began promoting him. People went to their salons, she explained, because they sought amusement. "Stein received in sandals and his wife in one garment fastened by a broach, which if it gave way might disclose the costume of Eve. Of course the curiosity was aroused and the anxiety as to whether it *would* give way. . . ."[48] Once there, the hapless visitor was made to feel inferior if he did not show the proper admiration for the art. When the advocates of the new style claimed Impressionism as its ancestor, Cassatt really put her foot down. This style, she said, is admired by those ignorant of art and rejected by artists; Impressionism, on the other hand, was understood by the elite, the artists, and rejected by the public, "no sound artist ever looked except with scorn at these cubists and Matisse."[49]

The depth of Cassatt's anger, which she tried so hard to keep in check, was ultimately betrayed by the racism that spills out in her arguments. The Steins were "not Jews for nothing. They—two of the brothers—started a studio, bought Matisse's pictures cheap and began to pose as amateurs of the only real art."[50] Their public was foreign, "at his exhibition in Paris you never hear French spoken, only German, Scandinavian and other Germanic languages."[51] Her implication is that it is the Jews and the Germans who are taking advantage of "the present anarchical state of things—not only in the art world but everywhere."[52] Cassatt assures her niece that this art is a fad, it "has only 'un temps'; it will die out. Only really good work survives."[53] But the first decade of the twentieth century had already closed and the new art had only gotten stronger. Today we see Matisse as following logically on the heels of the Impressionists; but to Cassatt the new style was a keen rival, and she felt that if it survived, then all she had worked for was for naught.

Cassatt's great misfortune in these years was not having a group of equally intelligent and sharp-witted artists and critics to challenge and advise her. The old Impressionist group no longer met socially and professionally to argue about art and throw vitriolic but useful barbs at one another. Morisot, Pissarro, and Caillebotte were dead; Degas was retreating into a fog; Monet and Renoir had removed themselves to country retreats far from Paris where they, like Cassatt, worked out idiosyncratic ideas in isolation. Cassatt had stopped making contact with the younger intellectuals in the 1890s and now found she was hopelessly out of touch. Even though she could not tolerate the flamboyant Steins, she might have allowed Sarah Sears to introduce her to more palatable progressives such as Alfred Stieglitz or Maurice Prendergast, both of whom were in Paris in 1907–8 and might have given her some insight into the new movements that they were currently discovering and evaluating themselves.

Instead, Cassatt used as a sounding board not the new intellectuals but her old friends—now conservative—and her dealers. Durand-Ruel, with his identification with the Impressionists and old masters, was by now completely bypassed by the avant-garde. He and his sons had a lucrative business in their chosen field and saw no reason to encourage their old standbys, such as Cassatt, to update their thinking or their art. Ambroise Vollard, on the other hand, was already leaning toward the new art and would follow the avant-garde well into the 1910s. Cassatt might have found in him a friendly foil, but instead, he seems to have preferred to have her continue in her already established niche and use her steady sales to finance his experimentation with more radical art. Both dealers took unlimited numbers of mother and child compositions and heaped praises on their steady producer.

In consequence, the art Cassatt exhibited and sold from 1905 to 1910 was an extension of the art that had won her prizes in 1904. The figures grew larger and heavier, were more richly dressed, often wearing enormous hats, and were engaged in more sentimental gestures. The paintings of these years in some ways are a return to her early Salon style. Like her earlier work, they are well painted and ambitious but are heavier than her Impressionist paintings and the gestures appear somewhat self-conscious.

In spite of their drawbacks, the paintings have a great deal of charm and were well received at the time. Durand-Ruel, sensing Cassatt's uncertainty now that her own circle was becoming history and she had no contact with the current avant-garde, gave her the reassurance that she needed. Periodically, he would take a look at the new work she was bringing him and tell

120. Mary Cassatt,* Children Playing with a Cat, *1908
Oil on canvas, 33 x 41 in.
Private collection

her she was still improving. As she wrote to Havemeyer, "I took two pictures to town with me & D.R. said one was the best picture I ever did."[54] Furthermore, Durand-Ruel could promote her work extravagantly in France and the United States. For example, *Children Playing with a Cat* (figure 120) was shown in Durand-Ruel's 1908 exhibition of Mary Cassatt in Paris and then sent on a tour of the United States, which took it to New York, Pittsburgh, and Washington, D.C. It was also reproduced in at least four publications in the next five years.

Years later, Cassatt would look back on this period with displeasure. When the admiring young art student Anna Thorne gushed, "Oh, but everyone loves your paintings!" Cassatt replied bitterly, "I sold my soul to the dealers, that's all. It was the dealers who stole my life!"[55] While she was in the midst of this period, any uneasiness she might have had about becoming stale and mannered was silenced by the adoration that surrounded her. Not only the dealers but the young art students, the collectors, and the critics did nothing but sing her praises. After hearing Clemenceau call her "one of the glories of France,"[56] and seeing articles about her titled "The Most Eminent of Living American Women Painters,"[57] she could hardly utter a complaint. As she realized that she had become fashionable at this time of her life, she began to wonder "perhaps they are right when they say I will survive, who knows—"[58]

Chapter IX

Hard Times
(1911–1926)

Toward the end of 1910 Cassatt decided to take an extensive trip with her brother Gardner's family through Europe to Constantinople and then down the Nile in Egypt. She felt she could afford to take a few months off because it had been an exceptionally good year. In addition to receiving extensive coverage in French and American publications, she had doubled her income from sales. In anticipation of the arrival of her brother's family in December, she refurbished the apartment in Paris and tied up all the loose ends of her business affairs.

After a brief reunion in Paris, Cassatt and her fellow travelers started their grand tour (figure 121). From the beginning, Cassatt felt odd about this trip. She immediately missed the work routine that had always been her mainstay. Never in her adult life had she taken a major trip that was just for leisure—art and collecting had always been the guiding principles. Furthermore, she had some trouble adjusting to traveling with people who weren't as fervent about art as she was, even though she loved them dearly, and to traveling with two teenaged girls. Ellen Mary was sixteen, Eugenia was thirteen.

Nevertheless, she bore these new circumstances with good cheer and absorbed all she could of Munich, Vienna, Budapest, Sophia, and Constantinople, while reacquainting herself with her family. Gard and Jennie encouraged her to take an interest in her young nieces, whose activities she observed with amusement and affection. As with Aleck's children, she immediately began to make plans for their education, recommending that Eugenia be sent to a boarding school founded by Theodate Pope, and that

121. Photograph of Mary Cassatt with the family of Gardner Cassatt at Versailles, 1910 (from left: Ellen Mary, Eugenia, Gardner, Jennie, Mary Cassatt) F. A. Sweet Papers, Archives of American Art, Smithsonian Institution

they both spend some time studying in Paris when they got older. Cassatt began to feel that the girls were "half hers."[1]

By the time they got to Cairo in early January 1911 Cassatt was on an even keel. In Cairo she saw an old dealer-friend from Paris, Dikran Kelekian, who specialized in art from the Middle East, and his friend the Boston collector and educator Denman Ross. With this infusion of intellectual contact, and with the spectacular art to be seen at the Cairo Museum and the pyramids, she wrote to her friends that she was glad she came. By this time she also began to see a return to normalcy and had settled her plans to return to Paris on March 1. At Cairo the family boarded a luxury dahabeah for the journey down the Nile. They were to be towed with only a few stops to Aswan and then left to float leisurely back to Cairo on the current of the river—a trip of about two months (figure 122).

Before they had been on the Nile for a week, Gard fell ill and required a three-day stay in Luxor while he was attended to by doctors. With Gard incapacitated, it seems that the ties that bound everyone else together quickly unraveled. Such forced intimacy on a relatively small boat exaggerated everyone's anxieties—Jennie became melancholy, the two girls withdrew into adolescent sullenness, and the tightly coiled Mary Cassatt began

122. Photograph of Mary Cassatt asleep on the Cassatts' dahabeah, Egypt, 1911
F. A. Sweet Papers, Archives of American Art, Smithsonian Institution

to feel trapped. She missed work more and more. She had brought her box of watercolors to do some sketching on the trip and tried to capture some of the exotic physical types of the Egyptian sailors around her, but the extremely windy and cold weather made working outdoors impossible.

The effect of the illness of her brother, the uncomfortable closeness of the rest of the family, and Cassatt's inability to work was made even worse by being projected against an Egyptian backdrop that was unnerving to her (figure 123). She was alternately bored by the deserted temples at Luxor, Karnak, and Aswan ("I am looking for Art not Archeology"[2]) and crushed by the strength of their design and scale. She felt that it was a masculine art against which she could not begin to measure her own graceful pictures of women and children. In spite of her respect for the achievements of ancient Egypt, she felt she was in an uncivilized land, and it made her shudder to think of "dying in this strange place."[3]

By the time the bedraggled family docked again in Cairo, Mary Cassatt, without knowing it, had been badly damaged, both physically and psychologically. The overpowering experiences had sapped her strength and her self-confidence. She also guessed that she had lost twenty pounds on the trip—weight she could not afford to lose since it brought her five-foot-six-inch frame to under a hundred pounds. In spite of her weakened condition, in the days following her disembarkation from the dahabeah, she followed a

123. Photograph of Mary Cassatt on a camel, Egypt, 1911 Private collection

strenuous schedule of seeing art and traveling by stages through Italy and back to Paris.

She did not immediately feel the devastating impact of the trip on herself because it was clear from the moment they started down the Nile that the sick one was Gard, even though his symptoms were never considered life-threatening. At various times he had diarrhea and hives, an affliction dismissed as Nile Fever, and he was treated by seven doctors, none of whom felt he had to interrupt the trip. By the time they returned to Cairo, everyone was worried that he had not recovered. Mary attributed her own lengthy bout with sleeplessness to her anxiety over him. She went home to Paris ahead of the others so that she could make advance arrangements for his comfort when he arrived. From Paris the family would then proceed home to Philadelphia.

When Gardner and his family reached Paris at the end of March, they all saw the severity of his illness. Cassatt met them at the train station with a doctor and ambulance and had Gard and Jennie taken to the Hotel Crillon, and brought the two girls home with her. On April 5, 1911, Gard died. Soon after, in spite of the fact that Jennie and the girls still needed her to negotiate the transporting of the body and their own return to Philadelphia, Mary Cassatt collapsed. Her doctor ordered strict bed rest and solitude. Young Gardner soon arrived to help his mother and sisters and take them home. By May, Cassatt was alone.

It was only then that she began to realize the enormity of her situation. In less than four months she had plummeted from the heights of activity, success, and self-confidence to the depths of physical pain and spiritual paralysis. For the next two years her body would suffer terribly, but even more distressing was her inability to restore the will to work that had been her life force for the past fifty years. To the outside world, nothing had changed. As usual she moved out to Beaufresne when the weather got mild; she revived the habit of going to the South of France for the winter; and she spent the intervening time trying to keep up with things in Paris. Her work continued to be exhibited, thanks to Durand-Ruel and Vollard, and the press continued to heap praises on her. But from 1911 to 1913 she could do little else but toss and turn through sleepless nights, combat the pain in her arms and legs with a myriad of treatments, and wonder if she would ever find the strength to stand in front of her easel again.

The physical pain was never properly diagnosed, but apparently it was the result of a combination of the diabetes that had long been incipient, the disastrous loss of weight that certainly began to attack her muscles and organs, and the onset of rheumatism. She, who had drawn on her immense reserves of wiry physical strength for so long, was now paying the price. She distrusted doctors and thus saw many at once, picking and choosing treatments that could be as "modern" as electricity and radium doses, or as ancient as drinking glasses of herb mixtures and adding extract of pine needles to her bath. Massage soothed her aching limbs, particularly when done by her dearest friends—Mathilde, whom she had to call in the middle of the night when she couldn't sleep, and Louisine Havemeyer, when she was finally allowed to see Cassatt several months after the doctor lifted his ban on visitors.

After a year even the doctors began to be alarmed when her physical body began to heal and yet she would not go back to her painting. "All my doctors want me to work! How is it possible, they don't know what it is to paint, they say only ten *minutes* a day."[4] While Cassatt was right that serious art took time and great physical stamina, she was avoiding even the small amount she could do. This hiatus of two years bespeaks more than physical distress, it shows a fundamental loss of nerve. What could have caused such a sudden breakdown in someone who had had, just months before, a deep reserve of self-confidence?

She claimed it was the art of Egypt: "I fought against it but it conquered, it is surely the greatest Art the past has left us . . . how are my feeble hands to ever paint the effect on me."[5] She would be well again "only if I can paint something of what I have learnt, but I doubt it—"[6] "fancy going back to babies & women, to paint . . . I am crushed by the strength of this Art. I wonder though if ever I can paint again."[7] Cassatt, who had fed off of challenges in the past, who had taken the strongest and most powerful art of her day and let it drive her own art to new heights, no longer had the will to fight.

One wonders if she would have been so crushed by Egyptian art if she had had different companions on her trip down the Nile. If she had had the Havemeyers, or even Haldeman or Sartain, if she had someone who knew and understood art, particularly her art, she might have come back refreshed and ready to begin again. As much as she loved them, Gard, Jennie, and the girls were not in the art world. They did not know how to nurture Mary's artistic ego, which increasingly depended on strong doses of praise from those around her: Louisine Havemeyer, the dealers Vollard and Durand-Ruel, the critics Duret and Marx, and the worshiping crowds of American art students. It became abundantly clear to Cassatt as she traveled with Gard's family that they were only slightly more sensitive to art and artists than Lois was, and that, in the end, they were merely "Philadelphia." She saw herself reflected in their eyes as a beloved sister, but not much more. As devoted as they were, they could not give her the recognition as an artist that was as precious as life to her.

After three months with them, even though she could not see it herself, she was deflated, diminished. Even her loss of weight might be attributed to living in the little Philadelphia that was her dahabeah; she always claimed that Philadelphia enervated her and made her lose her appetite. Since there was no overt quarrel, she had nothing to fight against; but in a thousand small ways her companions made her lose touch with her most powerful self. When she made the inevitable comparisons between Egyptian art and her own, as she had always done when studying the art of the past, she had no support from those around her and could not summon enough residual self-confidence to turn the comparison to her benefit. After Gard's death, she wondered why she could never restore the old warmth between her and the members of her brother's family, but increasingly she pushed them away from her, taking offense at small things and insisting they had nothing in common. If she had made this trip down the Nile under other circumstances, she might have fought Egypt and won, but she could not fight Egypt and Philadelphia at the same time. The combination nearly killed her.

Although she struggled to recover, death was very much on Cassatt's mind during her two-year bout with mental and physical exhaustion. Her previous interest in psychic phenomena and exploration of possible ways to make contact again with her lost loved ones had led her to see death as merely "over the border" from life, an alternate form of existence hidden from us by an impenetrable veil. Her curiosity about what lay behind the veil made her envy those who had already gained that knowledge—all of her immediate family, Harry Havemeyer, and other friends—although she would not take any steps except in imagination to fulfill that curiosity.

She confronted death on a practical level as well. She tended to the tombs of those of her family who had died in Europe. Gathering them all together, she transported the remains of her mother, father, sister Lydia and brother Robbie to the town cemetery of Mesnil-Théribus and had a large granite slab engraved with their names, and her own. She also revised her will within a month after Gard's death. Partly, this was a practical matter, since Gard had been her executor and she now needed to name someone new. But she was also keenly aware of the desirability of having her affairs in order.

Cassatt's contact with her remaining relatives in Philadelphia over these matters only highlighted her sense of loss and the disintegration of everything she had held dear in her lifetime. Lois and Jennie were themselves in a depressed state and unable to keep up their normal roles as family anchors. Their children had gone separate ways causing unusual alliances and deep rifts. Rob had allied himself with his uncle Gardner, who had taken him into Cassatt & Co. Elsie and Ed were estranged from Rob and the Gardner Cassatt family and consequently were not included in the family pews at Gard's Philadelphia funeral. Katharine Cassatt, Aleck's oldest daughter, had died from a very sudden illness in 1905.

In her will, Mary Cassatt showed how skewed her own relationship to her nieces and nephews had become. She had shown a preference for Gardner's children in her previous will, in which she divided her property so that one quarter would go to Ed, Rob, and Elsie, while three quarters would go to Gard, Jr., Ellen Mary, and Eugenia. When she decided to revise her will in 1911, her dealings with the families made her decide to cut out Aleck's children entirely while splitting the whole among Gardner, Ellen Mary, and Eugenia. Elsie and Ed were indignant about the situation, but as Elsie wrote to her mother, they would only have gotten fifteen thousand dollars each, a sum too small to worry about.[8] Elsie had inherited millions at her father's death and would inherit millions more from her mother. Cassatt's relationship with Rob was actually very cordial in spite of the fact that he was not mentioned in her will. She had taken a liking to his son Anthony and decided to leave him one of her pictures.

Rob and his wife, Minnie, visited Cassatt during the summer of 1911, as did many friends and family from back home, including Louisine Havemeyer. Havemeyer had wanted to rush to Cassatt's side when she first collapsed, just as Cassatt had done in 1908, when Havemeyer was in deep distress. When she finally did see her the following August, she was shocked at the change. All Louisine could do was to sit with her through her sleepless nights and rub her aching legs. Cassatt was sixty-seven years old.

By December of that year she was sleeping again and had put on some weight. She began to take an interest in her surroundings again, visiting the galleries once she returned to Paris from Beaufresne. Her closest and most solicitous friend in Paris was the American banker James Stillman (figure 124), who had maintained a house there since the 1890s, but settled there finally in 1909. The two had presumably met through their mutual friends, the Havemeyers, and Stillman had consulted her on his purchases of old master art over the years. Try as she might, she could not persuade him to like "modern art" (the Impressionists) although he considered a few Degas's and Manets worth having. He did, however, greatly admire Cassatt's paintings and bought them regularly, ending up with twenty-four, the largest single collection of her work outside her family.

Once Stillman settled in Paris, he saw a great deal of Cassatt, particularly

124. "James Stillman in the later years of his life," from Anna Burr,* The Portrait of a Banker: James Stillman, 1850–1918, *New York, 1927, after p. 248

in the year before her trip to Egypt. She got to know his three children as well as his two sisters, whom she found charming. He had been separated from his wife for more than fifteen years. Stillman was the type of man with whom Cassatt was comfortable. He was a successful businessman, like her father, brother, and Harry Havemeyer, knowledgeable about investments and fearless in negotiations. He was president and then chairman of the board of National City Bank in New York. Once away from the office, he showed an unbounded interest in the finer things of life: art, beauty, and ideas. Cassatt found this type of person exhilarating because she could let loose her own wide-ranging ideas without fear of offending or leaving him behind. Perhaps because of his open admiration and affection for her, she was touched by Stillman in a way few people had touched her, and during her illness she turned to him for support.

In spite of their mutual admiration, Cassatt was not always satisfied with their relationship. When she went on her trip to Egypt she found that she missed their daily interaction and was puzzled that he did not write to her more often. When she returned she saw him as much as her health permitted, and then agreed to join him when he took his annual trip to Cannes for the winter season. They drove separately, but took the same route so that they might meet up along the way. Cassatt found that he did not like to stop and sight-see as she did, and so she was disappointed when they met only when they got to Cannes. It is generally believed that Stillman had asked Cassatt to marry him. But although she liked him very much and appreciated everything he did for her while she was ill, she found too many differences in their habits to believe that she would be happy in such a marriage. As with Degas, she found him very affectionate but not very reliable. She wrote to Louisine Havemeyer, "I won't allow him to have me on his mind."[9]

While in Cannes, Cassatt explored the region she had not been to since she bought Beaufresne in 1894. Motoring through the diverse landscape of seacoast and mountains relaxed her as did the sunbaths in the garden of the Hôtel Californie. When she was younger she loved cold weather, but in her late sixties she began to appreciate the restorative power of the sun and looked around her with the idea of retiring to this area. If she did, she decided, it would not be in Cannes, so close to the water, but in the hills behind the coastal city, in the green pine woods.

On the return trip, Stillman took Cassatt in his own car, forcing her to forgo her incessant sight-seeing and, in an effort to keep her from exerting herself, even forbidding her to talk. These restrictions, as sensible as they were, were not calculated to please a person as restless as Cassatt, and afterward she said with some acrimony, "I think he must be glad to be rid of this sick old woman. I think I would be in his place."[10] They continued to be good friends and met frequently in Paris and Cannes until he made a final return to New York in 1916. He died in 1918.

The progress she had made in Cannes was unfortunately reversed as soon as she got back to Paris. By the time she moved out to Beaufresne in mid-May she was, if anything, worse than she had been the summer before. Jennie and the girls were in Europe again that summer and were shocked to see her—she weighed only eighty-six pounds.

The writer Achille Segard found her in this state when he visited Beaufresne in June of 1912. Segard, a poet and novelist, also wrote art and literary criticism, and had gotten a commitment from the Paris publisher Paul Ollendorff for a book on Mary Cassatt. It was a time of great interest in the original Impressionists, of whom only Cassatt, Degas, Renoir, and Monet were still alive. Several books on Degas, Renoir, and Cézanne had appeared in German and French by 1912, and Vollard had published a volume of Van Gogh's letters in 1911. Cassatt had been included in books on Impressionism and the history of American art, but never before had she been approached about a book on herself alone. She was wary of the writer and his book, but seemed pleased to accept it as a natural outgrowth of the interest in her that had building for the last few years.

It is also possible that Segard hastened to write his book hearing that Cassatt was in a weakened state and might not survive much longer. Surely when he saw her for the first time walking gingerly toward him down the path at Beaufresne with the help of a cane, he would have gotten that impression (figure 125). Although he described how her smile lit up her face and her eyes flashed as she began to talk about art, even he, a stranger, must have been aware of her extreme fragility.[11] After serving him lunch and spending the afternoon with him, Cassatt was exhausted; "I can not talk or listen to much talk," she wrote to Havemeyer, "silence and solitude are best for my state."[12] If Segard was hoping to elicit a large amount of information from her—to succeed where others had failed—he was disappointed. Her natural reticence coupled with her physical weakness made her even less communicative than she had ever been before, and thus Segard had to base the book largely on published sources and his own observations of Cassatt's paintings and prints. In spite of the lack of information from Cassatt herself, Segard's *Mary Cassatt: Un Peintre des Enfants et des Mères* was a substantial achievement in putting her work into its historical context and offering valid

125. Photograph of Mary Cassatt, Grasse, 1913
Hill-Stead Museum Archives

insights into her style and subject matter. An attempt to have it translated into English and published in New York unfortunately failed for unknown reasons, but even in French it stood as the major text on Mary Cassatt for several decades.

When Segard visited her again in late October, he found her much improved. "[He] thought I looked so well he could not see why I don't work."[13] Indeed, Cassatt's diabetes was now under control, she had gained back much of the weight she had lost, and her outlook on life was growing rosier. Although she still felt working would be too painful, she was planning to return to the South of France at the end of November and would take her box of pastels with her.

This year, instead of staying in a hotel in Cannes, she had rented a small villa in Grasse, the perfume-making center of France situated about fifteen miles above Cannes in the Alpes-Maritimes. The house, called the Villa Angeletto, was a *bonbonnière,* a cozy candy box of a house with three floors, glassed-in studio, and a garden with a view over the curving hills down to the Mediterranean Sea (figure 126). When Cassatt was there, Grasse was not only the home of the perfume distilleries but also the site of the immense fields of flowers grown primarily for their fragrance. Today, when the flowers for the perfume factories are imported from elsewhere, only the olive groves remain of the breathtaking view that Cassatt would have had from her terrace. From 1912 to 1924 Cassatt spent at least six months a year at the Villa Angeletto in a kind of semiretirement.

In the winter of 1912–13, the weather was unusually cold, but Cassatt managed to get the sunbaths she now felt were as healing as any medicine. She read a great deal and even managed to take the pastels in her hand once in a while, although she "gave out in less than an hour."[14] The Stillmans—James and his two sisters—were in Cannes for the winter and came often with their friends to the Villa Angeletto. Cassatt saw many art friends as well. Soon after arriving, she went to see the Fèvres, the family of Degas's sister who lived in a beautiful villa near Nice. She reported on Degas's declining health—she had seen him recently at an art auction "looking very old"[15]—and also on his immense fame and the increasing value of his

126. View of the Villa Angeletto, Grasse

pictures. "They did not know!" she wrote to Havemeyer.[16] One of Degas's nieces subsequently visited him in Paris and ended up caring for him during the last few years of his life. Cassatt was grateful to them for making his declining years comfortable, and they, in turn, were grateful to her for letting them know the situation. Through their kindness, they ultimately became his primary heirs.

Cassatt also revived her old friendship with Renoir, who had built a comfortable villa overlooking the sea about thirty miles away in Cagnes (figure 127). Renoir was now virtually immobile because of the rheumatoid arthritis that crippled his feet and hands, but he could still paint. Cassatt hated his latest work, "enormously fat, red, women with very small heads,"[17] but admired his courage and his ability to believe that each new painting was the best he had ever done. In some ways Renoir took Degas's place in Cassatt's life during these years, now that Degas was no longer in full command of his mental powers. Renoir had grown very philosophical without losing the sharp tongue of his youth, and Cassatt was fond of quoting his observations on the modern world.[18]

This time the healing powers of the South made a permanent improvement in her health. The inspiration of seeing Renoir work and reading the recently published biography of the famous naturalist Jean Henri Fabre, *Poet of Science,*[19] which exhorted "Let us work while it is day,"[20] improved her mental outlook while the sun and healthy diet improved her physical stamina. By the time she returned to Paris at the end of May she was finally ready to go back to work:

> Perhaps, who knows? I may have still something to do in this World. I never thought I would have. I felt as if I were half way over the border. I am so much better I think I may be still stronger, strong enough to paint once more. Perhaps I may astonish Segard yet, who rather finishes me in his book. . . .[21]

The summer of 1913 saw Cassatt's rebirth. Moving out to Beaufresne, she gradually began to work in the mornings, and by mid-July she was able to show Joseph Durand-Ruel a nearly completed pastel when he came to visit with his family. Four months later she could deliver to her dealer seven pastels, the first he had gotten since the fall of 1910.

In some respects, the almost-three-year hiatus made no difference in her work—she picked up where she had left off in terms of monumental mothers and children in intimate poses (figure 128). But she was no longer

127. Photograph of Auguste Renoir in his studio, 1912
Document Archives Durand-Ruel, Paris

as fastidious in the handling of the pastel strokes. This was partly due to the inevitable loss of facility that resulted from inactivity. Her fingers could not manipulate the pastel sticks with the sureness that had been almost instinctual after so many years of constant practice. The pain and weakness in her arms no doubt were also a factor in the lack of control seen in these pastels.

But it is also very likely that Cassatt's recent acquaintance with the late style of Renoir, as well as her awareness of the enormous attention being

128. Mary Cassatt, **Mother and Child,** *1913–14 Pastel on paper, mounted on canvas, 32 x 25⅝ in. The Metropolitan Museum of Art; H. O. Havemeyer Collection, bequest of Mrs. H. O. Havemeyer, 1929*

given by the American press to Matisse and the modernists in New York's Armory Show of February 1913, had an impact on her new pastels. Although she hated Renoir's red nudes and dismissed Matisse as a publicity hound, she took note of the fact that contemporary taste was for expressionistic colors and looseness of handling. She was pleased when the Durand-Ruels told her, as they had in the past, that these pastels were the best she had done,[22] and she concurred, pointing out that they were "more freely handled & more brilliant in color."[23]

She was especially pleased to have an income again, after having to live off her capital for the last three years. Prices were going up in prewar Paris, including the rent on the apartment in the Rue Marignan, and, in addition, she had added the rent on the Villa Angeletto to her annual expenses. As a citizen of the United States, she also had to begin paying the new income tax that had been imposed that year. In 1910, she felt she was getting rich; in 1913, after three years of added expenses and no new income from painting, she was reduced to worrying about money.

Nevertheless, the thrill of reclaiming her life and her art at the age of sixty-nine could not be diminished by concerns about money, or even the nagging difficulties she began to have with her eyes. These she and her doctor dismissed as temporary and insignificant. More important was the excitement of work, which lifted her spirits and drove her beyond her actual physical limits. Soon the doctors, who had been urging her to work again, began to caution her to slow down. Once she had gotten her models together and her studio set up again, she began to work without stopping —newly awed by the magic of making a baby's skin come alive on her drawing board in a thousand small strokes of pastel. It was so compelling to her that she forced herself to simplify for the sake of her health: "I have had to drop nude children for the moment, it is too absorbing."[24] Tired as she was by November when she left Beaufresne to head south again, she was profoundly grateful that her life had been given back to her. When she prowled around antique shops looking for old frames, she could once again look forward to putting her own pictures in them.

The winter in Grasse in 1913–14 was milder and more beautiful than she had ever seen it. She went about finding new models—as she had never painted there before, she had no old faithfuls to rely on as she had at Beaufresne—and easing back into her newly restored routine. Once again she saw Renoir regularly, as well as Degas's nieces, and was visited by Durand-Ruel, Vollard, and all the Paris art crowd who came south for the holidays.

Most important was a long visit from Louisine Havemeyer, who arrived on March 21 and stayed two months in the Villa Angeletto. The two women made an imposing sight as they strolled around the gardens or through the ancient streets of the hillside town of Grasse. Cassatt maintained her erect carriage (figure 129) even though she now leaned on a cane or on her friend's arm; the robust Havemeyer measured her brisk walk to that of her older companion. They both dressed simply, but in the dramatic fashion of the day with large hats and sweeping skirts. The picturesqueness of these two proud white-haired women was made more piquant by their intense observation of all around them and their incessant and urgent style of conversation.

Their daily habits were so similar that they fell into a routine at once; Cassatt painted and Havemeyer wrote in the mornings while the rest of the day was spent motoring around the region, taking long walks, and settling down after dinner for discussions that lasted well into the night. The burning issue for them both at this time was women's suffrage, the long-standing battle for votes that the international women's movement had been waging for more than sixty years. In the 1910s, victory seemed tantalizingly near, and Louisine Havemeyer was in the forefront of organized political activities in New York to help bring this about. Havemeyer was an active member of

129. Photograph of Mary Cassatt at Villa Angeletto, Grasse, c. 1914 Private collection

the Women's Political Union, which was led by Harriet Stanton Blatch, the daughter of the famous nineteenth-century feminist organizer Elizabeth Cady Stanton. She helped to organize the Union's annual marches down Fifth Avenue for women's suffrage that had become a national focal point for the movement and traveled around the state to establish new chapters of the organization (figure 130).

In 1912 Havemeyer had put her art collection at the service of the cause in organizing a benefit exhibition of El Greco and Goya at the gallery of M. Knoedler and Co. in New York. In 1914 she wanted to hold another benefit exhibition—this time of a modern master, Degas. Cassatt was amused and enthusiastic about the poetic justice of Degas's art being shown to raise money for feminism, remembering that sexist remarks had always been a staple of his biting wit, and that with his old-world conservatism he would have been as thoroughly antisuffrage as he was anti-Dreyfus. She remembered that when he stood in front of *Two Women Picking Fruit* for the first time, he scoffed, "No woman has the right to draw like that."[25]

130. Louisine Havemeyer (right) passing the torch of liberty to the New Jersey contingent, c. 1915, from Scribner's Magazine *vol. 71 (May 1922), p. 528*

In watching Cassatt work at the Villa Angeletto, and discussing the possibilities of such an exhibition with her, Havemeyer gradually came to feel that a suffrage exhibition of Degas would be incomplete without the representation of his closest female counterpart, Mary Cassatt. While neither Havemeyer nor Cassatt believed that it would be an exhibition of true equals (Cassatt wrote "I am surprised at the coolness I show in thinking of exhibiting with Degas alone"[26]), they both felt that Cassatt came out creditably in comparison with Degas and would do justice to the advancement of women.

When Cassatt returned to Paris after her heady conversations with Havemeyer and a portfolio of new pastels to show, she had the additional pleasure of attending the first major exhibition of her art in Paris since 1908. With the new 1913–14 pastels in stock, Paul Durand-Ruel, now working with his sons, staged another retrospective survey of one of their prized artists. For this show and possibly for the future suffrage show with Degas, Cassatt went deep into her storage areas in the Paris apartment and rediscovered the old portrait she had done of her mother's cousin Mary Dickinson Riddle, when she visited Paris in 1883. Mrs. Riddle's daughters, Annie Scott and Bessie Fisher, had rejected the portrait and it had been in storage ever since. Cassatt immediately offered it to the Durand-Ruels, who gave it a place of honor in their exhibition, where it caused a sensation. Both the Luxembourg and the Petit Palais wanted to acquire it, as did the Metropolitan Museum a year later. Cassatt added the sweetness of vindication to the other triumphs of her year of rebirth.

Unfortunately, Cassatt's return to health and life-giving work lasted only one year. She moved out to Beaufresne as usual in the summer of 1914, but does not seem to have been able to settle down to work before she was distracted by the arrival of Jennie, Ellen Mary, and Eugenia for a lengthy visit. Cassatt's two nieces were now nineteen and sixteen, smoked, and considered themselves "twentieth-century girls."[27] Cassatt's patience with their teenaged concerns was severely tried and the strain began to weaken her. While her visitors were still at Beaufresne the Germans began their long-dreaded campaign through Belgium and into France, signaling the start of the First World War.

Her relatives left for home as soon as they could, but Cassatt stayed on at Beaufresne confident that the Germans would be stopped before they reached her region of France. Before she knew it, they had penetrated to within a few miles of her château, and she was forced to evacuate. Not only did this involve a change of location, but it disrupted her entire household and thus her long-familiar way of life. Mathilde Valet, as an Alsatian German, was not safe in France and was forced to try to find her way into neutral Switzerland. Pierre, the chauffeur, was drafted into the army. Before long Cassatt was left with only one servant, Hulda Brune, a Swiss chambermaid, to help her negotiate her travels and new wartime lifestyle. She seriously considered returning to the United States, which all Americans were officially urged to do, and which her friends and family pleaded with her to do, but she feared the disastrous effect the transatlantic voyage would have on her fragile health. Instead, she decided to follow her regular routine and retreat to Grasse and the Villa Angeletto at the end of November.

When she arrived in Grasse her friends there were sorry to see how much her health had deteriorated since she left just six months before. Mathilde had managed to slip into Italy with her sister and, while waiting to proceed to Switzerland, was staying only a short train ride away. Cassatt was able to visit her occasionally and to keep sending her money in spite of the difficulties, but both women suffered from their first separation in more than thirty years. To make matters worse, Cassatt's eyesight was beginning to be seriously impaired. The weakness of vision Cassatt and her doctors had dismissed as temporary turned out to be cataracts. Cassatt had to begin the lengthy process of waiting for them to ripen, undergoing the operation, and then waiting to see if her eyes would heal.

Cassatt's one consolation in the midst of such unhappy developments was the upcoming exhibition of her work with Degas's for the benefit of women's suffrage. Havemeyer had been working in her usual efficient manner to organize the exhibition and had settled its location (Knoedler Galleries) and its dates (April 7–24, 1915). She and Cassatt had also decided that it should be broadened beyond just Degas and Cassatt, and, in a bold move, included works by old masters. This highly unusual format has seldom been duplicated in exhibitions before or since, but it perfectly expressed Cassatt's philosophy that the old and the new should always be intelligently juxtaposed. Naturally the lion's share of the loans were from that carefully groomed work of art, the Havemeyer collection, but many additional loans from the Whittemores, Sarah Sears, Joseph Widener, Henry Frick, and Durand-Ruel broadened the exhibition's scope. For those who could not make the intellectual leap required by viewing old master and modern pictures side by side, the exhibition was hung in a more conservative way—Degas, Cassatt, and the old masters each were hung in their own discrete areas—so that if necessary they could be experienced as three separate exhibitions (figure 131).

Of the eighteen works shown by Cassatt, virtually all were done after 1900 and four were from the previous spring, when Havemeyer and Cassatt worked side by side in the Villa Angeletto. Havemeyer wanted to showcase

131. Installation photograph of the "Loan Exhibition of Masterpieces by Old and Modern Painters," at Knoedler Gallery, 1915
(view of wall showing works by Mary Cassatt to the left of the doorway and works by Edgar Degas to the right)
Photo courtesy Knoedler Gallery, New York

these not only because she had a personal attachment to them, but also because she wanted to portray Cassatt as a still-active artist rather than a figure from the past, as was beginning to happen with Degas and all of the Impressionists. The only work from Cassatt's earlier periods was the rediscovered portrait of Mrs. Riddle, which was given a central position in light of its newfound fame. Even if she had wanted to, Havemeyer would have been unable to gather together a substantial representation from Cassatt's work of the 1870s through 1890s because the war precluded borrowing from French collectors and the American owners of these works were not willing to lend. Havemeyer, Cassatt, and Durand-Ruel had none of the early works in their own hands.

The exclusion of Cassatt works from the earlier periods had one beneficial effect and that was to minimize the similarities between Cassatt's style and Degas's. In contrast to Cassatt's showing of late mother and child compositions, Degas's was rich in early ballet, racetrack, milliner, and café scenes. The two sections showed distinctly different artistic personalities—not always to Cassatt's credit because of the preponderance of very late works—who had formulated their own styles independently while maintaining a close friendship. This was a point both Cassatt and Havemeyer were eager to make because both resented the assumption, already being voiced, that Cassatt had been Degas's pupil and that she merely copied his style. Havemeyer in the text of her introductory lecture and pamphlet accompanying the exhibition was quick to deny any pupil-teacher relationship, and went on to imply that he, of the two, was the one who gained more from their friendship: "She could do without him, while he needed her honest criticism and her generous admiration."[28] Cassatt herself was outraged at the suggestion that she copied Degas, and welcomed this exhibition if for no other reason than to prove her originality "in this age of copying."[29] She went on to stress that *she* was the one who was forever being copied: "I cannot open a catalogue without seeing stealings from me."

As much as this exhibition served as a vehicle for the private aesthetic ideas and pronouncements of Cassatt and Havemeyer, they never lost sight of its primary motive, which was to bring attention to and raise money for women's suffrage. Havemeyer's dedication to this cause was public and carried out within the principles and beliefs of an organized political movement. Cassatt's own feminism was shaped and expressed in a private forum, which made it less consistent than Havemeyer's and more personal in nature. There is no doubt that Cassatt was profoundly feminist from an early age. She held women in as high esteem as she held men, if not higher in some ways. She believed in a woman's right to education and advancement in the world outside of the home. She was fully aware of and did not hesitate to raise her voice against the vast injustices suffered by women in modern life.

However, she hated being classified as a "woman artist." When women organized their own exhibitions to advance their cause, she refused to join them, and she forbade Durand-Ruel and Havemeyer to lend to them. Furthermore, she avoided being doctrinaire in her feminism and always reserved the right to judge a person or a situation on its own merits. She could repeat some of Degas's antifemale comments with an affectionate chuckle, while others would cause her to stop speaking to him for months. She could be very critical of women she found silly, pretentious, or grasping, or those who, she felt, had achieved fame without deserving it. Among her colleagues, she dismissed Cecilia Beaux, Marie Laurencin, and Romaine Brooks as unworthy artists. In other fields, she had similar doubts about the writers Vernon Lee and Edith Wharton as well as the scientist Marie Curie. But nothing made her angrier than women who ridiculed their own sex. She once lost her temper at a dinner party when two female guests claimed that women were not fit to vote: "I said I hated to hear that women despise women. These youngish women have never done a stroke of work in their lives."[30]

Cassatt also considered her art an expression of respect for women. When she was younger she painted women of substance and intelligence: women at the theater, driving carriages, reading newspapers, or caught in a moment of serious contemplation. Her later mothers and children celebrate one of women's main experiences of pleasure and love and show them as sturdy adults, carrying out life's responsibilities. Although she began to add overtly charming touches to these mothers and children after 1900, she prided herself on what critics had always stressed, that she did not fall into overly sweet sentimentality. In fact, when the holiday Mother's Day was proposed in Congress in 1913, she thought the idea was absurd, and that the congressman's mother should box her son's "conceited ears."[31]

Havemeyer's increasing involvement in the suffrage movement and her plans for the exhibition swept Cassatt up in the type of organized political effort she normally avoided. Although she was not tempted to join any of the groups active in France, she expressed a willingness to support the cause financially and, of course, through her art. She thought that excluding women from the vote was unconscionable simply on principles of equality, but was spurred to greater outrage once the income tax was instituted and brought the issue of taxation without representation. The outbreak of war in 1914 put yet another new twist on her thinking. She, like many feminists, believed war was the result of excluding women from decision-making processes—in this case the vote. In particular, she saw aggressive Germany as a bastion of male *Kultur.* Only when German women had a say in society would it become more peaceful. She harped on this same theme for the duration of the war and took heart that the current catastrophe would eventually bring equality for women and a lasting betterment of society.

Given her strong feelings about women's suffrage, it was a personal trial for Cassatt that her sister-in-law Jennie and both nieces became involved in the antisuffrage movement. Try as they might to avoid this basic disagreement, their equally warm feelings on opposite sides of the issue wreaked havoc upon their already-strained relationship. It was inexplicable to Cassatt that these women, who were themselves active in the world, would want to prevent women from voting. If they did not want to vote, they wouldn't have to; but she couldn't understand why they would take the right away from someone who did. Cassatt attributed their misguided opinions to Philadelphia society, which encouraged women to stay within a very restricted sphere and to make their contributions to the world behind the scenes. Jennie, who had been far less conventional than Lois in devotion to her home, and her daughter Eugenia, who was independent and wanted a career in business, were now applying their great organizational powers to a cause that they believed in, just as Havemeyer was doing for the opposite side.

There was an inevitable collision between the two opposing sisters-in-law, and it came over the suffrage exhibition in New York. Naturally Jennie and her family could not endorse it by lending any of their works or by attending, and they were backed in their stance by Lois and her family as well as Annie Scott and Bessie Fisher. In fact, none of Philadelphia society, nor much of New York society could be found at an exhibition that would normally have attracted them in droves. Cassatt was furious. Although the exhibition was a critical and popular success, it was boycotted by the antisuffrage elite—her own family!

Cassatt struck back the only way she could. She began selling or donating all the remaining important art works she had been saving for her heirs. Ellen Mary, her namesake and favorite, was to have gotten *The Boating Party.* Cassatt immediately turned the painting over to Durand-Ruel, and it is now in the National Gallery of Art. A large round painting she had done for the Pennsylvania Statehouse was also to have gone to the family, but she sold it to Harris Whittemore. Her major Degas pastel of a bather and two other lesser Degas's would also have gone to Jennie's children; she sold them instead to Louisine Havemeyer. When the family showed some belated interest in the portrait of Mrs. Riddle, she scoffed at them. She eventually gave the painting coveted by the Luxembourg and the Petit Palais to the Metropolitan Museum. She took the family's antisuffrage position as a personal affront, believing that if they had no respect for the advancement of women, they had no respect for her, and therefore should not be allowed to have her art. In the next ten years Cassatt sold large groups of lesser works that she had in storage—prints, drawings, and sketches—rather than let them fall into the hands of her family and be cast aside, unappreciated.

The feeling of being betrayed by members of her own family never left her, despite the fact that in the years to come she kept up a regular correspondence with them and often showed the warm feelings that were too deeply rooted to be banished entirely. Jennie's sociability touched her as it always had. When the war was over, they resumed their normal visits to her in Paris and Beaufresne. In the end they did inherit a number of art works from her, although none was of such significance as those Cassatt disposed of in the wake of the suffrage exhibition.

Cassatt's tendency to respond to obstacles with uncontrolled anger, which had been so marked in her hot-tempered youth, began to surface again as she faced increasing blindness. By the summer of 1915, after the tumultuous suffrage exhibition was over, she could barely see to travel from Grasse back to Paris and Beaufresne. In her more philosophical moments she vowed to use her only remaining eyesight to read Milton: "When one can read but little, one must read the best."[32] In her darker moments she began to face the possibility that she might never work again, and that old age, which she had imagined as "the best part of life," would instead be nothing but "weariness and dispair."[33] Prevented from painting and from reading—her two most important activities—she had more time to mull over real and perceived offenses. Her helplessness fed the fear that everyone, from her old dealer Durand-Ruel to her servants to her doctors, was taking advantage of her.

She was not sure she should go back to Beaufresne that summer of 1915. The Germans were still occupying northern France and battles raged within earshot of her château. But it was too hot in Grasse and too uncomfortable in Paris, and she couldn't afford to rent another house somewhere else when she was already maintaining three residences, so back to Beaufresne and the *zone des armées* she went. After two difficult months there she returned to Paris, where the doctors, after examining her eyes, scheduled her for cataract operations on both, which took place in October.

As soon as she was able to travel again she headed south to the healing warmth of the sun. Now that she was a convalescent, she became involved with the hospital in Grasse that was treating the war wounded from all over France. With the war in its second year, private citizens like Cassatt were drawn into the enormous task of caring for the devastated and displaced populace that the war had left on their doorsteps. Cassatt enlisted Havemeyer and the two took on a number of charity cases by person-to-person benevolence and donations to small charitable foundations. An outgrowth of her interest in nursing was an invention that she had patented in the United States—a hammock for fractured legs.

In the summer of 1916, Cassatt returned again to Paris and Beaufresne, where, she was happy to report, "the cannon is not so loud, so the heavy artillery is not in action."[34] Her eye doctor in Paris, the Philadelphian Louis Borsch, was pleased with the progress her eyes were making and even believed she would be able to work again. Cassatt, suspicious as usual, did not. She did manage to see some art while in Paris and even, at the age of seventy-two, climbed the interminable Paris stairs to see a Courbet at her old friend Duret's apartment. When she finally got her clearance to go to Beaufresne, she was visited by a number of friends, including the artist George Biddle and Jennie's nephew, a young Mr. McCall. As the Americans made plans to enter the war and when war was declared in 1917, she began to see more and more young men of her acquaintance in Paris, including her nephew Gardner.

The doctor's prediction that she would work again did not come true. Either the operations were not successful or the cataracts continued to grow back, but Cassatt was deprived of sufficient eyesight to be able to work. From 1917 to 1921, she had several more operations. Her sight fluctuated, but never improved enough to allow her to read freely or to paint. In 1920 she began wearing eyeglasses to maximize what little sight she did have. She continued to devour books, however, with the help of a servant, nurse, or friend who would read to her, and was able to keep up her correspondence by having letters in English read to her by her maid Hulda, who could pronounce English words even though she did not understand them. Cassatt wrote her own letters except when she was completely deprived of sight immediately before or after an operation.

The loss of her eyesight was particularly frustrating because otherwise she was in good health. Always careful with her diet, she maintained her weight and kept her diabetes under control. She was still very mobile—she could walk better than she could during her illness of 1911–13, she could ride on trains and be driven in her car. In 1917 she turned seventy-three.

At her age her parents were still vigorous and in full command of their faculties. If she hadn't lost her vision, she could easily have worked for several more years. When the dullness of the last ten years of her life was relieved by some important art event, she was roused from her spiritual invalidism and showed how much energy she really had left.

It was the time of her life when she no longer produced anything new, but was periodically confronted with works of the past that had the power to meld past, present, and future. The accidental discovery of Mrs. Riddle's portrait was one such case in which she relived its creation in the past, arranged to have it exhibited in the present, and planned for its future destination. This telescoping of time was intensified because each re-surfaced work brought with it a review of her own place in history and the question of whether her work would stand up to time.

This process was triggered most often these days by the death of one or another of her contemporaries who had collected early and held works unseen for many decades. The large collections were usually put up for auction by the heirs and thus were exhibited, reviewed, discussed, and finally sold in a highly public manner. Such had been the case with the collection of Henri Rouart, friend of Degas and later Cassatt, which had been auctioned in December of 1912, a year after his death. The death of the dealer Manzi in 1915 also resulted in a large public auction in 1919. In both, early works by Degas and Cassatt were seen for the first time in many years and their careers reviewed.

The most personally wrenching of these reminders of her past was the death of Degas, on September 28, 1917. Cassatt was in Paris at the time, awaiting her second cataract operation and was able to go to the funeral. "We buried him on Saturday," she wrote to Havemeyer, "a beautiful sunshine, a little crowd of friends and admirers, all very quiet and peaceful in the midst of this dreadful upheaval of which he was barely conscious."[35] She was sad to lose the oldest friend she had left in Paris, but it had been years since he had been able to function on his own and his death was, as she said, "a deliverance."[36] Thanks to her intervention, his niece, Jeanne Fèvre, had been his nurse for the last two years of his life. Cassatt had continued to see him regularly, although not frequently, since she now spent only about two months a year in Paris. He had continued to work until about 1907, but then, troubled by weakened eyesight and deafness, he began to retreat into a more circumscribed life. By 1914 he had trouble recognizing his friends, although he did attend Cassatt's Paris exhibition of 1914. Soon afterward Jeanne Fèvre came to stay with him.

At his death, the vast studio/apartment complex he had crammed with art work was systematically explored and cleaned out. The immense collection of his own paintings, pastels, drawings, prints, and sculpture was supplemented by works by other artists he had acquired over the years. Four auctions were required to dispose of all the objects. Among the treasures unearthed were the Cassatts that Degas owned—a painting, a pastel, and several prints. Cassatt was flattered to hear that the people cataloguing the collection thought at first that they were his. The pastel was one of the theater subjects from 1879, none of which had been publicly shown in Paris since her exhibition of 1893, when Degas bought this one. The other work brought back fond memories for Cassatt, since it was *Girl Arranging Her Hair* (figure 132), the painting she had done after a quarrel with Degas and showed in the Impressionist exhibition of 1886. Degas had graciously apologized and offered to trade one of his famous nudes from the exhibition for the painting. The Degas nude was one of Cassatt's proudest possessions and one that she designated for Havemeyer rather than giving it to her family. Havemeyer appreciated the significance of the exchange between her two favorite artists so many years ago and wanted both for her collection—she bought Cassatt's painting from the Degas estate auction the next year.

The excitement generated by the Degas sales ultimately caused conflicting emotions in Cassatt's heart. She fully understood the honor of being recognized as Degas's friend and colleague, and of standing alongside such a giant. At the same time, she would have given up fame to be active once more—work being the only thing that had meaning to her. In her weariness, she wrote of her dilemma to Louisine Havemeyer, "In looking back over my life, how elated I would have been if in my youth I had been told I would have the place in the world of Art I have acquired, and now at the end of life how little it seems, what difference does it all make?"[37]

The winter of 1917–18 was particularly bleak because going to Grasse meant leaving all the Americans, including her nephew Gardner, in Paris. Wartime Cannes and Grasse were not the holiday spots—full of tourists from all over the world—they normally were. Instead they were full of the wounded and the infirm, like Cassatt herself, and she was intensely lonely. To compound her misery, she was forced to stay at Grasse through the summer because, with the German army advancing toward Paris, it was too dangerous to return to Beaufresne. When she heard of James Stillman's death in July, she was miserable from the unrelieved heat, the loneliness, and news from the front, and could only gasp, "Life is hard at present. What is humanity after all?"[38]

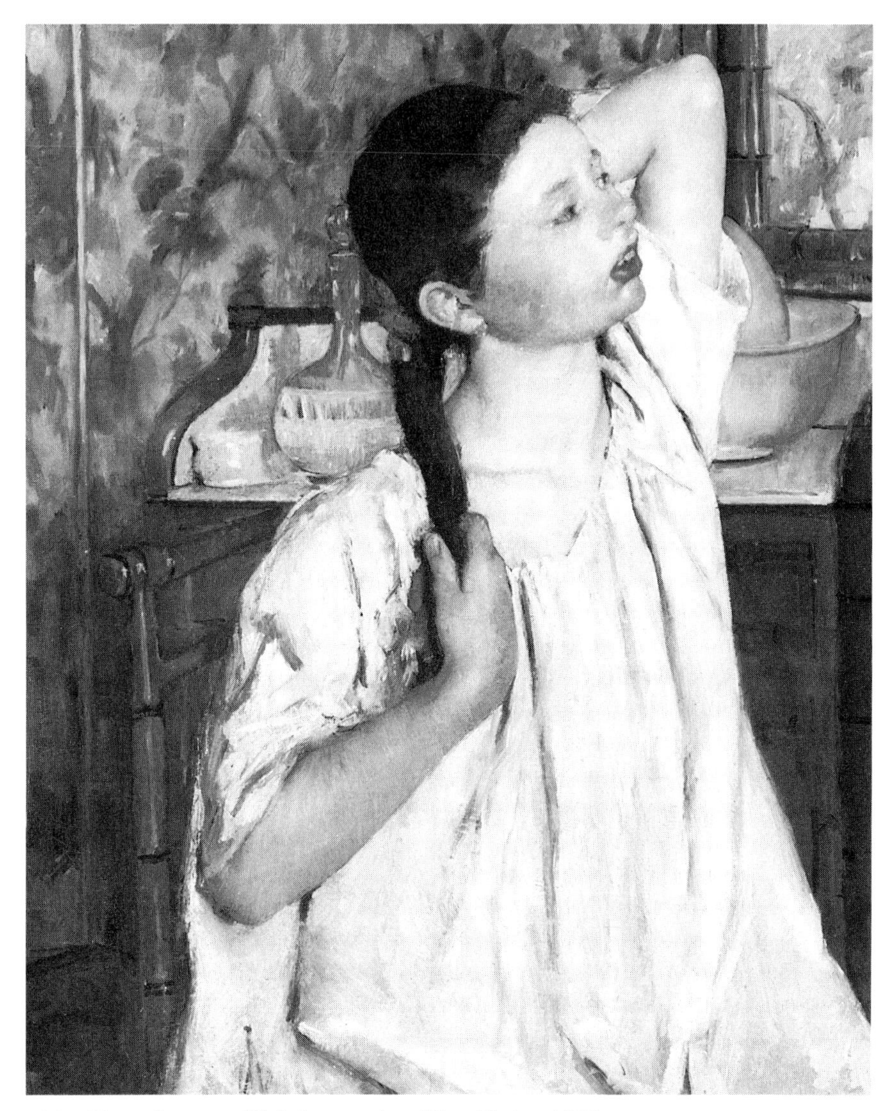

132. Mary Cassatt, **Girl Arranging Her Hair,** *1886*
Oil on canvas, 29½ x 24½ in.
National Gallery of Art, Washington; Chester Dale Collection

Cassatt was able to return to Paris in September, after the battle of the Marne and the retreat of the German army, but peace did not immediately improve her difficult living circumstances. She had her third eye operation that fall and retreated back to Grasse once more as a convalescent, only to return to Paris in May 1919 for her fourth. She spent the summer at Beaufresne merely waiting for the fifth operation that fall. Gradually the Paris art world was returning to normal, and she was involved to some extent in acting as an adviser to Jeanne Fèvre, who was having Degas's wax sculptures cast into bronze. Fèvre would have liked to sell his only exhibited sculpture, the *Little Dancer of Fourteen Years,* to Louisine Havemeyer as a unique wax piece, rather than making several bronze replicas of it; but she asked an exorbitant price and Havemeyer declined. Cassatt, as usual, was at the center of these negotiations, which took place both in Paris and in Grasse. At the end of 1919, before her departure for Grasse, Cassatt sold Durand-Ruel almost one hundred finished prints and proofs she had kept in storage for two decades, one of several groups of works she would dispose of in the next few years.

In January of 1920 Lois Buchanan Cassatt died. Mary Cassatt had had little to do with her since Aleck's death in 1906, and it had been many years before that since they had actually been friends. Lois's death did not soften Mary Cassatt's feelings toward her. After fifty years of alternating clashes and closeness, Cassatt concluded, "She was an unhappy woman & made those around her unhappy."[39] But she felt with a pang the loss of the last person with whom she had shared her youth.

As with the death of Degas, Lois's death triggered the unearthing of paintings Cassatt had not seen or thought of in many years, and with them, memories of the past and anxiety for their future disposition. Although Cassatt did not actually see any of the paintings from Aleck and Lois's collection that were being taken out of their houses and divided among the children, she remembered them well and was anxious to know how Ed, Elsie, and Rob would handle the legacy she had provided for them.

In going over the paintings in her mind, she immediately thought of how she might arrange for Havemeyer to buy some of the important early Degas's and Monets that she rightly guessed would go on the market almost immediately. Then, she reflected in leisure on the many family portraits she had done for Aleck and Lois over the years, and was particularly anxious to know who would get the large portrait of her mother, to which she was sentimentally attached. She had little hope that these paintings would be appreciated by their new owners, since she had long understood that Lois's "society" conservatism had been passed on to her children. She remembered when a young Elsie had complained without thinking to her grandmother about having such "modern" pictures in the house, "Grandmother we have to look at them!"[40]

As Cassatt predicted, all the paintings Ed had inherited that were not family portraits were immediately sold. Having inherited his father's love of horses, Ed was always in need of money. Elsie inherited all the Degas's and the portrait of her grandmother as well as many other important pictures. Although her aunt could not forgive her for her lack of appreciation of modern art, her mother loved her very much and gave her the lion's share of the collection. Rob, who had been estranged from his mother for many years, was given fewer things than Elsie, but not excluded entirely.

Cassatt discovered that Rob was the one who cared the most about the pictures and remembered that when the nieces and nephews were children, it was Rob who had painted alongside of her. When Ed put up for sale Cassatt's painting of his aunt Lydia crocheting in the garden at Marly (figure 66), Rob bought it as a gesture of affection and appreciation. When Rob and Minnie resumed their trips to Europe, Cassatt went through her storage closets once again and found the unfinished portrait of Aleck (figure 64) she had started in 1880, when the children first came to stay with her. This she had repaired and relined and gave to Rob as a memento of the summer he was an artist.

Cassatt's family feelings were further tested in 1920, when Jennie, Ellen Mary, and Eugenia came to Europe for the summer, now that normalcy was returning after the war. She had agreed to the visit because she thought *she* would be back to normal, but as the time approached she could only dread the strain they would put on her. Jennie was still an "anti" (antisuffrage) and was at Beaufresne at the time the Woman Suffrage Amendment was ratified in August of 1920, an ironic event to commemorate their first meeting in many years.

Gradually the effects of the war and Cassatt's other troubles began to subside, and by the fall of 1920 her world looked a little brighter. The most important improvement was the return from Switzerland of Mathilde Valet, whom Cassatt had been trying to get back into France since the war ended. As time dragged on and Mathilde's clearance was still not approved, Cassatt sank to her lowest point, hoping for a speedy conclusion to her life, but with only one wish: "I wish I could have Mathilde with me at the end."[41] Finally, in August Mathilde did return, equally grateful to be reunited with Cassatt after five years of separation. She immediately set to work getting the neglected woman and the neglected household back into shape. Gardner Cassatt sent her new seeds to plant in the garden at Beaufresne, and Cassatt's sight was good enough to let her see, over the rolling hills of the Oise valley, "a rainbow & beautiful sky."[42]

Now that the suffrage campaign had ended successfully, Louisine Havemeyer could turn her full attention to personal matters once again. The National Association of Women Painters and Sculptors invited her to speak on Mary Cassatt in April of 1920 and thus began a series of talks and exhibitions in the next few years in which Havemeyer promoted the work of her best friend. Cassatt was touched by Havemeyer's tribute to her and only wished that she had a way to return the compliment. In the summer of 1921 Havemeyer took her first trip to Europe since 1914 and divided her time between Paris and Beaufresne to renew their old friendship.

Cassatt, Havemeyer, and Valet were now tightly woven in a three-way relationship. Cassatt depended heavily on Valet's ability to carry out the business affairs she wanted to maintain but was increasingly unable to handle herself (figure 133). Valet wrote the letters to dealers, collectors, and friends that could be dictated in French, although Cassatt herself took care of the English correspondence with a shaky hand. Valet was also responsible for searching through the storage areas that Cassatt had already plundered several times for works to be sold, given away, or exhibited. The Durand-Ruels, for instance, periodically came back to her for new works and were increasingly satisfied with the sketches and unfinished efforts that were now in demand. Cassatt was also asked to check for exhibitable works when the Grolier Club in New York held an exhibition of her prints in 1921 and the Durand-Ruel Gallery held a retrospective show in New York in 1923.

In 1923, on one of these missions of discovery, Valet came across a stack of copper drypoint plates that appeared not to have been previously printed. Cassatt had an American artist friend, George Biddle, and a professional printer, Delâtre, check them and they confirmed her assessment. Cassatt had the plates printed, yielding nine sets of twenty-five different images. Durand-Ruel shipped several sets to New York, where Louisine Havemeyer and William Ivins, the print curator of the Metropolitan Museum, discovered that most of them had, in fact, already been printed and the original impressions were already in major collections. Havemeyer explained the mix-up to Cassatt, but Cassatt thought she was unfairly accusing her, Mathilde, and everyone else involved of dishonesty. The ensuing barrage of letters to Durand-Ruel, Ivins, the Havemeyers, and other friends such as Harris Whittemore showed the level of her outrage. Although she was furious with Havemeyer and would not write to her for months, she reserved her greatest contempt for Ivins in the well-worn tradition of the artist's contempt for the curator:

133. Photograph of Mary Cassatt at Beaufresne, 1925
F. A. Sweet Papers, Archives of American Art, Smithsonian Institution

I have had a joy from which no one can rob me—I have touched with a sense of art some people once more—They did not look at me through a magnifying glass but felt the love & the life. . . . Can you offer me anything to compare to that joy to an artist? . . . Do not allow yourself to be upset. All the same plates had never been printed before.[43]

Cassatt agreed to recall the sets, and donated one partial set to the Petit Palais. It indeed includes a few images that had not been printed before.

In the spring of 1924, perhaps because of the bitterness of this exchange, Cassatt decided she was no longer able to keep up some of her more strenuous activities. She decided to give up the Villa Angeletto and the annual trip to the south, preferring to stay in Paris and Beaufresne. She also announced that her exhibition that spring in Paris would be her last,[44] although she, of course, had not produced any new work for ten years. She was eighty years old.

For the next two years, she maintained a fairly normal routine. When in Paris she would go to exhibitions or see art that interested her, although she saw with great difficulty. She went with Mathilde to an exhibition of Americans in Paris, including George Biddle, who recalled, "I think I was never more flattered than when she told me that she had been led in front of one of my paintings and could make out that it was a still life. 'But the others,' she said, 'I could not see very distinctly. It must have been a bad light.' "[45]

At Beaufresne she enjoyed her beautiful gardens, which had now been restored since their period of neglect during the war. She had more than two hundred varieties of chrysanthemums and knew the colors of the rosebushes by heart. To the distress of her friends, she had had many different dogs over the years, Brussels griffons, terriers, a spitz, and in these days she was always accompanied by "two ill-natured and overfed griffons," which would bark furiously at visitors and then, exhausted, would "settle like withered chrysanthemums upon the rugs."[46] Every day she would be taken for a drive in the car she had bought in 1906, a "20 horsepower Renault landau,"[47] which was always kept in perfect running order.

As in the past, she entertained a variety of visitors, including old friends from the art world, curious young art students, and assorted members of her family traveling in Europe. Ellen Mary and Eugenia were now married and visited with their husbands, and she still maintained cordial relations with Gardner and Rob (both at Cassatt & Co.) and their wives. Through Mathilde she reestablished her old friendship with Louisine Havemeyer. One of her last visitors, George Biddle, painted this picture of her entertaining him in her room:

> There she lay, quite blind, on the green painted bed which I knew so well from the painting in the Metropolitan Museum. . . . She was terribly emaciated. Her hands, which used to be such big, knuckled, capable hands, were shrunken and folded on the quilt. When she began to talk they waved and flickered about her head; and the room became charged with the electric vitality of the old lady.
>
> "Well," she fairly shouted, "have you ever seen such weather! My doctor says that in forty years there has not been such a storm."[48]

Biddle goes on to describe how her mind "galloped along" as he and Mathilde followed attentively, interjecting a word only when her passion would momentarily subside.

The ills of old age—a fall from her bed, increasing rheumatism, and occasional losses of mental focus—gradually sent her into a decline that was the subject of constant correspondence between Mathilde Valet and Louisine Havemeyer. In January of 1926 she went into a diabetic coma while in Paris, but she recovered and was able to make the move to Beaufresne to see the roses one last time. She died on June 14. "I am sure," Mathilde wrote to Louisine, "although she had many friends, nobody in the world loved her as Madame [Havemeyer] and I have loved her, and she knew it well."[49] She was accorded a ceremonial funeral as befitted her rank as Chevalier of the Legion of Honor and buried in her family's plot in the town cemetery of Mesnil-Théribus.

Chapter X

THE HISTORICAL CASSATT

When Mary Cassatt died, she turned over her reputation and her art to the forces of history. In the almost seventy years since, all those who knew her well have also died, leaving only written words and, of course, her art to evoke the character and spirit that were once hers. How each succeeding decade interpreted these sources has depended on changing circumstances, and on the individuals who have come forward to shape their own version of Mary Cassatt. A review of the literature shows that the "historical" Cassatt has been as affected by the values and concerns of the art world after her death as the "real" Cassatt was during her own lifetime.

In fact, she had the rare opportunity of seeing how her reputation was being shaped even before her death, since Segard's very influential book appeared in 1913, only about a year before she stopped painting. Segard provided his readers with very little biographical information, but characterized her first and foremost as an intensely loving person who used her art to convey an emotional message to the world. This interpretation, which was consistent with a late version of symbolism popular in art criticism in the 1910s, was based mainly on Cassatt's mother and child paintings after 1900. Cassatt herself, at this time of her life, tended to stress the joy of touching people with her art and wanted the message of "love and life" to come through.[1] This differed from earlier statements she made about her artistic purposes, most of which emphasized technique in her art, such as studies of light and shade, line and color, and other formal qualities of painting. However, it does echo her earliest ideas, formed in the era of Romanticism, which revolved around lost love and contemplation. Since

Cassatt did not disavow Segard's book, it must have been very close to her own image of herself at that time and perhaps represented some of her oldest beliefs that had never been too far beneath the surface. The book was immediately taken up by subsequent writers in the 1910s and early 1920s, and remains one of the most important writings on her because of its firsthand information and its portrayal of the aesthetics of the last part of Cassatt's career.

By the twenties another version of Mary Cassatt had emerged that was not actually based on her art. Though she was infirm and no longer working, she made her presence felt through her own continued interaction with dealers and younger American artists and with frequent exhibitions. Because of this presence, she acquired a legendary status, even among those who felt her style was out-of-date. Like the art students who had begun pursuing her as early as the turn of the century, the successive generations of Americans coming to Paris made a role model of her as a hero of Impressionism.

As Impressionism began in the twenties to gain "old master" status among American collectors, art critics, and curators, her works were in steady demand. This coincided with the birth in the 1910s and 1920s of most of the major American museums, which vied with one another to amass overnight collections of Impressionist art. As a member of the original Impressionist group *and* an American, her works quickly entered major museum collections. By the mid-twenties she was represented not only in the French museums, such as the Petit Palais and the Louvre (formerly the Luxembourg), but also in innumerable American museums, such as the Metropolitan Museum of Art, the National Museum of American Art (then the National Gallery of Art), the Corcoran Gallery of Art, the Philadelphia Museum of Art (then the Wilstach Collection of the Pennsylvania Museum), the Pennsylvania Academy of the Fine Arts, the Museum of Fine Arts (Boston), the Carnegie Museum (Pittsburgh), the Detroit Institute of Arts, the Cleveland Museum of Art, the Wadsworth Atheneum (Hartford, Connecticut), and the museum of the Rhode Island School of Design.

Cassatt's death in 1926 sparked widespread eulogizing. Her obituaries, usually based on Segard's book, appeared in newspapers and journals across Europe and America. In addition, within a year, memorial exhibitions were held at the Durand-Ruel Gallery in New York, the New York Public Library, the Metropolitan Museum, the Art Institute of Chicago, and the Philadelphia Museum of Art (then the Pennsylvania Museum). The people who organized the exhibitions and wrote tributes to her were those who knew her well in her last years: the artist George Biddle, the critic Forbes Watson, the curators Frank Weitenkampf (New York Public Library) and the "contemptible" William Ivins (Metropolitan Museum), the dealer Charles Durand-Ruel, and, of course, Louisine Havemeyer. Since most of these were associated with the New York art world, where Cassatt had gained acceptance years before, the most miraculous of all the tributes was the one in Philadelphia.

Under the diplomatic guidance of the director and staff of the Philadelphia Museum, all the quarrels of the last ten years among Cassatt's family and friends were put aside in order to assemble an exhibition in 1927 of approximately 150 paintings, pastels, and prints that would be a fitting tribute to the artist. Among the lenders were both sides of the Philadelphia family—Jennie Cassatt *and* Elsie Cassatt Stewart—as well as the one caught in between, Robert Cassatt. Furthermore, peace was made with their opponent in the women's suffrage movement, Louisine Havemeyer, who was not only a lender but was asked to write the introduction to the catalog that was published in the museum's bulletin. Havemeyer's health was no longer good (she suffered a minor stroke that year), but she managed to write a brief note and allowed passages from her 1915 lecture on Cassatt to be reprinted. Havemeyer took one last trip to France in 1928, the year before her death, and, in a symbolic gesture, planted roses on Cassatt's grave. In 1930 her *Sixteen to Sixty: Memoirs of a Collector* was published posthumously, showing Cassatt at the center of Havemeyer's Paris art world.

Havemeyer's feminist portrayal of her friend in this context differed from Segard's symbolist interpretation and the art world's conferral of legendary status in that it stressed the person rather than the art or the legend. Havemeyer established her historical Cassatt as independent, hardworking, and eloquent. She was anxious to discourage those who might view Cassatt's paintings as biographical and imagine Cassatt leading a life of endless tea parties. Havemeyer, as a socialite and a feminist, knew firsthand how a prominent woman's work could easily be dismissed as the insignificant acts of a dilettante. Because *she* had worked hard during her lifetime to make a difference in the world around her, she emphasized these traits in Mary Cassatt. If Cassatt had not had such a feminist advocate as she had in Louisine Havemeyer, she might easily have been accorded a smaller role in the history of art.

In Paris, Cassatt's passing was marked by the customary sale of works from the studio, which took place on March 30, 1927. In this case, the heir was not from the family; it was Mathilde Valet, who had been given approximately three hundred paintings, pastels, drawings, and prints as a type of pension. Exactly when these works were given to Valet is unclear, since Cassatt's 1912 will had designated for her maid/companion only a cash amount and one object of Valet's choice. It is likely that in later years, as Cassatt periodically combed through her storage areas, she set aside these works for Valet rather than selling them to Durand-Ruel or leaving them to her family. It is evident in the purposeful way they were put on the market that they were intended to be used as a source of income rather than to remain with Valet as a permanent collection of sentimental or artistic value. The sale of the objects was handled by the Galérie A.-M. Reitlinger, which exhibited them and then had them auctioned in two groups four years apart (1927 and 1931). The works in these sales were stamped with an oval collector's stamp that read "Mary Cassatt: Collection Mathilde X" and the auctions were subsequently referred to as the Mathilde X sales.

Unfortunately, Valet, unlike Havemeyer, was not invited to put her version of Mary Cassatt into print. Therefore, Valet's contribution to the shaping of the historical Cassatt was solely in the act of exposing such a large number of minor and unfinished works to the public. French critics appreciated the chance to see them because these works gave insight, more than the more formal, finished ones to be seen at Durand-Ruel, into the thought processes and working methods of this artist. Cassatt's reputation as a printmaker and draftsman was already very high, and this exhibition as well as others that emphasized the prints and drawings established Cassatt in these mediums for decades to come.

In the twenty years following Cassatt's death, as historical perspective was gained, Cassatt went through a period of reevaluation, as connoisseurs and art historians attempted to find her proper context and ranking vis-à-vis other artists of her generation. As an Impressionist, her place had been established as early as the 1890s, when she found herself in the second tier, behind Degas, Renoir, and Monet, but vying (not always successfully) with Sisley, Morisot, and Pissarro and definitely ahead of Caillebotte and Guillaumin. This ranking changed very little since that time.

However, in terms of her place in American art, critics were anxious to find a way of claiming her in spite of her long career in Paris. Her "Americanism" was consequently seen in stylistic qualities, such as her "sharp, clear lines"[2] and her "individuality."[3] Two shows at Durand-Ruel in New York (1930 and 1939) pitted Cassatt against Morisot and underscored Cassatt's "American" solidity versus the "French" fluidity of Morisot. By 1946, when the National Gallery of Art organized an exhibition of "Two Hundred Years of American Painting" to travel to the Tate Gallery in London, Cassatt was considered to be seventh in importance among American artists, after Copley, Stuart, Homer, Eakins, Ryder, and Whistler. The British, interestingly enough (according to a poll of British critics conducted by the exhibition's organizer, John Walker, then chief curator of the National Gallery), ranked Cassatt second, after Whistler.[4]

France's hold on Cassatt grew weaker during these years in terms of exhibitions and publications, but Europeans in general tended to think of Cassatt first in a French context and only second as an American. In the first few decades of the twentieth century, many of Cassatt's works that had originally been purchased by French collectors came on the market and were bought by Americans. As a consequence, the European public, which could not see her work easily, lost awareness of her.

Cassatt's ranking among women artists underwent the same process of refinement. Although she was often touted during her lifetime as "the most eminent American woman painter," other contemporaries were generally listed as her competitors. In an article on "Famous American Women Painters" in 1914, she was discussed along with Elizabeth Gardner, Cecilia Beaux and at least sixteen others.[5] In the twenties, she was still compared with Beaux: "with the possible exception of Cecilia Beaux, Miss Cassatt is our most distinguished woman artist."[6] By the time of her death in 1926 she was elevated above her American rivals: "considered by the critics of two continents one of the best women painters of all time."[7] In the thirties she had no rivals among the Americans and had only Berthe Morisot among the Europeans.

During these years, most of Cassatt's important contemporaries—Emily Sartain, Elizabeth Gardner, Elizabeth Nourse, Lilla Cabot Perry, Cecilia Beaux—dropped from public awareness primarily because their academic or middle-of-the-road styles were less interesting to generations steeped in twentieth-century modernism. The few nineteenth-century artists who had worked in academic or conservative styles and were still in the public's consciousness were the big names of the generation: Bouguereau, Gérôme, Sargent, and a handful of other male artists. Therefore, as their art went out of style, the many women artists working in this period were lost to history. Cassatt and Morisot, the women practitioners of Impressionism—the one style that gained in popularity and importance as time went on—suddenly seemed to be the *only* women artists of their epoch.

With this limited view of history, younger writers were forced to explain why there were only two women artists working in the late nineteenth century. They concluded that the obstacles must have been enormous, and

Cassatt and Morisot therefore must have been exceptional, almost superhuman, to overcome them. They went on to assume that Cassatt and Morisot must also have been insufficiently recognized by their contemporaries. Contrary to all the evidence, writers such as Jeannette Lowe in a 1939 article titled "Important Unfamiliar Works by Morisot and Cassatt," asserted that Cassatt and Morisot were dismissed by their fellow artists as "dilettantes" and that "neither received much critical acclaim during their lifetimes."[8] Thirteen years after Cassatt's death, in spite of the fact that her reputation, which had been established by 1900, was holding firm, writers had already begun to "rediscover" her.

The major research and writing on Cassatt has been done by women. Two general monographs on the artist appeared in 1930 and 1944 by the writers on art Edith Valerio and Margaret Breuning. In 1936 Adelyn Dohme Breeskin, curator of prints at the Baltimore Museum of Art, organized the first major museum exhibition of Cassatt's works on paper since the memorial exhibitions of the late 1920s. Breeskin had become acquainted with Cassatt's prints while acting as a curatorial assistant to William Ivins at the Metropolitan Museum from 1918 to 1920. Although she never met Mary Cassatt, she had a vivid sense of her through Cassatt's dealings with Ivins. Breeskin rose from curator of prints to director of the Baltimore Museum in 1942. After her retirement from that post in 1965 she became senior curatorial consultant to the National Museum of American Art, a position she held until her death in 1986. During her lengthy museum career, Breeskin organized eight major Cassatt exhibitions. They were held in 1936, 1941, 1960, 1962, 1967, 1970, 1978, and 1982. In addition, she also published catalogues raisonnés of the prints (1948, revised edition 1980) and the paintings, pastels, watercolors, and drawings (1970). Breeskin was the recognized authority on Cassatt's work for fifty years.

Like Louisine Havemeyer, Breeskin emphasized Cassatt's hard work and professionalism. But, as an art historian and curator, she preferred to concentrate on elements of style and technique in her art rather than on biographical details. She also drew heavily on Segard for information, but reflected the new modernist aesthetic that emphasized abstract qualities of style, particularly line, over emotional content. In personal terms, however, she was of the same generation as Cassatt's nieces Ellen Mary and Eugenia, and, like them, was a "twentieth-century girl" who saw anyone from Cassatt's generation as from another world. Ignorant of the other women artists of Cassatt's time, Breeskin portrayed Cassatt as an anomaly in an age that barred women from professional art careers, an isolated "exception" in a world of only men. She stressed Cassatt's privileged background and the restrictions it imposed:

> No respectable, refined lady could be a professional artist. Ladies were permitted to paint roses or pansies on china plates, even to make pencil sketches or watercolors in their enclosed gardens, but to study art seriously, learning anatomy from nude models and having a studio of their own—it was never done and therefore was unthinkable.[9]

Breeskin's Cassatt triumphed over these attitudes and was admirable, but not quite human.

After World War II the "exceptional" status of Mary Cassatt came to be a liability. As writers lost touch with the realities of women artists in the nineteenth century, many felt that the paucity of women artists in history resulted from an inherent lack of ability. In the late 1940s women artists in general, and Mary Cassatt in particular, suffered jarring criticism that bordered on ridicule unlike any that had ever been written during her lifetime or afterward. In 1948 and 1949 a series of articles written by the prominent art historians John Walker, Albert Ten Eyck Gardner, and Douglas Cooper praised Cassatt's work while raising questions about the value of it in comparison to her "failed" personal life.

John Walker, who, only two years before, in his exhibition of American Art for the National Gallery, had placed her among the top artists America had ever produced, asked in an article in the *Ladies' Home Journal* whether this high place in the history of art was worth the sacrifice. "She ended her life a lonely woman, living in self-imposed exile, surrounded in her chateau by beautiful works of art which blindness . . . prevented her from seeing."[10] Walker suggests that her series of mother and child paintings were an acknowledgment that women *should* have children, and that she had made a serious mistake in her life. In December of that year, Gardner echoed this assertion. In one of the most patronizing histories of women artists ever written, Gardner ended with the observation "It was still maintained, in some quarters, that the greatest contribution to the world of art that could be made by any woman was to be the mother of a genius."[11] Douglas Cooper, a month later, in a review of Breeskin's catalogue raisonné of the graphic work of Mary Cassatt, went so far as to say that because there have been few women painters in the history of art, one concludes that painting is a man's job. "This is especially true to-day when the ever-increasing array of female practitioners makes them increasingly conscious of their artistic ineptitude."[12]

The harsh dismissal of all women artists—indeed women's professionalism of any kind—in favor of devotion to family life was clearly part of the glorification of motherhood that fed the postwar baby boom. Such overt antifeminist comments continued sporadically, but, as a whole, were at their worst in this particular historical moment. Unfortunately they came at the time when art history as a discipline was being established on a widespread scale in American colleges and universities. Women artists, including Mary Cassatt, were conspicuously absent from the new canon established by textbooks and course outlines.

In the public arena, Cassatt was back in the limelight by 1954 in an exhibition of the triumvirate of American expatriates, Sargent, Whistler, and Cassatt, which was organized by curator Frederick Sweet of the Art Institute of Chicago. The exhibition, which traveled to the Metropolitan Museum, brought renewed attention to all three artists, although Sargent and Whistler fared better in this particular grouping than did Cassatt, whose sturdy and unlovely models clashed with the elegant society beauties favored by her colleagues. Her exclusively female world in which contemplative women dominate their gardens and parlors came under attack by the art historian Edgar Richardson as being monotonous and, finally, not important enough to spend so much time on. He expressed genuine admiration for her luminosity of flesh and "dry elegance," which would, he felt, always win a place for her in the history of art, "But—" he concluded in a now-famous phrase, "tea, clothes and nursery; nursery, clothes and tea."[13]

Despite the antifeminist tone, Richardson's accusation of monotony was valid. Cassatt wrestled with the mother and child subject for twenty-five years and, even when painting other subjects, tended to produce a series of works using certain models over and over again. It was almost thirty years after her death and time for a fresh look at her work and reputation. So many of the early writers had been too preoccupied with her exceptional or legendary persona to look carefully at her work and reevaluate it for a new generation of viewers. When this was done in the 1950s, Cassatt's inflated reputation from the 1920s was cut down to a more realistic size.

In spite of Richardson's objection to Cassatt's often repeated imagery, her hold on both the art world and the public imagination continued to grow stronger. Sweet, who had conducted extensive research for his exhibition, published several biographical articles on Cassatt in conjunction with it that appeared in *Vogue* and *Art Institute of Chicago Quarterly* in 1954, and *Art Quarterly,* 1958. In addition, he had gathered family letters and documents together for microfilming by the Archives of American Art. Drawing on these resources, he published the first actual biography of Mary Cassatt in 1966, *Miss Mary Cassatt, Impressionist from Pennsylvania.* The biography uses extensive quotes from the letters (which had been available to other scholars, such as Breeskin, in the past but never published) and brought to the public its first glimpse of Cassatt in a personal setting.

The Mary Cassatt that emerged from Sweet's biography was not significantly different from the woman described by Havemeyer and Breeskin for the reason that Sweet used Havemeyer as his major source and shared with Breeskin the same information available from both Havemeyer and Cassatt family materials. But since he focused on her life rather than her art, his Cassatt was rounded out—her various life phases were defined and her relationships with family and friends explored. Sweet was a very conscientious researcher and thus established reasonably accurate dates for events. He also interviewed Cassatt's surviving nieces, Ellen Mary Cassatt Hare, Eugenia Cassatt Madeira, and Lois Cassatt Thayer, as well as others who knew her well, such as Harris Whittemore, Helen Sears Bradley, and various neighbors in Mesnil-Théribus. The result was a gossipy book that includes, among other things, anecdotes about her dogs and where she bought her hats. While Sweet does not condescend to Cassatt—he is convinced of her stature as an artist and a person—he relies heavily on the stereotype of a well-bred Victorian spinster. One reviewer described Sweet's approach as "gentlemanly."[14]

Sweet's biography was followed four years later by the publication of *Mary Cassatt: A Catalogue Raisonné of the Oils, Pastels, Watercolors and Drawings,* by Adelyn Breeskin, which brought a new level of clarity and understanding to Cassatt's art. Laying out the entries in chronological order, a catalogue raisonné documents every known work by an artist, with a photograph and the available factual information concerning its ownership over the years (provenance), exhibition history, and where it has been published. The appearance of such an encyclopedic treatment of an artist settles questions of authenticity, dating, and overall evolution of an artist and is the indispensable tool of the art historian and connoisseur. Breeskin's *Cassatt,* although inaccurate in some ways, was nevertheless a spur in the following decades to the increasingly complex art historical inquiries into Cassatt's work. Its appearance was celebrated by an exhibition of about one hundred works at the National Gallery of Art.

This milestone in the evolution of the historical Mary Cassatt coincided with the modern revival of the women's movement in the United States. Not since the last great period of feminism in the 1910s, which included the campaign for the vote in which Cassatt and Havemeyer participated, had American women pushed so hard for equal rights in society. Beginning in the late 1960s, feminism spread among artists and art historians and resulted in renewed attention to the place of women artists in the contemporary art world and in the writing of art history.

By the 1970s the upswing of feminism coupled with the new tools available to scholars brought more attention than ever to Cassatt. Not only were there three small Cassatt exhibitions at Newport Harbor in 1974, National Museum of American Art and Museum of Fine Arts, Boston, both in 1978, but she was included in numerous other exhibitions of Americans, Impressionists, printmakers and now, women. For instance, Cassatt was prominent in a small but important exhibition of women artists from the Renaissance to the nineteenth century that was organized by Ann Gabhart and Elizabeth Broun at the Walters Art Gallery in Baltimore.

Another full-scale biography was published in 1975, *Mary Cassatt: A Biography of the Great American Painter,* by Nancy Hale, a writer for the *The New Yorker* who had already published sixteen books on various topics including women, art, and fiction. Like Sweet, Hale also relied on the stereotype of the Victorian spinster but enlarged it with Freudian speculations, particularly about Cassatt's relationship with her father and her love of horses. It was also more discursive than Sweet's, which was built around lengthy excerpts from letters and other source materials, and more inquiring into Cassatt's psychological and emotional life. Ironically, the Mary Cassatt it portrayed was less professional and serious than the version of this artist most writers since Louisine Havemeyer had offered and was thus inconsistent with the feminist tenor of the times.

The rebirth of feminism did not have exclusively positive results for Mary Cassatt. The move to rectify art history so that women artists were reinstalled in their proper places and rewarded for their accomplishments led to the rediscovery of the many women who had genuinely been forgotten over the years. It was soon acknowledged that although Cassatt had suffered from the same patronizing attitudes as all women artists, she had by no means ever been "lost," and that researchers and writers should devote more of their time to those women, such as Emily Sartain for example, who truly had been forgotten. Because of the work of Breeskin and Sweet, Cassatt was already relatively well documented.

Cassatt was also problematic to feminist art historians in that her signature theme was the mother and child, a subject closely associated with a conservative view of women's roles. The subject was broached with great care by feminist art historians such as Linda Nochlin in her article "Women Artists in the Twentieth Century."[15] Nochlin stressed the variations of the theme among women artists as diverse as Cassatt, Morisot, Käthe Kollwitz, and Paula Mödersohn-Becker as an argument that it cannot be interpreted as uniform or predictable.

Nochlin and Ann Sutherland Harris included Cassatt to great advantage in their monumental exhibition, "Women Artists: 1550–1950," which opened at the Los Angeles County Museum of Art in 1976 and traveled to three other museums across the country. In 157 works representing over eighty artists the history of art was retold in a fresh and vivid way with an all-female cast. This exhibition also brought together the new research being done on individual artists and its catalog still stands as the most important book on women artists published in this period.

Feminist activity in the 1970s sparked new scholarly inquiries into the art of Mary Cassatt that would bear fruit in the 1980s. The first two doctoral dissertations were begun (my own, "Mary Cassatt and the 'Modern Madonna' of the Nineteenth Century," and Frances Weitzenhoffer's, "The Creation of the Havemeyer Collection, 1875–1900") and completed in 1980 and 1982, respectively. We were both primarily concerned with re-creating the cultural context for Cassatt's activities as an artist and an adviser to art collectors and would publish books based on this research throughout the 1980s. I published *Mary Cassatt and Her Circle: Selected Letters* (1984), *Mary Cassatt* (1987), and *Mary Cassatt: The Color Prints* (with Barbara Stern Shapiro, 1989), while Weitzenhoffer published *The Havemeyers: Impressionism Comes to America* (1986). A third art historian, Suzanne Lindsay, researched Cassatt's association with the Philadelphia art world and published the results in her catalog *Mary Cassatt and Philadelphia,* which accompanied an exhibition at the Philadelphia Museum of Art in 1985. My work, along with Weitzenhoffer's and Lindsay's, continued the tradition established by Louisine Havemeyer of treating Cassatt first and foremost as a professional artist, clarifying her goals and methods in that regard, and establishing the historical circumstances under which she worked.

The publication of the letters of Cassatt and her circle gave scholars and writers a new documentary source from which to draw insights. It was the first time Cassatt had been restored to her place among her friends and family, and one of the revelations was how many professional women were among her acquaintances. Far from being an exception in her generation, she was but one of many who led similarly productive lives. My monograph, *Mary Cassatt,* was also an attempt to publish new and accurate information about the artist in an introductory manner for the student and art lover. The study of Cassatt's color prints was a revision of that section of Breeskin's catalogue raisonné of the graphic work and accompanied an exhibition of the color prints and their various preparatory drawings and preliminary states. Each of these three books shows Mary Cassatt at work, facing the day-to-day problems of inspiration and choice of subject, evolving style, and the intransigencies of artists' materials.

An alternate view of Cassatt and her art was proposed with the publication in 1980 of the short monograph, *Mary Cassatt,* by the British art historian Griselda Pollock. She concentrated on interpreting Cassatt's art from a feminist point of view. She took the approach, popular since the 1930s, that Cassatt and Morisot were exceptions in a restrictive period that produced very few professional women artists and discussed Cassatt's imagery in terms of her ignorance of other themes—men, the city, etc.—which resulted from her limited access to society at large. While this exaggerated portrayal of life in the Victorian age does not jibe with the actual facts of Cassatt's life, Pollock's desire to get at the circumstances that make women's lives different from men's was consistent with the interest in analyzing gender issues that was rapidly growing in the scholarly arena and was very influential. In addition, she employed techniques of formal analysis to interpret specific paintings. For example, an unfinished, "evolving" painting of a mother and child was read as an attempt on Cassatt's part to suggest the "evolution" of the child from infancy into future stages of growth. Her approach appealed to deconstructionist approaches to art and literature, which were also becoming common in academic circles.

The scholarly Cassatt of the 1980s was also accompanied by the popular Cassatt—the beloved subject of magazine articles, picture books, children's books, calendars, note cards and numerous other museum-shop products. A half-hour documentary on Mary Cassatt produced and aired on PBS in 1977 by Perry Adato Miller has since been made available on videocassette, and a novel by Joan King, *Impressionist: A Novel of Mary Cassatt,* appeared in 1983. In the popular imagination, Mary Cassatt balanced the forcefulness of the successful career woman with the appealing female imagery of her art. Taking her life and art in their general outlines, the popular Cassatt seems to be all things to all women.

Mary Cassatt rode the crest of the women's movement into the 1980s and was further propelled by the prosperity of that decade, which brought the market values of Impressionist and American art to new levels. The insurance values of Cassatt's paintings rose accordingly, forcing museums to limit extensive borrowing for major exhibitions and making owners reluctant to lend their most popular works. However, the demand for Cassatt's work continued unabated and appears likely to spur carefully tailored exhibitions into the next century. The periodic renewal of American feminism has also promised an ongoing examination of issues concerning women and art.

Based on the publications of the 1980s and the plans for the 1990s, Mary Cassatt today is viewed as a much more complex person and artist than ever before. Reflecting current feminist ideals, she is now seen as a feminist herself, consciously or unconsciously using her art and her eloquent speech to advance the cause of women in her own day. Her efforts in this regard are perceived as ranging from the use of female subject matter to make an abstract point about women's psychology to the more obvious association with the women's suffrage movement. Also reflecting today's concerns, writers portray her as a successful career woman, using her talent as well as her understanding of market forces to rise to the top of her profession. Her choice to remain unmarried has been separated from her choice of mother and child imagery so that the first falls into the conduct of her personal life and the second into the realm of professional decisions. Today her art tends to be searched for clues about her attitudes and values within a nineteenth-century world of home, garden, and theater, rather than approached from a stylistic or connoisseurship point of view. Ultimately, she is considered as much a modern woman now as she was when she was invited to paint a mural on that subject one hundred years ago.

It is impossible to know how closely the evolving "historic" Cassatt approximates the actual person. She, like all human beings, had too many sides and too many stages in her development to be accurately described even during her lifetime. The most faithful chronicler is the one who uses all the sources available and interprets them in a convincing manner, but who, at the same time, acknowledges her human complexity and the complexity of the circumstances under which she lived. The only possible goal is to make her live as vividly in words as she did in her life and to pass on the baton to the next decade or generation. That the baton has been eagerly accepted by all generations since her death bodes well for the immortality she worked so hard for—and may yet be hers.

Notes

All letters are in private collections unless otherwise noted.

ABBREVIATIONS

MC	Mary Cassatt
EH	Eliza Haldeman
LH	Louisine Havemeyer
ES	Emily Sartain
MMA	The Metropolitan Museum of Art
PAFA	The Pennsylvania Academy of the Fine Arts

Chapter I

1. By the eighteenth century the name had been changed to Cassart and then Cassat. By 1830 some members of the family had added an extra *t*, but Robert Cassatt did not do so until sometime in the 1840s. Misspellings were rampant and give some indication of changes in pronunciation. Robert Cassatt's name was often misspelled Cassit in the 1840s (1840 census, 1849 Lancaster County tax records). However, the 1850 census taker recorded his name as Cassatte.

2. His statement is to be taken as somewhat tongue-in-cheek: "So you perceive I am about to relinquish a *profession called honourable* to exercise the calling of a money changer." Joseph Gardner to his cousin, Mary Pearson, 20 August 1834, Chester County Historical Society.

3. After discussing an article that predicted that painting was no longer needed by modern civilization, Cassatt wrote, "If painting is no longer needed, it seems a pity

that some of us are born into the world with such a passion for line and color." MC to Bertha Palmer, 11 October [1892], Chicago Historical Society.

4. Preregistration for this class was apparently not even required. Most of the students, including Cassatt's friend Eliza Haldeman, signed up after the class began on October 1. Cassatt and one other student registered in April. Cassatt may have been waiting for this moment for a long time, since the academy would not accept students younger than sixteen. Class Registration Lists, PAFA.

5. EH to Samuel Haldeman, 26 January 1861, PAFA. This letter is dated 1860, but it can be determined by the context that it was actually written the following year and that Haldeman mistakenly wrote 1860 for several weeks into 1861.

6. Earl Shinn [Edward Strahan], "The First American Art Academy," *Lippincott's Magazine* (February–March, 1872); reprint, unknown publisher, 3–4, PAFA.

7. Ibid., 36–37.

8. EH to Samuel Haldeman, 7 March 1862, PAFA.

9. Pennsylvania Academy of the Fine Arts Visitors' Register, 20 March 1861, PAFA.

10. Achille Segard, *Mary Cassatt, un Peintre des enfants et des mères* (Paris: Librairie Paul Ollendorff, 1913), 6.

11. "It is remembered that . . . Mary, a girl of artistic aims, . . . one day took M. Filmore Taylor, a little lad, into her home and had him pose for her while she sketched his portrait." Obituary, Alexander J. Cassatt, West Chester *Daily Local News,* 29 December 1906, from clipping in Chester County Historical Society.

12. Alice Buchanan to Lois Buchanan Cassatt, 19 August 1869.

13. MC to EH, 18 March [1864], PAFA.

14. MC to EH, 13 June [1864?]. She also teased Eliza about a certain Theodore, "I painted a small portrait of Whiskey [horse or dog?] for Aleck which he said was very good, and it also had the approval of Theodore who was here the other day. I suspected from something he said that he had either seen you in town or at Chiques, am I right?"

15. Alexander Cassatt to Lois Cassatt, 27 November 1867, Philadelphia Museum of Art.

16. If Alexander Cassatt hired a substitute, there is no record of it in the Chester County Archives. He may have done so in Philadelphia before the family moved to Chester County in 1862.

17. Eliza Haldeman's mother counseled her daughter, "Be careful how you talk politics. I fear there will be but little chance of electing [illeg.]. The soldiers' vote

has been taken and they are for Lincoln and what our country will come to in another 4 years is certainly one of which we cannot speak of at the present time." Mary Haldeman to EH, 14 October 1864.

18. Segard, 5, n. 3. "Le départ ne se décida pas sans difficultés. Peu Américain, le père de Miss Cassatt s'effrayait de ce voyage. 'J'aimerais presque mieux te voir morte.' " ["Her departure did not take place without difficulties. Not very American, Miss Cassatt's father expressed his alarm at the prospect of such a trip, 'I would almost rather see you dead.' "]

19. Their passports are on file in the National Archives, Washington, D.C.

Chapter II

1. Thomas Eakins to Emily Sartain, 16 November 1866, PAFA.

2. Thomas Eakins to Charles Fussell, 18 December 1866, PAFA.

3. EH to Mary Haldeman, 15 May 1867, PAFA.

4. Nathaniel Hawthorne, *The Marble Faun* (Boston: Houghton, Mifflin & Company, 1887), 80–81.

5. EH to Mary Haldeman, 28 May 1868, PAFA.

6. Henry James, *The American* (New York: Penguin Classics, 1986), 36.

7. See above, Chap. I, n. 18.

8. Mary Haldeman to EH, 18 December 1866. The Haldemans were Catholic and viewed all the Cassatts (not just Mary), who were lukewarm Episcopalians, with some caution. But Mrs. Haldeman knew Mary well from her six years of friendship with Eliza and was aware that she had an impulsive nature.

9. EH to Mary Haldeman, 28 October 1866, PAFA.

10. EH to Samuel Haldeman, 4 December 1866, PAFA.

11. Mary Haldeman to EH, 19 November 1866.

12. EH to Samuel Haldeman, 4 December 1866, PAFA.

13. EH to Mary Haldeman, 19–20 February 1867, PAFA.

14. For example, see Edward Dicey, *Spectator of America* (reprint, Chicago: Quadrangle Books, 1971), 12, detailing this Englishman's trip to the United States in 1862. "Undoubtedly, out-of-doors, you see evidences of a public equality, or rather absence of inequality, among all classes which cannot fail to strike an inhabitant of

the Old World. In the streets, the man in the hat and broadcloth coat and the man in corduroys and fustian jacket never get out of each other's way or expect the other to make way for him. In the cars and omnibuses ladies and washerwomen, gentlemen and laborers, sit huddled together without the slightest mutual sense of incongruity. In the shops and by the servants it is your own fault if you are not treated with perfect civility—but with civility as to an equal, not as to a superior."

15. EH to Mary Haldeman, 19–20 February 1867, PAFA.

16. EH to her sister Frances Haldeman, February 1867, PAFA.

17. EH to Mary Haldeman, 15 May 1867, PAFA. "I think I forgot to tell you we were invited to dinner at Mr. Bacons Sunday before last and went with them in the evening to see the ball the Peasants had at the fête. They are another poor set of artists though now Mr. B. is out of the mire, gets good prices for his pictures and has a pretty house and garden to keep his wife in."

18. EH to Samuel Haldeman, 1 October 1867, PAFA.

19. EH to Mary Haldeman, 15 May 1867, PAFA.

20. Elizabeth Gardner to her sister Ria, 25 May 1868.

21. EH to Samuel and Mary Haldeman, 8 May 1868, PAFA.

22. Ibid.

23. Ibid.

24. EH to Frances Haldeman, 13 May 1868, PAFA.

25. EH to Samuel Haldeman, 22 May 1868, PAFA. "Will you believe that yesterday we were at the Mabille. I have had great curiosity since I have been in Paris to see something of the kind, so have been satisfied. . . . The garden was beautiful and lighted up magnificently. . . . We were escorted by a young gentleman friend of [Cousin Sarah's] from Pittsburg who politely turned his back on the performances so that we might look on at ease 'as he had already been there half dozen times.' "

26. EH to Frances Haldeman, 13 May 1868, PAFA.

27. Ibid.

28. Alexander Cassatt to Lois Cassatt, 24 August 1868, Philadelphia Museum of Art.

29. Ibid.

30. Thomas Eakins to his mother, 1 April 1869, PAFA.

31. Ibid.

32. EH to Mary Haldeman, 15 October 1868, PAFA.

33. Samuel Haldeman to EH, 2 March 1863.

34. Ibid.

35. MC to EH, 17 August 1869, PAFA.

36. Ibid.

37. Ibid.

Chapter III

1. Alexander Cassatt to Lois Buchanan [Cassatt], 12 November 1868.

2. MC to Katherine Cassatt, unknown date, quoted in Katherine Cassatt to Lois Cassatt, 19 December 1868.

3. Eliza Buchanan to Lois Cassatt, 14 December 1870.

4. James Buchanan to Lois Cassatt, 9 October 1870.

5. Lois Cassatt to Harriet Buchanan, 6 August 1880.

6. Annie Buchanan to Lois Buchanan [Cassatt], 30 January 1865.

7. Nancy Hale, *Mary Cassatt: A Biography of the Great American Painter* (New York: Doubleday & Company, Inc., 1975), 41. The source of this quote is uncertain. Hale attributes it to "one Old Philadelphian."

8. Alexander Cassatt to Lois Buchanan [Cassatt], 15 August 1868.

9. MC to EH, 17 August 1869, PAFA.

10. MC to ES, 22 May 1871, PAFA.

11. Ibid.

12. Ibid.

13. MC to ES, 7 June 1871, PAFA.

14. MC to ES, 10 July 1871, PAFA.

15. U.S. Census, 1860.

16. MC to ES, 27 October 1871, PAFA.

17. ES to John Sartain, 7 March 1872, Moore College of Art.

18. Ibid.

19. William Sartain to John Sartain, 25 March 1872, Historical Society of Pennsylvania.

20. MC to EH, 2 June [1872], PAFA.

21. MC to ES, 5 October 1872, PAFA.

22. MC to ES, 13 October 1872, PAFA.

23. MC to ES, 27 October 1872, PAFA.

24. ES to John Sartain, 7 November 1872, Moore College of Art.

25. MC to ES, 1 January 1873, PAFA.

26. Ibid.

27. Ibid.

28. The choice of Mary Stevenson as a pseudonym recalls the name of an artist who studied in the all-male life class at the Pennsylvania Academy when Cassatt was there, "A. May Stevenson." A landscape of West Chester, Pennsylvania, Cassatt's hometown, was shown in the annual academy exhibition of 1861 under this artist's name.

29. See Lois Fink, *American Art at the Nineteenth-Century Paris Salons* (Cambridge: Cambridge University Press, 1990), 114–15.

30. ES to John Sartain, 8 May 1873, Moore College of Art.

31. Ibid.

32. Henry James, *Roderick Hudson* (New York: Penguin Books, 1987), 119–20. It was first published in the *Atlantic Monthly* in installments from January to December 1875.

33. STOP (pseudonym of L.P.G.B. Morel-Retz), *Le Journal amusant* (27 June 1874), caricature no. 326.

34. Segard, 35.

35. ES to John Sartain, 17 June 1874, Moore College of Art.

Chapter IV

1. Elizabeth Gardner, for example, had been exhibiting regularly at the Salon. In 1879 she won an Honorable Mention, which enabled her to bypass the jury in entering future exhibitions, and in 1887 she won a Gold Medal, the highest Salon award. Perhaps more important, by the early 1870s she was able to support herself

by the sale of her own works, by the sale of copies, and by miscellaneous activities such as publishing "letters from Paris" in American journals and by aiding collectors in obtaining French works of art. For a survey of Gardner's career, see Madeleine Fidell-Beaufort, "Elizabeth Jane Gardner Bouguereau: A Parisian Artist from New Hampshire," *Archives of American Art Journal* 24–25 (1984–85), 2–9.

2. MC to Eugénie Heller [c. 1 February 1896], MMA.

3. *Paris by Night: Sketches and Mysteries of Paris High Life and Demi-Monde* (Boston: Boston and Paris Publishing Company, 1875), 6.

4. May Alcott described a party at Cassatt's studio, where they ate "fluffy cream and chocolate, with French cakes, while sitting in carved chairs, on Turkish rugs, with superb tapestries as a background, and fine pictures on the walls looking down from their splendid frames. . . . Statues and articles of *vertu* filled the corners, the whole being lighted by a great antique hanging lamp. We sipped our *chocolat* from superior china, served on an India waiter, upon an embroidered cloth of heavy material. Miss Cassatt was charming as usual in two shades of brown satin and rep, being very lively and a woman of real genius, she will be a first-class light as soon as her pictures get a little circulated and known, for they are handled in a masterly way, with a touch of strength one seldom finds coming from a woman's fingers." May Alcott to Abigail May Alcott [November 1876], in Caroline Ticknor, *May Alcott: A Memoir* (Boston: Little, Brown and Company, 1928), 151.

5. Very little is known about this trip to the United States, Cassatt's last until 1898. She left Liverpool for Philadelphia on May 31 (S.S. *Illinois* passenger list) and returned by August 7, 1875 (list of Americans newly arrived in Paris published in the Paris newspaper, *The American Register*).

6. ES to John Sartain, 25 May 1875, Moore College of Art.

7. Émile Zola, *His Masterpiece [L'Oeuvre]* (Phoenix Mill: Alan Sutton Publishing Limited, 1986), 264. Trans. E.A. Vizetelly. *L'Oeuvre* was first published in Paris in 1886; this English translation was first published in London in 1902.

8. Louisine Havemeyer, *Sixteen to Sixty: Memoirs of a Collector* (New York: Ursus Press, 1993) ed. Susan A. Stein, 269–70.

9. Louisa May Alcott, *Diana and Persis* in *Alternative Alcott,* Elaine Showalter, ed. (New Brunswick: Rutgers University Press, 1989), 400. The novel was begun in 1879 but never finished. It was first published in 1978.

10. Ibid.

11. Ibid., 407.

12. Henry Bacon, *A Parisian Year* (Boston: Roberts Brothers, 1882), 70–72.

13. Zola, *His Masterpiece,* 263.

14. Ibid.

15. Louis Leroy, "L'exposition des impressionnistes," *Le Charivari* (25 April 1874): 2–3.

16. Edmond Duranty, *La nouvelle peinture,* 1876, and Georges Rivière, "Les intransigeants de la peinture," *L'Esprit Moderne* (13 April 1876), 7–8.

17. Bacon, 80. In spite of their long acquaintance, he does not mention Mary Cassatt's participation in the group.

18. Ibid., 81.

19. As Cassatt told Segard, ". . . Degas m'engagea à ne plus envoyer au Salon et à exposer avec ses amis dans le groupe des Impressionnistes. J'acceptai avec joie. Enfin je pouvais travailler avec une indépendance absolue sans m'occuper de l'opinion éventuelle d'un jury! Déjà j'avais reconnu quels étaient mes véritables maîtres. J'admirais Manet, Courbet et Degas. Je haïssais l'art conventionnel. Je commençais à vivre. . . ." [Degas asked me not to send to the Salon again but to exhibit instead with his friends in the Impressionist group. I accepted with joy. Finally I could work with an absolute independence without being concerned with the ultimate opinion of a jury. I already knew who my true masters were. I admired Manet, Courbet, and Degas. I hated conventional art. I began to live. . . .], Segard, 7–8.

20. Armand Silvestre, *Au Pays du Souvenir*, 1892, in Bernard Denvir, *The Impressionists at First Hand* (London: Thames and Hudson, 1987), 71.

21. Gustave Geffroy, *Claude Monet,* 1922, in Denvir, 167.

22. Quoted by Louisine Havemeyer in *Mrs. H.O. Havemeyer's Remarks on Edgar Degas and Mary Cassatt* (New York: M. Knoedler & Co., 1915), [2].

23. Silvestre, in Denvir, 72.

24. George Moore, *Confessions of a Young Man,* 1888, in Denvir, 78.

25. Bacon, 60.

26. *The Americans in Paris* (Paris, 1887), 56.

27. J. Monroe & Co., *The American Traveller's Guide to Paris* (London: W.H. & L. Collingridge, 1869), 2.

28. Bacon, 50–51.

29. MC to J. Alden Weir, 10 March 1878.

30. Ibid.

31. These and other details about the Impressionist exhibitions can be found in Charles S. Moffett, *The New Painting: Impressionism 1874–1886* (San Francisco: The Fine Arts Museum of San Francisco, 1986), 192.

32. Robert Cassatt to Edward Cassatt, 1 April 1878, Philadelphia Museum of Art.

33. Émile Zola, Preface to *L'Assommoir* (New York: Penguin Classics, 1970), trans. Leonard Tancock, 21.

34. *Paris at Night,* 82–83.

35. George Moore, *Reminiscences of the Impressionist Painters* (Dublin: Maunsel & Co., 1906), 35.

36. MC to Ambroise Vollard [1903], Archives of American Art.

37. Katherine Cassatt to Alexander Cassatt, 18 October 1878.

38. Robert Cassatt to Alexander Cassatt, 26 May 1879.

39. Robert Cassatt to Alexander Cassatt, 13 December 1878, Philadelphia Museum of Art.

40. Katherine Cassatt to Alexander Cassatt, 18 October 1878.

41. Robert Cassatt to Alexander Cassatt, 13 December 1878, Philadelphia Museum of Art.

42. MC to J. Alden Weir, 10 March 1878.

43. MC to Ambroise Vollard [1903], Archives of American Art.

44. Elizabeth Gardner to Ria Gardner, 23 May 1878.

45. M. Louis Gonse, *Exposition Universelle de 1878: Les Beaux-Arts et les Arts Décoratifs* (Paris: Gazette des Beaux-Arts, 1879), 210.

46. See Robert Cassatt to Alexander Cassatt, 4 October 1878, Philadelphia Museum of Art: "Mame had a very fine [frame] bought, a bargain in Rome, in which the picture was exhibited here."

Chapter V

1. Gustave Goetschy, *Le Voltaire,* 5 April 1881, in *The New Painting,* 250.

2. F.-C. de Syène [Arsène Houssaye], "Salon de 1879," *L'Artiste,* May 1879, 292.

3. George Lafenestre, "Les Expositions d'art," *Revue des Deux Mondes,* May–June 1879, 481.

4. Robert Cassatt to Alexander Cassatt, 21 May 1879, Philadelphia Museum of Art.

5. Ibid.

6. "The Exhibition of Independent Artists," *The American Register,* 17 May 1879, 4.

7. Gustave Caillebotte to Claude Monet [mid-May 1879] in *The New Painting,* 265, n. 114.

8. Robert Cassatt to Alexander Cassatt, 1 September 1879, Philadelphia Museum of Art.

9. Ibid.

10. EH to Samuel Haldeman, 21 December 1861, PAFA.

11. ES to John Sartain, 8 May 1873, Moore College of Art.

12. ES to John Sartain, 17 June 1874, Moore College of Art.

13. Katherine Cassatt to Alexander Cassatt, 9 April [1880], Philadelphia Museum of Art.

14. Edgar Degas to Ludovic-Napoléon Lepic [1878–79] in *Degas Letters* (Oxford: Bruno Cassirer, 1947), ed. Marcel Guérin, trans. Marguerite Kay, p. 144–45. The dog in question was probably the one she named Baptiste, or "Batty," who was her constant companion for the next decade.

15. Berthe Morisot to Edma Morisot, 2 May 1869, in *The Correspondence of Berthe Morisot* (London: Camden Press, 1986), ed. Denis Rouart, Kathleen Adler, and Tamar Garb, 36.

16. Havemeyer, 244.

17. Ibid., 244–45.

18. Katherine Cassatt to Alexander Cassatt, 9 April [1880], Philadelphia Museum of Art.

19. Henry Havard, "L'Exposition des artistes indépendants," *Le Siècle,* 2 April 1880 in *The New Painting,* 321.

20. Philippe Burty, "Exposition des oeuvres des artistes indépendant," *La République Française,* 10 April 1880, in *The New Painting,* 321.

21. Lois Cassatt to Annie Buchanan, 6 July 1880.

22. Lois Cassatt to Harriet Buchanan, 6 August 1880.

23. Ibid.

24. Lois Cassatt to Eliza Buchanan, 10 July 1880.

25. Lois Cassatt to Eliza Buchanan, 26 July 1880.

26. Goetschy, in *The New Painting,* 358.

27. G.G. [Gustave Geffroy], "L'exposition des artistes indépendants," *La Justice,* 19 April 1881, in *The New Painting,* 359.

28. Robert Cassatt to Alexander Cassatt, 18 April 1881, Philadelphia Museum of Art.

29. Katherine Cassatt to her granddaughter Katharine Cassatt, 15 April 1881, Philadelphia Museum of Art.

30. Katherine Cassatt to Lois Cassatt, 18 July 1881.

31. Berthe Morisot to Eugène Manet [spring 1882], in *Correspondence of Morisot,* 125.

32. Eugène Manet to Berthe Morisot [spring 1882], *Correspondence of Morisot,* 126.

33. Robert Cassatt to Alexander Cassatt, 18 September 1882.

34. Lois Cassatt to Eliza Cassatt [December 1882].

35. Ibid.

36. Lois Cassatt to Eliza Cassatt, 26 December 1882.

37. Berthe Morisot to Edma Morisot [May 1883], in *Correspondence of Morisot,* 131.

38. Lydia Gardner to Robert Cassatt, quoted in Robert Cassatt to Alexander Cassatt, 2 August 1882, Philadelphia Museum of Art.

39. Robert Cassatt to Alexander Cassatt, 14 April 1886, Philadelphia Museum of Art.

40. Katherine Cassatt to Alexander Cassatt, 30 November 1883, Philadelphia Museum of Art.

41. Adelaide M. Nevin, *The Social Mirror: A Character Sketch of the Women of Pittsburg and Vicinity during the First Century of The County's Existence,* Pittsburgh: T. W. Nevin, 1888, 21. Katherine Johnston Cassatt is not mentioned.

42. MC to LH, 4 February [1915], MMA.

43. Henri Meilhac and Ludovic Halévy, *La Cigale* (New York: Happy Hours Company, 1879), vii.

44. Lois Cassatt's travel diary for 1882–83, 20 April 1883.

45. Ibid., 23 April 1883.

46. MC to Lois Cassatt, 15 June [1883], Philadelphia Museum of Art.

47. MC to Alexander Cassatt, 14 October [1883], Philadelphia Museum of Art.

48. MC to Lois Cassatt, 29 December [1884], Philadelphia Museum of Art.

49. Cassatt's paintings cannot be taken as a literal reflection of the apartment because until 1887 she painted in her studio on the Rue Duperré using furniture she kept there. But the paintings do give an indication of her taste in furniture and decoration.

50. Paul Durand-Ruel to George Lafenestre (l'Inspecteur des Beaux-Arts Commissaire générale des Expositions), 18 September 1885, National Archives, Paris.

51. See Frances Weitzenhoffer, *The Havemeyers: Impressionism Comes to America* (New York: Harry N. Abrams, 1986), 42.

52. Robert Cassatt to Alexander Cassatt, 14 April 1886, Philadelphia Museum of Art. "Mame is pretty well and working like a beaver getting ready for an exhibition which they propose having in May. She is now engaged on a little Red Headed Girl in Demi costume dressing her hair before a glass, etc. (figure 167). The two or three experts and artists who have seen it praise it without stint, as for Degas, he was quite enthusiastic for him."

CHAPTER VI

1. Lois Cassatt to Harriet Buchanan, 1 March 1888.

2. MC to Alexander Cassatt, 2 September 1886, Philadelphia Museum of Art.

3. An impression in the New York Public Library is inscribed and dated "Jan/88."

4. Yveling Rambaud, "Miss Cassatt," *L'Art dans les Deux Mondes* (22 Novembre 1890), 7.

5. Katherine Cassatt to Alexander Cassatt, 23 July 1891, Philadelphia Museum of Art. "Mary is at work again, intent on fame & money she says, & counts on her fellow country men now that she has made a reputation here—"

6. Henry James, *The Ambassadors* (New York: Penguin Classics, 1986), 166–67. First published in serial form in 1903 by *The North American Review*.

7. Ibid., 167.

8. Havemeyer's memory may have been incorrect on this point, since it is more likely that Cassatt broke her leg in Septeuil. Degas wrote at the time, "The horse

must have put its foot in a hole made by the rain on soft earth. HE (meaning Mr. Cassatt) hides his daughter's *amour-propre* and above all his own." Edgar Degas to Henri Rouart [1889], in *Degas Letters,* pp. 125–26.

9. Havemeyer, 280.

10. MC to Berthe Morisot [April, 1890].

11. MC to George Lucas [June 1890], Baltimore Museum of Art.

12. Félix Fénéon, "Cassatt, Pissarro," *Le Chat Noir* (11 avril 1891), in *Félix Fénéon: Oeuvres Plus que Complètes* (Geneva: Librairie Droz, 1970), ed. Joan Halperin, 185.

13. "Exhibition of the Society of French Painters-Etchers," *The American Register* (11 April 1891), 6.

14. Camille Pissarro to Lucien Pissarro, 25 April 1891, in *Camille Pissarro: Letters to His Son Lucien* (Santa Barbara: Peregrine Smith, Inc., 1981), ed. John Rewald, 204.

15. Segard, 87.

16. Robert Cassatt to Alexander Cassatt, 28 July 1891, Philadelphia Museum of Art.

17. Katherine Cassatt to Alexander Cassatt, 23 July 1891, Philadelphia Museum of Art.

18. Robert Cassatt to Alexander Cassatt, 28 July 1891, Philadelphia Museum of Art.

19. Lois Cassatt to Harriet Buchanan, 6 August 1880.

20. Havemeyer, 288.

21. Ibid.

22. MC to Bertha Palmer, 11 October [1892], Chicago Historical Society.

23. Ibid.

24. André Mellério, Preface to *Exposition Mary Cassatt* (Paris: Durand Ruel Galleries, 1893). In describing the central panel of the Chicago mural, Mellério points out the figure carrying a basket of fruit, "[elle] a le geste empreint de grandeur et de simplicité d'une jeune prêtesse dans les processions antiques."

25. MC to Bertha Palmer, 11 October [1892], Chicago Historical Society.

26. T. W. Higginson, "Ought Woman to Learn the Alphabet?" in *Women and the Alphabet: A Series of Essays* (Boston: Houghton, Mifflin and Company, 1900), 2.

27. Ibid., 5.

28. Lois Cassatt to Edward Cassatt, 23 September 1892. "We all spent Sunday with your Grandmother and had a very pleasant visit and to my surprise Aunt Mary did come in on Wednesday and stayed with us for lunch although I really think she came in to attend the funeral of Durand Ruel's son, who died very suddenly on Sunday. I went to the service at the church with her. The music was splendid and I saw all the great artists there and Aunt Mary pointed them out to me."

29. I am grateful to Gary Allison for information about William Milligan Sloane and his family. In addition to Sloane's scholarly activities, he was one of the founders of the modern Olympics, which was organized in 1894. This research has been conducted by the 1st Century Project and World Sport Research & Publications, courtesy of the United States Olympic Committee.

30. MC to Bertha Palmer, 11 October [1892], Chicago Historical Society.

31. MC to Bertha Palmer, 1 December [1892], Chicago Historical Society.

32. MC to Samuel Avery, 2 March [1893].

33. Mary MacMonnies to Bertha Palmer, 23 January 1893, Chicago Historical Society.

34. Ibid.

35. MC to Bertha Palmer, 11 October [1892], Chicago Historical Society.

36. Camille Pissarro to Lucien Pissarro, 2 October 1892, in *Pissarro Letters,* 259.

37. Ibid.

38. Berthe Morisot to Louise Riesener [June 1892], *Correspondence of Morisot,* 194.

39. Eleanor B. Caldwell, Introduction to and translation of André Mellério, *Exposition Mary Cassatt, Modern Art* (Winter, 1895), 4. ". . . the best to me was a lady in a lace hat, in a garden, working, with gloves on, at knitting [see figure 66]. The face was so exquisite in tone, with the out-door light, and so refined in sentiment—she looked *thinking.*"

40. MC to Sarah Hallowell, quoted in Sarah Hallowell to Bertha Palmer, 6 February [1894], Chicago Historical Society.

Chapter VII

1. MC to John H. Whittemore, 22 December [1893].

2. MC to Joseph Durand-Ruel, 2 February [1894], Collection Durand-Ruel, Paris.

3. MC to Eugénie Heller, 30 January [1894], MMA.

4. Ibid.

5. MC to Rose Lamb, 26 April 1895, Museum of Fine Arts, Boston.

6. Robert Cassatt's fortune at the time of his death is not known. It was probably less than $200,000, which was the amount of Mary Cassatt's holdings around 1912, the bulk of which was inherited from her parents.

7. Vernon Lee to Kit Anstruther-Thomson, 28 July 1895, in Frederick A. Sweet, *Miss Mary Cassatt: Impressionist from Pennsylvania* (Norman: University of Oklahoma Press, 1966), 143.

8. Ibid.

9. MC to Paul Durand-Ruel [August 1894], Collection Durand-Ruel, Paris.

10. Ibid.

11. "Pictures by Mary Cassatt," *New York Times* (18 April 1895), 4.

12. William Walton, "Miss Mary Cassatt," *Scribner's Magazine* (March 1896), 356.

13. "Pictures by Mary Cassatt," *New York Times,* 6.

14. Havemeyer, 284.

15. Ibid.

16. Sweet, 144.

17. Havemeyer, 272.

18. Havemeyer, 273.

19. MC to Eugénie Heller, 24 February [1896], New York Public Library.

20. MC to Rose Lamb, 14 January 1898, Museum of Fine Arts, Boston.

21. Ibid.

22. Camille Pissarro to Lucien Pissarro, 24 February 1895, *Pissarro Letters,* 331.

23. She refused an invitation to visit the Whittemores in Connecticut, saying, "it would give me great pleasure to see you both in your home . . . [but] going out in

a boat to study the reflections of the water, on the bay here has made me seasick, what would an ocean voyage be!" MC to John H. Whittemore, 15 February [1894].

24. MC to Rose Lamb, 14 January [1898], Museum of Fine Arts, Boston.

25. *Daily Evening Telegraph* (15 January 1898), 7, in Suzanne G. Lindsay, *Mary Cassatt and Philadelphia* (Philadelphia: Philadelphia Museum of Art, 1985), 24.

26. Homer Saint-Gaudens, *The American Artist and His Times* (New York, 1941) in Sweet, 154.

27. R. Riordan, "Miss Mary Cassatt," *The Art Amateur* (May 1898), 130.

Chapter VIII

1. MC to Ada Pope, 7 April 1900, Hill-Stead Museum.

2. André Mellério, *L'Exposition de 1900 et l'Impressionnisme* (Paris: H. Floury, 1900), 9.

3. Camille Mauclair, *The French Impressionists: 1860–1900* (London: Duckworth & Co., 1903), trans. P. G. Konody, 146–50.

4. Camille Mauclair, "Un Peintre de l'Enfance: Miss Mary Cassatt," *L'Art Décoratif* (August 1902) 177–85.

5. Havemeyer, 107–8.

6. Ibid., 109.

7. Ibid., 110. The painting was subsequently proved to be by Francesco Montemezzano rather than by Veronese. But Cassatt at the time had no reason to question the attribution to Veronese, an attribution that had been accepted by the art world since at least 1849.

8. Since they were not making the attributions to famous artists themselves but trusting attributions that were widely accepted, they cannot be too strongly condemned for making mistakes. However, if they had gone through prominent dealers, the pictures offered to them would have been better known and more likely to have solid evidence of their authorship.

9. Havemeyer, 131.

10. Havemeyer, 145.

11. MC to Berthe Morisot [fall 1879].

12. Havemeyer, 111.

13. MC to LH, 6 February [1903], MMA.

14. Havemeyer, 278.

15. Ibid., 97.

16. Ibid., 135.

17. MC to LH, 5 January [1905], MMA.

18. MC to LH, 26 January [1903], MMA.

19. MC to LH, 2 February [1903], MMA.

20. Havemeyer, 292.

21. MC to LH, 26 January 1903, MMA.

22. Charles H. Caffin, "American Studio Talk: Pennsylvania Academy Exhibition," *International Studio* (March 1904), 239.

23. MC to Harrison Morris, 29 August [1904], PAFA.

24. Ibid.

25. MC to John W. Beatty, 5 September [1905], Archives of American Art.

26. Ibid.

27. Allan Sidney, "The Value of the Apparently Meaningless and Inaccurate," *Camera Work* (July 1903), 18.

28. Ibid.

29. Sweet, 170.

30. MC to LH, 27 December [1907], MMA.

31. Anna Thorne, "My Afternoon with Mary Cassatt," *School Arts* (May 1960), 11. This interview probably took place around 1913.

32. In Écouen and again in Parma, she suffered a bout with an undiagnosed stomach ailment. Her stomach also rebelled whenever she went out in a boat.

33. MC to Electra Havemeyer Webb, 27 May 1909, Shelburne Museum.

34. MC to LH, 23 November [1906], MMA.

35. MC to LH, 27 December [1906], MMA.

36. Havemeyer, 276.

37. Florence Finch Kelly, "Painters of Sea and Shore," *The Hampton Magazine* (August 1907), 584. Cassatt was included by virtue of her 1894 painting *The Boating Party* (figure 95).

38. MC to LH, 27 December [1906?], MMA. Henderson had already included Cassatt in an article on the "Centenary Exhibition of the Pennsylvania Academy of the Fine Arts," *Brush and Pencil* (March, 1905), 145–55, but another one never did appear.

39. MC to John Beatty, 6 October [1908], Archives of American Art.

40. *North American* (March, 1907), in Lindsay, 25.

41. MC to Joseph Pennell, 8 November [1905], Library of Congress.

42. MC to LH, 21 December [1906], MMA.

43. Ibid.

44. According to Helen Sears Bradley's reminiscences to Frederick Sweet, p. 196.

45. MC to Ellen Mary Cassatt, 26 March [1913?], Philadelphia Museum of Art.

46. Sweet, 196.

47. MC to Ellen Mary Cassatt, op. cit.

48. Ibid.

49. Ibid.

50. Ibid.

51. Ibid.

52. Ibid.

53. Ibid.

54. MC to LH, 28 September [1910], MMA.

55. Thorne, 12.

56. Quoting a recent speech by Clemenceau in "The Most Eminent of Living American Women Painters," *Current Opinion* (February 1909), 167.

57. Ibid.

58. MC to LH, 25 January [1910], MMA.

Chapter IX

1. MC to LH, 12 March 1913, MMA.

2. MC to LH, 11 February 1911, MMA.

3. Ibid.

4. MC to LH, 1 August 1912, MMA.

5. MC to LH, 17 March [1911], MMA.

6. Ibid.

7. MC to LH, 8 March [1911], MMA.

8. Elsie Cassatt Stewart to Lois Cassatt, 7 May 1911.

9. MC to LH, 29 December [1911], MMA.

10. MC to LH, 12 March [1912], MMA.

11. "De silhouette mince et haute, très aristocratique, habillée de noir, s'appuyant sur une canne et s'avançant avec précaution sur les allées sablées de son parc aux arbres magnifiques, telle m'apparut Miss Mary Cassatt, le jour où je lui rendis visite pour la première fois. . . . Un sourire d'extrême bonté éclaira son visage grave, et, sous des boucles mêlées de fils d'argent, les yeux gris et bleu, couleur d'eau dormant, animèrent tout le visage aux méplats fortement accusés." [Tall and thin, very aristocratic, dressed in black, leaning on a cane and walking cautiously on the gravel walks among the magnificent trees of her estate: thus Mary Cassatt appeared on the day I visited her for the first time. . . . An extremely kind smile lightened her serious expression, and, beneath her silvered hair, grey-blue eyes, the color of still water, gave animation to a face of strongly chiseled planes.] Segard, 1.

12. MC to LH, 7 June [1912], MMA.

13. MC to LH, 1 November [1912], MMA.

14. MC to LH, 10 April [1913], MMA.

15. MC to LH, [March, 1912], MMA.

16. MC to LH, 12 December [1912], MMA.

17. MC to LH, 11 January [1914], MMA.

18. During World War I, Renoir told Cassatt that it was natural for Frenchwomen to sleep with the soldiers pouring into their country; after all, he said, "Nature is opposed to Chastity." He also felt that "the finest death is a soldier's," which set Cassatt to wishing they would send "all of us who are old and useless to the front." MC to LH, 24 August [1912], MMA.

19. C. V. Legros, *Fabre, Poet of Science* (New York: The Century Co., 1913), trans. Bernard Miall.

20. MC to LH, 7 May [1913], MMA. Fabre's life had great meaning to Cassatt. He had lost a beloved child as well as his wife, and he had fought against the academic

establishment in his field of entomology. He found solace in retreat to a country house in the South of France and in work: "We are never so happy as when work does not leave us a moment's repose. To act is to live." Legros, 124.

21. MC to LH, 21 May [1913], MMA.

22. MC to LH, 4 November [1913], MMA.

23. MC to LH, 4 December [1913], MMA.

24. MC to LH, 11 September [1913], MMA.

25. MC to Homer Saint-Gaudens, 28 December 1922, Archives of American Art.

26. MC to LH, 12 March [1915], MMA.

27. "Here is Eugenia smoking (all Ellen's friends smoke) & their Mother has succeeded in making them promise not to smoke more than *three* times a day! and only at *home.* There is no harm in a woman smoking if she is careful not to oversmoke, but a girl not yet sixteen! and Ellen only nineteen. I wrote to Jennie to say that it would be good for Eugenia to profit by this coming winter spent in Paris to study languages, she says I am an artist, but she is just a 20th Century girl." MC to LH, 16 July [1913], MMA.

28. Havemeyer, Remarks [3].

29. MC to LH, 12 March [1915], MMA.

30. MC to LH, 28 August [1913], MMA.

31. MC to LH, [May, 1913], MMA.

32. MC to LH, 17 May [1915], MMA.

33. MC to LH, 13 July [1915], MMA.

34. MC to LH, 3 August [1916], MMA.

35. MC to LH, 2 October [1917], MMA.

36. MC to George Biddle, 29 September [1917], Philadelphia Museum of Art.

37. MC to LH, 28 December [1917], MMA.

38. MC to LH, 4 August 1918, MMA.

39. MC to LH, 16 January [1920], MMA.

40. MC to LH, 31 March 1920, MMA.

41. MC to LH, 28 March [1920], MMA.

42. MC to LH, 20 October [1920], MMA.

43. MC to William Ivins, 17 January 1924, Archives of American Art.

44. "Mary Cassatt Has Her Final Exhibit," *The Art News* (March 8, 1924), 5. "Mary Cassatt is threatened with blindness, and will sell all of her pictures. She has opened at a Paris gallery what will probably be her last exhibition."

45. George Biddle, "Some Memories of Mary Cassatt," *The Arts* (August 1926), 111.

46. Biddle, 108.

47. Sweet, 207.

48. Biddle, 107.

49. Mathilde Valet to LH, 28 June 1926, in Weitzenhoffer, 250.

Chapter X

1. MC to William Ivins, 17 January 1924, Archives of American Art.

2. Lloyd Goodrich, "New York Exhibitions," *The Arts* (December 1926), 348. Goodrich conceded that her early work as an Impressionist was French, but "in the work of her later years she was absolutely herself, and if one may say it without seeming to wave the flag, quite American. Looking at this group of pictures it was impossible to miss the American tang in the sharp, clear lines of her later work, in its bright and slightly hard color and its immaculate technique."

3. "Notes on Current Art," *International Studio* (August 1926), 88. "She was a highly individual painter who found her own subject and remained faithful to it, so that there is some excuse for our considering her not as a French painter but as a truly American one."

4. John Walker, "American Painters and British Critics," *Gazette des Beaux Arts* (December 1946), 336.

5. Arthur Hoeber, "Famous American Women Painters," *The Mentor* (16 March 1914), 1–13.

6. "The Work of Mary Cassatt," *Arts and Decoration* (September 1922), p. 377.

7. "Mary Cassatt Dies in Paris Home," *The Philadelphia Inquirer* (c. 15 June 1926), in Sweet, 209.

8. Jeannette Lowe, "The Women Impressionist Masters: Important Unfamiliar Works by Morisot and Cassatt," *Art News* (November 1939), 9.

9. Adelyn D. Breeskin, *The Graphic Work of Mary Cassatt: A Catalogue Raisonné* (New York: H. Bittner and Company, 1948), 9.

10. John Walker, "Mary Cassatt," *Ladies' Home Journal* (January 1948), 42.

11. Albert Ten Eyck Gardner, "A Century of Women," *Metropolitan Museum of Art Bulletin* (December 1948), 118.

12. Douglas Cooper, review of *The Graphic Work of Mary Cassatt,* by Adelyn D. Breeskin, *Burlington Magazine* (January 1949), 26. As for Mary Cassatt: "Visually and emotionally she was at heart conventional but was not content to remain so. This is her great merit. But science absorbed her at the cost of emotion, and that is why one is conscious of a certain coldness."

13. Edgar Richardson, "Sophisticates and Innocents Abroad," *Art News* (April 1954), 62.

14. D.S. [Denys Sutton?] "Other Book Reviews," *Apollo* (September 1966), 248.

15. Linda Nochlin, "Women Artists in the Twentieth Century," *Studio International* (March 1977), 165–74.

Bibliography

Alcott, Louisa May. *Diana and Persis* [c. 1879] in *Alternative Alcott.* New Brunswick, N.J.: Rutgers University Press, 1989. Edited by Elaine Showalter.

The Americans in Paris; with names and addresses, sketch of American art, lists of artists and pictures, and misc. matters of interest to Americans abroad . . . Paris, 1887. Mary Cassatt's name does not appear.

Bacon, Henry. *A Parisian Year.* Boston: Roberts Brothers, 1882.

Biddle, George. "Some Memories of Mary Cassatt." *The Arts,* August 1926, 107–11.

Boggs, Jean Sutherland, Douglas W. Druick, Henri Loyrette, Michael Pantazzi, and Gary Tinterow. *Degas.* New York: The Metropolitan Museum of Art, 1988.

Breeskin, Adelyn D. *Mary Cassatt: A Catalogue Raisonné of the Oils, Pastels, Watercolors, and Drawings.* Washington, D.C.: Smithsonian Institution Press, 1970.

———. *The Graphic Work of Mary Cassatt: A Catalogue Raisonné.* New York: H. Bittner and Company, 1948.

Breuning, Margaret. *Mary Cassatt.* New York: Hyperion Press, 1944.

Burty, Philippe. "Exposition des oeuvres des artistes indépendant." *La République Française,* 10 April 1880, in *The New Painting,* 321.

Caffin, Charles H. "American Studio Talk: Pennsylvania Academy Exhibition." *International Studio,* March 1904, 239.

Caldwell, Eleanor B. "Exposition Mary Cassatt." [Introduction to and translation of André Mellério, Preface to *Exposition Mary Cassatt.*] *Modern Art,* Winter 1895, 4.

"Mary Cassatt Has Her Final Exhibit." *The Art News,* 8 March 1924, 5.

Cooper, Douglas. Review of *The Graphic Work of Mary Cassatt,* by Adelyn D. Breeskin. *Burlington Magazine,* January 1949, 26.

The Correspondence of Berthe Morisot. London: Camden Press, 1986. Edited by Denis Rouart. Newly edited by Kathleen Adler and Tamar Garb.

Daily Evening Telegraph, 15 January 1898, 7, in Lindsay, *Mary Cassatt and Philadelphia.*

Davis, Patricia T. *End of the Line: Alexander J. Cassatt and the Pennsylvania Railroad.* New York: Neale Watson Academic Publications, Inc., 1978.

Degas Letters. Oxford: Bruno Cassirer, 1947. Edited by Marcel Guérin. Translated by Marguerite Kay.

Denvir, Bernard. *The Impressionists at First Hand.* London: Thames and Hudson, 1987.

Dicey, Edward. *Spectator of America.* 1863. Reprint. Chicago: Quadrangle Books, 1971.

Duranty, Edmond. *La nouvelle peinture à propos du groupe d'artistes qui expose dans les galeries Durand-Ruel.* Paris: E. Dentu, 1876.

"The Exhibition of Independent Artists." *The American Register,* 17 May 1879, 4.

"Exhibition of the Society of French Painters-Etchers." *The American Register,* 11 April 1891, 6.

Fénéon, Félix. "Cassatt, Pissarro." *Le Chat Noir,* 11 April 1891, in *Félix Fénéon: Oeuvres Plus que Complètes.* Geneva: Librairie Droz, 1970. Edited by Joan Halperin.

Fidell-Beaufort, Madeleine. "Elizabeth Jane Gardner Bouguereau: A Parisian Artist from New Hampshire." *Archives of American Art Journal* 24–25 (1984–85), 2–9.

Fink, Lois. *American Art at the Nineteenth-Century Paris Salons.* Cambridge: Cambridge University Press, 1990.

Frelinghuysen, Alice C., Gary Tinterow, Susan A. Stein, Gretchen Wold, and Julia Meech. *Splendid Legacy: The Havemeyer Collection.* New York: The Metropolitan Museum of Art, 1993.

Gardner, Albert Ten Eyck. "A Century of Women." *Metropolitan Museum of Art Bulletin,* December 1948, 110–18.

Geffroy, Gustave [pseud. G.G.]. "L'exposition des artistes indépendants," *La Justice,* 19 April 1881, in *The New Painting,* 359.

Geffroy, Gustave. *Claude Monet,* 1922, in Bernard Denvir, *The Impressionists at First Hand,* 167.

Goetschy, Gustave. "Exposition des artistes indépendants." *Le Voltaire,* 5 April 1881, in *The New Painting,* 250, 358.

Gonse, M. Louis. *Exposition universelle de 1878: Les Beaux-Arts et les arts décoratifs.* Paris: Gazette des Beaux-Arts, 1879.

Goodrich, Lloyd. "New York Exhibitions." *The Arts,* December 1926, 348–49.

Hale, Nancy. *Mary Cassatt: A Biography of the Great American Painter.* New York: Doubleday & Company, Inc., 1975.

Harris, Ann Sutherland and Linda Nochlin. *Women Artists: 1550–1950.* New York: Alfred A. Knopf, 1976.

Havard, Henry. "L'exposition des artistes indépendants." *Le Siècle,* 2 April 1880, in *The New Painting,* 321.

Havemeyer, Louisine. "The Cassatt Exhibition." *Pennsylvania Museum of Art Bulletin,* May 1927, 373–82.

Havemeyer, *Remarks.* Havemeyer, Louisine. *Mrs. H. O. Havemeyer's Remarks on Edgar Degas and Mary Cassatt.* New York: M. Knoedler & Co., 1915.

Havemeyer. Havemeyer, Louisine. *Sixteen to Sixty: Memoirs of a Collector.* 1930. Reprint. New York: Ursus Press, 1993. Edited by Susan A. Stein.

Hawthorne, Nathaniel. *The Marble Faun; or, the Romance of Monte Beni.* Boston: Houghton, Mifflin and Company, 1887.

Henderson, Helen. "Centenary Exhibition of the Pennsylvania Academy of the Fine Arts." *Brush and Pencil,* March 1905, 145–55.

Higginson, T. W. "Ought Woman to Learn the Alphabet?" in *Women and the Alphabet: A Series of Essays.* Boston: Houghton, Mifflin and Company, 1900.

Hoeber, Arthur. "Famous American Women Painters." *The Mentor,* 16 March 1914, 1–13.

James, Henry. *The Ambassadors.* New York: Penguin Classics, 1986.

———. *The American.* New York: Penguin Classics, 1986.

———. *Roderick Hudson.* New York: Penguin Classics, 1987.

Kelly, Florence Finch. "Painters of Sea and Shore." *The Hampton Magazine,* August 1907, 581–86.

King, Joan. *Impressionist: A Novel of Mary Cassatt.* New York: 1983.

Lafenestre, George. "Les Expositions d'art: Les indépendans et les aquarellistes." *Revue des Deux Mondes* 33 (May–June 1879), 481.

Legros, C. V. *Fabre, Poet of Science.* New York: The Century Co., 1913. Translated by Bernard Miall.

Leroy, Louis. "L'exposition des impressionnistes," *Le Charivari,* 25 April 1874, 2–3.

Lindsay, Suzanne. *Mary Cassatt and Philadelphia.* Philadelphia: Philadelphia Museum of Art, 1985.

Lowe, Jeannette. "The Women Impressionist Masters: Important Unfamiliar Works by Morisot and Cassatt." *Art News,* November 1939, 9, 17.

Mathews, Nancy Mowll. *Mary Cassatt.* New York: Harry N. Abrams, 1987.

———. *Cassatt and Her Circle: Selected Letters.* New York: Abbeville Press, 1987.

———. *Mary Cassatt: The Color Prints.* New York: Harry N. Abrams, 1989.

———. *Mary Cassatt and the 'Modern Madonna' of the Nineteenth Century.* Ph.D. dissertation: New York University, 1980.

Mauclair, Camille. *The French Impressionists: 1860–1900.* London: Duckworth & Co., 1903. Translated by P. G. Konody.

———. "Un Peintre de l'Enfance: Miss Mary Cassatt." *L'Art Décoratif,* August 1902, 177–85.

Meilhac, Henri, and Ludovic Halévy. *La Cigale.* New York: Happy Hours Company, 1879.

Mellério, André. Preface to *Exposition Mary Cassatt.* Paris: Galeries Durand-Ruel, 1893.

———. *L'Exposition de 1900 et l'Impressionnisme.* Paris: H. Floury, 1900.

J. Monroe & Co. *The American Traveller's Guide to Paris.* London: W. H. & L. Collingridge, 1869.

Moore, George, *Confessions of a Young Man,* 1888, in Bernard Denvir, *The Impressionists at First Hand,* 78.

———. *Reminiscences of the Impressionist Painters.* Dublin: Maunsel & Co., 1906.

"The Most Eminent of Living American Women Painters." *Current Literature,* February 1909, 167–70.

Nevin, Adelaide M. *The Social Mirror: A Character Sketch of the Women of Pittsburg and Vicinity during the First Century of the County's Existence.* Pittsburgh: T. W. Nevin, 1888.

The New Painting. Moffett, Charles H., et al. *The New Painting: Impressionism 1874–1886.* San Francisco: The Fine Arts Museums of San Francisco, 1986.

Nochlin, Linda. "Women Artists in the Twentieth Century." *Studio International,* March 1977, 165–74.

"Notes on Current Art." *International Studio,* August 1926, 88.

Paris by Night: Sketches and Mysteries of Paris High Life and Demi-Monde. Boston: Boston and Paris Publishing Company, 1875.

"Pictures by Mary Cassatt," *New York Times,* 18 April 1895, 4.

Pissarro, Camille. *Camille Pissarro: Letters to His Son Lucien.* Santa Barbara: Peregrine Smith, Inc., 1981. Edited by John Rewald. Translated by Lionel Abel.

Pollock, Griselda. *Mary Cassatt.* New York: Harper & Row, 1980.

Rambaud, Yveling. "Miss Cassatt." *L'Art dans les Deux Mondes,* 22 November 1890, 7.

Reed, Sue Welsh, and Barbara Stern Shapiro. *Edgar Degas: The Painter as Printmaker.* Boston: Museum of Fine Arts, 1985.

Galerie A.-M. Reitlinger. *Catalogue des Tableaux, pastels, aquarelles, dessins, gravures par Mary Cassatt . . . Composant la collection de Mademoiselle X.* Paris: A.-M. Reitlinger, 1927.

———. *Dessins, pastels, peintures, études par Mary Cassatt.* Paris: A.-M. Reitlinger, 1931.

Richardson, Edgar. "Sophisticates and Innocents Abroad." *Art News,* April 1954, 20–23, 60–62.

Riordan, Richard. "Miss Mary Cassatt." *The Art Amateur,* May 1898, 130.

Rivière, Georges. "Les intransigeants de la peinture." *L'Esprit Moderne,* 13 April 1876, 7–8.

Rubinstein, Charlotte Streifer. *American Women Artists.* New York: Avon Books, 1982.

Saint-Gaudens, Homer. *The American Artist and His Times.* New York: Dodd, Mead & Co., 1941.

Secrest, Meryle. *Being Bernard Berenson: A Biography.* New York: Holt, Rinehart & Winston, 1979.

Segard, Achille. *Mary Cassatt: Un Peintre des enfants et des mères.* Paris: Librairie Paul Ollendorff, 1913.

Shinn, Earl [Edward Strahan]. "The First American Art Academy." *Lippincott's*

Magazine, February–March 1872; reprint, unknown publisher, Pennsylvania Academy of the Fine Arts Archives.

Sidney, Allan. "The Value of the Apparently Meaningless and Inaccurate." *Camera Work,* July 1903, 18.

Silvestre, Armand. *Au Pays du souvenir,* 1892, in Bernard Denvir, *The Impressionists at First Hand,* 71.

Stuckey, Charles F., and William P. Scott. *Berthe Morisot: Impressionist.* New York: Hudson Hills Press, 1987.

D. S. [Denys Sutton?]. "Other Book Reviews." Review of *Miss Mary Cassatt: Impressionist from Pennsylvania* by Frederick Sweet. *Apollo,* September 1966, 248.

Sweet, Frederick. *Miss Mary Cassatt: Impressionist from Pennsylvania.* Norman: University of Oklahoma Press, 1966.

de Syène, F.-C. [Arsène Houssaye]. "Salon de 1879," *L'Artiste,* May 1879, 292.

Thorne, Anna. "My Afternoon with Mary Cassatt." *School Arts,* May 1960, 10–12.

Ticknor, Caroline. *May Alcott: A Memoir.* Boston: Little, Brown, and Company, 1928.

Valerio, Edith. *Mary Cassatt.* Paris: Crès et Cie., 1930.

Walker, John. "American Painters and British Critics." *Gazette des Beaux Arts,* December 1946, 331–44.

———. "Mary Cassatt." *Ladies' Home Journal,* January 1948, 42.

Walton, William. "Miss Mary Cassatt." *Scribner's Magazine,* March 1896, 356.

Watson, Peter. *From Manet to Manhattan: The Rise of the Modern Art Market.* New York: Random House, 1992.

Weitzenhoffer, Frances. *The Havemeyers: Impressionism Comes to America.* New York: Harry N. Abrams, 1986.

White, Barbara Ehrlich. *Renoir: His Life, Art, and Letters.* New York: Harry N. Abrams, 1984.

"The Work of Mary Cassatt." *Arts and Decoration,* September 1922, 377.

Zola, Émile. *L'Assommoir.* New York: Penguin Classics, 1970. Translated by Leonard Tancock.

———. *His Masterpiece* [*L'Oeuvre*]. Phoenix Mill, Gloucestershire, U.K.: Allan Sutton Publishing Limited, 1986. Translated by E. A. Vizetelly, 1902.

Index

Page numbers in *italics* refer to illustrations.

ABOUT THE AUTHOR

NANCY MOWLL MATHEWS began her research on Mary Cassatt in 1971 for her Ph.D. dissertation at the Institute of Fine Arts, New York University. She has gone on to publish four books on the artist as well as three more on the art of that period. She is the Eugenie Prendergast Curator of the Williams College Museum of Art and a recognized authority on American and European art of the Impressionist and Postimpressionist periods.